POLICE OCCUPATIONAL CULTURE: NEW DEBATES AND DIRECTIONS

SOCIOLOGY OF CRIME, LAW AND DEVIANCE

Series Editors: Mathieu Deflem   (Volumes 6 and 8)
                Jeffrey T. Ulmer   (Volumes 1–5)

SOCIOLOGY OF CRIME, LAW AND DEVIANCE   VOLUME 8

POLICE OCCUPATIONAL CULTURE: NEW DEBATES AND DIRECTIONS

EDITED BY

MEGAN O'NEILL
University of Salford, UK

MONIQUE MARKS
University of KwaZulu-Natal, South Africa

ANNE-MARIE SINGH
Ryerson University, Canada

ELSEVIER
JAI

Amsterdam – Boston – Heidelberg – London – New York – Oxford
Paris – San Diego – San Francisco – Singapore – Sydney – Tokyo
JAI Press is an imprint of Elsevier

JAI Press is an imprint of Elsevier
Linacre House, Jordan Hill, Oxford OX2 8DP, UK
Radarweg 29, PO Box 211, 1000 AE Amsterdam, The Netherlands
525 B Street, Suite 1900, San Diego, CA 92101-4495, USA

First edition 2007

British Library Cataloguing in Publication Data
A catalogue record for this book is available from the British Library

ISBN: 978-0-7623-1307-5
ISSN: 1521-6136 (Series)

For information on all JAI Press publications
visit our website at books.elsevier.com

Printed and bound in the United Kingdom

07 08 09 10 11 10 9 8 7 6 5 4 3 2 1

Working together to grow
libraries in developing countries
www.elsevier.com | www.bookaid.org | www.sabre.org
ELSEVIER   BOOK AID International   Sabre Foundation

For Aidan, my light
For Gabriel and Jamie for showing
the real meaning of wonder and of change

and

For Andrea for her strength of conviction

CONTENTS

PART II: POLICE REFORM, CULTURAL CHANGE AND CONTINUITY

PART III: POLICE AS CHANGE AGENTS

LIST OF CONTRIBUTORS

Bruce Baker	Applied Research Centre for Human Security, Coventry University, UK
Mark Bevir	Department of Political Science, University of California, Berkeley, CA, USA
Jennifer Brown	Department of Psychology, University of Surrey, Guildford, UK
Janet Chan	School of Social Sciences & International Studies, University of New South Wales, Sydney, Australia
Tom Cockcroft	Canterbury Christ Church University, Canterbury, Kent, UK
Simon Holdaway	School of Law, University of Sheffield, Sheffield, UK
Michael Kempa	Department of Criminology, University of Ottawa, Ottawa, Ontario, Canada
Ben Krupicka	Department of Political Science, University of California, Berkeley, CA, USA
Bethan Loftus	Centre for Criminological Research, University of Keele, Staffordshire, UK
Peter K. Manning	Brooks Professor of Criminal Justice, College of Criminal Justice, Northeastern University, Boston, MA, USA
Monique Marks	Sociology Programme, University of KwaZulu Natal, Howard College, Durban, South Africa
Megan O'Neill	School of ESPaCH, University of Salford, Salford, Greater Manchester, UK

Maurice Punch	Mannheim Centre, London School of Economics, UK
Anne-Marie Singh	Department of Criminal Justice and Criminology, Ryerson University, Toronto, Canada
David Alan Sklansky	University of California, Berkeley, CA, USA
Jennifer Wood	Australian National University, Canberra, Australia

ACKNOWLEDGEMENTS

This book would certainly not have happened without the generous support and advice from numerous people:

First of all, we wish to acknowledge the generosity and faith of the series editor, Mathieu Deflem, for inviting us to publish this volume in the *Sociology of Crime, Law and Deviance Series*, and for his sage advice in preparing the collection. While he was not able to contribute to the volume as an author, as we originally intended, his role of series editor had a profound impact in bringing the book into existence. For this, and for his patience with our repeated extension requests, we are very grateful.

The editors at Elsevier deserve our thanks as well, especially Ben Davie, Scott Bentley and Julie Walker. Again the words 'faith' and 'patience' come to mind, and we appreciate all they have done in bringing this book into the world.

No small amount of thanks is due to our copy-editor, David Newmarch, who invested very many hours in preparing the manuscript for publication. His intuition and clarity of expression have made these pages better than we had ever hoped possible. This is the second police-oriented book that David has edited and he is now very familiar with key debates in the policing literature. His contribution has at times been more substantive than copy-editing and many authors in this volume have benefited from these insightful interventions.

Of course, without the contributing authors there would be no book to publish. Many thanks go out to the scholars whose words fill these pages. Their generosity in time and energy in preparing their chapters was an inspiration to us, as well as their willingness to conform to our multiple deadlines. Thank you for these interesting and impressive chapters.

And we each have personal debts to acknowledge:

From Megan: Thanks go to Paul Bellaby, Mary Byrne, and the Institute for Social, Cultural and Policy Research at the University of Salford for their invaluable, and unrepayable, support. Former colleagues from the University of Sheffield also deserve thanks for their encouragement and advice in getting this project off the ground in the first place, especially, Jason Ditton, Simon Holdaway, Joanna Shapland and Maggie Wykes.

Monique and Anne-Marie also deserve thanks for coming on board this project with a person whom they have yet to meet in the flesh. This book would not be the success it is without you two. Finally, Boab McMillan must be acknowledged for possessing the patience of a saint in listening to much ranting during the more stressful points of the editing process. My thanks and my love are yours.

From Monique: My ongoing appreciation to Jennifer Wood, Clifford Shearing, Jenny Fleming and Peter Grabosky for being fantastic academic collaborators over the past three years when we were all based at the Regulatory Institutions Network at the Australian National University. We have all gone our separate ways now, but my thinking has been fundamentally shaped through working with you. Thanks also to the Sociology Department at the University of KwaZulu-Natal, my home base, who have always given me the space to complete projects such as this one. Thanks to my co-editors, Megan and Anne-Marie, for their personal support through the difficult times of moving country and home and through bouts of illness. And, of course, I'll slip in a love note to my two little boys, Gabriel and Jamie.

From Anne-Marie: I gratefully acknowledge the friendship of Michael Kempa who first introduced me to this project and with whom I co-authored a chapter. I also owe a great deal of thanks to Megan and Monique for their generous offer to me to participate as a co-editor in this project. The experience has been most rewarding. Colleagues at Ryerson University also deserve thanks for their encouragement and support and for their tolerance of what must have seemed like never ending spools of printing.

Megan O'Neill
Monique Marks
Anne-Marie Singh

ABSTRACT

This book brings together experts in the field of police studies from across the globe to assess contemporary police occupational culture: how it has changed since the classic research of the 1960s and what forms it may take in the future. It considers some aspects of the occupational culture that have been absent in research, areas like the role of police unions and the affect of civil war. The book also questions the concept of police culture itself, especially in light of the current pressures on the police to work in partnership with a variety of other policing agencies.

Megan O'Neill
Monique Marks
Anne-Marie Singh
Editors

INTRODUCTION

Megan O'Neill and Anne-Marie Singh

In the fields of police research and reform, there is an inescapable, controversial, surprisingly stubborn and recurring theme: the police occupational culture. It has been a topic of interest since research of the public police began in the 1960s; it has been the focal point of every conceivable variety of literature (from academic to pulp), film (from documentary to farce) and television (from evening news to morning cartoons). The importance of the police presence and its culture has even been linked to the idea of nationhood generally (Loader & Mulcahy, 2003). Police culture has been seen as both the object of policing and political reform in developing democracies and a barrier to such reforms. In more established democracies of 'the west' police occupational culture has been held up to public scrutiny, as in the 1999 inquiry into the London Metropolitan Police's handling of the racially motivated murder of a young black man, Stephen Lawrence (Macpherson, 1999). All this makes it a topic of immense interest and importance both within the police and beyond. However, as this book will demonstrate, some of the original texts on police culture still have a considerable influence on the way it continues to be understood, despite the passage of over 40 years and numerous research projects of varying methods and fields of interest, many of which suggest a broader view is needed.

It is not just the passage of time or developing research methods and fields that demands a book such as this. There have been many significant events and changing contexts for police work in the course of the intervening decades and these are reflected in the contributions to this volume. For example, the police, in many countries, now work in a radically different

Police Occupational Culture: New Debates and Directions
Sociology of Crime, Law and Deviance, Volume 8, 1–16
Copyright © 2007 by Elsevier Ltd.
All rights of reproduction in any form reserved
ISSN: 1521-6136/doi:10.1016/S1521-6136(07)08019-0

legal environment, with greater demands for police accountability – and not just in the practice of their craft or in their use of force. It also includes their role as employers – their willingness to embrace the diversity of their workforce – as well as their ability to be responsible agents of the state. Other internal issues too are increasingly salient, such as acceptance and enabling of post-secondary education for all ranks of employee. The police now also find themselves with a mandate to work in partnership with a wide spectrum of groups and organisations, from highly organised and multi-national security companies to local individuals or voluntary community security groups. The police can no longer be viewed as an isolated 'force', but must become a community 'service', whether they welcome such a change or not, and one that is representative of the community it serves. It is very important for policing studies to take stock of the cultural implications of these changes, and to that end we hope this book will be a timely and, so far as its scope permits, a comprehensive analysis of current work on these issues.

In this introduction it seems to us better to defer any definition of 'police occupational culture', however much it is of the essence. For each contributor in this volume has her or his distinctive perspective on the phrase and to try to summarise or consolidate the diversity of interpretation would be a disservice to our authors. Instead, we offer here a primed canvas on which they can paint their various perspectives, namely that police occupational culture can best be considered as the 'way things are done around here' for the officers, not always 'by the book', but not always without it either. Police, both public and private sector, have socially constructed ways of viewing the world, their place in it, and the appropriate action to take in their jobs. These waters may seldom be entirely clear but we hope this book will help the reader to navigate them.

The purpose of this book is to engage with some of the most recent research on the police occupational culture in order to update and advance the discussions around it. Represented here are not only some of the earliest writers on the topic but also emerging scholars, yielding both reflection on and extension of established discourse and fresh and new perspectives. A key element of this book is the international dimension it brings. Much of the best-known work in this field comes from the United States and the United Kingdom. These perspectives are present, but so are those of several countries in Africa as well as Australia and Canada, showing a degree of continuity with the classic research locations, but also interesting points of departure. Organised policing is present in every national state and much insight can be gained into policing culture by looking beyond the typical

Anglo-American perspective. Indeed, the book's Conclusion argues for much more comparative work in police cultural studies.

BACKGROUND TO CURRENT POLICE CULTURE RESEARCH

Before considering in more detail the chapters in this volume, let us look briefly at some of the work that continues to exert a powerful influence on police culture research. The earlier works (such as Westley, Rubinstein, Skolnick and Bittner) were groundbreaking in that a previously unresearched organisation became a new site of academic interest. The police organisation did not necessarily open its doors to all academic researchers, but the few who were able to negotiate access provided a rich account of a powerful group in western democratic society. These initial ethnographies and other studies may portray a police service that no longer exists in exactly the same form, but they have provided inspiration and insight to police culture researchers all over the world, and are still widely cited, both for their valuable insights and, in some cases, for their now usefully recognised shortcomings. The following brief look at prominent writers from the 1970s onwards (some of whom are contributors to this book and who continue to develop and expand their contribution to the field) is offered not as a comprehensive list but to indicate some of the key lines of debate.

One of the earliest police researchers was William Westley (1970). He conducted his research in the United States in the 1950s, although it was not published until the 1970s. He describes a police force that perceives a very hostile public. Officers usually only meet the *policed*, rather then the ones they are protecting, and as such it is easy to see why the public comes to be seen as a threat. This then leads the police to bind together in isolation and secrecy for self-protection. This isolation and secrecy is 'an occupational directive, a rule of thumb, the sustenance and the core of meanings. From it the definitions flow and conduct is regulated for the general and the particular' (Westley, 1970, p. 49). His work was influential in its time but it has since been criticised for oversimplifying police relations with the public (Holdaway, 1989, p. 70). It makes no allowance for non-hostile police encounters with the public to enter police thinking. It also presents a monolithic view of the police occupational culture, assumed to apply generally to all Anglo-American police groups.

Rubinstein (1973), in his study of an inner city area in the USA (pp. 435–436), picks up this theme of isolation, though he does not attribute it to a perceived public hostility; he sees the police as isolated because of the nature of their work. Not only do they often work alone, but also due to their hours and the issues they have to face they tend to be friends only with other police officers. He also finds pervasive secrecy in the force, but unlike Westley (1970) who saw the police group as secretive towards outsiders (p. 141), Rubinstein (1973) sees individual officers as being secretive towards everyone else, including other officers. For him, 'a policeman's information is his private stock, which nobody else may presume to make claims on, unless invited to share' (p. 439). In this way, officers protect the work they have done so that no one else can claim rights to it and if they are involved in illegal activities no one else can be implicated.

Skolnick (1966), another American researcher, has proposed the idea of a police 'working personality', which is generated by a combination of three elements of police work: danger, authority and efficiency. He acknowledges that not all police officers are alike in this personality, but that it is reflective of distinct cognitive tendencies in the police as an occupational group. The elements of danger and authority isolate police officers. Because their work is unpredictable when it comes to the potential for danger, police officers tend to be suspicious of everyone and this can be socially isolating. Their authority requires them to enforce laws of 'puritanical morality' that they could never hope to adhere to themselves, making them seem hypocritical and inviting hostility towards them from the public. All this inclines them to be more socially isolated and thus encourages solidarity with each other (Skolnick, 1966, pp. 42–44), as Westley suggested. But what makes Skolnick's 'working personality' thesis unique is his added element of the pressure on police to produce, to appear efficient. The demand both internally and from the public that officers maintain order and make arrests, coupled with danger and authority mean that official procedure and the law may be modified or even set aside so that the desired end result is achieved. Skolnick argues that the police want to appear to be competent craftsmen, and so do the best they can through the pressures they face (Skolnick, 1966, pp. 110–111). Reiner (2000, pp. 87–88) cites Skolnick's work as the 'locus classicus' for studying the police culture, but adds that it neglected to consider how this model may vary within and between forces or to take account of the relationship between the police and the wider social and political structure (Westley is also open to these criticisms). Reiner argues that the police reflect and influence power differences in society and he feels that Skolnick could have taken heed of this.

In his now classic study in the USA, Bittner (1967) describes how uniformed officers on 'skid-row' keep the peace. Building on the work of Banton (1964), who argued that police are more 'peace officers' than 'law enforcement officers', Bittner notes how, rather than enforcing the law as an end in itself, skid-row officers will invoke the law only if it will lead to a more tranquil environment. They use their powers strategically; they get to know their beat and the people in it and they learn what is the best way to respond to any situation. Bittner's study makes the case that the two police tasks of law enforcement and peacekeeping go hand in hand and cannot be regarded separately. However, it could be argued that in practice this is an overly simplistic analysis of police work, especially for present-day officers whose duties are multifarious. Wright (2002), for example , proposes four overlapping police 'modes': peacekeeping, crime investigation, management of risk and community justice.

The scholars who have made significant contributions to this field are not just Americans or men. The next author of note, Maureen Cain, is a British researcher who conducted groundbreaking work into police culture in the 1970s. Hers is one of the first examinations of the differences within police culture. Cain (1971) compared urban and rural police forces and found marked differences in their experiences. For instance, both types of officers developed coping techniques (easing behaviour) for their long periods of boredom, but the nature of these techniques would vary depending on the type of area the police officer patrolled. She also found differences between the urban and rural officers in how they approached members of the public. Thus while some aspects of police culture were similar, their actual expression will vary depending on context, and this is a theme that will be taken further in many of the chapters in this book as authors consider police culture in a variety of countries and contexts.

The 1980s saw the publication of a major piece of British research into the workings of the public police, specifically the London Metropolitan Police. Smith and Gray's (1985) report for the Policy Studies Institute brought to light and openly criticised many expressions and characterisations of police culture. This groundbreaking study is still cited for its detailed analysis of police officers in their working practices, highlighting numerous aspects not so far touched upon in previous research. For example, Smith and Gray draw attention to the largely explicit and accepted racist language of the officers they were observing, concluding, nonetheless, that these same officers did not act in a racist way when carrying out their duties. This is a similar argument to that of Waddington (1999), that 'canteen' talk is not indicative of actual police action.

One key British writer who might disagree with this assumption is an author in this volume, Simon Holdaway. Holdaway began his research into police culture as a serving officer in the 1970s. He has published many works on the experiences of minority ethnic police officers and the 'racialisation' of policing (Holdaway, 1996). The racialisation process suggests that routine and mundane police work and relationships can take on a racial 'framing' that need not be there. People and events can be seen in a way that prioritises race (or, ignores race when it is actually pertinent), and in consequence police officers can inadvertently act in racist ways without completely realising it if that is how their 'usual' practice has always been. In this assessment, regarding police talk as easily separable from and thus not representative of police action is too simplistic. Holdaway's work on race and ethnicity in police work and police culture continues to be highly influential (see, for example, Rowe, 2004).

Another prominent writer in the police culture genre who is a contributor to this book is Peter K. Manning. Manning's work in the 1970s and 1980s on uniformed police officers (in the US and the UK) and detectives (in the US) remain core texts for any police culture researcher (see, for example, Manning, 1980, 1997). He has conducted ethnographies in several police forces, and through them has made contributions to many areas of sociological thought, such as dramaturgy and semiotics. Manning continues to be a prolific writer in this field, more recently in the areas of technology in policing and democratic policing approaches. His works portray the symbolism and meaning inherent in police action, an approach taken up by writers such as Loader and Mulcahy (2003).

It is not just Britain and the US that have served as sites for the 'classic' police culture research. Maurice Punch found fruitful scholarly opportunities in the Netherlands. His work began in the 1970s and continues to this day, as exemplified by his chapter in this volume. Punch (1985) has written extensively about his observations on the beat with Dutch police, providing a detailed account of their working practices, both above-board and otherwise. Much of his work focuses on police corruption and the internal reactions to it. Being a British writer in the Netherlands allowed Punch (1979) to bring a new international dimension to the Anglo-American dominated police culture field. His emphasis on the inherent (and inextricable) social service aspect of police work is one that has subsequently been taken up by many other writers.

One final writer (and author in this book) who deserves note in this overview also brings a much-needed international dimension. Janet Chan (1997), who began her work in the 1980s, conducting research in Canada and Australia, has made a particularly deep impression on the police culture field. She argues that police culture cannot be fully appreciated without consideration of the wider social context in which it is located and the agency of the individual officers. Chan challenges the orthodox character-isations of police culture with a call for a more specific (perhaps inductive) approach where the particularities of police dispositions and the power relations and social relations that frame these are investigated preferably through a more case-study approach and using ethnographic methods. Her influence can be felt throughout this book in which many of the authors draw upon it for inspiration, and her attention to variety in police culture both between and within police forces is a notably recurring issue in the chapters that follow.

There are many other writers on police culture that we could mention here (such as Muir, Fielding, Reuss-Ianni, Reiner, Heidensohn, Norris, Maguire and more) and their omission reflects only the exigencies of space. What we do hope to have shown is that while writings on the police did not start out with an idea of 'culture', over time one began to emerge, often focused on characteristics like secrecy, suspicion, isolation, racism, sexism and informal working practices. In turn, subsequent writers begin to question the concept, with the improbability if its being universally generalisable in all societies and across time. But one very notable omission from the main thrust of the work we have been surveying is a consideration of the growing private security and private policing market and any occupational culture there. Nor is it only the commercial sector that has muscled in on the state's claimed monopoly on policing and the use of force: at the local level, voluntary community-based structures actively perform policing functions, sometimes in co-operation with the public police (i.e. Neighbourhood Watch) and sometimes quite independently of them (i.e. Guardian Angels), and undoubtedly there is work that still needs to be done on the cultures of these voluntary groups and how they compare to those of the public police.

We hope the chapters that follow will help to unravel some of the principal factors that construct police culture – public sector, private, voluntary, in a variety of sites, with a variety of actors – to provide a more rounded analysis of that culture.

NEW DEBATES AND DIRECTIONS IN RESEARCH

The book is structured according to four broad themes. The first looks directly at the key analytical concept: 'police occupational culture'. Chapters

by Sklansky, Manning and Cockcroft each offer a critical assessment of the
traditional interpretation of police culture as a homogeneous and
homogenising phenomenon. The second theme, developed in the Punch,
Chan, Bevir and Krupicka and Brown chapters, focuses on the impact, on
the occupational culture, of various police organisational reforms. The third
theme, pursued in the chapters by Marks, O'Neill and Holdaway, and
Wood and Marks, investigates how police occupational culture is created,
given meaning, shaped and transformed 'from below', through the agency,
actions and activities of police unions, associations and individual officers.
The final theme, explored in two chapters by Singh and Kempa, and Baker,
concerns new policing cultures in the contemporary plural field of security
governance.

PART I: DECONSTRUCTING THE NOTION
OF POLICE OCCUPATIONAL CULTURE

David Alan Sklansky (Chapter 1) revisits the meaning of 'police
occupational culture' in light of contemporary developments in policing.
Lawyers, scholars and police reformers in the United States, he notes, have
long assumed that police officers share a monolithic occupational mindset,
and that this mindset – paranoid, insular, intolerant and inflexible – is the
chief impediment to better law enforcement. What he terms the 'Police
Subculture Schema' helped shaped American police reform by supporting
the top-down control mechanisms of police professionalism, the judicial
oversight model at the centre of the Supreme Court's 'criminal procedure
revolution', and systems of civilian oversight. But while this 'Police
Subculture Schema' made a good deal of sense in the 1950s, 1960s and
early 1970s, he argues that it makes less sense today. According to Sklansky,
increasingly the idea of a monolithic, reactionary police subculture hinders
clear thinking about the police, by obscuring differences between officers,
new complexities of police identity and dynamic processes within the police
workforce. It diverts attention from important avenues of reform. Sklansky
points to neglected questions pertaining to institutional redesign of police
agencies, the characteristics of effective, trustworthy police and the
participatory decision-making of rank-and-file officers. The 'Police Subculture Schema' also directs focus away from new, emerging challenges in
policing such as the growth of police managerialism and the risk that
diversification of police agencies is stalling if not backsliding.

Like Sklansky, Peter K. Manning (Chapter 2) offers a robust critique of the traditional model of police occupational culture, a model that owes much to the work of William Westley. For Manning, that model, as a benchmark for all matters police, has become an unwelcome filter that precludes deeper analyses of policing as an organisation and as a practice. This has come about because the visible and obvious aspect of policing, the officer's culture, is too easily taken as globally indicative of the organisation and its politics, the mandate and intra- and inter-organisational dynamics. Manning protests at the way research has seized on police–citizen interactions, a single aspect of public policing, as fundamental to an understanding of policing as an activity. In addition, he suggests that 'the dramaturgical properties of "profiling" and a resentful negative force make it an easy intaglio on which textbook writers can further inscribe'. This has made the analysis of policing superficial and misleadingly reductionistic, stripping the organisation of its politics and nuance and its larger field of municipal and local politics, along with its inter-organisational dynamics. It is unwarrantable, Manning demonstrates, that the small-scale sketch provided by Westley should now stand as a synecdoche for the entire organisation and its practices and politics.

Manning reviews literature relevant to understanding the occupational culture of policing (considered as segments – officers, middle management/supervision and top command – not sub-cultures) and argues for recognition of complexity in the use of the concept. He insists that the police occupation must be located within its organisational context: its ecology (spatial and temporal elements), material constraints, patterned interactions and shared understandings. He also points to the necessity of investigating inter- and intra-organisational relationships for better understanding of the role of the top command and staff in organisational governance. He provides details from a case study of two examples of policing mass public occasions in Boston in 2004 to illustrate his argument.

Tom Cockcroft (Chapter 3) reflects on the utility of oral history for rethinking police culture and identifies some of the attendant definitional, methodological and analytical issues. Oral history studies of the police rely on narrative accounts by retired officers of their past (including recent past) experiences. Based on a review of the extant research, Cockcroft argues that the oral history approach challenges us to differentiate between police organisational influences and the influences of wider society. This emphasises both the complex linkages between police officers at the organisational level and the complicated relations that exist between the police and the wider social environment in which they are necessarily located and function. This approach, Cockcroft maintains, also highlights the difficulties associated with assuming a degree of universality between police cultures. Drawing on Janet Chan's work, he notes the failure of conventional analyses to examine variations in police occupational culture. The oral history method, he argues, gives voice to the organisational, social and historical contexts of policing and attends to differences in police role, behaviours and values within and between jurisdictions and over time. The oral history approach also encourages a close look at the tricky relationship between language and behaviour that Waddington and others have pointed to, by exploring the disparity between police narration (what is said) and police action (what actually happened).

PART II: POLICE REFORM, CULTURAL CHANGE AND CONTINUITY

Having critiqued the concept of police culture, the book now turns to an analysis of the cultural implications of police reform projects. Maurice Punch (Chapter 4) provides an analysis of organisational reform efforts to transform the police into a 'professional' institution with well-educated leaders. He outlines how the British Police began in 1829 as an 'artisan' institution that would develop its own leaders and not recruit the 'educated'. Senior officers (and also police constables) tended to be 'respectable' upper working class males with limited formal education. However, by the 1960s pressure for change led to support for university education for officers. The Essex Police, in an experiment partly aimed at preventing the imposition of leaders from outside of the police organisation, sent officers to university to learn about society through both formal study for a social science degree and informal interaction with a diversity of fellow students. Punch draws on oral history material involving interviews with officers who studied in that period, examining their experiences as students, their return to policing and their reflections on having graduates within the service. These officers' experience in attending tertiary education institutions and then returning to the police organisation points to some of the changes that emerged within police occupational culture and within police leadership styles from as early as the 1960s.

Punch argues that educating officers at university has contributed substantially and positively to the police organisation and its culture, particularly through fostering a more analytical approach to understanding practical problems and developing solutions. These early experiments to improve officers' educational qualifications are now far more common and a series of formalised relationships have now been established between universities and the police in the United Kingdom, but also in other parts of the world like Australia. Punch warns, though, that some of these positive effects may be limited or even contradicted by other factors in recent reforms such as 'new public management' and the 'professionalising' of policing.

Janet Chan (Chapter 5) examines the relationship between police stress and occupational culture, an under-researched area. She notes that danger and trauma in police work have long been linked to the development of a suspicious and cynical 'street cop' culture. Nevertheless, there is evidence, she contends, that stress among police officers in Western democracies is more likely to be produced by organisational pressure and management practices than by actual traumatic experience. The chapter uses data from a follow-up study of police recruits in New South Wales, Australia to consider the impact of organisational changes on police officers' perception of their work and culture. Chan demonstrates the way changes in the *field* of policing had generated organisational stressors – i.e. increased account-ability, competitive promotion systems – that had modified some aspects of the occupational *habitus* while reinforcing others. She argues that police reforms and organisational changes may have further embedded certain negative aspects of police culture such as cynicism and self-protection even while putting an end to other negative features such as the 'code of silence'.

Mark Bevir and Ben Krupicka (Chapter 6) attempt to understand police reform in the United Kingdom and United States during the latter half of the twentieth century by exploring the various narratives that have inspired it. They indicate that many of these narratives are elite ones and bear similarities to wider public sector reform narratives. They identify and describe three distinct and competing sets of elite beliefs: a progressive narrative tied to bureaucratic modes of governance; a neo-liberal narrative emphasising markets and new management practices; and a community policing narrative promoting partnerships and networks. While policy experts and public officials formulate narratives, the reforms are imple-mented and enacted in part by local police officers. Bevir and Krupicka point out that rank-and- file officers will necessarily interpret and extend the elite-inspired reforms through the lenses of their own local beliefs. According to the authors, the inability of the elite narratives to adequately recognise the impact of local cultures means that the reforms are often incomplete and give rise to unintended consequences. They suggest that a better understanding of this process of reform and its implications for democratic governance might orientate reformers and scholars towards more bottom-up approaches to police reform (a point more fully explored in Part III of the book).

Bethan Loftus's ethnographic study (Chapter 7) of a provincial English police force exposes a contradiction that emerged between the new police organisational emphasis on diversity and the enduring axes of class. Loftus notes that efforts aimed at changing police culture both within and beyond the organisation focus on notions of equity, anti-discrimination and respect for diversities of race, gender and sexuality. However, it was predominantly poor and low status white males who occupied a central position in the police's practical workload and in their occupational consciousness. She demonstrates that contempt expressed towards the under-class constitutes a prominent yet relatively unexamined aspect of police culture: police officers often saw themselves as protecting the moral majority from the morally worthless underclass; this accentuated their sense of solidarity and their moral conservatism and also marked out a 'common enemy'. She observes that class contempt goes largely unchallenged in contemporary police institutions, and that this confirms the status of poor white males in particular as legitimate targets of contempt and more generally reinforces societal disregard for its poor. Thus, reform efforts missed a large aspect of police practice; they were intended to be holistic but were interpreted thematically.

In some contrast to Loftus, Jennifer Brown (Chapter 8) argues that it is gender that has been eclipsed by demands of other diversity agendas: the recent urgency in tackling racist language did not extend to sexist or homophobic language and behaviour. Brown proposes that whilst operational policing and its management may have changed, the masculine ethos of police officers has not. She notes that the introduction of equality legislation, new managerialism in the public sector and initiatives in community policing presaged a potential transformation of policing through adoption of more co-operative and collaborative styles that might be held to be more feminine in orientation. Yet, her review of recent research shows that organisational attention to gender issues has slipped and she claims that police occupational identity remains privileged by a masculine orientation which values danger, excitement and 'good arrests'. She examines why this is so and concludes that male officers, finding their identity under threat from a raft of managerial and operational reforms, deploy ritual arguments to preserve gender continuity, distinctiveness, self-esteem and self-efficiency. A similar process is hypothesised for police organisations facing adverse conditions more generally.

PART III: POLICE AS CHANGE AGENTS

Change in police culture does not just happen from above. Officers and staff themselves can instigate change in the culture or be directly involved in change projects. Monique Marks (Chapter 9) highlights the possibility of effecting police reform 'from below' in her discussion of cultural influences of police unions, a little researched area. As a subcultural grouping, police unions exhibit specific characteristics and identities while sharing the core values of the dominant organisational culture. Drawing on first-hand empirical data from Canada, the US, Australia, New Zealand and South Africa, Marks shows that adherence to traditional cultural norms structures union responses to the organisational reform initiatives of police leaders and managers. But she suggests that there is evidence of police unions that break from cultural traditions and that potential exists for unions to play an important role in directing more responsive and forward thinking reform agendas, including ways of repositioning the police, as providers of public goods, in policing networks.

Marks points out that in some countries, such as South Africa, police unions have promoted more democratic policing practices through their identification with a range of social justice organisations. She concludes that police unions, as important insider groupings, have the capacity to reshape police culture in new, progressive directions. But she argues that this role as change agents is dependent on police unions broadening their understandings of police professionalism and on their willingness to forge new identities and alliances.

Megan O'Neill and Simon Holdaway (Chapter 10) undertake a parallel assessment of the impact of identity-based police associations on the occupational culture. They argue that in recent years, Black Police Associations (BPAs) have become key forces of change within police services throughout the UK. These are voluntary groups composed of minority ethnic police officers and support staff. O'Neill and Holdaway observe that the majority of police services in England and Wales now have an officially recognised BPA. Using data from their recent research project on BPAs, O'Neill and Holdaway examine issues of ethnicity and diversity in police work. They explore issues such as the decreasing importance of rank and grading in the police culture, whether a parallel, 'black' occupational culture is emerging alongside the traditional 'white' one, and the interplay between changing individuals and changing the institution as a whole. The authors argue that the impact of BPAs on the police occupational culture occurs within the context of wider 'field' events and situations and in individual encounters between minority ethnic police officers and their white colleagues. In contrast to the findings of previous research on minority ethnic police officers, this study suggests that ethnicity plays a central role in their self-identities as police officers.

Much more than in the two previous chapters, police officers in Jennifer Wood and Monique Marks's study (Chapter 11) appear as innovators, playing an active role in reshaping their work practices and in generating (not simply implementing) change programmes. Wood and Marks propose that cultural transformation is not cataclysmic but occurs through small shifts in the way police practitioners think and act within the context of a constantly changing and plural field of policing. Police officers do not simply acquire new knowledge but must become knowledge producers and brokers. In this respect the authors discuss the 'Nexus Policing Project', a joint venture of the Victoria Police and the Australian National University. Wood and Marks attend to the emphasis that Nexus places on mobilising and enhancing the capacity of individual police members to be self-reflective and to respond innovatively to new problems. Police officers who participate in Nexus are provided with the space both to review their existing ways of seeing, being and doing and to engage with other groups (academics, schoolchildren, etc.) whose worldviews and problem-solving approaches may be quite different. While Nexus has been successful, Wood and Marks identify and elaborate some of the challenges associated with police–academic partnerships.

PART IV: NEW POLICING CULTURES IN A PLURAL POLICING FIELD

It is of course not just public bodies who undertake policing, and these other groups deserve consideration of their own occupational cultures. Anne-Marie Singh and Michael Kempa (Chapter 12) address similarities between public and private police cultures with particular attention to post-apartheid South Africa. They describe the co-existence and inter-penetration of state and non-state policing agencies in the contemporary security landscape. The authors observe that there is no function performed by the public police that is not also performed, in some manner, by private security agents. However, the cultures of private policing agents have been far less studied than those of public police officers. With the private security industry employing a wide array of coercive techniques and in many cases operating punitive strategies for controlling crime and maintaining public order, this chapter suggests that sectors of this industry exhibit a reactive and punitive organisational culture resembling the dominant culture of the public police in the mid-twentieth century. Singh and Kempa focus upon the relevance for private policing cultures of issues and themes traditionally raised in analyses of public police cultures. In particular, they discuss the relevance of concerns pertaining to individual psychology, institutional structure and broader 'field' influences for analysing, accounting for and thereby reforming private policing cultures. The authors conclude by raising some questions about what the surprising culture and practices of the private security industry may signal about the emergent political economy of human security. In so doing, they point to the need to go beyond the traditional binary division between public police and private security cultures.

That policing is not the sole prerogative of the public police is also central to Bruce Baker's study (Chapter 13). He investigates the role of non-police security agencies and their relationship with the state police in contemporary Uganda, Rwanda and Sierra Leone. Relying on primary interview material, he compares the everyday practices and values of the public police in these three African countries arguing that police culture is shaped by its socio-political context, particularly recent experiences of civil war. Following successful rebellion, Uganda and Rwanda chose to rely on a form of local popular justice, supplemented by the police. Sierra Leone, where the rebellion was defeated, has adopted a more western-style police model of a professionalised force with a monopoly on policing functions. All three have, with substantial international assistance, undertaken management reform to restructure mechanisms of state policing. Baker notes that donor programmes focus on training senior personnel in strategic and operational planning aimed at improving accountability, co-ordination, efficiency, effectiveness and community/police relations. He observes that the new values and approaches have differentially penetrated the senior, middle and lower ranks. Baker suggests this divergence of cultures, along with the disparity between the discourses and actual practices of state policing pose problems for the reform efforts of government, police leaders, international donors and foreign police trainers.

Collectively, these chapters map out new lines of debate and directions for research on police occupational culture. A concept that began life as a largely negative, inflexible and monolithic construct has become one that is multi-faceted and intricate. This is indeed a vibrant and exciting field and one that is amenable to diverse methodological and conceptual tools. By opening up the terms of the debate, this book seeks to stimulate further research and discussion. In the concluding chapter, we explore the key challenges to police cultural studies and point to possible future areas of research.

NOTE

1. The obvious gendering of the earlier police research will be explored later in this introduction.

REFERENCES

Banton, M. (1964). *The policeman in the community*. New York: Basic Books.
Bittner, E. (1967). The police on skid-row: A study of peace keeping. *American Sociological Review, 32*(5), 699–715.
Cain, M. (1971). On the beat: Interactions and relations in rural and urban police forces. In: S. Cohen (Ed.), *Images of deviance*. Harmondsworth: Penguin.
Chan, J. (1997). *Changing police culture: Policing in a multicultural society*. Cambridge: Cambridge University Press.
Holdaway, S. (1989). 'Discovering structure. Studies of the British police occupational culture'. In: M. Weatheritt (Ed.), *Police research: Some future prospects*. Aldershot: Avebury.
Holdaway, S. (1996). *The racialisation of British policing*. Basingstoke: Macmillan.
Loader, I., & Mulcahy, A. (2003). *Policing and the condition of England: Memory, politics and culture*. New York: Oxford University Press.
Macpherson, W. (1999). *The Stephen Lawrence inquiry: Report of an inquiry by Sir William Macpherson of Cluny*. Cm 4262-I. London: HMSO.
Manning, P. K. (1980). *The narcs' game: Organizational and informational limits on drug law enforcement*. Cambridge, MA: The MIT Press.
Manning, P. K. (1997). *Police work: The social organization of policing* (2nd ed.). Prospect Heights: Waveland Press.
Punch, M. (1979). The secret social service. In: S. Holdaway (Ed.), *The British police*. London: Edward Arnold Press.
Punch, M. (1985). *Conduct unbecoming: The social construction of police deviance and control*. London: Tavistock.
Reiner, R. (2000). *The politics of the police* (3rd ed.). Oxford: Oxford University Press.
Rowe, M. (2004). *Policing: Race and racism*. Cullompton: Willan Publishing.
Rubinstein, J. (1973). *City police*. New York: Ballantine Books.
Skolnick, J. H. (1966). *Justice without trial: Law enforcement in democratic society*. New York: Wiley.
Smith, D. J., & Gray, J. (1985). *Police and people in London: The PSI report*. Aldershot: Gower.
Waddington, P. A. J. (1999). Police (canteen) sub-culture: An appreciation. *British Journal of Criminology, 39*(2), 287–309.
Westley, W. A. (1970). *Violence and the police: A sociological study of law, custom, and morality*. Cambridge, MA: The MIT Press.
Wright, A. (2002). *Policing: An introduction to concepts and practice*. Devon: Willan Publishing.

PART I:
DECONSTRUCTING THE NOTION OF POLICE OCCUPATIONAL CULTURE

CHAPTER 1

SEEING BLUE: POLICE REFORM, OCCUPATIONAL CULTURE, AND COGNITIVE BURN-IN

David Alan Sklansky

ABSTRACT

Lawyers, scholars, and police reformers in the United States have long assumed that police officers share a monolithic occupational mindset, and that this mindset – paranoid, insular, intolerant, and inflexible – is the chief impediment to better law enforcement. These assumptions made a good deal of sense in the 1950s, 1960s, and early 1970s, but they make less sense today. Increasingly, the idea of a monolithic, reactionary police subculture hinders clear thinking about the police by obscuring differences between officers, new complexities of police identity, and dynamic processes within the police workforce. It diverts attention from important avenues of reform and from new, emerging challenges in policing.

Plasma televisions, like old-fashioned cathode-ray sets and first-generation computer screens, are prone to a problem called 'image burn-in'. If a stationary picture or graphical feature is shown for long enough, it can leave a permanent, ghostlike trace. What happens is that the light-emitting phosphors coating the screen deteriorate over time, and the speed of the

Police Occupational Culture: New Debates and Directions
Sociology of Crime, Law and Deviance, Volume 8, 19–45
Copyright © 2007 by Elsevier Ltd.
ISSN: 1521-6136/doi:10.1016/S1521-6136(07)08001-3

process depends on how often each phosphor is triggered. So if a particular image is displayed on the screen for an extended period, it leaves an imprint, altering how later signals are processed.

Something similar happens with ideas. We view the world through schemas – mental constructs that sort and organise experience (see, for example, Blasi, 1995). Schemas are powerful conceptual tools. We need them in order to make sense of the blizzard of information we face every day. But schemas used for too long without interruption can become difficult to dislodge. A sort of cognitive burn-in can permanently alter our perceptions. Paraphrasing Marcus Aurelius, we might say that the mind becomes dyed with the colour of its thoughts.

A story of cognitive burn-in has long been part of the received wisdom about the police subculture. New recruits, the story goes, have a range of different outlooks. But they quickly become assimilated into a powerful occupational culture with its own ways of seeing, and they adopt those ways of seeing as their own. After a while it can be difficult for them to see the world in any other way. Their minds are dyed blue. In the words of one officer (Conlon, 2004, p. 320), 'Over time and in the main, cops tend to think like other cops'.

I am interested here in a different kind of cognitive burn-in, also associated with the police subculture – a cognitive burn-in not *caused* by that subculture but rather consisting in ideas *about* it. For over half a century, police reform in the United States has been guided by a broadly shared set of assumptions about the nature of the police subculture and its central importance in shaping the behaviour of the police. Those assumptions – that police officers think alike; that they are paranoid, insular, and intolerant; that they intransigently oppose change; that they must be rigidly controlled from the outside, or at least from the top – themselves constitute a schema.

First developed in the 1950s, this schema made sense of much of what lawyers and social scientists were then beginning to learn about the police. Its explanatory power grew in the 1960s, as the police felt themselves increasingly under siege. By the early 1970s this view of the police – call it the Police Subculture Schema – had achieved the status of unquestioned orthodoxy. A process of cognitive burn-in was underway.

Much has changed in American policing since the early 1970s. Community policing has replaced police professionalism as the taken-for-granted ideal of police reformers and law enforcement administrators alike (see, for example, Livingston, 1997). Civilian oversight, once resisted tooth-and-nail by the police, has become unexceptional (Walker, 2001). The virtually all-white, virtually all-male departments of the 1950s and 1960s have given way to departments with large numbers of female and minority officers, often led by female or minority chiefs; openly gay and lesbian officers, too, are increasingly commonplace (Sklansky, 2006a). College educated officers are no longer a rarity; increasingly they are the norm (Carter & Sapp, 1990). Police solidarity has declined, and with it police insularity; the profession is 'less and less a fraternity' (Conlon, 2004, p. 9). Police ethnographers find that the 'unified occupied subculture' of policing is being replaced by workforces marked by 'segmentation and division' (Haarr, 1997, p. 66; see also, for example, National Research Council, 2004, pp. 80–82). Police benevolent associations look more and more like other labour unions (Delaney & Feuille, 1987), and increasingly they compete for influence with identity-based caucuses of minority officers, female officers, and gay and lesbian officers (Barlow & Barlow, 2000, pp. 235–241). The self-identity of police officers is more complex and more varied today than 40 years ago. Police departments are marked by less consensus and more debate. Policing is not what it used to be.

But legal regulation of the police and new efforts at police reform in the United States continue to be shaped by the Police Subculture Schema. Partly this is a matter of institutional inertia, and partly it is a matter of cognitive burn-in. Lawyers, scholars, and reformers still tend to think of the police rank-and-file as sharing a monolithic occupational mindset and still tend to treat this mindset as the chief impediment to policing that is fairer, more effective, and more humane. The Police Subculture Schema makes it hard to see differences between officers, new complexities of police identity, and dynamic processes within the police workforce. When we look at the police, all we see is blue.

My goals here are twofold: to trace the imprint that the Police Subculture Schema has left on American police reform and the ongoing legal regulation of the police; and to identify some of the opportunities and dangers that the schema has made harder to perceive. I will start by describing how the Police Subculture Schema helped to shape the 'criminal procedure revolution' of the 1960s and broader patterns of police reform. I will then discuss important avenues of reform the schema may have led us to neglect. These include questions of institutional design, insights to be gained by focusing on differences between officers, and the possibility of giving rank-and-file officers a larger, collective role in the shaping of their work. Finally, I will address two problems the schema has tended to make less visible. The first of these is the risk that diversification of police departments may be stalling. The second is the set of challenges posed by the recent expansion of private policing and its characteristic culture of managerialism.

There is a real danger here of overstating. The Police Subculture Schema retains explanatory power. Police officers still tend to derive a good part of their self-identity from their work, and many of the defining qualities of that work – the unpredictability; the physical danger; the routine exposure to failure, folly, and meanness – remain largely unchanged. Understanding the police, and crafting intelligent strategies of police reform, still require sensitivity to the powerful and distinctive ways in which the day-to-day experiences of law enforcement officers influence their behaviour. Nor are police racism, sexism, and homophobia things of the past. But 'every way of seeing is also a way of not seeing' (Lynd, 1958). The Police Subculture Schema has always obscured certain critical dimensions of policing and police reform, and changes in policing over the past few decades have made it more important than ever to rectify those blind spots.

I focus here on American scholars, American police departments, and American reform efforts. The Police Subculture Schema may have a looser hold elsewhere. In Australia, for example, Janet Chan (1996, p. 110) has influentially criticised the entire concept of 'police culture'. In Britain, Robert Reiner (1992, p. 109) has warned that police occupational norms are 'neither monolithic, universal, nor unchanging', and Nigel Fielding (1988, p. 9) has stressed both the multiplicity of cultures found within law enforcement agencies and the way in which individual recruits mediate workplace influences, 'constructing an "organisational reality" special to themselves' by selectively resisting and embracing the norms they encounter. In the end, though, Chan (1996, pp. 119–122) replaces the concept of police culture in part with an account of the police 'habitus' that replicates most of the key elements of the Police Subculture Schema, and Reiner emphasises 'commonalities of the police outlook ... as discovered by many studies in several different places and periods' (Reiner, 1992, pp. 109, 136). So the story I tell here may have parallels outside the United States.

ORIGINS OF THE POLICE SUBCULTURE SCHEMA

The notion that police officers tend to share a distinctive outlook is at least as old as police departments themselves. But the Police Subculture Schema, as a rounded, fully articulated theory of how to think about the police, dates from the mid-1950s, when William Westley (1953, 1956) published two highly influential articles based on his firsthand observation of and interviews with working police officers. The articles were adapted from Westley's (1970) doctoral dissertation, later published in its entirety. Earlier studies of policing had tended to be the work of journalists, blue-ribbon commissions, or reform-minded police executives. Westley helped to inaugurate a new field of interdisciplinary, academic inquiry, which we can loosely call police studies.

The field burgeoned in the 1960s and 1970s, as more and more social scientists and legal scholars turned their attention to the police. In critical ways Westley's work set the pattern for these later studies. Westley thought the key to understanding the police was to see them 'as a social and occupational group' (Westley, 1970, p. 8). More precisely, the police were a 'conflict group', united by the manner in which their work isolated them from the community and threatened their collective sense of status. The police officer came to regard himself as a 'pariah' and came to 'regard the public as an enemy' (Westley, 1953, p. 35; 1956, p. 256). The shared alienation of police officers led to the creation of a distinctive set of group norms, into which new recruits were systematically indoctrinated. The internal group norms of the police were at war in important respects with their formal legal mandate. The norms of the police approved the selective use of illegal violence against suspects, for example, and forbade officers from testifying against each other.

Westley thus argued that the key to understanding the police was to understand their shared mentality – their subculture – and that the key to their shared mentality was the nature of their job, including the ways in which it estranged them from the community and threatened their collective sense of self-esteem. This set of premises – what Cain (1993) calls 'the Policeman as Other' – became the central motif of police studies in the 1960s and 1970s. It linked together, in particular, the work of the two most influential social scientists to write about American police in the 1960s, James Q. Wilson and Jerome Skolnick. As Simon (2002) points out, Wilson and Skolnick differed fundamentally in their attitudes towards policing: Wilson was very much a conservative, and Skolnick was very much a liberal. But they both shared, with Westley, the Police Subculture Schema.

Wilson and Skolnick agreed, too, on an important extension of that schema. Like other police scholars of the era, they believed that the psychology of law enforcement officers was shaped not just by occupational role and outcast status, the factors Westley had stressed, but also by certain inclinations that officers brought with them to the job. Wilson (1968) speculated that the 'working-class backgrounds' of police officers predisposed them to view violence as legitimate and gave them 'a preoccupation with maintaining self-respect, proving one's masculinity, "not taking any crap", and not being "taken in"'. Skolnick (1966) thought it plain that 'a Goldwater-type conservatism was the dominant political and emotional persuasion of the police'. The worldview of the police included a simplistic, acontextual understanding of criminality, an apprehensive traditionalism, an intolerance for nonconformity, and a hostility to permissive childrearing (Skolnick, 1969).

THE POLICE SUBCULTURE SCHEMA AND AMERICAN POLICE REFORM

The Police Subculture Schema made sense to scholars in the 1960s in part because it fit nicely with then-prevalent ideas about democracy and social relations. Those ideas included the fundamental role of interest groups in modern democratic politics and the existence of an 'authoritarian personality'. As to the first, the Police Subculture Schema resonated strongly with the view, held by many if not most social scientists in the middle decades of the twentieth century, that groups – including occupational groups – were 'the primary, though not the exclusive, means by which the individual knows, interprets, and reacts to the society in which he exists' (Truman, 1971, p. 21). As to the second, the distinctive mentality that scholars like Wilson and Skolnick saw in the police 'was almost a classic example of the authoritarian personality' (Balch, 1972, p. 107), that cluster of dispositions widely thought to characterise the bulk of ordinary, working-class citizens and to make them a dangerous force in democratic politics (see Adorno, Frenkel-Brunswik, Levinson, & Sanford, 1950).

In turn, the Police Subculture Schema supported and helped to motivate the two major lines of police reform in the 1960s: the 'police professionalism' agenda of law enforcement executives and the 'criminal procedure revolution' mounted by the United States Supreme Court. Police professionalism, which reached the peak of its popularity in the 1950s and 1960s, aimed to raise the quality of law enforcement by streamlining operations, improving task specification, strengthening lines of command, tightening standards, and leveraging personnel with technology. The models were the Chicago Police Department under Superintendent O. W. Wilson and the Los Angeles Police Department under Chief William Parker (see, for example, Fogelson, 1977). Police leaders like Wilson and Parker fought hard for, too, for the political independence of police departments; this was part of what they meant by 'professionalism'. But autonomy for the rank and file, individually or collectively, was no part of the programme – quite the contrary (see, for example, Bittner, 1990, pp. 357–366).

The Police Subculture Schema, which understood police officers in terms of a pervasive and dangerous set of characteristic predispositions – what Skolnick (1966) called their 'working personality' – made police professionalism, with its commitment to rigid top-down control of officers, much more attractive. In a similar way, the Police Subculture Schema lent support to the Supreme Court's 'criminal procedure revolution', led by Chief Justice Earl Warren. Warren took office in 1953, the same year Westley published the first results of his fieldwork. Under Warren's leadership, the Supreme Court reined in the discretion of police officers, most notably by beefing up systems of judicial oversight. The Police Subculture Schema was never articulated and defended in these decisions, but it plainly lurked in the background. The Court sometimes deferred to judgements of forward-thinking law enforcement executives, but it was distinctly distrustful of line officers (see, for example, Sklansky, 2005, pp. 1736–1745).

That distrust helped motivate the most characteristic tool of the criminal procedure revolution – the requirement that searches and seizures be authorised in advance with a judicial warrant. The constitutional text does not explicitly require warrants; it requires only that searches and seizures be reasonable, and that warrants, when they do issue, be appropriately narrow and based on probable cause. The Court's efforts to harmonise these two commands were always erratic, but by the time Warren took the bench the Court seemed inclined to the general view that searches and seizures were constitutional if they were reasonable, regardless whether they were pursuant to warrant. The Warren Court emphatically rejected that position. Again and again, the Court insisted that, with certain narrow exceptions, every search and seizure required a warrant. The point was that judges should be in control, not police officers. The Court liked to quote Justice Jackson's famous warning in United States v. Johnson (1948) that the decision should not be left to 'the officers engaged in the often competitive enterprise of ferreting out crime'. So fond was the Court of this formulation that it was hard not to see it as a diplomatic expression of worries about the police that went beyond their excessive zeal. Justice Jackson himself voiced concern that the point of constitutional guarantees was 'often not grasped' by the police – even, presumably, in their reflective moments – and that concern found echoes in the Court's later opinions (see Sklansky, 2005, p. 1734).

Herbert Packer (1966, p. 241), a leading legal scholar largely sympathetic to the direction the Warren Court took in criminal cases, suggested that the Court saw the police as 'suspect'; the justices were 'unconvinced that the police regard[ed] the rights of the accused as anything but a nuisance and an impediment'. Packer shared that scepticism, as did many if not most scholars writing about the police in the 1960s – and, for that matter, in the 1970s. Their concerns about the police mentality, and their attraction to the Police Subculture Schema, were only heightened by the heavy-handed, reactionary police responses to the rioting and political protests of the late 1960s and early 1970s, and by the knee-jerk hostility that law enforcement administrators and police unions showed to key Warren Court rulings and to emerging proposals for civilian oversight boards (see, for example, Fogelson, 1977). The turmoil of the late 1960s and early 1970s made it seem more obvious than ever that police officers shared a distinctive and dangerous mentality – rigid, insecure, inclined towards violence, and hostile to anyone 'different'.

The Police Subculture Schema pictured the police as a discrete and unified group, alienated from mainstream society and inherently hostile to democratic values. It thus encouraged the notion that effective regulation of the police required strong oversight from the outside, or at least from the very top. And it contributed to the great pessimism shown by scholars in the 1960s and afterward about the potential for police forces ever to regulate themselves effectively, or even to cooperate voluntarily with systems of outside review. Herbert Jacob (1974, p. 10) was fairly typical in perceiving, 'deeply embedded in the norms and work routines of policemen', a 'gigantic conspiracy against the outside world'. This perspective helps to explain why the major institutional reform drive in American policing over the past four decades has focused on civilian review boards. Samuel Walker (2001) counts roughly 100 police agencies across the United States now subject to some form of civilian oversight, including 80% of the departments in the 50 largest cities. Most commonly the oversight consists of civilian involvement in, or review of, police disciplinary proceedings.

Walker notes that civilian oversight, which existed virtually nowhere in the United States at the end of the 1960s, is now 'firmly entrenched as an important feature of American policing'. The criminal procedure revolution has faltered significantly since Earl Warren retired from the Supreme Court in 1969, but in many ways the Warren Court innovations still provide the doctrinal framework within which the police operate (see, for example, Steiker, 1996). Mid-twentieth-century police professionalism, on the other hand, fell into disfavour in the 1980s and never recovered. 'Community policing', the new shared orthodoxy of police reformers and forward-thinking law enforcement executives, is notoriously ill-defined; its core, though, may be a rejection of the kind of policing championed in the 1960s by O. W. Wilson in Chicago and William Parker in Los Angeles. But community policing, like police professionalism, is fully compatible with the view of the Police Officer as Other – the view lying at the heart of the Police Subculture Schema. The rhetoric of community policing calls for the police to be *partners* with the community, not *part* of the community. In reality, the relationship falls short of true partnership: community policing as practised rarely intrudes much on the operational autonomy of the police. But community policing does even less to challenge the longstanding view of police officers as necessarily a breed apart. Almost always, a police department engaged in community policing remains 'a force of outsiders' (Frug, 1998, p. 81).

It is telling in this regard that the reinstatement of residency requirements for police officers is rarely part of the community policing agenda. Requirements that officers live in the communities where they work were widely discarded in the era of police professionalism. A few departments brought back residency requirements in the early 1970s, but police unions strongly opposed the idea, and in most cases the opposition was successful (see, for example, Fogelson, 1977, pp. 306–307). Since the 1970s, the number of departments imposing a residency requirement appears to have declined (see Waldeck, 2000, pp. 1295–1296). Through the lens of the Police Subculture Schema, residency requirements seem pointless: police behaviour is shaped by occupational norms, not by the lives officers lead off-duty.

NEGLECTED AVENUES OF REFORM: INSTITUTIONAL DESIGN

The Police Subculture Schema has helped to shape American police reform not only by supporting the top-down management style of police professionalism, the judicial oversight model at the heart of the Supreme Court's criminal procedure revolution, and more recently the agenda of civilian oversight. It has also left a mark by diverting sustained attention *away* from certain other avenues of reform – notably those avenues of reform that focus on institutional design rather than occupational culture, differences between officers rather than similarities among them, and rank and file participation rather than top-down control. I will address each of these three large categories of reform possibilities in turn, starting with institutional design.

The Police Subculture Schema has encouraged academics and reformers interested in the police to train their sights on the shared mentality of law enforcement officers and away from the internal structure of police departments. Police administrators tinker endlessly with organisation of their departments, but generally with an eye to efficiency, not with any real expectation of significantly changing the nature of policing. The civilian oversight boards for which so many outside reformers fought so long and so hard are also, of course, a kind of restructuring, but a relatively modest kind, consisting essentially of an added layer of review. Most academics, like most police reformers, persist in stressing the group psychology of the police and in treating the internal organisation of police departments as largely irrelevant. In the words of Edward Maguire (2003, p. 39), '[r]esearchers have generally neglected studying police organisations in favour of studying police work – including situations, encounters, strategies, and occupational characteristics – and police officers – their attitudes, feelings, beliefs, behaviours, and interactions'. The blue-ribbon commissions appointed after each police scandal in the United States typically take the same tack, stressing the importance of changing the 'culture' and 'mindset' of whatever department is at issue. The questions that rarely get asked about policing are the ones that would have seemed most obvious to, say, the eighteenth-century framers of the United States Constitution, had they foreseen the emergence of modern police departments: How should law enforcement be organised to best assure that the powers given to police officers are used wisely and fairly? What departmental structures will best harness and counterbalance the ambitions of police officers, aligning their collective objectives with public purposes?

For example, virtually every American police agency of significant size now has an internal affairs department, which investigates allegations of wrongdoing by officers (see Perez, 1994). These departments vary widely in their functional organisation, lines of reporting, operational protocols, and policies for rotating officers into and out of internal affairs work. We know very little about internal affairs departments and what features of institutional design work best, in large part because most scholars and reformers have written off the whole idea of internal review as a joke. How can police misconduct be addressed by police officers themselves, when the root problem is the shared mentality and culture of the police?

The widespread pessimism about internal review is not entirely baseless; officers obviously can experience divided loyalties when investigating their colleagues. But line officers do not view internal affairs investigations lightly, nor should they. In fact, internal affairs departments on average sustain allegations against officers at significantly higher rates than civilian oversight boards. No one thinks internal affairs departments can take sole responsibility for improving the quality of policing: wholly aside from conflicts of interest, internal affairs investigations tend by their nature to be punitive rather than forward-looking, and to focus on specific incidents rather than systemic failures. But some internal affairs departments function better than others, and some even depart from a pure incident-by-incident focus (see, for example, Armacost, 2004). Writing off internal affairs departments as hopeless makes no sense. Finding the best ways to organise and to run internal affairs departments is an important, largely neglected strategy of police reform, and it is part of a broader category of neglected questions pertaining to institutional redesign of police departments. Some of the blame for this neglect can be laid at the feet of the Police Subculture Schema.

NEGLECTED AVENUES OF REFORM: GOOD COPS AND BAD COPS

The Police Subculture Schema has also diverted attention from another set of approaches, focusing on differences between officers rather than on similarities among officers. Since the 1950s, the overwhelming bulk of research on the police has tried to explain the characteristics of police as a group. The question it poses is, 'Why are the police the way they are?' Much rarer is research that tries to understand why some police officers wind up more effective and more trustworthy than others. Precisely because it *did* ask this latter question, the justly celebrated study of Oakland, California, police officers by William Ker Muir, Jr. (1977) has been far less influential than the work of scholars like Skolnick and James Q. Wilson, who focused on group characteristics and group behaviour – the matters highlighted by the Police Subculture Schema, and the matters on which police researchers have continued to train their sights.

Police reformers, too, have tended to pursue measures that treat all cops alike and all recruits as essentially fungible. Recruiting practices have received less attention than they deserve, and all officers are generally treated as needing the same degree and kind of supervision. One encouraging departure from this approach is the increasing emphasis on the use of data management systems to identify and to track officers with a history of violent encounters and disciplinary actions. There is growing recognition that a small subgroup of officers accounts for a large share of police abuse, and that identifying these officers and closely monitoring them is a particularly promising strategy for reducing violence and illegality in the ranks (see Walker, 2003). Tracking systems of this kind are required under the settlements negotiated in civil rights lawsuits brought against police departments by the United States Department of Justice, and in some case by private plaintiffs (see, for example, Johnson, 2004). But the systems are still far from universal (see Armacost, 2004). More importantly, they differentiate officers only at the low end, distinguishing 'problem officers' from the great majority. They do not pursue the agenda suggested by Muir's work: identifying excellent officers, rewarding them for their excellence, and learning from them.

NEGLECTED AVENUES OF REFORM: PARTICIPATORY DECISION-MAKING

The third category of reform possibilities the Police Subculture Schema has tended to slight consists of efforts to enlist rank-and-file officers in the collective reshaping of their work. In ways discussed above, the police professionalism movement of the 1950s and 1960s and the Supreme Court's 'criminal procedure revolution' both operated on a model of rigid, top-down reform of the police. In the late 1960s and early 1970s, when many people saw workplaces as ideal venues for experiments in participatory democracy, several scholars – including Westley (1970) – argued for bringing a degree of workplace democracy to policing (see also, for example, Berkley, 1969; Angell, 1971). The core idea was that officers who participated collectively in the shaping of police work would be less alienated, more effective, and more acculturated to and comfortable with democratic values and practices. There even were scattered efforts to implement these ideas, and they met with some success. In Oakland, for example, Toch, Grant, and Galvin (1975) led a team of officers that developed a novel institutional mechanism for reducing police violence – a mechanism that itself drew heavily on the involvement of rank-and-file officers, and that actually enjoyed a promising degree of success before it fell victim to budget cuts (see Toch & Grant, 2005, p. 100).

As it happened, the late 1960s and early 1970s were about the worst possible time to argue for giving police officers a larger role in reshaping their work. Police unionism and rank-and-file activism were surging at the time, and they took distinctly unattractive forms. The rallying issues included not only working conditions and compensation but also, and more strikingly, opposition to civilian review boards and related efforts at police reform. And those were some of the tamer forms of police politics in the late 1960s and early 1970s. The less tame forms included active participation in far right-wing organisations, vigilante attacks on black activists, organised brutality against political protesters, and open defiance of civilian authorities (see, for example, Fogelson, 1977). The Police Subculture Schema seemed to fit events better than ever.

As a result, liberal academics and reformers who might otherwise have been sympathetic to giving police officers a collective say in the nature of their work instead concluded that democracy and the rule of law required that police officers be followers, not innovators (see, for example, Skolnick, 1969). By the end of the 1970s, enthusiasm largely disappeared for bringing workplace democracy to law enforcement, and it has never really reappeared. 'Team policing' and 'problem-oriented policing', two important predecessors of community policing, each incorporated elements of participatory management (see Livingston, 1997). But those elements became much more muted as time went on and as team policing and problem-oriented policing were absorbed into mainstream thinking about law enforcement. Theories of 'cooperativist' management, which became popular in industrial relations circles in the 1980s and 1990s (see, for example, Wilms, 1996), had little impact on law enforcement.

Today, policing clings stubbornly to authoritarian management practices long discredited in other, traditionally hierarchical sectors of the American economy – including, ironically, the military (see Cowper, 2004). Little has changed in this regard in the decade and a half since the assessment by Herman Goldstein (1990, p. 27) that '[t]he dominant form of policing ... continues to view police officers as automatons' and to ask them for 'nonthinking compliance'. An extreme, but telling illustration: The city of New London, Connecticut, went to court several years ago to defend, successfully, its policy of refusing to hire applicants who scored too high on a test of 'cognitive ability' (see Allen, 1999). The publisher of the test recommends its use to screen out employees unsuited for jobs 'where creativity could be a detriment'. New London's deputy police chief told a reporter that the department had adopted the test because '[p]olice work is kind of mundane'. The president of the test publishing company agreed: 'You can't decide not to read someone their Miranda rights because you felt it would be more efficient, or you thought they knew them already'. All of this would make perfect sense to Frederick Taylor, the Progressive Era champion of top-down, thoroughly regimented workforces, and who warned that '[t]he man who is mentally alert and intelligent is for this very reason entirely unsuited' for monotonous work (Taylor, 1911, p. 59). Taylorism has few fans today among management theorists and other students of employment, but law enforcement has remained a bastion of something not too distant, in some ways, from the Taylorist faith in 'scientific management'.

The Police Subculture Schema is part of the reason. The sense lingers that the self-perpetuating occupational norms of law enforcement are inherently antithetical to democracy. For some scholars, the power of those norms in shaping police behaviour is reason to couple top-down reforms with management practices that 'obtain "buy-in" from the ground up'. But in the main the Police Subculture Schema has dulled the interest of academics and reformers in efforts to 'mobilise ... the energy, passion, commitment, and expertise' of the police rank-and-file. (Armacost, 2004, p. 546). It has kept them wedded to a command-and-control model of police reform.

Because departures from that model have been so limited, we have little evidence about how well they work. But the evidence we do have is encouraging. The success of the Oakland violence reduction project has already been mentioned. The Madison, Wisconsin, Police Department, which began experimenting with participatory decision-making in the 1980s, found that it increased job satisfaction, made officers more open to reform, and improved the level of police service in the eyes of the public (see Wykoff & Skogan, 1993). More recently, the police department in Broken Arrow, Oklahoma, has turned much of its policy-making over to a 12-member committee of management officials, union leaders, and rank-and-file officers, a move that appears to have contributed to greater productivity (as measured by arrest and clearance rates), a sharp drop in citizen complaints, and higher levels of job satisfaction (see Wuestewald & Steinheider, 2006).

These results are consistent with the growing body of research on participatory management in workforces outside law enforcement. That research suggests that involving employees in decision-making does more than boost morale; it improves the quality of decisions by capitalising on the diffused, hands-on knowledge that workers gain by actually doing their jobs (see, for example, Wilms, 1996). Mobilising the energy and expertise of the rank and file may be particularly important in policing, given the large amounts of discretion that police officers exercise and the extent to which good police work relies on localised, ground-level intelligence – points stressed by Goldstein (1990). Valuing the intelligence and initiative of police officers may also be the best way to get the kind of educated, highly qualified recruits that most departments (contra New London) seem to want these days – and that they report increasing difficulty attracting (see McGreevy, 2006).

These are not the only ways in which participatory decision-making may have special advantages in policing. A long tradition – dating back to John Stuart Mill and G. D. H. Cole and revived in the wake of the 1960s by scholars like Carol Pateman (1970) and Jane Mansbridge (1980) – sees the workplace as the ideal training ground for democratic citizenship and argues against rigid, autocratic workplaces on the ground that they stunt the political development of employees, not only depriving them of full, satisfying lives but also weakening democracy in the broader society. This viewpoint remains controversial. But even if democracy does not depend on fostering the political growth of *all* employees, there are two special reasons to want *police officers* to internalise democratic values and habits. First, the police are often placed in positions where they can actively support or actively threaten democratic activities: they can protect political protesters, for example, or they can attack them; they can help create a climate of respect for individual privacy and autonomy, or they can make privacy insecure and nonconformity difficult; they can enforce norms of tolerance, or they can reinforce bias and prejudice; they can teach citizens that authority may safely be challenged, or they can teach the opposite (see, for example, Goldstein, 1977). Second, there are reasons to think that effective policing *in general* – at least the forms of effective policing most congenial to a free and open society – depends on some of the same values and skills often thought important for democratic citizenship more broadly.

This is one of the great lessons of Muir's extraordinary study of Oakland police officers in the early 1970s. Trying to determine what made some police officers more effective and more trustworthy than others, Muir concluded that good police officers had democratic virtues: a comfort with moral ambiguity, an ability to see shades of grey, a broad capacity for tolerance and empathy, and, perhaps most important, 'an enjoyment of talk' – an affinity, that is to say, for conversation, argument, deliberation, advocacy, and compromise (Muir, 1977). Police officers developed these virtues, in part, by working in a department that itself embraced them. Among the heroes of Muir's book is Chief Charles Gain, a legendary reformer who ran Oakland's police force from 1967 to 1973. Gain ruled with a heavy hand and was never popular with the rank and file; in 1972 the Oakland Police Officers' Association voted no confidence in his administration (see Jackson, 1979). Muir admired him nonetheless for infusing the department 'with a sense of purpose', which gave his officers 'dignity and moral meaning'. Much of that was accomplished, Muir thought, through a training style and a workplace climate that invited 'participation, discussion, argument, and questioning'. What Muir liked about the Oakland Police Department, in short, was the way it seemed to operate as a school for democratic citizenry – or, more precisely, democratic leadership. Muir saw police officers as 'streetcorner politicians', and they were most likely to grow in that role if they worked in departments that within themselves fostered 'widespread political participation' (Muir, 1977, pp. 253, 281).

Now is a propitious time to explore the potential of participatory decision-making in policing. There is a large literature on cooperative decision-making in other workplaces and organisations, and a small but instructive body of work experimenting with these ideas in policing. Police unions, implacable foes of reform in the late 1960s and early 1970s, have since moderated their rhetoric and their politics, and in some cases they have become active proponents of reform (see Marks & Fleming, 2006). Increasingly, police unions are rivalled for influence by identity-based groups of police officers – groups of minority officers, of female officers, and of gay and lesbian officers – many of which are quite vocal in pushing for reform (see, for example, Barlow & Barlow, 2000). And police workforces have grown more educated and more diverse; they are more hospitable venues than they used to be for experiments in employee empowerment (see Sklansky, 2006a). To take advantage of these changes, though, we need to recognise them, and recognition has been hindered by the lasting hold of the Police Subculture Schema.

OVERLOOKED DANGERS: DIVERSIFICATION AND AFFIRMATIVE ACTION

In addition to making certain reform possibilities harder to see, the Police Subculture Schema has also obscured a pair of increasingly pressing problems. The first is the risk that the diversification of police departments, which has done so much to clear space for debate and disagreement within the ranks, may be stalling prematurely, as court-ordered affirmative action remedies grow less common. The second is the set of challenges posed by the growth of police managerialism. Let me take each of these in turn.

First, diversification and affirmative action. Much of the reason the Police Subculture Schema now seems out of date is that police workforces are no longer unified and homogeneous. Minority officers, female officers, and openly gay and lesbian officers are slowly but dramatically transforming a profession that 35 years ago was virtually all white, virtually all male, and uniformly homophobic. Blacks, for example, made up somewhere around 6% of sworn officers in the 300 or so largest American police departments in 1970; today the figure is around 18% (see McCrary, 2003). In 2005, for the first time in the history of the New York City Police Department, a majority of the new officers graduating from its academy were members of racial minorities (see Lee, 2005). In some major cities – including Los Angeles, Detroit, and Washington, D.C. – the entire police force is now majority minority (see Reaves & Hickman, 2000). Women were 2% of sworn officers in large police agencies in 1972; today they are close to 13% (see National Center for Women and Policing, 2002). Again, the figure in some departments is significantly higher, although it tops out around 25%. Like minority officers, female officers remain concentrated in lower ranks – although, as with minority officers, the extent and uniformity of the concentration is less than one might expect. It is difficult to estimate the number of gay and lesbian police officers, or even those who are, to a greater or lesser extent, open about their status. The latter category is clearly growing, though, to the point where, in some departments, 'the presence of self-disclosed gay and lesbian officers has become normalised' (Belkin & McNichol, 2002, p.78; see also Miller, 1999). And the mere fact that there are *any* openly gay officers, let alone gay police executives, is a sea change from the situation 30 years ago (see, for example, Leinen, 1993; Miller, Forest, & Jurik, 2003).

All of this has made the Police Subculture Schema, with its picture of police departments as insular, homogeneous bastions of unchallenged patriarchy, racism, and authoritarianism, increasingly out of date. Police officers today report lines of division, distrust, and resentment not only between white officers and minority officers, but also between male and female officers, between gay and straight officers, and sometimes between black officers and Latino officers, Latino officers and Asian-American officers, and so on. In the words of one white, male officer, 'It used to be we were all "blue", but that has changed over the past years. Today there is black, white, and female segregation' (Haarr, 1997, p. 66).

The decline in solidarity does not seem to have impaired police effectiveness; for operational purposes it appears still to be true that 'blue is blue' (see, for example, Myers, Forest, & Miller, 2004). In between calls to service, though, police officers are a less cohesive group than they used to be, and that turns out to be a largely good thing. It has made the internal cultures of police departments less stifling, and it has opened up space for dissent and disagreement. Studies of police departments today read far differently than those of 30 or 40 years ago: investigators rarely find a single police perspective on any given issue, but rather a range of conflicting perspectives (see, for example, Barlow, Barlow, & Stajkovic, 1994; Haarr, 1997).

Moreover, the social fragmentation has gone hand in hand with a decline in police insularity. For identity binds as well as divides (see Oberweis & Musheno, 1999). Minority officer organisations frequently work closely with minority organisations outside law enforcement; to a lesser extent, female officers sometimes form organisational ties with women working in other historically male professions. The National Center for Women and Policing, for example, is part of Eleanor Smeal's Feminist Majority Project. Organisational alliances like this operate alongside, and help to foster, less formal ties of affinity between minority cops and minority citizens, female cops and women more broadly, and gays and lesbians inside and outside law enforcement (see Barlow & Barlow, 2000). Both the formal, organisational alliances and the less formal ties of affinity create channels for expanding civilian involvement in the shaping and directing of law enforcement.

The growing, still far from complete acceptance of openly gay and lesbian officers may contribute in a particularly powerful way to the social realignment of law enforcement – in part by accelerating the fragmentation of the police subculture, in part by creating new channels of communication with groups outside of law enforcement, and in part by challenging the endemic homophobia of law enforcement. There is good reason to think that the suppression of homosexuality has played a central role in cementing police solidarity, in part by rendering professional male–male partnerships sexually unthreatening, and in part by helping to shape a whole, hyper-masculinised professional ethos (see, for example, Harris, 2000; Messerschmidt, 1993). The presence of openly gay and lesbian officers, particularly once they begin to rise through the ranks, challenges the easy, taken-for-granted homophobia of law enforcement, and all that it has helped to foster – the nominally desexualised police workplace, the hyper-masculinised ethos of the profession, and the tacit acceptance of extra-legal violence. All of that is on top of the ways in which gay and lesbian officers, like minority officers and female officers, will help to fragment the police subculture and to build identity-based bridges to groups outside of law enforcement.

The clear weight of the evidence suggests that the diversification of American police departments over the last four decades owes much to race-conscious and gender-conscious affirmative action remedies, typically under court order (see, for example, Sklansky, 2006a). Some of the most striking evidence is the progress over time in particular departments. In Pittsburgh, for example, the percentage of women officers went from 1% in 1975, when court-ordered hiring quotas were imposed, to 27.2% in 1990, the highest figure at the time for any large city in the nation. When the quota was lifted in 1991, the female share of new hires plummeted from 50% (required under the court order) to 8.5%, and by 2001 the percentage of women in the rank of police officer had dropped to 22% and was continuing to decline. (National Center for Women and Policing, 2003). The clear implication – that court-ordered affirmative action has played a pivotal role in diversifying police departments – is confirmed by more sophisticated and broad ranging statistical analyses of police hiring in the United States (see, for example, Martin, 1991; McCrary, 2003). Because the statistics regarding gay and lesbian officers are so paltry, it is more difficult to assess the role of lawsuits here. Anecdotally, though, lawsuits appear to have played a significant role in spurring departments to become more welcoming to, and tolerant of, openly gay and lesbian cops, just as earlier lawsuits were pivotal in bringing more race and gender diversity to policing (see, for example, Belkin & McNichol, 2002; Hernandez, 1989).

All this gives reason to be concerned about the recent contraction of court-ordered affirmative action in the United States. Turnover in police departments is low – typically about 4% annually – so it takes many years for changes in hiring practices to have their full effect on workforce composition (see McCrary, 2003). With affirmative action increasingly under fire in the United States, hiring and promotion quotas are often lifted before the demographics of police forces are brought fully in line with the communities they serve. Backsliding at that point is a real possibility – as Pittsburgh discovered. The Pittsburgh experience serves as a warning about what may happen elsewhere, and may in some respects already be happening. The nationwide increase in the representation of women in large police departments, for example, appears to have stalled since 1999, and the percentage of officers who are female in these departments may have ticked slightly downward (see National Center for Women and Policing, 2003).

The danger of losing ground in the gradual diversification of American police forces has received less attention than it deserves. Part of the reason may well be the Police Subculture Schema, which conditions us to see police officers as fungible, police occupational norms as unchanging, and police demographics as functionally irrelevant. Cognitive burn-in has made it harder to see the dramatic though still incomplete ways in which the internal dynamics of police forces have been transformed, and how much rides on continuing that progress.

OVERLOOKED DANGERS: POLICE MANAGERIALISM

The Police Subculture Schema focuses attention on the occupational norms and practices of the police rank-and-file. Police leaders almost always start their careers as patrol officers and work their way up the ranks, but by the time they become managers, it is generally assumed, they are no longer part of the subculture. The police professionalism movement was predicated, in part, on this assumption; much of the point of police professionalism was to replace unwritten, rank-and-file norms with explicit rules imposed from above. An influential study in the early 1980s argued that 'management cops' have their own culture, separate and distinct from 'street cop culture'. But 'management cop culture' essentially consisted of a commitment to rules and regulations and a faith in 'the theories and practices of scientific management and public administration'. In contrast, street cop culture was a real culture, replete with socialisation practices, informal role assignments, and an elaborate set of unwritten maxims of conduct – 'the cop's code'. (Reuss-Ianni & Ianni, 1983, pp. 257, 266). Not surprisingly, then, it is the street cop culture, not the management cop culture, that has continued to receive the lion's share of the attention from scholars and reformers, and the lion's share of the blame for the weaknesses and pathologies of law enforcement.

But alongside the social realignment within police forces, described above, there is another cultural change brewing in law enforcement, and focusing on the rank and file makes it harder to see. There has been a pronounced shift towards managerialism in American policing, and the change is most apparent in the command ranks.

The new managerialism of law enforcement has been driven in part by a shift of policing responsibilities to the private sector, discussed more extensively elsewhere in this book. Borrowing terms from Philip Selznick (1969), Elizabeth Joh (2004, pp. 65–66) suggests that at bottom the difference between private policing and public policing may be the difference between 'management' and 'governance' – between organisations that emphasise 'efficiency and goal achievement', and organisations that 'take into account broader values such as integrity, the accommodation of interests, and morality'. Selznick developed this distinction in the course of an argument for workplace democracy; he was part of a broad intellectual movement in the late 1960s and early 1970s that saw workplaces as particularly promising sites for participatory democracy. I discussed earlier the reasons why efforts to extend that kind of thinking to policing proved largely abortive. The frightening forms that police activism took in the late 1960s and early 1970s dulled the appetite of scholars and reformers for bringing any kind of participatory management to law enforcement. The idea was pretty much dead by the end of the 1970s, and it has never really been revived.

In some respects, though, democratic values *have* been brought into the internal operations of police workforces. Over the past three decades, police departments have become heavily unionised, and police officers have been given, by statute and court decision, a robust range of due process protections against adverse employment decisions. As we have seen, police workforces are also far more diverse than they were 30 years ago, far less monolithic, far less insular, and far more open to dissent and disagreement. Police privatisation puts these gains at risk. In a recent, illuminating study of a large Canadian security firm, George Rigakos (2002) found a workplace marked by extraordinary efforts at monitoring, controlling, and disciplining employees, and by levels of alienation and cynicism remarkable even in comparison with what we have come to expect from public law enforcement officers. There is no reason to think other security firms would look strikingly different in these regards. It may be possible, of course, to bring public values of employee due process and participatory decision-making to the private security industry. The industry is currently the target of a major organising campaign (see Greenhouse, 2006), and workplace democracy could be imposed by statute on private security firms – just as on any other private firm. At bottom, though, what a private security firm offers its customers is, as Rigakos puts it, 'a management system for hire' (Rigakos, 2002, p. 148). This will likely make public norms regarding the *internal* operation of police forces the hardest to export to the private sector. Their internal operations – overwhelmingly non-union, unburdened by civil service rules and 'police officers' bills of rights', relentlessly focused on efficiency and narrowly drawn performance goals – are precisely what the private firms have to offer. It is what distinguishes one firm from another, and what still, despite the spread of public sector managerialism, most strongly distinguishes private policing as a whole from public law enforcement. If the current trend towards police privatisation has any single point, after all – other than retreating from a collective commitment to egalitarian protection against illegal force – the point is to escape, to circumvent, or to limit the domain of the organisational styles associated with public law enforcement, and to move the internal operations of policing some distance from governance towards management (see Sklansky, 2006b).

Rather than serving as the model for private policing, public police agencies may find themselves copying the strategies, rhetoric, and self-conception of the private police – much as Henry Fielding's Bow Street Runners brought the entrepreneurial spirit of thief-taking to the eighteenth-century London magistracy, and J. Edgar Hoover later mimicked the marketing tactics of Alan Pinkerton (see Sklansky, 1999). Some police departments may already be drifting in this direction, pulled along by the mounting tendency for the public and private police to see themselves as partners, 'with similar goals but different approaches and spheres of influence' (International Association of Chiefs of Police, 2004, p. 1; see also Joh, 2004).

In principle, the expanding cooperation between public law enforcement and the private security industry, and the growing feeling of affinity between the two sectors, could facilitate a transfer of norms in either direction. In practice, though, there is little evidence so far of private security firms becoming more mindful of values beyond efficiency and the achievement of narrowly-defined goals. It is easier to find signs of police departments becoming more 'managerial', both in their practices and in their sense of organisational mission. Probably the best example is Compstat, the New York Police Department's statistics-based system of performance evaluations for mid-level supervisors, now emulated throughout the nation (see, for example, Walsh & Vito, 2004). But the growing managerialism of police departments is a much broader phenomenon (see, for example, Garland, 2001; Loader, 1994; Wood, 2004). Even the 'client-driven mandate' of private security firms may be crossing over to the public sector: one of the many plausible definitions of 'community policing' is 'police treating a neighbourhood the way a security guard treats a client property' (Sherman, 1995, pp. 338–339). Police unions, with their guild instincts, may slow the growth of managerialism in some public law enforcement agencies (see Fleming & Lafferty, 2000; O'Malley & Hutchinson, 2005). But there are signs that police unions, too, are beginning to adopt, out of necessity, the rhetoric of managerialism (see McLaughlin & Murji, 2001).

None of this is unambiguously bad. Managerialism has its strengths. Compstat, for example, may have contributed to New York City's unusually sharp decline in crime rates in the 1990s (see, for example, Moore & Braga, 2003; Walsh & Vito, 2004) – although this is very much a matter of debate (see, for example, Levitt, 2004; Rosenfeld, Fornango, & Baumer, 2005). The rapid spread of managerialism in public policing is cause for concern, though, because of the way in which it threatens to supplant older – and some newer – traditions of governance in public law enforcement with a focus on efficiency and narrowly defined goal achievement. 'Community policing', for example, has at times meant something quite different from adopting the mindset of private security firms; it has meant reducing the organisational insularity of participating police departments by opening new channels of communication and cooperation with a variety of outside groups, both governmental and nongovernmental. Officers in these departments have been forced, regularly and systematically, to confront and to accommodate conflicting views of their mission and conflicting notions of how best to balance liberty and security (see Thacher, 2001). They have been pushed away, in other words, from a single-minded focus on a narrow set of performance goals; they have been driven from management towards governance. It would be a mistake to overstate the extent of this trend in public policing. But there is no corresponding trend whatsoever in the private security industry.

A final caveat: there are grounds for strong scepticism about how strongly the official ethos of a police organisation, public or private, shapes the behaviour of officers out on the streets. Rigakos found that the private security guards he studied thought and acted, in many respects, much like public law enforcement officers engaged in similar work, and for much the same reasons. Among private police, just as among public police, 'conditions of dependent uncertainty', 'status frustration', and physical risk breed 'a strong occupational ethic of interdependence in the face of immediate or impending dangers' – 'not unlike the occupational codes of public police agencies' (Rigakos, 2002, pp. 119–120).

That is exactly what the Police Subculture Schema would predict, of course. It is one more piece of evidence that the schema retains considerable explanatory power. But the grounds for concern about the Police Subculture Schema have to do less with what it suggests than with what it obscures. The problem with a burned-in image, even a good one, is what it prevents us from seeing.

REFERENCES

Adorno, T. W., Frenkel-Brunswik, E., Levinson, D. J., & Sanford, R. N. (1950). *The authoritarian personality.* New York: Harper.

Allen, M. (1999). Help wanted invoking the not-too-high-IQ test. *New York Times*, Sept. 19, p. D4.

Angell, J. E. (1971). Toward an alternative to the classic police organizational arrangements: A democratic model. *Criminology, 9*, 185–206.

Armacost, B. E. (2004). Organizational culture and police misconduct. *George Washington Law Review, 72*, 453–545.

Balch, R. W. (1972). The police personality: Fact or fiction? *Journal of Criminal Law, Criminology, and Police Science, 63*, 106–119.

Barlow, D. E., & Barlow, M. H. (2000). *Police in a multicultural society.* Long Grove: Waveland Press.

Barlow, M. H., Barlow, D. E., & Stajkovic, S. (1994). The media, the police, and the multicultural community: Observations of a city in crisis. *Journal of Crime and Justice, 17*, 133–166.

Belkin, A., & McNichol, J. (2002). Pink and blue: Outcomes associated with the integration of open gay and lesbian personnel in the San Diego Police Department. *Police Quarterly, 5*, 63–95.

42   DAVID ALAN SKLANSKY

Berkley, G. E. (1969). *The democratic policeman.* Boston: Beacon Press.
Bittner, E. (1990). *Aspects of police work.* Boston: Northeastern University Press.
Blasi, G. L. (1995). What lawyers know: Lawyering expertise, cognitive science, and the functions of theory. *Journal of Legal Education, 45,* 313–397.
Cain, M. (1993). Some go forward, some go back: Police work in comparative perspective. *Comparative Sociology, 22,* 319–324.
Carter, D. L., & Sapp, A. D. (1990). The evolution of higher education in law enforcement: Preliminary findings from a national study. *Journal of Criminal Justice Education, 1,* 59–85.
Chan, J. (1996). Changing police culture. *British Journal of Criminology, 36,* 109–134.
Conlon, E. (2004). *Blue blood.* New York: Riverhead Books.
Cowper, T. J. (2004). The myth of the 'military model' of leadership in law enforcement. In: Q. C. Thurman & J. Zhao (Eds), *Contemporary policing: Controversies, challenges, and solutions* (pp. 113–125). Los Angeles: Roxbury.
Delaney, J. T., & Feuille, P. (1987). Police. In: D. B. Lipsky & C. B. Donn (Eds), *Collective bargaining in American industry: Contemporary perspectives and future directions* (pp. 265–306). Lexington, MA: D. C. Heath & Co.
Fielding, N. G. (1988). *Joining forces: Police training, socialization, and occupational competence.* London: Routledge.
Fleming, J., & Lafferty, G. (2000). New management techniques and restructuring for accountability in Australian police organizations. *Policing, 23,* 154–168.
Fogelson, R. M. (1977). *Big-city police.* Cambridge, MA: Harvard University Press.
Frug, G. (1998). City services. *New York University Law Review, 73,* 23–96.
Garland, D. (2001). *The culture of control.* Chicago: University of Chicago Press.
Goldstein, H. (1977). *Policing a free society.* Cambridge, MA: Ballinger.
Goldstein, H. (1990). *Problem-oriented policing.* New York: McGraw-Hill.
Greenhouse, S. (2006). Borrowing language of civil rights movement, drive is on to unionize guards. *New York Times,* July 26, p. A13.
Haarr, R. N. (1997). Patterns of interaction in a police patrol bureau: Race and gender barriers to integration. *Justice Quarterly, 14,* 53–85.
Harris, A. P. (2000). Gender, violence, race, and criminal justice. *Stanford Law Review, 52,* 777–807.
Hernandez, M. (1989). 2 LAPD officers join homosexual bias suit. *Los Angeles Times,* Nov. 22, p. B3.
International Association of Chiefs of Police. (2004). *National policy summit: Building private security/public policing partnerships to prevent and respond to terrorism and public disorder.* Retrieved on July 3, 2006, from http://www.cops.usdoj.gov/mime/open.pdf?Item = 1355.
Jackson, B. M. (1979). *Leadership and change in public organization: The dilemmas of an urban police chief.* Doctoral dissertation. University of California, Berkeley.
Jacob, H. (1974). *The potential for reform of criminal justice.* Beverly Hills: Sage Publications.
Joh, E. (2004). The paradox of private policing. *Journal of Criminal Law and Criminology, 95,* 49–131.
Johnson, C. (2004). Oakland's new system to weed out bad officers. *San Francisco Chronicle,* May 31, p. B1.
Lee, J. 8. (2005). In police class, blue comes in many colors. *New York Times,* July 8, p. B2.
Leinen, S. (1993). *Gay cops.* New Brunswick: Rutgers University Press.
Levitt, S. D. (2004). Understanding why crime fell in the 1990s: Four factors that explain the decline and six that do not. *Journal of Economic Perspectives, 18,* 163–190.

Livingston, D. (1997). Police discretion and the quality of life in public places: Courts, communities, and the new policing. *Columbia Law Review, 97,* 551–672.

Loader, I. (1994). Democracy, justice, and the limits of policing: Rethinking police accountability. *Social and Legal Studies, 3,* 521–544.

Lynd, H. M. (1958). *On shame and the search for identity.* New York: Harcourt, Brace & Co.

Maguire, E. R. (2003). *Organizational structure in American police agencies: Context, complexity, and control.* Albany: State University of New York Press.

Mansbridge, J. J. (1980). *Beyond adversary democracy.* Chicago: University of Chicago Press.

Marks, M., & Fleming, J. (2006). The right to unionize, the right to bargain, and the right to democratic politics. *Annals of the American Academy of Political and Social Science, 605,* 178–199.

Martin, S. E. (1991). The effectiveness of affirmative action: The case of women in policing. *Justice Quarterly, 8,* 489–504.

McCrary, J. (2003). *The effect of court-ordered hiring quotas on the composition and quality of police.* Retrieved on June 29, 2006, from http://www-personal.umich.edu/~jmccrary/mccrary2004.pdf

McGreevy, P. (2006). LAPD is under the gun on recruitment. *Los Angeles Times,* July 2, p. B1.

McLaughlin, E., & Murji, K. (2001). Lost connections and new directions: Neo-liberalism, new public managerialism and the 'modernization' of the British police. In: K. Stenson & R. Sullivan (Eds), *Crime, risk, and justice: The politics of crime control in liberal democracies* (pp. 104–121). Cullompton: Willan.

Messerschmidt, J. W. (1993). *Masculinities and crime: Critique and reconceptualization of theory.* Lanham: Rowman & Littlefield.

Miller, S. L. (1999). *Gender and community policing: Walking the talk.* Boston: Northeastern University Press.

Miller, S. L., Forest, K. B., & Jurik, N. C. (2003). Diversity in blue: Lesbian and gay police officers in a masculine occupation. *Men and Masculinities, 5,* 355–385.

Moore, M. H., & Braga, A. A. (2003). Measuring and improving police performance: The lessons of Compstat and its progeny. *Policing, 26,* 439–453.

Muir, W. K. M. (1977). *Police: Streetcorner politicians.* Chicago: University of Chicago Press.

Myers, K. A., Forest, K. B., & Miller, S. L. (2004). Officer friendly and the tough cop: Gays and lesbians navigate homophobia and policing. *Journal of Homosexuality, 47,* 17–37.

National Center for Women and Policing (2002). *Equality denied: The status of women in policing, 2001.* Retrieved on June 29, 2006, from http://www.womenandpolicing.org/PDF/2002_Status_Report.pdf

National Center for Women and Policing (2003). *Under scrutiny: The effect of consent decrees on the representation of women in sworn law enforcement.* Retrieved on June 29, 2006, from http://www.womenandpolicing.org/pdf/Fullconsentdecreestudy.pdf

National Research Council. (2004). *Fairness and effectiveness in policing: The evidence.* Washington, DC: National Academies Press.

Oberweis, T., & Musheno, M. (1999). Policing identities: Cop decision making and the constitution of the citizen. *Law & Social Inquiry, 24,* 897–923.

O'Malley, P., & Hutchinson, S. (2005). *Police culture and the new police corporations.* Unpublished manuscript.

Packer, H. L. (1966). The courts, the police, and the rest of us. *Journal of Criminal Law, Criminology and Police Science, 57,* 238–243.

44   DAVID ALAN SKLANSKY

Pateman, C. (1970). *Participation and democratic theory*. Cambridge: Cambridge University Press.
Perez, D. W. (1994). *Common sense about police reform*. Philadelphia: Temple University Press.
Reaves, B. A., & Hickman, M. J. (2002). *Police departments in large cities, 1990–2000*. Washington, DC: U.S. Government Printing Office.
Reiner, R. (1992). *The politics of the police* (2nd ed.). Toronto: University of Toronto Press.
Reuss-Ianni, E., & Ianni, F. A. J. (1983). Street cops and management cops: Two cultures of policing: Street cops and management cops. In: M. Punch (Ed.), *Control in the police organization* (pp. 251–274). Cambridge, MA: MIT Press.
Rigakos, G. (2002). *The new parapolice: Risk markets and commodified social control*. Toronto: University of Toronto Press.
Rosenfeld, R., Fornango, R., & Baumer, E. (2005). Did *Ceasefire, COMSTAT*, and *Exile* reduce homicide?. *Criminology & Public Policy*, *4*, 419–449.
Selznick, P. (1969). *Law, society, and industrial justice*. New York: Sage.
Sherman, L. W. (1995). The police. In: J. Q. Wilson & Petersilia Joan (Eds), *Crime* (pp. 327–348). San Francisco: Institute for Contemporary Studies Press.
Simon, J. (2002). Speaking truth and power. *Law & Society Review*, *36*, 37–50.
Sklansky, D. A. (1999). The private police. *UCLA Law Review*, *46*, 1165–1287.
Sklansky, D. A. (2005). Police and democracy. *Michigan Law Review*, *103*, 1699–1830.
Sklansky, D. A. (2006a). Not your father's police department: Making sense of the new demographics of law enforcement. *Journal of Criminal Law & Criminology*, *96*, 1209–1243.
Sklansky, D. A. (2006b). Private police and democracy. *American Criminal Law Review*, *43*, 89–105.
Skolnick, J. H. (1966). *Justice without trial: Law enforcement in a democratic society*. New York: Wiley.
Skolnick, J. H. (1969). *The politics of protest*. New York: Ballantine Books.
Steiker, C. (1996). Counter-revolution in constitutional criminal procedure? Two audiences, two answers. *Michigan Law Review*, *94*, 2466–2551.
Taylor, F. W. (1911). *The principles of scientific management*. New York: Harper.
Thacher, D. (2001). Conflicting values in community policing. *Law & Society Review*, *35*, 765–798.
Toch, H., & Grant, J. D. (2005). *Police as problem solvers: How frontline workers can promote organizational and community change* (2nd ed.). Washington, DC: American Psychological Association.
Toch, H., Grant, J. D., & Galvin, R. T. (1975). *Agents of change: A study in police reform*. New York: Wiley.
Truman, D. B. (1971). *The governmental process: Political interests and public opinion* (2nd ed.). New York: Alfred A. Knopf.
United States v. Johnson (1948). 333 U.S. 10.
Waldeck, S. E. (2000). Cops, community policing, and the social norms approach to crime control: Should one make us more comfortable with the others? *Georgia Law Review*, *34*, 1253–1310.
Walker, S. (2001). *Police accountability: The role of citizen oversight*. Belmont: Wadsworth.
Walker, S. (2003). The new paradigm of police accountability: The U.S. Justice Department 'pattern or practice' suits in context. *Saint Louis University Public Law Review*, *22*, 3–52.
Walsh, W. F., & Vito, G. F. (2004). The meaning of Compstat: Analysis and response. *Journal of Contemporary Criminal Justice*, *20*, 51–69.
Westley, W. (1953). Violence and the police. *American Journal of Sociology*, *59*, 34–41.

Westley, W. (1956). Secrecy and the police. *Social Forces, 34*, 254–257.

Westley, W. A. (1970). *Violence and the police: A sociological study of law, custom, and morality.* Cambridge, MA: MIT Press.

Wilms, W. W. (1996). *Restoring prosperity: How workers and managers are forging a new culture of cooperation.* New York: Random House.

Wilson, J. Q. (1968). *Varieties of police behaviour: The management of law and order in eight communities.* Cambridge, MA: Harvard University Press.

Wood, J. (2004). Cultural change in the governance of security. *Policing and Security, 14*, 31–48.

Wuestewald, T., & Steinheider, B. (2006). Shared leadership: Can empowerment work in police organizations? *The Police Chief, 73*(January), 48–55.

Wykoff, M. A., & Skogan, W. K. (1993). *Community policing in Madison: Quality from the inside out.* Washington, DC: National Institute of Justice.

CHAPTER 2

A DIALECTIC OF ORGANISATIONAL AND OCCUPATIONAL CULTURE

Peter K. Manning

ABSTRACT

This chapter maps the police occupational culture according to configurations of organisational structure, career lines, interactional patterns, and value conflicts. Organisational features of policing are highlighted according to stratifications in the strategic import of different modes of police work (inspectorial; bottom-entry socialisation; fact-rich/ information thin; secrecy suffused practices; risk-making and taking) and a hierarchy of interactional segmentations among personnel (investigators, patrol officers, middle management, top-command). In these segmentations of the police occupation, patterns of tension (independence/dependence; autonomy/collective obligation; authority/lack of authority; certainty/uncertainty) interlink with various exchanges and reciprocities that unify the organisation. The organisational dynamics take on a specific cast of meaning for individual officers according to the officer's position in one or another of the segments.

Police Occupational Culture: New Debates and Directions
Sociology of Crime, Law and Deviance, Volume 8, 47–83
Copyright © 2007 by Elsevier Ltd.
All rights of reproduction in any form reserved
ISSN: 1521-6136/doi:10.1016/S1521-6136(07)08002-5

INTRODUCTION

The core source of integration in modern industrial society is the occupation, and the modes of coping manifested in occupations are the most powerful windows into the workings of a democratic society. Since many occupations now manifest their course within large bureaucratic organisations, organisations, and occupations are a kind of crucible in which expansion and contraction of power, a dialectic, takes place. The argument of this chapter is that it is not beliefs or attitudes, or even a 'culture' that drives the dialectic; it is the practices that make work possible within this organisation and its constraints.

The study of occupations and their cultures is the study of the emergence of modern industrial societies in which complementarity of functions, reciprocity, and equality interact. If one is to study modern occupations they must be seen in organisational context, for there are few occupations not entangled in a subtle and enmeshing bureaucratic web. This suggests that occupations be studied as organisationally located. This means further that named occupations have an ecological feature, a temporal organisation or history, and a role structure that shapes the range of coping called a culture. Van Maanen and Barley (1984), in a classic statement , argue that the study of occupations in organisational context involves a description of several features of organisations: *ecology* (their material, temporal and social location); modes of *interaction* of the relevant segments of the occupations based on role differentiation; and the ways in which these shape *collective understandings* that are assembled in the name of the occupation as a culture. In this way, action-choices of individuals, variations on group practices, emerge. These features of organisational life interact with and shape the cultures that arise.

The chapter begins with an overview of the five structural features of the Anglo-American police organisation, discusses the role of careers in shaping policing, summarises the conventional wisdom on the police occupational culture, and then presents a scheme for analysis of the culture, both the uniformed and investigator segments. The final section suggests a dialectic between the organisational, occupational and individual forces that animate police organisations.

Let us first consider the police in Van Maanen and Barley's terms. The police license and mandate expand and contract with political trends and beliefs, not withstanding their masterful elevation of crime control as their enduring lasting and requisite function. As the guardians of order, and surrogates for deeper matters of trust and the sacred, the police do what others may not. Enabled to violate the law, they must act violently and intrusively, shoot, maim, and kill. In this sense they violate the law daily with impunity. They are also required to rationalise or justify the necessary – what they have done. Action and deciding precede rationalisation. Ironically, it would appear that by adopting the façade of law enforcement as their virtually exclusive job, they have been constrained to avoid direct responsiveness to the often self-interested pressures of political interest groups. They are of course neutral on the side of the current government. As a tentative definition, I would suggest: the police in Anglo-American societies, constituted of many diverse agencies, are authoritatively coordinated legitimate organisations that stand ready to apply force up to and including fatal force in specified political territories to sustain political ordering.

While the police are an occupation within an organisation, policing is a *practice* that takes place in the auspices of a police organisation. Police work has naturally dramatic aspects because it is above all a performance to sustain an impression of control. The drama persists because variation in the quality of performances before others and pressures to mystify it conceal its vicissitudes from others and smooth over mistakes and failures (Manning, 2003). These moves require a collection of 'tricks of the trade' that while common, differentiate officers one from another. As is perhaps obvious, the police at root hold out violence: they have an obligation to coerce, apply violence when and if they deem it advisable and keep a jail. They must always maintain a degree of social distance between themselves and those they serve.[1] Without an understanding of the mandate granted to the police, their oddly violent, vast range of powers, and court-based protections, especially their success in defining their work as 'crime control' and being granted virtually unlimited powers to pursue this nominally defined goal, cannot be fathomed.

While there are many modes of adaptation to a mandate, what might be called policing cultures, those arising from ad hoc and informal policing – such as the historically venerated and undisciplined and unsupervised semi-vocational Texas rangers (Klockars, 1985; Robinson, 2001; Samora, Bernal, & Pena, 1979; Webb, 1935), policing associated with civil regulation and inspection (Hawkins, 2003; Hutter, 1985), undercover, high policing and 'homeland security' (Brodeur, 1983, 1999; Marx, 1989), private contract and proprietary policing (Shearing, 1992) (Forst & Manning, 1999), federal, state and county policing using the criminal sanction, and local municipal policing[2] – what is most studied is large city urban policing done by patrol officers. There is, however, a growing body of research on policing in

Anglo-American societies, some of which is comparative and some case-focused (see Brogden & Nijhar, 2005).

Functionally, others police, or apply sanction to alter behaviour, but the primary distinctive characteristic of the public police is that they employ the criminal sanction and can thus via the district attorneys access the courts and their sanctions with impunity. This facility is denied all other policing occupations. Police organisations are held legally 'accountable' in a very loose fashion. By accountable is meant that a *rhetoric* espousing responsibility is required that is somewhat consistent with the mandate claimed. The police organisation's spokespersons have to be able to explain police actions but their representations are not legally binding. What being made accountable comes down to for the police is a requirement that they give 'institutional accounts' or explanations for their actions. This claim and its validation have little to do with everyday facts, even in a specific circumstance, but rather tap broad public expectations and beliefs. These expectations, varying as they do by class, race, and age, as well by neighbourhood, make the police rather impervious to casual criticism.[3] The extent to which police officers are individually accountable varies by state in the United States, and most organised means of holding police agency accountable to some written standards or policies are weak because most localities grant wide powers and flexibility in line with local practices and preferences.

The police organisation is constituted by several occupations and specialties, and this makes cultural conflict between interacting groups likely (Van Maanen & Barley, 1984). The police organisation employs civilians (about 25% of the employees of local police organisations): janitors, cooks, maintenance employees, clerks, secretaries, part-time, and full-time expert consultants, lawyers and researchers, and other short-term employees. These are called 'civilians' in the organisation to distinguish them from sworn officers.

The expressed ideology of uniformed police occupational culture, that of crime control, rapid and sometimes risky action, individualistic job entrepreneurship, cynicism about the trustworthiness of citizens, and a distrust of bureaucracy, supervision and 'politics', dominates the several occupational groups within the organisation. This focus on the *expressed ideology* of the patrol officer and one aspect of routine work has made the analysis of policing-as-occupation – studies of the conventional occupational culture – superficial and misleadingly reductionistic. The concept of occupational culture itself seems a tool for criticism rather than analysis (Waddington, 1998). This conception has stripped the organisation of its politics and nuance, and its role in the field of municipal and local politics, as well as its inter-organisational dynamics. It ignores the situated nature of the work and its complexity (Manning, 2004), and overlooks the administration and paperwork, constraints on action, and tensions between the organisational reality and socially patterned individual commitments, loyalties and careers. It echoes the false idea that top command (TC) are semi-competent idealists, who have lost touch with the reality of policing as seen from the front seat of a patrol car.

Most significantly for the argument made here, this roots the causes of police practices entirely in attitudes towards the public, danger, rules, citizens, without questioning the negotiated socio-organisational reality – the politically organised, segmentalised organisations that are home to the networks of power, sponsorship and tightly articulated bureaucratic rules within which such matters are played out daily.

STRUCTURAL FEATURES OF ANGLO-AMERICAN POLICE ORGANISATIONS THAT DIVIDE AND UNIFY THE OCCUPATION

Policing as a practice is shaped by five structural features of police organisations. These are traditional ways in which policing is done. The features vary empirically from force to force, and the salience of one or the other may vary by local political context. The first is the inspectorial strategy of policing, which deploys a large number of low-ranking officers who are ecologically dispersed to monitor and track citizens in the environment and take complex, difficult decisions, usually alone, with minimal supervision and/or review. The second is the localistic, common-level entry and apprenticeship-training pattern of police. In the United States, most officers serve their entire careers in one organisation, and only TC officers join as a result of lateral mobility. Few rise above the initial rank of officer or constable. In the UK, officers above superintendent are moved with promotion and are required to have served in several constabularies as they rise in the hierarchy. The third feature is that the police organisation is both fact rich and information thin. Facts become information when placed in a context and the police supply the several contexts. Despite the notion that the police are information processors and knowledge workers (Ericson & Haggerty, 1998), they actually work within a confusing, disorganised set of information systems and caches, none of which are widely and generally shared within the organisation (Manning, 2003) or with other policing organisations. The police mission, to penetrate and control problematic environments, leads them to overemphasise secrecy and deception as mean of achieving organisational ends. Police information consists in collections of scraps of data, quasi-secret and secret intelligence files, an amalgam of out-dated context-specific information, and a layered archaeology of knowledge. Although secrecy is not the highest value amongst officers, it is safe to say that the conditions under which information is shared (rarely) are carefully observed. This secrecy is a fourth structural feature of policing. The fifth structural feature is that police are risk takers and risk makers (positive and negative consequences of high uncertainty). The police seek risks in high-speed chases, arrests, raids, and other interventions, and act on behalf of society in taking on risks. While the amplification of risk is a part of the ideology, or belief system, the actuality of the risk remains, and it is reproduced and elaborated upon in the stories told (Waddington, 1998). These features turn officers inward, away from the public, and laterally to their colleagues for support.

Practices differentiate individual officers and serve to highlight other less visible variations within the occupation. Practices are actions, ways of doing, designed to carry out tasks and get work done. The core tasks (individual acts) and routines (sequences of tasks) of policing are uncertain and unpredictable as to their appearance and consequence. Officers share assumptions about the nature of the work (risky, exciting, worthwhile, 'clinical' in nature), and operate in an environment perceived or created by such work routines, and by codified definitions of relevant tasks. In urban policing, the cynosure of 'the job' is 'working the streets', patrol response to radio calls. Boredom, risk, and excitement oscillate unpredictably. The technology, unrefined people-processing recipes (i.e. judgements of officers working with little direct guidance), pattern work, and a rigid rank structure officially organises authority. In many ways, it remains a kind of entrepreneurial activity – lonely, undertaking tasks with uncertain outcomes and dynamics, and largely self-defined as to its scope and intensity.

Policing is realised within a bureaucratic, rule-oriented, hierarchical structure of command and control on the one hand, and a loose confederation of colleagues on the other. The operation of these factors stratifies and differentiates the organisation and partitions officers' experience. Investigative work, specialised squads such as SWAT teams, and staff functions such as internal affairs are much more skill based in that they display to each other competence in their everyday work. Patrol officers, however, rarely see the skill of other officers, although they may hear about 'cock-ups' and successes, because they work alone generally and are ecologically dispersed, transferred from division to division and may rotate shifts frequently. While the officer on the ground feels committed to the job, it is in terms of the freedom to 'work outside', 'be my own boss', work with people, and the security and short-term obligations typically involved (20 plus years). The constraints and supervision and tedium are structural – given meaning by the everyday choice of practices and workload. The emotional attachment is more likely to be the job rather than abstractions. As one rises in rank, rewards are attached to new mini- and situated rhetorics – such as espousing service to the city, asserting obligation to the community's quality of life and the like – and to emotional groundings in making policy-like decisions and 'putting out fires', fending off and dealing with the media.

CAREERS

Career is a summative notion but unfolds one day at a time. A career, stripped to bare minimum features, is a series of positions, or stages, a life course, held over time by a social actor – an organisation, a group or a person. It can be viewed subjectively, from the actors' perspective, objectively as a set of named positions or ranks, temporally or cross-sectionally, and either individually or in cohort terms. The central feature of the work career in modern industrialised society is that, it is the active link between an individual's paid work life, and the contours of the division of labour. Movements occur within and across occupational careers. Occupational mobility has both a vertical dimension as measured by individual movement between or within occupations, and horizontal movement within an organisation, occupational category or grouping of similar occupations. Occupations as entities also have careers and movements as exemplified by the changed status of policing as a career in the past 35 years. Careers are not merely individual pursuits or choices; they are much shaped by gender, ethnicity and the market in which the career is enacted (industry, service, the professions, pink, blue, or white collar).

Policing historically was and still is a stable, blue-collar manual job with good pay, benefits, and early retirement potential. Perhaps because it lacks the glamour of high-paying prestigious occupations, the shape and contours of police careers have been little studied. The study of police careers, seen as a longitudinal matter from the academy to termination (resignation, firing, retirement or disability), has not yielded a rich harvest of insights. It has in large part been ignored as a facet of the work and its politics. There is no full study of police careers using a large sample, nor any recent panel study involving re-interviewing (Fielding, 1988; Van Maanen, 1975). Chan's work (Chan, 2001; Chan, Devery, & Doran, 2003) focuses on changes in attitudes and to a lesser extent on practices, in the first years of the job. There are no studies of the career lines of federal officers, even in the most important and prestigious forces such as the FBI, DEA, and what is now called Homeland Security as a result of the consolidation of customs and immigration, border patrol and the coast guard. There are no studies of state police careers (there are 49 state police forces). Chiefs' biographies, such as those recently published by Bratton, Gates, Moose and Stampfer, are very informative albeit a bit self-aggrandising, while only two studies have focused on the careers of chief constables (Reiner, 1991; Wall, 1998).[4]

Perhaps, this absent substance arises because the vast majority of its practitioners do patrol work (some 60 plus per cent at any given time of the entire organisation are in the patrol division) and serve at the same rank throughout their careers.[5] This pattern is reinforced by powerful unions that defend seniority as a basis for advantage, suppress merit and competition as bases for salaries, and shape the conditions of work. While they may move from a top position in one city to another or from the second in command spot to the TC spot in another organisation, in the United States there is no systematic scheme for developing and training police officers beyond the academy or the odd certification scheme. In the UK, the national approach integrates training, promotion, and transfer from one constabulary to another.

The police organisation is roiled from time to time by four forces that alter this bottom-heavy, single-rank stasis. The first is *reciprocated loyalty* to those above in the organisation and sponsorship that increases chances of promotion or assignment to political niches that attract ambitious officers (the chief's office, Internal affairs), and special squads in current favour in the organisation (the gang squad, SWAT teams). These loyalties become either assets or liabilities in succession crises when the organisation is temporarily decapitated and attempts are made to assert power by competing cliques. The second force is *a political career-shattering downward or lateral move* due to major 'cock-ups' and affairs that turn banana-shaped or return to destroy the sender.When Superintendent Claiborne of the Boston Police Department, an heir apparent to the job of chief superintendent (or chief in fact) failed to organise a fully manned and prepared police response to a celebration that in time turned into a riot, he was demoted to the training academy (generally seen as a 'Siberia');[6] another Superintendent, Mr. Hussey, at the time acting chief (just under the commissioner and also the heir apparent to the role of commissioner), was forced to resign and retire for similar failures in the demonstration after the Red Sox victory over the American league villains the New York Yankees in October 2003. These lateral-demotion moves are not always successful, such as when a power base remains (the above-mentioned captain who returned to command a district after a trip to Siberia). An additional example is found when Charles Ramsey became chief in the Washington, DC metropolitan force in 1998 and demoted an assistant chief. The assistant Chief had sufficient power to find an office, furnish it and label his non-existent task force as an inquiry into juvenile crime in the district. In other ways, lateral transfer, such as movement of a patrol officer to a 'desk job', is used to mark time and although seen as a punishment is not defined as such by the union contract. A third is the *rare inter-organisational transfer*, permitted in some states, from one to another specialised role in another police organisation. Such transfers allow advancement without regard to union-based considerations of seniority. A fourth career-changing contingency also involves an organisational change or an advancement, as a result of being hired in: the *outside hire over one's head*. Big city chiefs are an unusual and small group; they are increasingly appointed as a result of a search and may be hired from 'outside'.

The published research on police careers is thus an unsatisfying mosaic that does not produce a definitive picture of the dynamics, diachronic matters, nor correlates of achieving a given rank, role (a particular short-term task force assignment) or organisational position (one not based on rank, but a niche such as a computer repair man or driver for the chief's office). Little is known about investigators' careers. They are both organisational and inter-organisational as they encounter district attorneys (and defence attorneys), investigators from other departments, city, state, and federal, evidence technicians and forensic scientists and judges. This 'politicking' is necessary but viewed ambivalently within the department. They are selected by political means and hold their positions in large part by merit. Selection to a unit signifies that the person has the potential to be trusted and loyal – a 'team player'– and has investigative skills. Finally, like the segmented officer, detectives live in a world that is gender and ethnically biased in a dramatic fashion (Corsianos, 2003, 2004; Martinez, 1996; Simon, 1991). Females, African–Americans and/or Latinos are selected to enter a white, male world. There is some indication that female detectives experience the job differently, have innovated in detection styles and suffer different sources and kinds of stress than their male counterparts (Corsianos, 2003, 2004).[7]

Several generalisations can be offered about police careers.

- Very few officers experience upward rank-based mobility.
- Most types of mobility in police organisations are horizontal. Some of these are moves into special units (gang squad, dynamic entry team), some are niches or favoured positions within the organisation that are dependent more on skill than upon rank, or that maximise some sorts of rewards (overtime, time off, prestige). These include a position in research and development, an assignment to a task force as a cover for other work. In the Washington DC department, a crime analysis unit was in place, headed by a sergeant who had created a software program and produced daily reports (this passed for analysis at that time). He was deposed by a new leadership in crime analysis while on his annual leave, and shifted out of the unit. The chief was developing a crisis management centre in part for the coming inauguration, and the sergeant, using his influence, was named the technical advisor to the new command centre. The rewards sought vary by the niche.
- Transfers from one district or position to another are sought for any and all of the following: convenience, workload variation (either more or less work), action or finding a niche conforming to a person's special skills or interests (research, laboratories, property room, shooting range), political advantage because of assignment to certain squads (homicide, SWAT) that are fast tracks or essential to achieving higher rank or a sinecure in which little or no police work is required.
- All mobility is patterned strongly by matters out of the hands of individual officers – retirement rates, disability levels, attenuation due to dismissals and firings, city budgets, and patronage patterns (more relevant in strong major city governments such as Boston and Chicago and less so in cities in the Far West).
- The complex dynamics of federal consent decrees, city politics, and corruption shift 'reformers', females, and people of colour to the top (and to the bottom) unexpectedly (see Sklansky, forthcoming).
- Lateral moves that do not alter the rank of the officer may be seen as symbolic demotion (see above on the demotion to 'Siberia'). These are usually transfers from active crime focused units to training, totally administrative or marginalised units.

Actively running a policing career is a series of gambles or bargains. A second parallel and simultaneous career has advantages but also associates officers with risks and associations that may not bode well for a police career. A police career facilitates pursuing another parallel career such as repair work, construction, managing security in hotels or dealing in real estate or insurance. It provides access to various forms of non-rank reward – perks such as overtime, comp time for overtime worked as a favour from a sergeant, assignment to paying police work called 'details' in Boston (private contracts from sports franchises and contractors). In Washington DC in the late seventies, a sergeant in the drug squad was running a real estate business from his office, making calls, and showing houses to clients; in Chicago, a sergeant in 1998 was head of security at two downtown hotels at night while acting as head of a special hate crimes unit during the day. In Boston, the overtime associated with the 'details', although technically facilitated through the department (money is paid by contractors and sports teams and laundered through the departments' accounting office), is a very lucrative second job, which covers bribes, corruption, and other illicit opportunities. For some officers, designated by union contract, it is a source of substantial wealth. Low-level temptations such as having another officer sign in, using sick days on one job to facilitate the second job, asking the contractor on site to sign for a 'non-show' or padding the number of people present are routine forms of corruption. For TC, working on exit strategies, typically the post-retirement job, involves cultivating private security firms, or entering local politics (a striking number of ex-chiefs, for example, in St. Louis, Houston, Minneapolis, and Portland, Oregon, have been elected mayors). Kathleen O'Toole, commissioner of the Boston Department for about 18 months in 2005–2006, had served previously as a member of the Commission for the Reorganisation of Police Services in Northern Ireland (the 'Patten Commission'), and in late spring 2006, when she was offered the job as inspector general for the Garda, the police service in Ireland, she resigned and moved to Dublin.

In general, however, it can be said that prestige in the job flows to those serving in specialised units, investigative work, especially homicide, and positions most associated with crime control and crime suppression. The track to a top rank usually involves passage through the favoured special squad in the department such as the gang squad, juvenile squad or the SWAT team, and always involves at least one or two positions within the detective division. In most departments, skilled detectives are favoured for higher spots, if not chief. The learned skills of policing as a patrol officer are not transferable to other occupations or occupational clusters. In other words, the low horizon of entrants, lack of upward mobility through the work, little transferable skill, and modest educational attainment means that the work is a calculated trade off between retirement security, a second part-time job (and the possibility of overtime on the job) and the risks of the current work. Top managers are hired for management skills and for the name recognition or local prestige, but very few officers achieve these ranks.

Policing (and policing careers) are anchored in the present and this orientation shapes the way policing is seen over time. Careers of these kinds, anchored in a bureaucratic organisation, produce commitments and side bets (Becker, 1961) – structural constraints that limit the horizon, stifle reforms and mitigate even modest change (see Herbert, 2006).[8] For example, retirement pay in police departments is often based on the average of the last few years on the job, so that quitting short of the retirement age is punitive. Career lines and the organisational structure shape what is called the occupational culture.

AN OVERVIEW OF STUDIES OF POLICE OCCUPATIONAL CULTURE

The first public acknowledgement of the violence of policing, its potential for corruption and veniality, was found in the National Commission on Law Observance and Enforcement Report, Lawlessness in Law Enforcement (called the Wickersham Report, 1931). This federally sponsored study found widespread local police, corruption and violence. The classic studies in the Chicago school tradition (Short, 1971) in which the connection of policing and police officers to local politics was noted, also suggested that policing was a political matter and linked to the local political climate. The idea of a vibrant, forceful and abiding police occupational culture was set forth first by William Westley (1970 [1951]). Westley did fieldwork in Gary, Indiana sponsored by Joe Lohman (at the time the Sheriff of Cook County and a University of Chicago graduate). Westley emphasised the ways in which police defined their role in a rather grandiose and independent fashion and combined violence with authority. These themes were amplified in Jerome Skolnick's (1966) original and creative fieldwork-based study, *Justice Without Trial*. *Justice Without Trial* displayed a discourse in which 'legal' variables were contrasted with 'extralegal variables', which modified or shaped outcomes. In the book, based on fieldwork in two Californian cities, a combination of police authority, their sense of risk and their cultural and social isolation was the principle explanatory operative for whatever kind of justice was done by police 'on the streets' and 'without trial'. The title was a pun: his rather pained discussion of policing showed how little justice was meted out. The Westley sketch, based on a small sample of officers in a Midwestern city almost sixty years ago, often cited with reference to

Skolnick, has become a synecdoche for the police organisation, its practices and politics.[9] In these works there are no sergeants, no supervision, no corrective bureaucratic rules that impede 'doing the job', and the street-level hero or villain emerged.

This scholarly view has arisen because the visible and obvious aspect of policing, the patrol officer's practices, are easily cast as a synecdoche for the organisation and its politics, its leadership and management, its policies and practices, broader questions of the mandate, and all manner of intra- and inter-organisational dynamics. The resultant academic, or should one say the textbook treatment of the police occupational subculture is disproportionately influenced by a handful of studies of American or English uniformed patrol officers serving in large urban areas, and it has been reified in textbooks. Although rich ethnographic treatments of policing exist (Banton, 1964; Bittner, 1990; Holdaway, 1983; Rubinstein, 1972; Simon, 1991; Van Maanen, 1974, 1988; Westley, 1970[1951]), the police are often flattened, desiccated and displayed like insects pinned on a display board. Since the police officers studied have in the past been very largely (90% or more in most forces) white, working class origin males of modest educational accomplishment, what has been described is a one time-slice through one organisational level in handful of forces (those employing 500 or more officers for example). The best police ethnographies, discussed below, are dated, most being done over thirty years ago. The idea has unfortunately come to be used as a touchstone and nexus for explaining all matters police (Crank, 1998; Paoline, 2003; Reiner, 2001). The police organisation, occupation, and the changing demographic characteristics of the entrants have been conflated into a caricature.

Certainly, observers have noted the differentiation and segmentalisation of policing, using attitudes and/or role types (Terrill, Paoline, & Manning, 2003), conceptions of external publics (Reiner, 1991, pp. 117–121), distinctive subcultures such as a 'street cop culture' and a 'management culture' (Punch, 1983), and they have also noted the conflicts within forces based on ethnicity and gender (Foster, 2004; Martin, 1977; Miller, 1999). Interest in interactional tactics is somewhat shaped by the recent popularity of 'community policing' (Bayley & Bittner, 1986; Mastrofski, Snipes, Parks, & Maxwell, 2000). Research has seized on police–citizen interactions, especially those involving coercion (1–5% of all interactions) and traffic stops – one aspect of public policing – as fundamental to an understanding of policing as a practice. It is unclear whether the tendency to use less force, be more inclined to explain decisions to people, and be less concerned with crime fighting as an abstract mission for policing is a function of ageing and experience rather than the imposition of an ideology (Mastrofski, 2006). Expressed value variations are based in part on task differentiation within departments (Jermier, Slocum, Fry, & Gaines, 1991). Other social forces, especially technology, management training, the law – coupled with 'pressures to produce', traffic ticket quotas and case clearances in detective work – also impact the level of work and output. Some recent studies have worked towards a generalised model of the patrol officer culture (Klinger, 1997; Paoline, 2003), while Janet Chan's (1997) work is the most theoretically informed effort at contrasting modes of deciding in police organisations. She takes a complex Bourdieu-influenced perspective arguing that policing is organised around various forms of knowledge and practice shaped continuously by a habitus or way of being and doing.

Exceptions to this street level and micro-interactional focus, such as Wilson's (1968) early work, Sheingold's (1991) sensitive analysis of the politicisation of crime, Hunt and Magenau's (1989) sketch of the role of the chief, and Brown's (1977) public administration-focused work, point to the limits of other less broadly cast scholarship on police and policing. With the focus centred on the occupation and its overt manifestations, the role of structural constraints within the organisation and its place within a network of power is little discussed (but see Hunt & Magenau, 1989). Police claim they are disinterested and eschew, and even abhor politics, yet they are the most deeply and profoundly political of organisations (Thacher, 2005). This is because they enforce the law which is a political force, in part reflecting elected interests and in part compromises with interest groups, lobbyists and the media; it is because the top positions, certainly the chief, in the department are appointed by the mayor (in the USA); and fundamentally, it is because they are the most visible and powerful 'face' of city government services. In 'old fashioned', party-based strong patronage cities such as Boston and Chicago, the police are a central link in the political machine that delivers city services to huge numbers of potential voters. As Skogan (2006) observes, '[community policing is] a political program' (p. 1).[10]

The most consistent emphasis in these studies of the occupational culture is individualistic and reductionistic. It focuses on the attitudes and tactics of the lower participants (LP), positing a fearful environment replete with and redolent of risk, a sense of isolation and abandonment (in extreme, a feeling of lack of support from the public), a basic distrust of people, and an expressed sense that the work is complex and difficult – crime-focused and crime-punctuated; that the authority of the officer is problematic and negotiated often at great length, and that the 'culture' is masculine and derived from working class ideas about manhood, sex and gender, and social relationships in general. The dramaturgical properties of 'profiling' and a resentful negative force make them an easy intaglio on which textbook writers can further inscribe. In contrast, Waddington (1998) argues that these attitudes are in fact a reversal of the everyday experience of officers, who seldom make an arrest, are bored and lethargic during tedious periods of time driving aimlessly through city streets and on motorways. They are less than violent and certainly are not fearful. Waddington sees these as a kind of flattering potted version of the work, tales told to each other and social researchers, and calls such ideas not the occupational culture, but the 'canteen culture', an oral culture, a configuration of stories, successes and miscues, cautionary tales and myths that arises from causal interactions at meals, tea and coffee breaks, and parties and annual affairs such as Christmas parties. Recall that the police canteen culture reflects the social values of Anglo-American societies such as individualism, material success, bias against various others (minorities, people of colour, women), and preference for the company of others like themselves. It is particularly shaped by local politics, situational pressures arising from issues in the polity at large and media dramatisations of untoward incidents. This is a very penetrating insight, and cries out for further specification. How do beliefs, encapsulated in stories, shape practices?

Pointing out this narrowed vision of policing and its practices leaves aside how it functions as a binding and organising account of the job, especially as it is seen by patrol officers. It has tenacity and power. Steve Herbert's (2006) book, *Citizens, Cops and Power*, for example, presents a succinct summary of how these ideas shape interactions with the public. The police organisation is replete with individualistic, power-oriented actors who work in isolation in large part, unsupervised and not directed to targets, goals, or short-term objectives. Officers speak of good police work involving crime, but this is individualistic, ad hoc and variously defined. It cannot be pointed to as a thing – crime work can range from running plates and registrations, towing cars away, noting garbage on the streets, or arresting crack dealers. The police do not see 'communities', and eschew the term as a 'buzz' word. They see only shifts, places, divisions, and patrol beats. Some of these police-defined locales are not full of dangerous and violent criminals; the villains are rather some sort of 'bad apple' whose families, religion, and education have failed them. These are the people who should be identified, coerced, controlled, and sanctioned. These moves are seen as restorative of order. The police, in this view, according to Herbert (2006), see themselves as a political professionals, isolated, and authorised as 'agents of expulsion' who need to relate to citizens primarily as sources of information 'about those who need to be expelled' (p. 95). This is a view that elevates the police and sanctions their violence, denies any obligation to citizens, sees the problem of crime as targeting hot spots, and controlling a few offenders with whatever tools can be marshalled.[11] What is missing from this portrait are other aspects of police work – the short cuts to avoid work, overlooking crime and disorder, the kindness shown daily to the mad, crazed, sad and lost, the patience and tolerance of officers show to angry and misguided complainants, and true regard for civil liberties and privacy.[12]

SEGMENTATION OF THE POLICE OCCUPATION

What is called the occupational culture is not that but a set of routines, practices, and other means for coping with the vicissitudes or uncertainties arising routinely in the course of doing a paid named job. It is a configuration of concerns rather than a thing (Shearing & Ericson, 1991). The facets of interest are revealed in the practices that sustain the interaction order (Goffman, 1983; Rawls, 1983): that which is the on-going means of ordering interaction in situations. This interaction is not a culture. The interaction order that emerges, one sequence at a time, is not a single reified culture. The resultant thing called a culture is an artefact, an abstraction, sediment of past interactions around which grows a core of meaning and tradition to which members refer. It is a reflective and dialectic matter that cannot be reduced to a minimal set of norms, values, or attitudes. An occupational culture that arises and is sustained is a reduced, selective, and task-based *version* or account (Mills, 1940) that includes a potted or simplified history, some expressed traditions, etiquette and routines, rules and principles that serve to buffer practitioners from contacts with the public. It has an emotional aspect; it generates and reflects feelings that are constituted and reconstituted in the work. A kind of lens on the world, it highlights some aspects of the social and physical environment and omits or minimises others. It generates stories, lore, and legends. The sources of the conventionally expressed occupational culture are the repeated, well-routinised tasks incumbent on the members, a technology, largely verbal and interactional, that is variously direct or indirect in its effects (mediated by the organisational structure within which the occupation is done), and the reflexive aspects of talking about these doings. In this sense, an occupational culture reflects not only what is done, how it should be (and not) done, but also idealisations of the work. It summarises neatly the complex set of interactions that are characteristic of police work.

Rather than seizing upon attitudes, it is preferable to examine interactions and practices. A segment is a group of people loosely bound by intense, face-to-face interactions that are more concentrated with the specific network of interactants than with others outside that network.[13] In policing, the limits on interaction are tightly drawn around rank, although some interaction occurs laterally via sponsorship of protégés, political ties based on religion, union membership, past links in the academy, partnerships and participation in special units and ad hoc task forces.

There are four primary segments found within the occupation based on interaction. They vary in mode of selection or entry, the risks entailed, the audiences they regard as significant, the rewards sought, and how they view their authority.

The first is that of the LP or patrol officers, who work in response to calls directed from 911 (999 in the UK), interact widely with the public, are uniformed, heavily armed, equipped, and visible. They patrol in nominally delineated police 'beats' or patrol areas rotating by shifts of days and hours (4/10, working four days ten hours a day with three days off, or 5/8, working five days for eight hours a day with two days off). This is the largest number of officers and proportionally about 60% of the force. All enter here and few rise above this rank and are firmly anchored here emotionally and sociologically in terms of commitment. They view the risks as those of the street, they value overtime, time off and work that is interesting. Their audience, an almost exclusive significant audience, is their peers, and other patrol officers, past or present. They view their authority as fundamental, almost essentially individualistic, the job as 'on the streets'.

The second segment is that of the middle managers. They are typically appointed as a result of seniority, an exam and interviews. They supervise, handle paperwork, complaints and evaluation, and advise officers about problematic situations. They generally wear uniforms, usually without the jacket as they work 'inside', and are provided with a uniform allowance. Their claims for occupational prestige are aligned either up or down: towards administrative officers or their colleagues 'on the street'. Among them a distinction gets made between the 'station cats' and the 'Olympic Torches', sergeants who never venture out of the station, and those who are out 'chasing their men' (Van Maanen, 1983). It is done in American forces for the most part by white men in their forties. Few rise above this position and fewer still have aspirations to command positions. These officers view themselves as moderating and supervising the mistakes of others, a locus of their risks. They are 'middle-men', the face of authority in the organisation, and often face role conflict. Their authority is a blend of their personal charisma or reputation and their rank and its authority and powers.

The third segment is 'TC' or higher administrators. These may be as few as 1% of the organisation (in Boston, for example, the TC of super-intendents under the chief constitutes about 1% of the total sworn and civilian employees). They are selected by political processes which may include the consultation of the mayor, city council, or a hiring committee (in the USA). They typically have a network of power extending through the organisation, and when this is absent, as with appointments from outside, they may be weak leaders. They wear either uniforms or suits depending on the occasion, rarely have direct contact with patrol officers and see themselves in part at least as the representative of the organisation in local and state politics. Their risks are both symbolic, shifts in the views of the media and 'public opinion', and indirect such as corruption or a serious violent or fatal incident that is well publicised. Their staff is composed of ambitious young officers, civilian experts, consultants, and they are surrounded with those who owe them personal loyalty. The job is at least in part 'politics', the audiences both internal and external, the rewards largely symbolic as the differences in pay between the TC and officers is strikingly small.[14]

Finally, the detectives or investigators are sufficiently isolated politically, intellectually and symbolically to be considered a fourth segment. The detective segment is omitted in conventional descriptions of the police occupational culture, although several detailed monographs have been done (Ericson, 1993; Innes, 2000; Lucas, 1973; Manning, 2004; Sanders, 1977). Perhaps, the most detailed depiction of the work is done by a journalist (Simon, 1991). Because investigative work is ordered by status distinctions based on skill, interactions are squad and shift based rather than precinct based, and are not based on rank. The work of detectives can be either reactive or creative and proactive such as when they create a case against a drug dealer. Detectives have higher status than patrol officers in the department. They are information-processors who investigate, define, clear, and otherwise manage the tension between 'the case' as their property (Ericson, 1993) and the case as an organisational object of concern. While carrying out these functions, the modern detective, at best, is a careful and skilful bureaucrat who fits the organisational demands to 'produce' (clear cases) with career aims and the extant detective (occupational) culture. The role has changed considerably since World War II (Kuykendall, 1986). Investigators are appointed as a result of an exam and interviews and are usually known to officers in the detective units (several from the standard violent and property crimes units, vice/narcotics and special squads such as sexual assault or hate crimes) prior to their appointment. They undergo fairly brief 'in house' training but may be sent for special short courses during the time they serve. Senior detectives in skilled positions, such as in homicide, tend to have long tenure – twenty plus years. Their risks surround mistakes in court (lies, poorly delivered testimony, embarrassment in court – Corsianos, 1999) and with the media in 'high profile' cases (those involving a known celebrity, high status white person or a child). They are highly respected within the department, can be well known in the media and in court, and regarded as clever and articulate. Their authority – and their primary audience is their fellow investigators – in many ways is connected to their interpersonal skills: their ability to extract confessions, work with witnesses, and do their paperwork. As a skilled craftsperson, the detective values 'internal' rewards – good work, a clean case, self-esteem – but also enjoys flexible hours and movements (including often a car), overtime which may be linked to court time, and media attention in big cases. They certainly do not view the public as a fearsome 'symbolic assailant' (Skolnick's term) because they are utterly dependent on the public for information, cooperation, witness appearances and good will, and they feel much less isolated as their work brings them into many settings and places, and makes them very likely to be given gifts, legitimate and illegitimate, frequently by grateful citizens. They are also in a position to violate the trust put in them.

There are tensions across and within segments because of their different views of the rewards, audiences and purposes of the job. These are suppressed and diminished by the expressed ideology shared by all: the job is on the street. Within each of the segments are officers who are planning changes and reforms, are upwardly mobile, and yet oppose the current ruling cadre. Questions of succession in the organisation elevate the tensions because although networks of support cross segments, the interests of the segments are reflected in their leadership preferences and tensions within the segment. In the recent succession crisis in Boston, two of the internal candidates were divided on their approach to crime control. One was more 'community oriented' and the other a more crime-focused officer; in the end, the mayor appointed a commissioner from outside the force who was nationally known as an advocate of community policing. In Washington DC, when Charles Ramsey became chief he brought in his own cadre of civilian administrative people in research and planning, human resources, and 'quality control', about 10–15 people from Chicago (CPD); these were opposed in change by the past cadre surrounding the former chief. Tensions

within are reflected in the envy of these 'new people' and in fears about
whether they would be promoted ahead of or favoured more in informal
power relations than the 'old guard'. Tensions across segments are reflected
in the uncertainty of how the networks of sponsorship that run up, down,
and across ranks will be affected and who the new favoured officers might
be in the various segments. Since the new people were community policing
oriented, officers without alignment to any particular segment, but
nonetheless alert to issues of politics and advancement, were concerned
about their prospects. In general, police departments are divided by
'philosophy' in the sense of being divided into those who are 'tough on
crime' and favour active arrest-oriented practices, and those who are more
community oriented. These rough divisions cross the segments and unify
the organisation in one way and divide it in another. There are always those
who are in clique that oppose any organisation idea and are a conservative
resistance ensemble.

Turning to the matters revealed in practices, the *axes of concern to police*
revolve around questions of independence and autonomy on the one
hand and authority and certainty on the other. They can be seen as four
pairs: (A) independence–dependence, (B) autonomy-collective obligation,
(C) authority-lack of authority, and (D) uncertainty–certainty. They are
dynamic oppositions that take on significance from each other. These are
discussed here within the context of the four segments. The four pairs can be
aligned more generally: the first two concern tensions between individualism
and group obligations and the second two concern the locus of control
(internal vs. external). These tensions exist within and across segments,
binding and separating ranks, investigators and members of social units. As
I discuss below, these tensions are only partially effaced by the ideology of
policing, but more importantly they are reduced by gifts and reciprocity in
informal obligations. The axes of concern, which I call 'themes' in the
discussion below, are indicators of what people feel on the job as well as
their sentimental links to each other. Kai Erikson (1976, p. 83) argues that
'people think or feel different things in the service of an overall pattern of
coordination. In the same sense that people contribute different skills and
abilities to the organisation of work, so they contribute different
temperaments and outlooks to the organisation of sensibility'.

The occupational culture in some ways is a configuration of practices and
exchanges that are more or less salient from time to time. The primary
exchanges that unite are (a) between officers in the uniformed segment and
investigators in specialised units, (b) between sergeants and patrol officers,
and (c) between middle management (MM) and top command. An outline

of these interactive exchanges is indexed by a few examples taken from my field notes.

1. When patrol officers work together in a precinct or division, they defer to each others' skills in respect to negotiation (domestic violence calls Davis, 1983), arrests (Walsh, 1986), back-up, and tacit understandings about how calls will be reported (Manning, 2004). This means that trust must be displayed in the follow-up of any sequence of action, and if reciprocity is not observed, the officer becomes isolated. This is an exchange that unites the segment.

2. When drug officers need a patrol unit to appear (depending on departmental policy), it is considered something of a favour to the narcotics/vice officers because there is no direct reward for protecting the scene while a long search goes on, watching prisoners that are not uniformed officers' arrests (no credit is given to them), looking on when a shift change takes place and no overtime is given whilst waiting to be relieved, and in general acting more less as symbolic figures. However, officers who are interested in drugs, cultivating informants, and learning the craft are informally rewarded by their involvement in raids – the proximity, idle gossip and chitchat as they wait. This exchange of favours unites the uniformed and the specialised investigative units.

3. Sergeants rely on officers to avoid trouble, and reward them with time off, 'comp time', tolerance for missed roll calls, and overlooking errors of commission and omission such as failing to finish paperwork on drug cases, keeping money advanced in spite of a failed 'buy-bust', and other bad behaviour that leads to citizens' complaints. Officers in turn overlook sergeants' behaviour like drinking on the job. This unites the MM and the officers.

4. Officers and MM keep many complaints to themselves in the course of work, only to release them in 'times out' – parties with drinking and celebration – in which it is acceptable to violate the tacit rules about not responding to indignities, errors and insults by ranking officers. This unites MM and the officers they supervise.

5. Units without reciprocity, or something to give, are further isolated. Community police officers in Lansing, Michigan, were never told of drug raids in their areas, and citizens would respond in frustration telling the CP officers they were supposed to be in 'partnership' with the community and tell them in advance of such raids. However, when citizens become directly involved in actions to control or prevent drug dealing (Lyons, 1996, pp. 80–85) they are shunned and forced to desist. They have, in this

sense, nothing to offer the police. This absence of reciprocity between police and the public contrasts with the inter-organisational reciprocity, which is rewarded as shown above in item 2 of this list.

6. When TC deals with the officers as a segment, they must see the entire matter as a bargain with the union; any change means a concession of some kind to union conditions of work. This unites TC and middle management.

7. Very little direct exchange unites TC and officers and this relationship shows the greatest social distance, ambivalence, and animosity. This is revealed in situations in which officers are alleged to have acted badly – carried out a chase with a fatal consequence, beat up or shot someone, especially an unarmed person, or colluded to frame someone or conceal evidence. In these cases, TC almost automatically transfers the officer(s), puts them on leave or on leave without pay, and in general acts first and asks questions later. In departments with strong unions or officers' federations, the unions step up to protest, criticise the chief publicly and issue press releases.

Each of these illustrates tensions between individualism and group obligations of various kinds. The tensions, however, are meaningful only situationally, and during the 'as and when' of their relevance to the undertaking at hand. These concerns come in and out of salience and are not fixed possessions or features of individual actors. They exist and circulate in a network of signification and telling, not in people's heads or their attitudes. Their dynamic relationship surfaces primarily in crises in which the veneer of authority is shattered, the public performance is threatened or collapses, or the officer is embarrassed or fails to fill role requirements. In these situations, the officer reflects, and draws on the 'occupational perspective' for support and clarification. The residual of these encounters and their ambiguous outcomes is the basis for the narrative or story telling that reinforces and renews the coping-culture. It is not a constant, but a variable. Let us now consider the more detailed configuration of these pairs by segment.

Lower Participants

Lower participants (the LP segment) generally emphasise their dependence, autonomy, authority, and uncertainty. The uniformed officer works using his or her body in an uncertain environment where choice, action, and decision are emphasised, where the veneer of objectively guided decision-making is essential, and where an often tenuous authority must frequently be asserted with strangers in public. The officer is routinely dependent on fellow officers and the public to maintain a credible performance, combining authoritative assertions and action, yet the occupation emphasises autonomy. Working class culture, from which most police are recruited, supplies the most frequently noted emblems or symbols that collapse attitudes and practices into valuations of action characterising policing. Thus, emphases upon individual control of situations, toughness, machismo, hedonism, deprecation of paperwork and abstraction, concrete language and description, are 'imported' working class emphases that shade practices. Officers 'at the coal face' or 'on the street' appear to exchange a degree of organisational autonomy to maintain a working class style. The four axes of concern for the LP can be clustered into two metathemes: *metatheme 1* is 'the job', an index of the interrelated themes of (job) dependency and autonomy; *metatheme 2* is 'real police work', an index combining authority and uncertainty in relationships with the public. It is important to note that these are glossed by use so that either side of the worrying tension can be expressed failures to control and to be caught up in a situation that has an odd, amusing or disastrous outcome or one that is exemplary in its features and outcomes. Either or both can be called 'good police work' as it includes and encompasses both.

The Middle Management Segment

This segment (MM) is composed of officers in the rank of sergeant, lieutenant, inspector, chief inspector and superintendent or their equivalents. They are quasi-managers. Technological developments make management skill a likely consideration for promotion – attending night school for an MBA, for example, rather than seeking a law degree – although a degree is considered entirely secondary to political, sponsorship, reputation, and character. Computer-assisted dispatch, management information systems, computer-based records, and crime analysis applications have altered their workloads (although they have not necessarily increased them).[15] Organisational politics, both of careers and of the TC, is a keen interest and concern of middle managers. Symbolically located between command and other officers, they must adapt to organisational realities. They rarely earn overtime, and work shifts if not assigned to staff positions. The MM officers emphasise independence and collective obligations to form *metatheme 3*, namely 'politics' (of the job or the occupation, oriented partially to internal and partially to external audiences), while the twin themes of authority and certainty (the need to control contingencies through supervision) are clustered as a *metatheme 4*, which is 'management'.

The Top Command

This segment (TC) is composed of officers above the rank of superintendent (or commander) including chief, and deputy chief or assistant chief. Their speech and manner often emulate those they admire in the business world. They have options in dress – full or partial uniform, business suit, or casual wear, and some have adopted the term police 'CEO', mimicking business practice, and make reference to 'changing the way we do business'. Much of their work is 'fire-fighting': managing mini-disasters such as severe known (as opposed to those unknown, unreported to the department, or unknown to the media) public beatings, fatal shootings, crashes after high-speed chases, and periodic peaks in recorded homicides. In theory, they make 'policy' decisions, or at least consider issues enduring beyond the end of a shift or a day's work, yet there is little written policy in police departments; TC avoid written plans, policies, and even detailed budgets because of their situational and immediate view of the work and their need to avoid crises with the patrol segment. Union and civil service constraints limit their options to transfer and fire. The administrative cadre is dependent on the good will and discretion of officers, because 'working the streets' produces most of the known public scandals, media amplified incidents and political controversies. The tensions of the work that dominate the LP segment remain surprisingly salient: they function as a ground against which the 'perks', rewards and intrinsic satisfactions of command are seen. Some TC still think of themselves as 'good police officers', and emphasise their 'street smarts', 'toughness', or past crime-fighting successes, rather than their administrative skills, wisdom as 'people managers', or their educational achievements. Command officers' views of policing are reflexive, because they are obligated to manage the consequences of decisions made by others. They must 'read off' these value axes and metathemes to understand and interpret police work. Command officers emphasise that they manage the dependence and autonomy issues that LP label 'the job' and middle managers call 'office politics'. Top administrative officers also emphasise the 'politics' and 'management' themes of middle management. The refracted value tensions of LP and managers are an element of the command segment's work. One metatheme here, *metatheme 5*, is called 'managing the job'. They see their work bearing external responsibility, being accountable, while being dependent on LP. The second metatheme here, *metatheme 6*, 'policing as politics', glosses command responsibility. Command officers emphasise 'management' rather than 'the job', and view police management as paperwork and coping with and managing the LP' subculture. When a strong union exists, it is the union that provides the face of battle and a constant source of criticism for failing to 'back up the officers', bowing to public opinion, being too 'political'. Uncertainty reappears, although for these administrators, uncertainty focuses on their weak authority in the context of dependence upon the discretion (in both senses of the word), and competence of the LP. Finally, it appears that they combine two metathemes of other segments into a single idea: combining the MM metathemes of 'management' and 'politics', into one that might be called 'policing as democratic politics'. In some ways, TC would like to position themselves as leaders who protect their 'troops' while acting as skilful political community actors, and acting internally as wise bureaucrats. This formulation glosses their interest in sustaining and amplifying the political power and independence of the police in the criminal justice system and dramatises and displays the role of police in both the local and occasionally the national political system. Policing as democratic politics implies sensitivity to the encumbrances and political implications of policing. This is not easy to carry off. In the United States, police define their obligations as 'law enforcement' which is stripped of political meaning, and refuse to comment on matters they deem to be political, i.e. not to do with crime narrowly construed.

The Investigative Segment[16]

The detective or investigator stands in contrast to the visible, well-known uniformed patrol officer. Independence–dependence, autonomy-collective obligation' authority and its absence, and uncertainty also suffuse detective work. Investigative officers are, however, much more independent of the organisation than other officers. They are dependent on their investigative colleagues and to a lesser degree the public, but view themselves as independent operators: skilled artisans and puzzle-solvers. However, they are profoundly dependent upon their partners for joint work and the division of labour that emerges over time, and on witnesses and those willing or not to testify in court. The detective has autonomy because the hours are flexible hours, the work load is episodic and uneven according to day of the week, month, and season of the year, and is guided by the officer's own energies and imagination, his or her current case load, and pressures to produce clearances. Skills are validated in outcomes, a little-present matter for patrol officers in the United States, although they are monitored in the UK. Paperwork and interviewing skills are admired and required, even though paperwork is viewed ambivalently and usually disdained. The acknowledged skill of officers is validated by others within and outside the unit – while skill varies among detectives, the stratification system (respect given to each other) within a unit is generally well known and shared. This reduces the uncertainty of 'respect' and authority, which remain the burdens of working patrol officers. By working a case well, detectives mean manifesting and displaying 'flair', or imagination in anticipating what might go wrong; dealing with a problem in the event creatively, or constructing the right story or paperwork that puts the proper 'spin' on the events reported. Flair connotes the aesthetics and prosody one brings to the vicissitudes of the work. The authority of the investigator is far less problematic than it would be for a patrol officer or TC: the skills manifested are demonstrated and validated by colleagues, compliance of victims and witnesses is generally high and the suspects are seen as dangerous and unwanted, and the work arises, except in drugs, as a result of a complaint and a victim – although Ericson, however, sees detective work as also 'making crime', in part because by defining the case, its victims, suspects, evidence and relevant contingencies as their 'property' investigators constrain the contra-dictions implicit in many crimes and make unreviewed decisions about the suspects, the evidence, and who is the victim, and in the end manipulate the criminal justice system, magistrates, judges, district attorneys, to their advantage in rather devious fashion (Ericson, 1993, pp. 211–213). The uncertainty that is shared by investigators arises from cases that present various degrees of 'trouble' in so far as victims, witnesses and evidence can all go missing, be misplaced or leave. All are problematic to manage. It is assumed that things will go wrong: witnesses will disappear or recant testimony, evidence will be overlooked or contaminated, interrogations will go badly, and errors in procedure will arise (see Simon, 1991, pp. 195–220). How well these are handled is the basis for prestige within the occupation. Because there is agreement about the work, it is visible to other investigators, and the rankings by skill are agreed upon, there is less conflict about the job and the standards to be applied to it. Metathemes unify in the face of contradictions, and do not seem to be present among those in the investigator segment.

A DIALECTIC EXCURSION

The police organisation shapes policing practices and the careers possible. While the police present themselves as operating in the military model of a disciplined, directed, commanded, carefully nuanced machine to apply force across situations as needed, the organisation is a fairly loosely coupled one in which divisions, special units (SWAT team, tactical or 'tact' squad, hostage rescue, juvenile or gang squad), segments within (LP, MM, TC, and detectives), and networks that cross the segments and integrate them all interact according to here and now assessments of what is required to sustain order as they variously define it. Occasionally, operations, proactive sweeps, crackdowns, or moral panics about particular crimes, notably homicide, bring a focus on policing activities, typically around a place or an activity. There is little or no 'problem-solving', and lack of quick here and now deciding is generally criticised throughout the organisation (see Eck, 2006). This interaction between patrol duties, specialised actions, and policy-driven activities leads to what Herbert accurately (and in an understatement) calls 'bureaucratic disarray' (Herbert, 2006, pp. 101–106). The disarray comes because there is a deep and profound contradiction between running a police department in terms of situationally justified actions and the rule-guided, routinised, compression of expectations that characterises bureaux in the modern, industrialised world. Police work has a polar quality – it can go very badly, easily, or be amazingly banal and routine. Because officers view the organisation as a mock bureaucracy, capricious, unpredictable and punitive, rather than democratic and fair, they feel at risk from the internal machinations of politics, supervision, policies, and uncertain events or incidents. They are bound together by shared practices and torn apart situationally. This repeated uncertainty gives rise to the tricks of the trade. The conventional view of the occupational culture within the police organisation overlooks the complexity of the work and the individualistic solutions that have been developed on the ground to deal with contingencies. The practices of officers create islands of individual control that contradict rule-based modes of organisational control. Through their practices they make substantial efforts to create autonomy.

The practices are the work; the organisation is the abstraction that shapes and constrains them. A fine range of variations in practices that have been discovered ethnographically is available. Consider these

- Officers when dispatched to calls will jump them to get 'good calls' regardless of their area or present assignments (Van Maanen, 1988, p. 60).

- Officers will call to accept a call after they are on the way to shorten the official response time (Van Maanen, 1988, p. 60ff).
- Officers swarm to certain calls that seem promising, and/or 'swing by to check on a colleague' if they are concerned about the call (Van Maanen, 1988, p. 109).
- Officers will develop their own métier or specialty. Herbert (2006, p. 105) reports an officer who sat by a gas station, watched the drivers and cars, and ran plates to find citizens driving with suspended licenses (a ticketing and towing offence in Seattle), outstanding warrants or cars on the stolen list. Fielding (1988) reports similar patterns learned by emulating the field training officer with whom one worked.
- 'Running plates' in areas that constitute the boundaries of city – a function that both keeps up the numbers and produces 'profiling' since the selection of vehicles and drivers is not random: it disproportionately includes people of colour (Meehan & Ponder, 2002a, 2002b).
- Officers convert technology to their own uses and may sabotage it as a mode of rebellion, stating their autonomy, or both (Manning, 2003, p. 157). These include such things as turning off the video camera or microphone (or both) in a car, using the radar gun to warn of the appearance of a sergeant when an officer is sleeping, dismantling the seat belt so that the buzzer or light does not come on, driving under bridges or into 'dead spots' to truncate the radio signal or a transponder in the car (p. 155).

Officers manage threats to their authority in a variety of ways: by threats in advance (I will have to lock you up, or, we can discuss this here or at the station); by lies; by giving motorists a chance to apologise so that they will cop a plea (accept the guilt and responsibility); acquiescing by and large to the requests of the complainant in situations of conflict (more so in misdemeanour than in felon offences) (Black & Reiss, 1970; Mastrofski et al., 2000) and simple things like leaving the lights on to blind the driver while he waits for the officer to use the MDT (mobile data terminal) to check on the driver, car, insurance, and registration.

These tactics are not a product of beliefs but of pragmatic practices that work over time. It is these practices that reflect the segmentalised work and its contingencies. The accounts of police occupational culture in Crank (1998) and Reiner (2001), for example, put the emphasis on beliefs and attitudes, and see culture as a coherent, integrated whole based on value agreement and consensus. My view is that these explanations are vague surrogates for shared exchanges and practices that bind the segments and separate them within an organisational context. The practices are what sustains the segments, and the organisational context, by which I mean the distribution of power within, is what binds them in a constraining fashion. It is their ecology and modes of interaction which I call here practises that bind them (see Van Maanen & Barley, 1984).

Specialisation (within the uniform division and within the organisation at large) adds another level of organisational constraint on the practices viewed as the occupational culture. Consider these matters of local practice that were carried out within specialised units.

• One officer in a Metro division decided that he would try out all the tools he knew on his cases: working an informant; hand to hand buys; search warrants and raids; surveillance; 'hot busts' (eye-balling and swooping in and arresting open-air drug dealing places). No supervision altered his practices, even though a sergeant has to sign off on any affidavit for a search warrant.
• One unit in Motor City worked a place where drug dealing and prostitution were known to take place; the officers, if they needed overtime or court time (a result of an arrest), would drive over to the 'Good Times Motel', ask the prostitutes who was dealing and in what room and then go up and knock on the door and rush in making an arrest and perhaps a seize of drugs and or money (personal communication, Sean Varano, 13th July 2006). The record would show arrests, seizures and 'activity'.
• In one Michigan city (called Tanqueray in another work: Manning, 2003), a gang squad was formed in 1998 because of complaints made to the mayor. In a focus group, the officers on the squad could not name a local gang, its location, or any descriptive aspects, but said gangs were a problem and they were heavily involved in surveillance and evidence gathering.
• Community police officers in West Seattle were seen as not doing a job since they were not answering calls nor making arrests. They created a hot spot policing unit to serve search warrants and make dynamic entries, and thus emulate the uniform patrols and the SWAT team. Like weed and seed efforts generally, there is no seeding, only weeding (Herbert, 2006, pp. 1–2). A similar organisational move was made in a Midwestern US city I called 'Western', where community police officers were rotated into a squad that made arrests, planned little operations, and were crime focused (Manning, 2003, p. 198).

These are examples of the ways in which officers create a distance from the formal authority structure. The practices create uncertainty for MM and

TC and thus are a source of power for the LP beyond the particular practices in which they engage. On the other hand, the organisation acts as a buffer for the street officers. What has been too little emphasised is that the police organisation creates, maintains, sustains, and protects the deep myths of the job and the everyday practices that remain in its visible presence. Paoline (2003), for example, argues that the shape of the occupational culture reproduces itself in organisations and, thus, gives primacy to the occupation over the organisation rather than seeing it as dialectic (p. 209). Van Maanen and Barley (1984) suggest a mode of adaptation within organisations to the contours of occupational culture, but this is just one side of the dialectic.

What has been argued previously is that the organisation encodes the environment such that noise and equivocations are erased (Manning, 2004). The organisation sees, responds to and reifies what is brought to 'its attention'. Herbert's fine study of community and police relations in West Seattle shows how frustrated citizens are with the ways in which the 911 system puts them off: will not process calls; does not yield response; and when they try in writing, letters disappear into the bureaucratic maw. This is in middle-class neighbourhoods; in lower class areas and in housing estates police either do not respond at all, or respond proactively and aggressively; they can be relied upon to suppress crime in activist ways (Stotland, 2001; Venkatesh, 1998). This permits officers to withdraw, lay low or respond as they choose (see Paoline, 2003). The organisation resists penetration except when the formulaic call and response is uttered; calls are screened, filtered, defined, and redefined in terms of the organisational code (that which incidents can be seen as); officers filter and screen their calls shifting and attending as they choose. The result is differential by areas of the city, by the content of the call and the working premises of the officer. The insulation of the officer in the car from the demands and concerns of the citizen is consummate unless the officer chooses to do otherwise.

CONCLUSION

Studying occupations in the division of labour requires an examination of the organisation in which they are located: their ecology, material constraints, interaction patterns and collective understandings. The police are significant in the modern division of labour not only because they represent order and ordering, but also because they are a primary redistributive mechanism – they alter the fates of millions of people every year in a significant fashion. In police practices one sees axes of concern, a tension between independence–dependence, autonomy-collective obligation, authority-lack of authority, and uncertainty–certainty. They are paired and dynamic oppositions that take significance from each other. Officers within the four segments must balance over time the four oppositions. While the individualism/group oppositions and the locus of control oppositions are salient across all segments, each segment adds a connotation or *metatheme* to the oppositions and in effect 'relabels' them. In the LP segment, the oppositions are a contrasting set, 'the job' and 'real police work'; in the MM segment they become 'politics' and 'management'; in the TC they become 'managing the job' and 'policing as democratic policing'. Think of these in yet another way: while the LP see the contrast between the individual officer and the group or occupation as 'the job', MM see these tensions as doing 'politics' and the TC see it as 'managing the job'. To continue this contrast, the second set of oppositions, locus of control, is seen by the LP as how to do the job right or 'real police work'; the MM see it as 'management'; TC see it as bridging internal and external audiences for their work – 'policing as democratic policing'. All of these, in sum, are variously layered, emotional, and sentimentally sourced labels for on-going activities. These are tensions in the culture, while the practices are ways of making distance between the segments and the organisation as a political weapon of the most powerful members of the occupation. Resolutions via practice may have lasting importance in shaping the 'tricks of the trade', or what is done to maintain autonomy and distance from review and supervision within the organisation. In many respects, the bargain is between a loose connection to the organisation in some respects (how one works the streets or cases; how one deals with anomalies) in exchange for the occasional crackdown, disciplinary sweep, rash of transfers or demotions based on the façade of bureaucratic rules. Power inheres in the ways in which command deals with exceptions, not with the routines of the work.

The irony of looking more closely at what officers do is that they act in such a way in situations that their decision-making balances the rational legal bureaucracy and its public face with the personalistic day-to-day work that is policing. If the expectation of police is that they should reflect the broader societies and cultures in which they work, observations suggest that they do. Finally, the police are not the source of order; they deal with failures – hence the depressive quality of police discourse and the cynicism displayed in public pronouncements. The uncertainties with which they deal are endemic, not subject to police modification, and perversely salient – hence their dramatic role.

NOTES

1. This is why I argued that 'community policing' can never fundamentally reduce a degree of necessary social distance, 'serve' a client, be true and full 'partners' with any community nor give up the obligation to intervene regardless of conventional social constraints (Manning, 1997). Neither can policing be a business, or judged properly by 'business' standards of profit and loss because unlike a market-based business, public cannot refuse to support the police through taxation, are always subject to coercion regardless of their current attitude or disposition, and cannot refuse the 'services' rendered. The police and the community do share values and are not always in fundamental opposition. What might be called the 'reserve clause' that grants police in the event almost endless levels of force to produce a desired outcome, means that they will always in potential maintain and exercise distance and autonomy from the wishes of some segments of the public.

2. The commonwealth of Massachusetts has no less than 351 separate police forces. These forces are small, locally funded, and the officers have no arrest powers beyond their own jurisdictions. These organisations remain a shadow of the early revolutionary idea of limited governmental power. There are also miscellaneous state and specialised state agencies. The environmental police in the Commonwealth watch over alligators, plovers, and endangered species.

3. Here, I have reference to the group threat thesis as explicated by Weitzer and Tuch (2006). The dominant group tends to identify with the 'forces of law and order' as they were called in the late 1960s, the police in particular – see them as defending their interests against the threats of crime and against minorities perceived as threats – while minorities are more critical, dubious, and distrustful of the police in general. All groups, however, in national surveys, believe that the primary job of the police is crime control, and this perception is the basis for their evaluation of the police as an organisation. The data of Weitzer and Tuch, gained from national surveys and local interviews in Washington DC neighbourhoods, show that Hispanics and blacks, in part a result of their own experiences and those of the people they know, see greater corruption and violence as a feature of policing. Not only are whites more positive about policing in general, they also deny the existence of extensive corruption and are generally unmoved by reported media-amplified events.

4. These men (at that time, no women had reached chief constable rank) have achieved very high rank in a small number of organisations (53 in the UK since the late 1960s). The studies suggest some basic biographical facts. They are on the one hand exceptional, and on the other are non-exceptional when compared to other police officers of their era. They share class origins, modest initial ambitions, sponsorship and protection by those 'above them' and a definition of and understanding of what the job requires. In this respect, they are not unlike the physicians studied by Oswald Hall (1948, 1949) more than 50 years ago.

5. The politics that have sustained this local career pattern have never been challenged in the United States, but alternative schemes were adopted in India and tried for a time in the United Kingdom after World War II. The United Kingdom experimented for some years with a plan called the Trenchard scheme after a British air marshall. This plan permitted officers to enter as inspectors (lieutenants) or 'gazetted officers' thus bypassing the ranks of constable and sergeant. It was

abandoned although various efforts to create a 'fast track' or accelerated plans for those aspiring to officer rank remain in place, facilitated by the National Police College at Bramshill. These schemes have never affected more than a handful of officers. Only chiefs in very large American cities or British Constabularies, typically very visible and active media figures, operate in a national or rarely in an international career system. The changing schemes, the absence of large numbers of graduates and shifting organisational responsibilities for training in the past 15 years suggest there is no consensus on what role advanced degrees should play in a police career. For more, see Punch in this volume.

6. He bounced back and is now (late 2006) head of a police district and a candidate for a top position in the ruling cadre of the new Commissioner Ed Davis (in place as of December, 2006).

7. This bias is manifested in gossip about these officers being lazy, not being a hustler, being unable to clear cases. In Latino-based units, it is believed that Anglos cannot investigate cases properly because they cannot get people to talk with them, have no informants, do not know African–American or Latino neighbourhoods (Martinez, 1996). In Boston, for example, the clearance rate of below 35% in homicide cases in 2005 was at least in part attributable to the absence of experienced African–American investigators and distrust of police in disadvantaged areas of the city. Where ethnicity divides the unit, racial stereotypes also shape the prestige of officers. A corollary of this is that sponsorship to the unit is difficult for those from stereotypic categories, and power shifts amongst ethnic groups are revealed in the composition of the unit. When police organisations are divided by conflict between ethnic groups and this division exists between the top command and detectives, transfers and promotions indicate additional ethnically based power relations.

8. Steve Herbert (2006, p. 95) reports that the Seattle police referred to attending seminars on community policing as analogous to invitations to drink Kool-Aid by followers of sect leader James Jones in Guyana in 1978. Some 900 people accepted the invitation, drank and died. It is not noted in the text whether any police officers succumbed to community policing as a result of the being exposed to the ideology in the seminars.

9. The idea has been adopted widely in the Anglo-American research world. It has been reconsidered, refined and elaborated recently by scholars such as Chan, Marks, Shearing, Waddington, Holdaway and others studying the police. See the contents of this volume for detailed examples.

10. The number of ex-chiefs who have been elected mayor is quite striking- a quick list would include mayors elected in the past twenty years in Portland Oregon, Minneapolis, Minnesota, St. Louis, Missouri, Houston, Texas, and Philadelphia, Pennsylvania.

11. Needless to say this set of crude short-hand ideas can easily become a rationalisation. The broken windows approach to policing justifies fining and enforcing life styles, arresting indiscriminately for misdemeanor offenses, perceived ill-defined ad hoc notions about disorder, and virtually anything else an officer decides to call an instance of broken windows policing (Harcourt, 2000).

12. I draw here without detailed reference on my fieldwork in Boston, in London, Birmingham, and Manchester in the UK, in Warren and Lansing Michigan, and in Washington DC. It is perhaps not necessary to note that Herbert was given what

might be called the guided tour of 'interesting places' with commentary, sometimes including 'well, it's quiet today but ...'.

13. The idea of a segment is taken from anthropology and is derived from tribal groups in which villages or separate clusters break from the group and set out on their own, but maintain interactions with the larger tribal group (see also Van Maanen & Barley, 1984).

14. In Boston in 2006, the beginning officer makes about $50,000 and the commissioner about $125,000. The top command do not make overtime. However, officers can augment their salaries by overtime, and some 10–15% of the force makes more than the commissioner through overtime assignments paid by private corporations and the city called 'details'. This is a ratio of about 2.5–1. At Northeastern University, for example, the beginning assistant professor with a PhD makes about 55,000 and the president in 2006 made 350,000, a ratio of approximately 6.4–1.

15. In Massachusetts, where officers are given pay raises based on their level of educational achievement, education counts. Education and abstract knowledge have little bearing on the everyday evaluation of performance, competence or trustworthiness. They are likely to be a liability in these contexts.

16. Some of these points are taken from my entry on detective work in the Encyclopedia of Police Science, 3rd edition (Manning, 2007).

ACKNOWLEDGEMENTS

I am grateful to P. A. J. Waddington and John Van Maanen for comments on an earlier draft.

REFERENCES

Banton, M. (1964). *The policeman in the community*. New York: Basic Books.

Bayley, D., & Bittner, E. (1986). The tactical choices of police patrol officers. *Journal of Criminal Justice, 14*, 329–348.

Becker, H. S. (1961). *Sociological work*. Chicago: Aldine.

Bittner, E. (1990). *Aspects of police work*. Boston: Northeastern University Press.

Black, D. J., & Reiss Jr, A. J. (1970). Police control of juveniles. *American Sociological Review, 35*, 63–77.

Brodeur, J.-P. (1983). High policing and low policing. *Social Problems, 30*, 507–520.

Brodeur, J.-P. (1999). Cops and spooks: The uneasy partnership. In: T. Newburn (Ed.), *Policing: Key readings*. Cullompton: Willan.

Brogden, M., & Nijhar, P. (2005). *Community policing: International and international models and approaches*. Cullompton: Willan.

Brown, M. (1977). *Working the street*. New York: Sage.

Chan, J. (1997). *Changing police culture*. Melbourne: Cambridge University Press.

Chan, J. (2001). The technology game. *Criminal Justice, 1*(2), 139–159.

Chan, J., Devery, C., & Doran, S. (2003). *Fair cop: Learning the art of policing.* Toronto: University of Toronto Press.

Corsianos, M. (1999). *Detective work.* Unpublished Ph.D. dissertation, York University, Toronto.

Corsianos, M. (2003). Discretion in detectives' decision making and 'high profile' cases. *Police Practice and Research, 4,* 301–314.

Corsianos, M. (2004). 'Women' detectives and perceptions of 'oppressive' experiences. *Critical Criminology, 12,* 67–85.

Crank, J. (1998). *Occupational culture.* Cincinnati: Anderson.

Davis, S. (1983). Restoring the semblance of order. *Symbolic Interaction, 6,* 261–278.

Eck, J. (2006). Problem-solving policing. In: D. Weisburd & A. Braga (Eds), *Policing innovation.* Cambridge: Cambridge University Press.

Ericson, R. (1993). *Making crime.* Toronto: Butterworth.

Ericson, R., & Haggerty, K. (1998). *Policing the risk society.* Toronto: University of Toronto Press.

Erikson, K. (1976). *Everything in its path.* New York: Simon & Schuster.

Fielding, N. (1988). *Joining forces.* London: Routledge Kegan Paul.

Forst, B., & Manning, P. K. (1999). *Privatization of policing: Two views.* Washington, DC: Georgetown University Press.

Foster, J. (2004). Police cultures. In: T. Newburn (Ed.), *Handbook of policing* (pp. 196–227). Cullompton: Willan.

Goffman, E. (1983). The interaction order. *American Sociological Review, 48,* 1–17.

Hall, O. (1948). Stages of a medical career. *American Journal of Sociology, 53,* 327–336.

Hall, O. (1949). Types of medical careers. *American Journal of Sociology, 55,* 243–253.

Harcourt, B. (2000). *The illusion of order.* Cambridge, MA: Harvard University Press.

Hawkins, K. (2003). *Law as a last resort.* Oxford: Oxford University Press.

Herbert, S. (2006). *Citizens, cops, and power.* Chicago: University of Chicago Press.

Holdaway, S. (1983). *Inside the British police.* Oxford: Blackwell.

Hunt, R., & Magenau, J. (1989). *Power and the police chief.* Thousand Oaks: Sage.

Hutter, B. (1985). *Compliance, regulation and the environment.* Oxford: Oxford University Press.

Innes, M. (2000). *Investigating murder.* Oxford: Clarendon Press.

Jermier, J., Slocum, J. W., Fry, L. W., & Gaines, J. (1991). Organizational subcultures in a soft bureaucracy. *Organization Science, 2,* 170–194.

Klinger, D. (1997). Negotiating order in patrol work: An ecological theory of police response to deviance. *Criminology, 35,* 277–306.

Klockars, C. (1985). *The idea of police.* Thousand Oaks: Sage.

Kuykendall, K. (1986). The municipal detective. *Criminology, 24,* 175–201.

Lucas, N. (1973). *The C.I.D.* London: Mayflower.

Lyons, W. (1996). *The politics of community policing.* Ann Arbor: University of Michigan Press.

Manning, P. K. (1997). *Police work.* Prospect Heights, IL: Waveland Press.

Manning, P. K. (2003). *Policing contingencies.* Chicago: University of Chicago.

Manning, P. K. (2004). *The narcs' game: Organizational and informational limits on drug law enforcement* (2nd ed.). Prospect Heights, IL: Waveland Press.

Manning, P. K. (2007). Detective work/culture. In: J. Greene (Ed.), *Encyclopedia of police science* (pp. 390–397). New York and London: Routledge.

Martin, S. (1977). *Breaking and entering.* Berkeley: University of California Press.

Martinez, R. (1996). Unpublished fieldnotes from Miami police department. University of Delaware Department of Sociology.

Marx, G. (1989). *Undercover*. New York: Sage.

Mastrofski, S. D. (2006). Community policing. In: D. Weisburd & A. Braga (Eds), *Innovations in policing*. Cambridge: Cambridge University Press.

Mastrofski, S. D., Snipes, J. B., Parks, R. B., & Maxwell, C. D. (2000). The helping hand of the law. *Criminology, 38*, 307–342.

Meehan, A. J., & Ponder, M. C. (2002a). How roadway composition matters in analyzing police data on race profiling. *Police Quarterly, 5*, 306–333.

Meehan, A. J., & Ponder, M. C. (2002b). Race and place: The ecology of racial profiling African–American motorists. *Justice Quarterly, 19*, 399–430.

Miller, S. (1999). *Gender and community policing*. Boston: Northeastern University Press.

Mills, C. W. (1940). Situated actions and vocabularies of motive. *American Sociological Review, 5*, 904–913.

Paoline, E. A. (2003). Taking stock: Toward a richer understanding of police culture. *Journal of Criminal Justice, 31*, 199–214.

Punch, M. (1983). Officers and men in control. In: M. Punch (Ed.), *The police organization*. Cambridge, MA: MIT Press.

Rawls, A. (1983). The interaction order *sui generis*: Goffman's contribution to social theory. *Sociological Theory, 5*, 136–149.

Reiner, R. (1991). *Chief constables*. Oxford: Oxford University Press.

Reiner, R. (2001). *The politics of police*. Oxford: Oxford University Press.

Robinson, C. (2001). *Texas rangers*. New York: Modern Library.

Rubinstein, J. (1972). *City police*. New York: Farrar, Straus and Giroux.

Samora, J., Bernal, J., & Pena, A. (1979). *Gunpowder justice*. South Bend: University of Notre Dame Press.

Sanders, W. (1977). *Detective work*. New York: Free Press.

Shearing, C. (1992). Private policing. In: M. Tonry & N. M. Chicago (Eds), *Modern policing*. Chicago: University of Chicago Press.

Shearing, C., & Ericson, R. (1991). Culture as figurative action. *British Journal of Sociology, 42*, 481–506.

Sheingold, S. (1991). *The politics of street crime*. Philadelphia: Temple University Press.

Short, J. F. (Ed.), (1971). *The social fabric of the metropolis*. Chicago: University of Chicago Press.

Simon, D. (1991). *Homicide*. New York: Simon & Schuster.

Sklansky, D. (forthcoming). *Democratic policing*. Unpublished manuscript.

Skogan, W. (2006). *Police and community in Chicago*. New York: Oxford University Press.

Skolnick, J. (1966). *Justice without trial*. New York: Wiley.

Stotland, S. E. (2001). The multiple dimensions of trust: Resident police relations in Boston. *Journal of Crime and Delinquency, 38*, 226–256.

Terrill, W. E., Paoline, E., & Manning, P. (2003). Police culture and coercion. *Criminology, 41*, 1003–1034.

Thacher, D. (2005). The local role in homeland security. *Law and Society Review, 39*, 635–676.

Van Maanen, J. (1974). Working the street. In: H. Jacob (Ed.), *The potential for reform in the criminal justice system*. Beverly Hills: Sage.

Van Maanen, J. (1975). Police socialization: A longitudinal examination of job attitudes in an urban police department. *Administrative Science Quarterly, 20*, 2017–2028.

Van Maanen, J. (1983). The boss. In: M. Punch (Ed.), *Control in the police organization*. Cambridge, MA: MIT Press.

Van Maanen, J. (1988). *Tales from the field.* Chicago: University of Chicago Press.
Van Maanen, J., & Barley, S. R. (1984). Occupational communities: Culture and control in organizations. In: B. M. Staw & L. L. Cummins (Eds), *Research in organizational behaviour* (Vol. 6, pp. 287–365). Greenwich, CT: JAI Press.
Venkatesh, S. (1998). *American ghetto.* Cambridge, MA: Harvard University Press.
Waddington, P. A. J. (1998). Police (canteen) culture. *British Journal of Criminology, 39,* 287–309.
Wall, D. (1998). *The chief constables of England and Wales.* Aldershot: Ashgate.
Walsh, W. (1986). Patrol officer arrest rates. *Justice Quarterly, 2,* 271–290.
Webb, W. (1935). *The Texas rangers.* Austin: University of Texas Press.
Weitzer, R., & Tuch, S. (2006). *Race and policing in America.* Cambridge: Cambridge University Press.
Westley, W. (1970)[1951]. *Violence and the police.* Cambridge, MA: MIT Press.
Wickersham Report. (1931). *National Commission on law observance and enforcement.* Washington, DC: USGPO.
Wilson, J. Q. (1968). *Varieties of police behaviour.* Cambridge, MA: Harvard University Press.

CHAPTER 3

POLICE CULTURE(S): SOME DEFINITIONAL, METHODOLOGICAL AND ANALYTICAL CONSIDERATIONS

Tom Cockcroft

ABSTRACT

This chapter explores the use of oral histories in furthering our understanding of police cultures by expanding upon three main themes. First, the oral history approach challenges us in terms of the need to differentiate between police organisational influences and the influences of wider society. Second, the approach highlights the difficulties associated with assuming a degree of universality between police cultures. Third, the approach allows one to build upon the work of policing scholars such as Shearing and Ericson, and Waddington in drawing out further dimensions of the problematic relationship between language and behaviour in the context of police narratives.

Police culture is, in many respects, a contested term. Inter alia it can refer to specific (and almost prescriptive) modes of behaviour, the values that inform such behaviours and the narrative modes used by the police to describe or accommodate them. The purpose of this chapter is to highlight some of

Police Occupational Culture: New Debates and Directions
Sociology of Crime, Law and Deviance, Volume 8, 85–102
Copyright © 2007 by Elsevier Ltd.
All rights of reproduction in any form reserved
ISSN: 1521-6136/doi:10.1016/S1521-6136(07)08003-7

those definitional, methodological and analytical issues which emerge when
one explores police culture through the oral history method. This chapter
will aim to highlight the contribution of oral history to debates concerning
the clarity of the term police culture, the use of oral history in exploring
police culture and, finally, the challenges of making sense of police
testimony. First, though, we shall take a brief overview of oral history as
a methodology.

WHAT IS ORAL HISTORY?

Oral history is a broad-based methodological approach that focuses upon
the narratives of individuals recounting past experiences. Several of the
definitions of oral history provided by the existing literature highlight
disputes over its purpose and method. For example, the Library of Congress
(1971) states that oral history is, simply, information in oral form collected
through planned interviews. This definition fails to acknowledge that oral
histories have both an explicit historical dimension and can be based upon
spontaneous exchanges that really do not constitute 'planned' interviews as
such. Grele (1996), on the other hand, views oral history as 'the interviewing
of eye-witness participants in the events of the past for the purposes of
historical construction' (p. 63). Grele's definition describes some oral history
projects but does not adequately portray those studies that are concerned
with meaning rather than events (see Portelli, 1991) and, I argue, it is the
meaning that is imbued in oral histories that allows us to probe police
culture in more detailed ways.

Oral histories are subject to persistent debate regarding the 'nature' of the
data that they generate, an important factor in determining the type of
analysis that such data can and should be subjected to. This debate centres
upon two opposing viewpoints, outlined by Grele (1998), which fail to agree
on whether transcript data is 'raw' and unfiltered or, conversely, already
subjected to interpretive process. Given the disputed nature of what
constitutes oral history, it is perhaps of use to present the broad but helpful
definition provided by Starr (1977, p. 440) that suggests that, 'oral history is
primary source material obtained by recording the spoken words – generally
by means of planned tape-recorded interviews – of persons deemed to
harbour hitherto unavailable information worth preserving'.

Recent years, as Perks and Thomson (1998) note, have seen a renewed
interest in oral history on account of the growing popularity of emergent
qualitative approaches such as life history. This, and the growing

acknowledgement of oral history as an interdisciplinary tool, has served to, perhaps paradoxically, allow the method to weaken its links with history (where, as Sangster, 1994, notes it was seen by some as too *unhistoric*) and to reposition itself as a qualitative method of inquiry. Given that biographical approaches such as oral history have strong links with the symbolic interactionist 'schools' of sociology (Goodey, 2000) as well as with the socialist movement (Popular Memory Group, 1982; Selbourne, 1980), oral history has developed as a means of addressing the lives of those generally neglected by more orthodox historical approaches. In this way, oral history has provided a suitable way of addressing the hidden histories of marginalised groups such as rural women in South Africa (Bozzoli, 1991), labourers in 1930s Hackney (Hackney WEA, 1975), gay men and women (Kennedy, 1998) and the disabled (Walmsley, 1995).

DEFINITIONAL CONSIDERATIONS: THE MEANING OF POLICE CULTURE

Oral history can be a useful methodological tool in analysing the complicated concept of police culture. One of the challenges of making sense of police culture is that from a seemingly straightforward precept we are confronted by an array of separate yet inter-related issues. For example, if we take three straightforward explanations of police culture, several further avenues of inquiry become apparent:

a layer of informal occupational norms and values operating under the apparently rigid hierarchical structure of police organisations (Chan, 1997, p. 43)

accepted practices, rules, and principles of conduct that are situationally applied, and generalised rationales and beliefs (Manning, 1989, p. 360)

a patterned set of understandings which help to cope with and adjust to the pressures and tensions which confront the police (Reiner, 1992, p. 109)

These three definitions point to the informality within formal organisations; the situational application of beliefs; and the need for a cognitive lens within which to interpret the tensions which are integral to the job. These broad, all encompassing, definitions have come under wider scrutiny as is evidenced by the following extract from a report by Her Majesty's Introspectorate of Constabulary:

The journalistic shorthand that summarises the thinking of operational police officers as being explained by 'a canteen culture' is as misleading as it is mischievous. It is acknowledged that the location reference is merely evocative of what is seen as a collective attitude. These very canteens witness the conversations of officers who still see service to all members of the public as an intrinsic part of their vocation. The number of officers who are nominated each year for community awards are part of this same culture. (Her Majesty's Introspectorate of Constabulary, 1999, p. 29)

The complexity of organisational culture, its nature and effect is made especially difficult when applied to the police. The police are historically characterised as having a role that is difficult to define (a theme common to public sector institutions). Goldstein (1979) notes that there is a disparity between what the public perceive the police function to be and what it is that the police actually do. Goldstein therefore differentiates between the widely held view that the police are there to enforce the law and a contrasting view that the police enforce laws as a mere means of achieving their main goal – quite simply, solving problems. Such an approach was anticipated by Westley (1970) who drew on the work of Vollmer (1936) to show that there is a difference between the explicitly stated responsibilities of the police and that work that they actually undertake. Beyond such principal tasks and responsibilities lie the more social or service-oriented aspects of the police role and, significantly, these are subject to variation between areas and over time.

Increasingly, historical analyses of police work (see, for example, Brogden, 1991) demonstrate the ways in which the behaviours of officers within a particular force are inextricable from historically located industrial structures, employment patterns and the resultant secondary economies. Emsley (2005) in his analysis of the Sergeant Goddard[1] case notes that the Soho area of London provided both the motivation and the opportunity for corrupt police behaviour with two main features accounting for this. The financial wealth of Soho at the time served to highlight the relative modesty of the police salary and, perhaps more importantly, much of the wealth of the area was generated through unlawful pursuits. As Emsley's work suggests, any analysis of police occupational culture needs to acknowledge those features of the social environment that may increase the probability of, if not actively encourage, certain police responses.

Brogden (1991) shows how oral history allows us to focus upon 'the contextualisation of police life' (p. 165) through allowing the oral historian a glimpse of those occurrences and interactions which, according to Weinberger (1995), hold significance for the social actor. For Brogden, oral history allowed for an appreciation of what he saw as the complex class relations which characterised policing in Liverpool between the First and Second World Wars. Alternatively, Weinberger used oral history as a means of exploring both organisational relations and the changing dynamics of the police relationship with the public. Oral history is, therefore, one method of inquiry that can facilitate our understanding of the complex relationships that exist between police officers and both their immediate and wider social environments.

Oral histories appear to have also circumvented some of the criticisms that Chan (1997) raises with conventional analyses of police culture. The work of both Weinberger and Brogden provides several examples that appear to support Chan's assertion regarding the need for a more flexible conception of police behaviour. Each of Chan's criticisms will now be addressed with reference to examples from the police oral history literature that demonstrate its potential in identifying the fluid characteristics of police culture. Chan's first criticism is that of 'internal differentiation and jurisdictional differences' (1997, p. 65) and relates to the problem of traditional police culture theories insufficiently explaining cultural variations in police work. Weinberger's (1995) oral history of policing adequately conveys both the way in which individual officers in the same station adopted contrasting values and behaviours as well as identifying considerable differences in police role between locations. In particular, in Weinberger's work, the issue of 'internal differentiation' is highlighted through her findings in regard to police use of force. For example, despite the routine use of force by some officers to gain confessions, assert authority and informally resolve public order situations, other officers in her sample condemned the use of force by officers as poor police practice. Likewise, pronounced differences in policing between jurisdictions were evidenced by her comparison of rural and inner-city police divisions, with officers in the former priding themselves on the lack of 'action' that characterised their day to day work. In the latter, however, the pressure to be seen as efficient led, in some instances, to inner-city officers challenging neighbouring divisions to see who could generate the most arrests and summonses.

Chan's second criticism of traditional conceptions of police culture is that they portray police officers as being passively socialised into cop culture. Brogden's (1991) oral history of Liverpool policing between the First and Second World Wars goes some way towards highlighting alternative interpretations of the socialisation of officers. First, he suggests that the considerable amount of discretion enjoyed by officers allowed them to develop their own particular strategies for dealing with, for example, public order situations – a factor which perhaps undermines the notion that police officers, in all situations, have a prescriptive framework of reference for future action. Second, he suggests that the relative isolation of the beat officer's role simply did not allow for the sustained social immersion with one's colleagues which is required to prolong a strong occupational culture.

Chan also challenges traditional conceptions of police culture for neglecting the influence of wider external factors upon the context of policing. Weinberger's (1995) study is a good example of how using an oral history approach provides researchers with a means for contextualising police organisational culture both socially and historically. She examines the impact of the Street Betting Act of 1906 and shows how this piece of legislation was viewed by police officers as having far-reaching consequences for day-to-day policing given its impact upon police relations with the public and the role it played in encouraging bribery of officers. She also shows how the reversal of policy concerning the recording of crime, during the 1960s, led to CID officers being encouraged to record as much crime as possible. Over time, and as Weinberger illustrates, the advent of such policies had wide-ranging effects upon the CID in terms of their working practices, morale and relationship with uniformed officers.

Finally, Chan also questions the extent to which cultural change is possible within a restrictive and deterministic cultural framework, noting that any conception of police culture needs to account for change as well as opposition to change. Again, oral history approaches allow for an appreciation of cultural change within the police organisation and Weinberger demonstrates how the exigencies of wartime signalled a remodelling of the police relationship with the public in terms which emphasised the service role of the police. The narratives which constitute her work also describe how the advent of the post-war era heralded a swift decline in police relations with the public and, for the officers interviewed by Weinberger (1995), the 1950s onwards were characterised by 'strain and ambiguity' (p. 133), a growing detachment from the public and significant changes to police strategy. Tellingly, the narratives from the officers of the 1930s and 1940s suggest that those officers were quick to censure post-war society and the style of policing that they saw as characterising it. This distinction between pre- and post-war policing does suggest the possibility of considerable cultural change occurring over a relatively short period of time.

Oral history, therefore, allows for a reading of police culture that emphasises the possibility of cultural variation, the agency of the individual social actor, the impact of external factors and the possibility of cultural change. As Samuel (1976, p. 202) notes, 'people's memory of their work ... is often particularly vivid, and extends to incidents and events and stories which give precious insights into the workplace, as a total context and cultural setting – the ambiguities of foremanship and the difficulties encountered by authority, the nature of the learning process, the subdivision of the different classes of work'. By focusing on the individual officer in relation to 'local and national specificity, intra-organisational conflicts, and processes of temporal change' (Loader & Mulcahy, 2003, p. 182), oral history provides a framework that encourages investigation of the ways in which police officers relate to the complex environments they inhabit.

The pitfalls of investigating police culture without taking into account socio-political factors leads to a reading of police work that situates it in a sociological cul-de-sac devoid of sufficiently broad cultural appreciation – wider culture does not simply 'end' at the front door of the police station. Brogden (1991) provides an especially incisive account in this respect by drawing out the particular social, economic and cultural influences which characterised Liverpool in the first half of the twentieth century. He identifies the unquestionable influence of the city's economic infrastructure, built largely on its status as the largest seaport in Western Europe, as determining not only the class composition of the city but also its tradition of casual employment. Likewise, he describes the persistent undercurrent of tension between the police and ethnic minority groups in the city where a precursor to the 1981 Toxteth riots can be found in the 1919 race riots that the city witnessed. When we build into this picture a pronounced sectarian divide, we become acutely aware that Liverpool was a city where the job of policing was inextricably linked to the social relations (and tensions) of that particular environment.

This unique social milieu shaped not only the views of police officers but also the way they policed. As Brogden (1982) illustrates, outside of London, Liverpool was the only key location to witness widespread police strikes during 1919. That these strikes led to widespread public support for the police, in itself, highlights the 'messy [and] confused' (Brogden, 1991, p. 2) nature of class relations in the area. Likewise, Brogden (1982) describes a police force that itself was strictly divided by stratifications of social class with officers from the middle-classes being overtly antagonistic to unions and their members. Brogden's work is crucial in this respect as it draws out the historical and cultural underpinnings that not only shape a given environment but also prescribe the nature of social relations within that locale. Conceptions of police culture which fail to take into account distinct, yet complex, factors of this kind that provoke variations in police behaviour do little to acknowledge that police culture is 'neither monolithic nor unchanging' (Reiner, 2000, p. 106) and characterised by 'complexity and [a] multi-faceted nature' (Foster, 2003, p. 222).

One unfortunate consequence of approaches that fail to take into account the complexity of the context within which policing takes place is, according to Punch (1985), an over-eagerness to automatically view all police behaviours as artefacts of a specific and separate police culture. Punch advocates methodological styles that incorporate, 'historical, comparative (cross-cultural and cross-national), and organisational levels of analysis' (p. 186) to help us fully understand the shifting and nuanced nature of much police behaviour. Taking forward Punch's challenge, in the following section oral history will be explored in more detail in respect of how it might be used to successfully investigate both the universal and the variable aspects of police culture.

ORAL HISTORY METHODS AND POLICE CULTURE

One way of demonstrating the impact of shifting political and social contexts upon police culture is to utilise methodological approaches that can accommodate the variable historical relations between the police and wider society. This is not to disregard the fact that there appear to be some relatively consistent cultural reference points in police work. Skolnick (1994) argues that police culture serves as a cultural lens through which to make sense of the world and it might be fair to suggest that, over time, the focus of the lens may vary, accentuating some attributes and diminishing others. Brown (1995) further notes that core assumptions which constitute a culture will tend to remain relatively stable whereas the more ancillary assumptions will be prone to transformation. Such a distinction suggests that we are likely to witness cultural shifts which emphasise certain roles or values as important at different periods of time and in different environments.

Underlying this, however, is the assumption that policing, throughout much of the world, is characterised by generally similar structural features which tend to produce a 'typical cultural pattern' (Reiner, 2000, p. 106) amongst police officers. The extent to which police oral histories either substantiate or refute claims of cultural universality is arguable given the variety of forms that such histories can take. Abbott (1991, p. 223) noted that 'history limits generalisation by emphasising changing causal universes' and this is especially true of the work of Weinberger. The wide remit of her work, to create an oral history of British policing between the 1930s and the 1960s, was considerably more encompassing than Brogden's which adopted much narrower terms of geographical and temporal reference.[2] As such, Weinberger's work is characterised by a pervasive impression of change and contrast – in terms of changing social relations both inside and outside the police organisation, as well as the contrasting images she portrays of police work in different locations. Despite adopting such broad terms of reference, Weinberger does succeed in highlighting evidence of some cultural behaviours and values which appear common to many analyses of police culture. However, it should be noted that in many cases such cultural characteristics appear to lack universality amongst officers, with some apparently rejecting views held by colleagues, for example in regard to police use of force. In this respect, Reiner's (2000, p. 106) concept of the 'typical cultural pattern' is problematic when viewed in the light of such work as it implies that there is a dominant or uncontested set of cultural norms.

Traditionally, police culture has been viewed in terms that tend to gloss over many variations in police behaviour. Such an approach has allowed us to construct a conception of the police that highlights factors common to police environments but which fails to fully assimilate those factors that are not common to the occupational world of all officers. Accordingly, alternative methodologies and disciplinary approaches may serve to highlight the diversity of police experiences rather than the similarity. The oral history accounts collected by Brogden (1991) and Weinberger (1995) provide a vital dimension to our understanding of policing not only in a broader sense but especially in terms of understanding both the differences in what police officers do and in how they justify or explain their actions.

In some respects, the narratives generated by oral history projects appear little or no different to police narratives generated by more contemporary research projects in that they provide vivid first-hand accounts of police officers recounting the 'reality' of day-to-day policing. Where they do differ, however, is in what they offer us as a hitherto unavailable glimpse of the lives of former police officers, doing so, moreover, in a format that allows us to appreciate the wider legal, political and social contexts of that time. As Perks and Thomson (1998) note, oral histories not only alert researchers to new areas of interest but they are in addition instilled with a subjectivity and personal value borne of experience and reflection.

The methodology of oral history is, however, a broad and contested area. Slim and Thompson (1993), for example, highlight five main types of oral history method (life story interviews, family-tree interviewing, single-issue testimony, group interviews and, controversially perhaps, diary interviewing). Given the variety of ways in which oral testimony can be captured it is unsurprising that oral history methodology remains subject to continuing debate regarding both its form and function. It is possible, however, to tentatively suggest two main areas which make oral history different from more orthodox interviewing approaches. First, the historical dynamics of oral history, combined with its politicised roots, emphasise the importance of the narrator and his or her individual viewpoint. Subsequently, for oral historians like Anderson and Jack (1991), the methodology dictates that the narrator tells his or her story in his or her own terms rather than being treated by the interviewer as purely a source of information. Furthermore, the use of open-ended questions, and an increasing use of oral history as a means of exploring meaning and emotion rather than *fact*, allows the narrator, according to Samuel and Thompson (1990), to challenge the rigid and artificial partitioning of his or her public and private life. Ultimately, these factors are instrumental in emphasising not only the narrator's diversity of experience but also the ways in which individuals draw on common culture. Second, the literature of oral history, as noted by Grele (1998), has become increasingly dominated by debate regarding the complexity of relationships between the narrator and both the interviewer and his or her own 'historical conscious-ness' (p. 45). This appreciation of the importance of *orality* (Portelli, 1991) suggests that oral testimony allows for different levels of analysis (with regard to what Grele (1998, p. 45) termed 'hidden levels of discourse') to that of the written word. Thus, oral history can be presented as a methodological approach that highlights the importance of the narrator, of his or her past life, and of the subjectivity with which he or she recounts such experience, and that, importantly, also recognises oral testimony as an intrinsically distinct type of data.

The oral histories of both Weinberger (1995) and Brogden (1991) therefore have a wider purpose than merely 'filling in' gaps in our historical understanding of policing. Perhaps their greatest contributions have been in the voice they give to previously 'hidden' histories and the understanding they offer of the way police officers both comprehended and managed the social worlds that they inhabited. Both works succeed in demonstrating the contribution of historical methods to our understanding of the similarities and dissimilarities between the cultural dynamics of the past and the present.[3]

These oral histories suggest that, historically, police behaviour was influenced by less formalised instruction and supervision than nowadays and that, subsequently, police officers used their considerable discretion to exhibit a wide variety of behaviours. Significantly, where such work proves invaluable is in the way that it allows officers not only to explain the actions they carry out or the values that they hold, but also to contextualise these in terms of the pressures brought to bear upon them or, conversely, in terms of those aspects of their everyday lives which supported such actions or values. Both Brogden and Weinberger highlight use of force by police officers and show how it was used, variously, as a means of extracting confessions, asserting authority and pre-empting further trouble. These oral histories succeed in not only explaining such types of behaviour and their extent but also in clarifying the norms surrounding them and how they came to be viewed as 'acceptable' by some officers, and also sometimes by the public. In particular, oral histories have given us the opportunity to explore historical accounts of police work from what Seldon and Pappworth (1983, p. 49) termed 'non-elite witnesses'. The testimony of witnesses like these who have retired allows us to by-pass the problem of interviewees being reluctant to divulge information about their experiences, especially where doing so might undermine the official ideology of the institution. Oral history, according to Weinberger, therefore

> offers a particular advantage, as an especially useful means of inquiry in bureaucratic and hierarchical organisations where the gap between the officially stated means and purposes, and the reality on the ground is likely to be wide. (1995, p. 3)

Police oral histories point to the existence of possible alternative readings of police culture and its intensity, a point that may serve to partially reinforce Manning's (1978) assertion that policing is not endowed with a common culture. Primarily this is due to the broad nature of oral history narratives and the fact that the relatively unstructured interviews upon which they are largely based lead to significant amounts of diverse data from which it is often hard to extract common experiences despite the existence of some apparently persistent cultural reference points. Passerini (1979) makes a similar point regarding her oral history research into the attitudes of the Italian working class towards fascism. By adopting an approach that stressed the importance of spontaneous and in-depth responses she found that the data which emerged from her study was initially difficult to interpret. Her account details the difficulty with which she learned to 'read' the oral data that challenged her preconceptions regarding the narratives and the information they conveyed. Cogently, she notes that 'oral sources refuse to answer certain kinds of questions' (p. 91) whilst suggesting that, simultaneously, the narratives often provided information which had not originally been considered important but which nevertheless transpired to be of value. Passerini's work is important in that it reminds us of the need not only to engage with apparent discrepancies in data but also to realise that such 'anomalies' are often more important aids to our understanding than data which appear to reaffirm our presumptions. It might therefore be fair to suggest that the conceptualisation of police narratives in terms that overlook their true complexity obstruct us from gaining a more nuanced

understanding of police behaviour and police language. As the next section
will demonstrate, to equate language with action through a two-dimensional
axis of cause and effect underplays the use of language as a creative tool that
has different purposes in different situations.

MAKING SENSE OF POLICE NARRATIVES

Gennette (1980) draws out the complexities of narrative by suggesting that
any narrative has a relationship with both the occurrence it presents and the
act of narration itself. In short, to take a particular narrative and assume that
it is a 'true' account of what happened, where, and to whom is to ignore the
subtleties of the form and purpose of language. Instead, we need to
appreciate that the relationship between a narrative and an occurrence is not
inherently unproblematic and, correspondingly, that the act of narration is in
many instances a creative rather than a passive act.

In their 'Culture as Figurative Action' model that draws on what Ericson,
Baranek and Chan (1987) termed the 'vocabulary of precedents', Shearing
and Ericson (1991) provide a sophisticated account of police 'storytelling'
which denotes the ways in which language provides a 'cultural tool-kit'
(p. 500) for occupational behaviour. Shearing and Ericson note that this kind
of police narration allows a degree of creativity and flexibility in police action
and invites individuals either to be guided by the provided framework or to
extemporise within it. The sheer breadth of purpose presented by storytelling
invariably necessitates an appreciation of the inconsistent role and form of
police language. As such, police language is portrayed in terms that
emphasise its adaptive and versatile nature. Some police narrations,
therefore, are viewed by Shearing and Ericson as short-lived, static and
descriptive, whereas others may be persistent, perpetually evolving and
subjective – the distinction between the two ultimately depending on the
purpose which that testimony holds for the officer.

Such an account of the relationship between language and culture is
obviously of wide interest to those engaged in police culture research, not
least for the way in which it appears to challenge overly deterministic
conceptions of the relationship between police behaviour and police culture.
Shearing and Ericson's model has been criticised by other policing scholars
who aim to clearly delineate between those cultural influences associated
with police culture and those from wider societal culture. For example,
Waddington (1999) challenges Shearing and Ericson's model on a number
of points, the first of which asks quite simply whether officers might be more

influenced by those narratives which are generated outside of the culture of policing than those generated within it.

Perhaps Waddington's main contribution to the debate over police narratives is his suggestion that police culture might be bifurcated along the lines of a canteen culture and an operational culture. That is, the cultural rules which guide action on the street may be separate from those that guide the recounting of such actions amongst their peers. As Waddington shows, canteen storytelling can be a means of contextualising occupational experiences, a way of emphasising, and sustaining, the perceived 'them' and 'us' worldview of policing which disparages all who play down either the danger or the bureaucracy of the job. If the 'mean streets' are the battleground of policing, then, as Waddington (1999) observes, 'the canteen is the "repair shop"' (p. 295) and it is this distinction that raises some conspicuous challenges for research into policing. If canteen talk acts as a distorting lens through which officers accentuate their understanding of their work in relation to key cultural themes, just how 'valid' are such narratives to our understanding of what police officers actually 'do'?

Questions surrounding the ways in which police officers 'use' language to fill gaps in memory soon arise when one examines police oral history narratives, and the issue of memory and its impact on the narrating of past incidents is a recurrent theme of discussion within the literature of oral history (Lummis, 1983, provides a detailed overview of these issues). Frisch (1990), for example, draws attention to the concern that, even with recall of the recent past, interviewees are liable to *reflect* upon their past experiences rather than recall their feelings at the time. The impact of hindsight (Seldon & Pappworth, 1983, p. 25) remains a crucial issue that potentially can serve to remove a narrative from its original and personally situated context.

This point is addressed by Beckford (1975) who highlights the impact of 'plausibility structures' which are used by social actors to assemble their normative view of the social world. Such 'plausibility structures' refer to institutions which provide the basis for an individual's worldview and which sustain meaning through language and ritual denied to others not affiliated to that particular group and, crucially, which provide a framework through which individuals both articulate meaning and are socialised. Reiner (1992, p. 109) notes that police culture can be viewed in terms of, 'a patterned set of understandings' which, one might speculate, largely serves as a form of 'plausibility structure'. When one is removed from a particular 'plausibility structure' (through retirement, promotion or a change in occupational role or status within a force) we may need to consider the influence of that referential framework on subsequent narratives concerning that individual's past.

The study of police oral histories provides a potential historical angle to Shearing and Ericson's (1991) model of 'Culture as Figurative Action'. In the introduction to her oral history of English policing, Weinberger (1995) notes that the analysis of police oral history narratives compel the researcher to confront the inevitable intertwining of allegory and social identity and to recognise the fact that narratives 'tell us less about events than about their symbolic, cultural and personal meaning' (p. 3). A further factor that needs to be taken into account when assessing the narratives of those engaged in actions which occasionally might attract censure is that of the distinction between public and private memories. Thomson (1998) provides a case study of an Australian Anzac veteran recounting his recollections of the Battle of Gallipoli and charts how the recall and narrative representations of the past are mediated through public expectation and national mythology. Only with the passage of time and the influence of the anti-war movement has it become possible for Thomson's subject to recall the previously taboo subjects of tension between ranks and the hostility of many sections of the public to Anzac veterans on their return after the First World War.

We can speculate that this distinction between 'what actually happened' and 'what should have happened' might be an integral issue in our understanding of police narratives. Similarly, one might take such examples of individuals being reluctant to break with the prevalent discourses of the time as further evidence of the influence of external factors upon what individuals do and how they present such actions to 'outsiders'. As Susman (1964) notes, the dialectic tension between history and myth/ideology 'through combination and interaction ... produce[s] a variety of historical visions' (Grele, 1998, p. 46) which are ultimately dependent upon the individual who is narrating, the subject he or she is narrating, and the person to whom he or she is narrating.

Such discrepancies suggest a need to adopt approaches to understanding police narratives that draw away from simplistic methods that simply equate police language with police action. This complex relationship (already addressed by writers such as Waddington, 1999; Shearing & Ericson, 1991) becomes even more convoluted when one introduces a historical dimension. As Abbott (1991) implies, any true appreciation of social process requires an appreciation of the complexity of the changing environment within which those processes take place.

CONCLUSION

Police oral histories raise a number of interesting angles for further debate in the area of police culture, most notably in terms of the ambiguity over the influence of internal and external factors, the universality of police culture and the interpretation of narratives. The historical and subjective dimensions provided through such narratives allow for a more extensive appreciation of factors as diverse as responses to police scandals, the demographic factors peculiar to an area and the negotiated 'relationships' between the police and the policed in informing the cultural landscape of policing. By extracting the 'undercurrents, inconsistencies and quirks' (Fielding, 1997) of police officers' working lives they also provide explanations of 'why' officers act in the way they do rather than merely explain 'how' they act. Punch's (1985) contention that too much emphasis is placed upon the power of internal factors suggests that, until we more fully utilise research methodologies that allow us to examine police work within contexts which acknowledge the influence of wider societal factors, it is unlikely that this dialectic will be resolved.

The role of narrative and its importance to our understanding of police culture appears as an interesting but largely ignored area in many analyses. Recent years have seen the literature of oral history acknowledge the challenges of the spoken word and the complexity of its relationship to action, primarily due to its reliance on relatively unstructured interviewing methods. Barring the work of Shearing and Ericson (1991) and Waddington (1999) surprisingly little has been written on the specific area of police narrative. As Waddington notes, ethnographers engaged in studies of policing have been reluctant to suggest that the relationship between police narrative and behaviour is unproblematic. Notwithstanding the obvious methodological challenges of unthreading the complexities of such an entwined relationship, it stands to reason that the acknowledgement of the 'interpretive and active role' (Chan, 1997, p. 66) of individual officers in making sense of their environment should be replicated in an acknowledgement of their fluid and constructive use of language.

This chapter has attempted to address some concerns regarding what we mean by the term police culture, the opportunities provided by the oral history method, and some of the challenges of making sense of police testimony. In doing so, there is always a danger of being seen to promote a negative and problematic view of police culture that questions the value of further investigation. This is by no means the intention of this chapter.

Instead, such challenges should be used to enrich and inform our future research in this area. The need for further debate concerning what we mean by the term 'police culture' is perhaps timely regardless of issues of methodology. Newburn (2003), in particular, provides a coherent over-view of the changes to both the *police* and *policing* currently taking place whilst simultaneously reminding us that key aspects of the police role remain unchanged. Such an analysis suggests that the tasks of unravelling the cultural dynamics of policing, devising appropriate research methodologies and assessing the ways in which we 'evidence' police culture in the future will become even more challenging as we begin to unpick the various cultural issues associated with the increased complexity of 'policing' and its contexts.

NOTES

1. George Goddard, a sergeant in the Metropolitan Police Force, was convicted of accepting money from members of the public in 1929.
2. As mentioned earlier in this chapter, Brogden (1991) proposes that within his data there was no evidence to suggest that officers were part of a specific occupational culture.
3. The focus of oral history upon the testimony of living subjects can make the act of differentiating between the 'historical' and the 'contemporary' difficult. Popular Memory Group (1982, p. 219) view this distinction between the past and the present as an unhelpful but widely accepted part of the prevailing historical orthodoxy. Instead, they advocate a stance that stresses the importance of the role of memory in contributing to the 'contemporary consciousness'.

REFERENCES

Abbott, A. (1991). History and sociology: The lost synthesis. *Social Science History, 15*, 201–238.

Anderson, K., & Jack, D. (1991). Learning to listen: Interview techniques and analyses. In: S. B. Gluck & D. Patai (Eds), *Women's words: The feminist practice of oral history* (pp. 11–26). London: Routledge.

Beckford, J. (1975). *The trumpet of prophecy: A sociological study of Jehovah's witnesses.* Oxford: Basil Blackwell.

Bozzoli, B. (with Nkotsoe, M). (1991). *Women of Phokeng: Consciousness, life strategy and migrancy in South Africa:* 1900–1983. London: James Currey.

Brogden, M. (1982). *The police: Autonomy and consent.* London: Academic Press.

Brogden, M. (1991). *On the Mersey beat: An oral history of policing Liverpool between the wars.* Oxford: Oxford University Press.

Brown, A. (1995). *Organisational culture*. London: Pitman Publishing.

Chan, J. (1997). *Changing police culture: Policing in a multicultural society*. Cambridge: Cambridge University Press.

Emsley, C. (2005). Sergeant Goddard: The story of a rotten apple, or a diseased orchard? In: A. G. Srebnick & R. Lévy (Eds), *Crime and culture: An historical perspective* (pp. 86–104). Aldershot: Ashgate.

Ericson, R. V., Baranek, P. M., & Chan, J. B. L. (1987). *Visualizing deviance: A study of news organization*. Toronto: University of Toronto Press.

Fielding, N. (1997). Review of Chan, J. (1997). Changing police culture: Policing in a multicultural society. *Sociological Research Online 2*.

Foster, J. (2003). Police cultures. In: T. Newburn (Ed.), *Handbook of policing* (pp. 196–227). Cullompton: Willan.

Frisch, M. (1990). *A shared authority: Essays on the craft and meaning of oral and public history*. Albany, NY: State University of New York Press.

Gennete, G. (1980). *Narrative discourse*. Oxford: Basil Blackwell.

Goldstein, H. (1979). Improving policing: A problem-oriented approach. *Crime and Delinquency, 25*, 236–258.

Goodey, J. (2000). Biographical lessons for criminology. *Theoretical Criminology, 4*, 473–498.

Grele, R. J. (1996). Directions for oral history in the United States. In: D. K. Dunaway & W. K. Baum (Eds), *Oral history: An interdisciplinary anthology* (pp. 62–84). Walnut Creek: Altamira Press.

Grele, R. J. (1998). Movement without aim: Methodological and theoretical problems in oral history. In: R. Perks & A. Thomson (Eds), *The oral history reader* (pp. 38–52). London: Routledge.

Hackney WEA. (1975). *Volume 1: 1905–1945: A people's autobiography of Hackney*. Hackney: WEA.

Her Majesty's Inspectorate of Constabulary. (1999). *Winning the race- revisited: A follow up to the HMIC thematic inspection report on police community and race relations (1998/1999)*. London: HMSO.

Kennedy, E. L. (1998). Telling tales: Oral history and the construction of pre-Stonewall lesbian history. In: R. Perks & A. Thomson (Eds), *The oral history reader* (pp. 344–355). London: Routledge.

Library of Congress. (1971). *National union catalogue of manuscript collections: Information circular No. 7*. Washington, DC: Library of Congress, Descriptive Cataloging Division, Manuscript Section.

Loader, I., & Mulcahy, A. (2003). *Policing and the condition of England: Memory, politics and culture*. Oxford: Oxford University Press.

Lummis, T. (1983). Structure and validity in oral evidence. *International Journal of Oral History, 2*, 109–120.

Manning, P. K. (1978). Lying, secrecy and social control. In: P. Manning & J. Van Maanen (Eds), *Policing: A view from the street* (pp. 238–255). Santa Monica: Goodyear.

Manning, P. (1989). Occupational culture. In: W. G. Bailey (Ed.), *The encyclopedia of police science* (pp. 360–363). New York: Garland.

Newburn, T. (2003). The future of policing. In: T. Newburn (Ed.), *Handbook of policing* (pp. 707–721). Cullompton: Willan.

Passerini, L. (1979). Work ideology and consensus under Italian fascism. *History Workshop: A Journal of Socialist Historians, 8*, 82–108.

Perks, R., & Thomson, A. (1998). Introduction. In: R. Perks & A. Thomson (Eds), *The oral history reader* (pp. ix–xiii). London: Routledge.

Popular Memory Group. (1982). Popular memory: Theory, politics, method. In: R. Johnson, G. McLennan, B. Schwarz & D. Sutton (Eds), *Making histories: Studies in history-writing and politics* (pp. 205–252). London: Hutchinson.

Portelli, A. (1991). *The death of Luigi Trastulli and other stories: Form and meaning in oral history*. Albany, NY: State University of New York Press.

Punch, M. (1985). *Conduct unbecoming: The social construction of police deviance and control*. London: Tavistock.

Reiner, R. (1992). *The politics of the police* (2nd ed.). London: Harvester Wheatsheaf.

Reiner, R. (2000). *The politics of the police* (3rd ed.). Oxford: Oxford University Press.

Samuel, R. (1976). Local history and oral history. *History Workshop: A Journal of Socialist Historians, 1*, 191–208.

Samuel, R., & Thompson, P. (1990). Introduction. In: R. Samuel & P. Thompson (Eds), *The myths we live by* (pp. 1–22). London: Routledge.

Sangster, J. (1994). Telling our stories: Feminist debates and the uses of oral history. *Women's History Review, 3*, 5–28.

Selbourne, D. (1980). On the methods of history workshop. *History Workshop: A Journal of Socialist Historians, 9*, 150–161.

Seldon, A., & Pappworth, J. (1983). *By word of mouth: Elite oral history*. London: Methane.

Shearing, C. D., & Ericson, R. V. (1991). Culture as figurative action. *British Journal of Sociology, 42*, 481–506.

Skolnick, J. (1994). *Justice without trial: Law enforcement in democratic society* (3rd ed.). London: Wiley.

Slim, H., & Thompson, P. (1993). *Listening for a change: Oral history and development*. London: Panos.

Starr, L. (1977). Oral history. In: A. Kent, H. Lancour & J. E. Daily (Eds), *Encyclopedia of library and information science* (Vol. 20, p. 440). New York: Marcel Dekker.

Susman, W. I. (1964). History and the American intellectual: Uses of a usable past. *American Quarterly, 16*, 243–263.

Thomson, A. (1998). Anzac memories: Putting popular memory theory into practice in Australia. In: R. Perks & A. Thomson (Eds), *The oral history reader* (pp. 300–310). London: Routledge.

Vollmer, A. (1936). *The police and modern society*. Berkeley: University of California Press.

Waddington, P. A. J. (1999). Police (canteen) sub-culture: An appreciation. *British Journal of Criminology, 39*, 287–309.

Walmsley, J. (1995). Life history interviews with people with learning disabilities. *Oral History, 23*, 71–77.

Weinberger, B. (1995). *The best police in the world: An oral history of English policing*. Hampshire: Scolar.

Westley, W. A. (1970). *Violence and the police: A sociological study of law, custom and morality*. Cambridge, MA: MIT.

PART II:
POLICE REFORM, CULTURAL CHANGE AND CONTINUITY

CHAPTER 4

COPS WITH HONOURS: UNIVERSITY EDUCATION AND POLICE CULTURE

Maurice Punch

ABSTRACT

The British Police began in 1829 as an 'artisan' institution that would develop its own leaders and not recruit the 'educated'. By the 1960s, pressure for change led to support for university education for officers. The Essex Police sent officers to university and this paper draws on interviews with officers who studied in that period. It analyses their experiences as students, their return to policing and their reflections on having graduates within the service. This raises issues about policing, culture, education and leadership and how the police organisation has endeavoured to change to a 'professional' institution with well-educated leaders.

INTRODUCTION

The police have often been portrayed as a 'problem profession' afflicted by prejudice, violence and corruption (Manning, 1977; Westley, 1970; Skolnick, 1966; Sherman, 1964). Its culture was, apparently, one of racist,

Police Occupational Culture: New Debates and Directions
Sociology of Crime, Law and Deviance, Volume 8, 105–128
Copyright © 2007 by Elsevier Ltd.
All rights of reproduction in any form reserved
ISSN: 1521-6136/doi:10.1016/S1521-6136(07)08004-9

sexist, devious and blasphemous men (Manning & Van Maanen, 1978; Martin, 1980). This unwholesome image, particularly strong in American reports and media, contrasts with accounts in many of the early ethnographies of policing which conveyed empathetic portraits of bright-witted, street-smart maintainers of order (Bittner, 1967; Rubinstein, 1973). But there certainly was, and is, a large measure of ambivalence about policing, police officers and their abilities.

Turning, then, to the subject of officer abilities, historical material in Britain reveals that the vast majority of police officers were not 'well-educated'. In the model established by the Metropolitan Police of London, or 'Met', established in 1829 (Emsley, 1996), constables were typically 'respectable' upper working-class men with minimal educational qualifications. And, unlike Continental Europe, their senior officers came mostly from the same background, started as constables and had to work themselves up the hierarchy. Thus, among the competing images of the police in Britain, was one that cops were just not very 'bright'.

A lot depends, of course, on what one means by 'bright'. For, generally, they had a basic understanding of Law, a range of practical skills and social insights typical of front-line, emergency-oriented 'semi-professions', a capacity to judge evolving and unclear situations and a rich repertoire of formulations that could be employed to keep the peace and to render acceptable accounts for senior officers and/or the courts (Lipsky, 1980). In many research accounts, then, cops are portrayed as generally being smart and savvy in a peculiarly police way, which contrasts with the more prestigious professions drawing on academic knowledge (Muir, 1977).

In Britain, however, one recurring answer to rectifying this image, and to improving the quality of police performance, has been to enhance officers' educational qualifications. This is a debate that has taken place primarily in certain western democracies – particularly the USA, UK and Australia – whereas in many developing and transient societies, the level of education of police recruits is comparatively low and the emphasis is on improving basic police training, equipment and infrastructure. In continental European countries, the tendency is to provide high-quality education within the police service whereas in the 'Anglo-Saxon' countries, the accent is more on recruiting people with secondary school qualifications or a college education. In recent decades the focus has shifted towards tertiary education. Many problems would dissolve, proponents argue, if every constable had a degree.

But what if someone who was formally well educated had joined the police in Britain, say some thirty, forty or more years ago? What was the organisation like? And what sort of culture did it generate? In essence, the traditional structure and culture of that early post-war organisation generated a number of domain assumptions about work, operating style, values, expectations and interactions with colleagues, senior officers, outside agencies and civilians. One central assumption was that you did not need to be educated, as one officer with ten 'O' levels, conveyed about joining the police:[1]

> *So when you joined the police in 1975 how common was it at the time for officers to have a degree?* It didn't exist. God, my first posting as a probationary PC [police constable] was to Harlow; and the first ever words of my first ever sergeant on meeting me – and I've often quoted that nice, welcoming, warm face–were 'bloody hell, so you're the clever bastard with the ten 'O' levels; we'll soon knock that out of you'. Funny, isn't it, by today's standards. (Respondent 6)

THE RESEARCH

In this paper, I explore the impact that sending police officers to university, and recruiting graduates, has had on the police organisation and its culture. I contend that this has had a substantial and positive influence: but this is only one factor among many other interlocking elements contributing to the process of change. Some of those positive features may even have been contradicted by other factors in recent reform.

Nevertheless, I suspect that most commentators would agree that the general culture of policing has altered; that the police institution is less conservative and defensive and more professional and transparent than three decades ago. But there are many 'cultures' within policing and police 'culture' is not monolithic: it is more of a complex, matrix than an easily defined, one-dimensional concept. Police culture is, for instance, often used to refer to the culture of the lower ranks (Chan, 2003). Its focus is on the practical skills of street work, solidarity and impression management towards supervisors and managers. Some of the standard tenets and practices of the culture can be viewed as norms of mutual problem-solving and survival, drawing on many years of practical experience and occupational folk-lore (Schein, 1996). If these are embedded in the nature of the work, then you will not be able to change the culture unless you alter the nature of the work itself or its meaning for practitioners (Chan, 1997).

But if there is a strong, traditional culture that is held to resist change and that also supports rule bending, then this stands in clear opposition to the

contemporary 'professional' culture espoused at the top of the service. This
focuses on governance, managerial competence, performance standards,
external accountability and transparency. It could even be argued that the
dichotomy sketched by the Iannis (Reuss-Ianni & Ianni, 1983) between
'management cops' and 'street cops', based on research in New York in the
late 1970s, is not only acutely present today but in danger of amplification.
For it is possible to develop an expansion of the Iannis' dichotomy to a
fourfold typology of *street cops, management cops* (middle-ranking supervisors concerned with targets), *strategic cops* (concerned with planning and
external stakeholders) and *'frequent flyer cops'* who are into national and
international assignments. If this is accurate, then there exists greater social
distance between higher and lower ranks than before in terms of language,
conceptual lenses for viewing policing, qualifications, work experience and
orientation to outside stakeholders. This enhances the danger of alienation
and lack of communication.

Here, I wish to examine the process of police attending university through
interviews with police officers who studied full-time as serving officers. No
effort was made to seek a random sample and a convenience sample drew on
seven senior male officers from Essex (three of whom had retired), the
former chief constable (Sir John Nightingale), and two officers from other
forces who had joined as graduate entrants. At Essex one had reached the
rank of deputy chief constable, one of assistant chief constable and the
others had become either superintendents or at least chief inspectors. It is
impossible to say if this group is in anyway representative. It is conceivable
that they are particularly positive about their experiences as several can be
seen as pioneers who both broke new ground and who benefited
considerably from the scheme. All we can say is that, these interviews
provide us with insights into the experiences of a small number of officers
from the Essex Police who were selected to study at university – and who
remained in the police organisation afterwards. There is a biographical
dimension here as I met some of these officers in the late 1960s and early
1970s when I was teaching at Essex University and it was through these
contacts that I became interested in researching the police.

But to illustrate how the police organisation has changed, I wish to return
to the occupational environment that a young constable was likely to
encounter when joining the police in the post-war period to the 1960s. The
organisational style was rigidly conservative and locked into routine
responses to situations: these practices were virtually unassailable. Working
behaviour was posited on practical knowledge learned from a highly limited
training (with marching, sport and learning laws by heart), quick immersion

into standard ways of doing things and from imbibing the inviolable tenets of the occupational culture passed on by older men, many with military experience. The 'cop code' was posited mainly on staying out of trouble, covering up for others and regulating the work load (Reuss-Ianni & Ianni, 1983; Muir, 1977). Inside accounts often relate how considerable energy was spent in *avoiding work* and in the delights of 'mumping', 'sciving' and 'easy numbers'.[2] Working knowledge was practical, communal, 'common-sense' knowledge and academic learning was perceived as largely irrelevant, if not dysfunctional.

There was an elaborate hierarchy of formal ranks and informal status with considerable social distance and rigid rules of engagement. Until quite recently in Essex, for instance, someone from the Traffic Department would not dare enter the detectives' lair for fear of his life. There was, then, a sort of shifting, shadowy, 'matrix' institution of considerable complexity, containing dangerous sections to be avoided, which was tacked onto the formal structure and both had to be negotiated by newcomers. Even now most constables remain in that lowly rank throughout their service; a few reach sergeant but most never make it beyond that (and see Bayley, 1994). And in Continental European and 'colonial-style' forces, there was a clear distinction between officers and lower ranks and almost no-one moved into the officer caste (Bowling, 2005). But in this period movement up the hierarchy was painfully slow anyway: the image looking up must have been not of a pyramid but rather of the Eiffel Tower, with its pinnacle shrouded in mist. Promotion was based largely on performing well practically; and also, importantly, on not 'peeing beside the pot' (to use a Dutch expression).

Indeed, the Dutch system until fairly recently was based on advancement through strict seniority: when someone moved on, was promoted or died, then everyone automatically moved up a slot. Providing, that is, that they had cautiously and accurately aimed within the pot: because it was important not to make mistakes. This system created its own pathology of ritualism, sloth, indifference and lack of initiative: to display undue initiative was to be deviant (like the 'rate-busters' in the Hawthorne Studies: Roethlisberger & Dickson, 1939). The newcomer was also caught between the autocratic, rule-bound, punishment-centred bureaucracy and the rule-bending of the informal culture (Punch, 1985). Negotiating this friction enhanced solidarity and secrecy and encouraged uncritical conformity to the group.

Given the vulnerable nature of policing there was, and still is, an emphasis on fitting into the group, covering up for colleagues, fabricating convincing statements, manipulating supervisors and rule-bending (Crank, 1998). A senior officer recalled how as a young recruit the desk-sergeant told him that he needed 'court practice' and pointed to a 'prisoner'. This sort of predicament forms an instantaneous initiation into the informal culture, for the constable knew that it meant falsifying a statement and lying in court. He did not protest, set aside the legal requirements just learned in the training school, and acquiesced. There were, too, aggressive and humiliating initiation rituals that were 'pass–fail' tests conveying that acceptance into the informal culture was dependent on solidarity and secrecy (Scraton, 1999, p. 15).

Much of this analysis is familiar from descriptions of the occupational cultures and organisational distortions in the military, industrial plants, corporations and bureaucracies. Fitting in, conformity to the group, never letting colleagues down in a critical incident, never betraying a mate and not exceeding informal 'production' norms are often paramount (Goode, 1967). Some of these agencies were, and are, typically macho, male preserves with powerful informal cultures, strong prejudices, an antipathy to senior officers (and females) and outsiders and especially to 'theoretical knowledge'. To be educated was to be deviant: as in the quote above it was an occupational handicap to be swiftly erased.

This raises the key issue: to what extent has that traditional reflection of institutional practice and police culture been altered by the increasing number of officers who have attended university in the last three decades? And how did they fare in this rigid, traditional world of practical knowledge and antipathy to academic learning? In brief, my argument on this will be threefold.

Firstly, policing itself has changed considerably in recent years and the assumption is that the resilient cop culture is also inevitably changing (Foster, 2003). In Britain, people refer disparagingly to the supposedly plebeian and raucous 'canteen culture' (Waddington, 1999b). But, as one senior officer told me, in his canteen there were fervent chess players; Rose (1996) saw constables reading the progressive newspaper, the *Guardian*, in London canteens; and a leading researcher, Robert Reiner, spoke of visiting a station and being besieged by several officers wishing to pick his brains for their degree studies and research projects.

Secondly, educating officers at university has undoubtedly made a major difference, as we shall demonstrate in the material below.

But, thirdly, that has only been one of the interlocking strands among the many that have profoundly changed policing in the last two decades (Reiner, 2000; Newburn, 2003, 2005).

NO GENTLEMEN, PLEASE, WE'RE BRITISH

I shall summarise the material in this section by emphasising five points.

1. For several reasons the founding father of the Metropolitan Police, Robert Peel, 'was stubborn to the point of obsession that his "New Police" should be seen to be free of all taint of militarism and indeed he made it a cardinal principle that, as the force grew, it should be "*filled up from below*"' (Ascoli, 1979, p. 89, emphasis added). This created an institution that was not for the well-educated while Peel proved particularly averse to recruiting 'gentlemen'.

2. In essence, that traditional model remained largely intact until the 1960s. The rapid if not turbulent societal changes of the period stimulated efforts to improve the quality of training as well as providing opportunities for serving officers to attend university, to recruit more university graduates and to offer them the possibility of rapid promotion. A number of national initiatives were undertaken including 'Bramshill Scholarships',[3] introduced in 1966 to enable serving police officers with intellectual capabilities to go to university full-time. These initiatives were seen as particularly crucial in ensuring a steady supply of officers of the right calibre for future promotion to the higher ranks (cf. Royal Commission on the Police, 1962). They represented one of the most significant changes to the Peelite paradigm of policing in 130 years.

3. The recruitment of graduates has significantly altered the profile of senior officers. Reiner's (1991, pp. 59–60) study of chief constables holding office in the late 1980s suggests that nearly 70% of them came from manual working-class origins: one in four of the chief constables in the study obtained a university degree while in the service. Wall (1998) found that a similar proportion of roughly a quarter of chief constables held degrees while in office in the late 1970s and 1980s, respectively. But by 1996, the overall percentage with degrees had trebled to over two-thirds (Wall, 1998, p. 286). A survey in 200 of the 43 serving chief constables in England and Wales found that all but seven had degrees, five had a masters degree and another four had a PhD (*Daily Telegraph,* 17 May, 2000). In effect, *it has become a requirement for senior officers to have one, if not two, degrees.*

4. This interaction between the police service and university education fosters a range of intriguing issues. Bradley, Nixon, and Marks (2006, p. 3) remark that 'from the inception of the new police, the worlds of the public police and the public university, have been very separate, with

little if any formal interchange'. Furthermore, many commentators have identified an 'inherent anti-intellectualism' that permeates police thinking (Brewer, 1991), a history of police hostility to 'outsiders' (Punch, 1979) and a rejection of social research as 'clap trap' (Young, 1991, p. 20). Such an antipathy reflects a fundamental police worldview based on 'police common sense' (Holdaway, 1983, p. 65): and linked to this is the perception of the police officer as a 'craftsman' (Skolnick, 1966), with skills learned through practice at the 'sharp-end'. This enables one to become a 'good practical copper' (Manning, 1979, p. 49) and formal education is largely irrelevant.

In relation to the tension between these two contrasting worlds, Reiner (1994) has written of a 'war between the police and academe'. As Young (1991, pp. 37–38) has argued, the result was a paradox that the police service was still living out at the time he wrote: 'Even at the same time as it publicly commends higher education, seeking out the graduate entrant, spending large sums on publicity to this end, and funding access to degree courses on scholarships, it also holds to a central ethic of distrust of the academic'.

5. This conflictual picture has become less acute in that a closer relationship between the police and academic world has emerged. There is the proliferation of police research, with forces sponsoring university research and sharing in the research process: and there has been a substantial expansion of police studies courses, with many police officers taking part-time degrees. Some universities focus strongly on law enforcement and even receive a franchise to conduct segments of standard police education (e.g. the former Scarman Centre at Leicester University – now the Department of Criminology, Portsmouth University and Cambridge University).

Two main features are relevant here for placing this material in a contemporary perspective. Firstly, the occupational and technical 'professionalism' of policing (in terms of setting standards of performance and levels of expertise) has increased dramatically. In response to rising crime, terrorist threats, cross-border policing, technological advances and media exposure, the police service has become in many respects a well-resourced, well-equipped, well-trained, well-paid and sophisticated 'semi-profession' (Etzioni, 1969). Secondly, 'new public management', or NPM, has had a substantial impact on public services, including the police (Leishman, Savage, & Loveday, 1996). This brought in management speak, an obsession with targets and budgets, demands for improved service delivery and also a wave of organisational reform and new training for new skills. And, furthermore, what might be called growing 'secularisation' of the police world. Beforehand policing was normally a highly self-contained institution with a near monopoly on training and services with a highly insular culture. Now, under the influence of efficiency and budget discipline, there has come civilianisation, diversity, inter-agency cooperation and a breakdown in barriers with other agencies, links with the private sector and the outsourcing of some services. The impact of all this on police culture has been subject to much debate (Smith & Gray, 1985, p. 517; McLaughlin & Murji, 1997; Ericson & Haggerty, 1997).

THE ESSEX 'GUINEA PIGS'

In turning to the officers who went as 'guinea pigs' to the University of Essex, I can only present a fraction of the extensive 'oral history' material (Lee & Punch, 2006) and shall restrict my focus largely to the impact these graduates had on return to their force. The officers were mostly inspectors or were promoted to inspector on going to university, had around ten to twelve-years service, studied full-time for three years, took a degree in the School of Social Sciences (then Sociology, Law, Government or a combined degree), and usually received promotion fairly soon after returning. Invariably, they came from backgrounds where a university education had not been seriously considered: several had not performed well at school: but now they had been selected to attend university with the implication that it might be a stepping-stone to higher rank.

But to begin I wish to touch briefly on two features of the material: what was the motivation behind the Essex Scheme and how did these early cohorts experience university?

Firstly, we have seen that British policing was typically an 'artisan' institution that rarely attracted people with a university education. Indeed, in the 1960s the police service did not think that it could recruit many graduates directly and, therefore, turned to the policy of educating serving officers. There were national initiatives but also one particular local scheme within the Essex Police.

The then Chief Constable, John Nightingale,[4] decided in the late 1960s to send two officers a year to university to study full-time for three years, to allow them a free choice of subject within the Social Sciences; and *not* to tie them to a period of service after return.[5] This formed a substantial investment of resources. It appears that the chief constable felt that it was the *experience* of university, mixing with people from different backgrounds taking a wide range of subjects, that formed the valuable learning experience for his officers rather than gaining specific, occupationally focused knowledge. But Nightingale was also quiet clear that senior officers should *learn about society* and the officers should study one of the Social Sciences. According to one respondent, his main aim was to prevent the imposition of leaders on the force from outside

> Nightingale's view, when you get right down to it, was if we didn't provide our leaders then they would be provided from without ... . This was a pre-emptive strike against the possibility of lateral entry on the basis that the organisation's soul would be contaminated by something like that. It was as dramatic as that really. (Respondent 1)

He was selecting officers to lead the force in the future, providing them with full-time university education and, by so doing, adapting the institution to societal change while keeping lateral entry firmly at bay.

In a sense he was an enlightened conservative, preserving certain core values while bending to the wind of change. He was himself one of the rare graduate entrants to the police. In the 1930s, Lord Trenchard, a key figure in building the Royal Air Force, became Commissioner of the Met and founded the Police College at Hendon to give young talent the chance of swift promotion, including some outside the service. The emphasis, as in military training was on 'character building', and Nightingale was selected to attend. Hendon elicited sustained opposition from certain politicians and 'implacable hostility' from the new Police Federation for its elitism and lateral entry (Critchley, 1978, p. 204). This innovative institution was, then, conveniently shoved aside after only five years with war looming (Ascoli, 1979, p. 233). Nightingale was reviving Trenchard's idea of favouring those with 'character', while adding an emphasis on learning.

And, secondly, sending serving officers to university was not unproblematic in relation to their adjustment to full time studying and to their subsequent re-entry into operational policing. This unease is reflected in several police officers' accounts of their experiences of the academic world and their return to policing (indeed, several subsequently became academics, e.g. Waddington, Holdaway and Young). Young (1991) and Smith (1978) wrote of the 'feeling of potentiality' stimulated by the exposure to university life but convey as well the sense of frustration and of being 'cut off' that university-educated officers can experience on their return to service. Young's experience of reincorporation into the 'real world' of 'basic coppering' after a period of 'academic high flying' is echoed by our respondents (below). The 'real polises', according to Young (1991, p. 118), were invariably seen as possessing 'special knowledge', enabling them to master the art of 'doing the business on the job'. The receiving police organisations did not always see the practical relevance of university education, nor how to exploit the benefits gained by the individual officer (Smith, 1978, p. 154).

The research cohort attended Essex University, one of the new universities established in the early 1960s, with the first students from the Essex Police commencing in 1967. Several early student cops did particularly well, reaching high rank in Essex or elsewhere (the first two later became chief constable and deputy chief, respectively, in other forces). Several factors were apparent in their adjustment to moving from the policing to the university world. They tended to be highly motivated, conscientious and organised in their style of studying and, after an initially uneasy period of adjustment to the academic environment, they began to relish the intellectual challenge while most obtained good degrees. But most found the sudden shift from policing to studying tough and demanding.

> *What was it like at first?* Dreadful! The first term I thought I was going to pack it all in, thinking 'what am I doing here?' But after the first term I just thoroughly enjoyed it. It brought me up sharp, to a rigour that I hitherto had never ever been close to, in terms of my thinking or my ability to identify issues. It was a massive change of culture; and to be completely on my own, exposed in a sense, because this was all about me: it was sort of 'deliver', and thinking, 'God, this is really difficult: I'm not going to be able to cope with this'! So in the first term I felt out of my depth.
>
> *Did you start to enjoy it?* It was just a completely different environment; it was a challenge and I found I started to enjoy the richness of the work we were doing. (Respondent 2)

The 'dear, old police culture', as a respondent called it, in which they grew up and were returning to, was one where the 'educated' stood out and where operational ability was paramount. But that was about to change as our graduates filtered back, moved up the hierarchy and started to make their mark.

RE-ENTRY AND SUBSEQUENT CAREER

Re-entry

After three years of personal and academic freedom – exploring ideas purely for the sake of it and in some cases exulting in the pleasures of learning, and with no shift-work, no uniform and no superiors – our guinea pigs had to return to service. How did they fare in the process of re-entry and how did the organisation employ their new-found talents?

The policy was to put people into uniformed duty as re-immersion into the routines of policing and to catch up with the legal and operational changes of the intervening period. This meant operational shift work 'on division' at the rank of inspector, which was a new function for most of them. They encountered some ribbing and prejudice, the need to establish credibility, the demands of adjusting to new legislation and working practices, and somehow the need to take a stance with regard to the knowledge and insights gleaned and its relation to the realities of policing.

Did you find it difficult going back to Basildon as an Inspector? How were you received? No, I don't think it was problematic. Most people were able to put it to one side, you know, 'I'm not interested in what you did in the last three years; I'm interested in what sort of a shift inspector he is, whether or not he can stand up for the shift'. So to an extent it was there as a possible issue, but only as a factor in me establishing credibility early on, that I was running the shift. (Respondent 9)

They had to establish themselves without operational experience in that rank and having been to university was just one factor in that process.

Were there remarks made about being away for three years? I had one or two problems with one or two of my peers because you had just come out of university and because degrees were quite unusual. There was a stereotypical image of what you were like or what you would be like – 'oh, here they come out of the dream factory; here for a couple of years, then they will bugger off to Headquarters for greater and better things leaving us in the mud bath'. So there was a bit of resentment. (Respondent 6)

The impression conveyed by the interviews was that there were no great 're-entry' problems. There were some predictable prejudices from a few die-hards but to a large extent they fitted back, and were accepted back into, police culture. The 'troops' were mostly more concerned about the returned graduate's performance as the new boss than about his or her university background.

How were you received when you went back? Well, different reactions. My two immediate superiors at the training school felt threatened because of some of the things they used to say to me and clearly there was some distaste on their part. I found they were being a bit defensive. The CID didn't like graduates so that part of the hierarchy was antagonistic and there was definitely an element of hostility. (Respondent 4)

To a large extent the social and institutional problems on re-entry were more with the upper hierarchy and their unreflective, stereotyped and limited manner of thinking and operating. For these graduates had gained a measure of personal and intellectual self-confidence: this aided them professionally, both within the service and externally in their dealings with diverse stakeholders. In the following section we can see that the graduates challenged their superiors, did not automatically accept policies and were able to bring a new management approach and operational style to the functions they were given.

Subsequent Career

As noted, this early group all did reasonably well, either in Essex or elsewhere, while of the interviewees two became chief officers within Essex and the rest reached senior rank (superintendent level or at least chief inspector). No one ever hinted that there were any detrimental aspects to attending university and generally people were highly positive about its influence on their career. This respondent made rapid promotion after that initial re-immersion.

Do you feel it enhanced your career? All of a sudden, I didn't even seek promotion, it was just happening to me. Within two years I was chief inspector and within two years after that I was superintendent. I think you were used by the organisation, they wanted to make the best use of their graduates, so I'd be invited onto projects, even advising the divisional command team on certain aspects, in a sense unheard of before, but now I was seen as someone with a future.

What did you see as the benefits? You became comfortable with research and with quantification because it had just been very much a part of what you had been doing while getting your degree. You could be equal in debate with almost anybody, because you constructed your debates around evidence and substance. It gave you a much deeper confidence in any audience. Now you are sitting down with the Home Secretary, and senior Home Office officials, I work with them a lot on youth issues nationally, and after all that I think, 'thank God I got that degree'. It also helped with balanced decision making, because you don't just see an issue as it might appear first off, you want to know 'where is the evidence coming from?', before you're prepared to commit resources or commit yourself publicly to certain things. (Respondent 2)

In brief, although there was a 'back-to-reality' phase on re-entry, the organisation clearly perceived the graduates as a cadre of potential leaders and as spokespersons to represent the service externally. The benefits of a university education for serving officers can be seen in terms of social capital (self-confidence and status) and generic skills (ability to analyse material, ease of communication, report writing) while some respondents saw more specific institutional benefits in bringing reflection to an action-oriented institution or to questioning quite critically the underlying assumptions of policy.

I believe Essex Police has used you in the more strategic and planning roles. What has university education given you that aided you in those roles? It just made me a bit more insightful and self-reflexive, and less likely to accept an argument, however initially persuasive it might seem, without putting it under a magnifying glass just to see exactly what the strength of its appeal was. There is this expectation that policing is all about getting things done, being decisive, being busy, because people think 'ah, that's good, that's getting things sorted'. There are limitations and disadvantages with that but if I'd say 'I don't care how urgent the situation is, I need to spend as much time as I feel I need to have to exhaustively explore all my options', well you often can't really do that in reality. So it's a question of striking a balance that meets the urgency of the situation. But it's important to make the right decision, so it's just taking a second to step back before we commit ourselves. And there is a fair bit of tension around just where that right balance is. (Respondent 9)

The respondents maintained that it gave them benefits in decision-making but that often this conflicted with the operational style of the leadership: in the ensuing friction, it was the graduates who supported new approaches while other colleagues tended to go with the institutional flow.

What we found was that with the other graduates you could talk in ways you couldn't talk with your other colleagues; and this isn't elitist, this is just you had a shared language, a shared way of seeing things and you could talk about things in different ways. And also it affected what you did. There were one or two things that I did which I thought were quite important where you knew that the other graduates would understand what your concerns were and would back you, whereas other just didn't. (Respondent 4)

This respondent gives an example of the Coal Strike in the 1980s when picketing miners threatened to block imports of coal into two ports on his 'patch'. Elsewhere during the strike the controversial tactic was employed of a protective ring of officers that allowed working miners access to mines while preventing striking miners from entering that area.

We used to have policy meetings once or twice a week at Headquarters; and on one of those a decision was taken we would do the same here [as with the protective ring elsewhere]. We had had some violence at Wivenhoe and so we wouldn't let any striking miners down to Wivenhoe to protest on the grounds that we feared a breach of the peace.

Well I simply didn't fear a breach of the peace as I'd got so many police officers there. Twelve miners came up in a coach and what I said to them was 'look, a policy decision was taken yesterday at Headquarters not to allow you to go down to the port' and they accepted it so I didn't have a confrontation there. Well I wasn't happy with it so I conveyed it back and at the next policy meeting it was changed, but there was a lot of argument about that and the only other people who supported my argument were two other graduates. And we altered the policy so that the man on the ground would make a decision based upon how he felt. So that was the sort of thing that was happening but at first the other police officers didn't question it at all. (Respondent 4)

This respondent is referring to challenging policy decisions in relation to gaining more operational autonomy for officers on the ground. But he also speaks elsewhere of moral obligations, which he felt were being dismissed out of hand, and refers to the fact that the graduates brought not only a new vocabulary but also a deeper analysis of policy-making. With regard to the latter, he refers to setting up a new department with a fellow graduate

When did you start feeling that you could use some of these ideas from the university? Oh, all the time. You thought differently, say in doing a report or an inquiry then it would have been much better than it would have been before because I had a method. And I got used to handling large amounts of information and putting it on paper. And I remember writing some reports and they were challenged by some people. I remember using the words 'implicit' and 'explicit' and this caused a problem for someone above me: he didn't really know what they meant and I got severely criticised for using these words and he said to me 'I don't know why you read all those books. I only read books by retired policemen and that's good enough for me'. And that was an example of the sort of thing that you would get all the time.

How much of that is to do with your three years at University? I've always liked ideas, always been fascinated by ideas. But the process of joining the police, of conforming, is very, very powerful, certainly as a young man as I was at nineteen. So a lot of it gets knocked out of shape by this requirement to conform and your desire to conform; because you want to be part of it. But then the fact of coming from the university gave it a boost and enabled you to do things better; so that what you wanted to do before you could now actually do: it empowered you really.

He then gave an example of setting up a new department from scratch.

Was it always possible for you to translate these new ideas into practices and policies once you came back to HQ? It was possible to influence things. I remember doing something with Geoff Markham; it was about '79 and we were appointed to create a new unit, called the 'Community Services Branch' [concerned with juvenile liaison and polices for when, and when not, to prosecute juveniles]. And at that stage the received wisdom was that the police liaised with hospitals, schools, the social services, the probation services, and made a decision on whether to prosecute and proceeded from there. So we sat around saying to ourselves 'we've got to establish a system which brings the decision making process central; then you get equality decision-making for the force – and we've got to liaise on this with all these people'.

Now immediately when we said that I was thinking about the state; and I was thinking of all these other state agencies and we have to go to the school and tell the school, the social service and the probation service. And I said 'what are we talking about? What is all this for?' And with a first time offender you caution them anyway, so why do you go round telling all these people? So we set that up as the philosophy of the system that certainly the first offence was to be just between the police and the parents.

Now I was looking at it in political terms, the state agency, this 'phalanx' of agencies facing this child who'd perhaps only stolen an eye shadow, which is what they'd tend to do before. And we actually did a joint paper, which they wouldn't let us publish. We called it 'The Alternative View' because it went against the perceived wisdom which was then seen as liberal – the *police* talking to social workers, school teachers and probation officers – this is great, these wonderful, liberal policemen. But we said 'this isn't liberal at all, it's fascist'! You're creating this wonderful state alliance thing against these poor kids'. But it was completely against the prevailing theme and our system in Essex protected children in that first phase against the state thing. (Respondent 9)

Some respondents emphasised the more generic aspects of their university education, which played a positive but fairly diffuse role in their further career, whereas several perceived the intellectual capital as being of almost daily significance because it enabled them to challenge conventional ways of thinking and acting. This applied particularly to the two officers who had worked closely together in setting up a new Community Services Branch. They, with others, kept demanding from the leadership that they explain the philosophy behind their policies, were prepared to use a new conceptual vocabulary and were not afraid to bring the state, and abuse of state power (even with references to fascism), into discussions. And, as one recalled, when they asked senior officers to articulate their philosophy behind a decision, one chief officer replied 'how do you spell that? Is it with an "f"?' The graduates were far more likely to think in terms of a philosophy first, then policy and only after that practice and they claimed that superiors tended to work on the reverse principle – practice first and then a 'philosophy will evolve' (as one chief officer put it).

In short, the material of the interviews conveys images of officers who felt strongly that they were advantaged in their further careers by their university background and who could identify attitudes and skills that assisted them. We are dealing with some successful, self-confident people here, and there may well be an element of retrospective rationalisation about the perceived benefits of university. What they do believe, however, is that it brought them social 'capital', a set of skills (verbal, analytical, in writing, etc.) and, above all, a sort of critical, questioning style to problem-solving and decision-making. This enabled some of them to be used in setting up new and innovative departments, to pose fresh and critical questions about the 'philosophy' underpinning these and to be given challenging roles in strategy formation. Sometimes this enhanced standard practice but at other times it posed fairly fundamental issues about institutional ideology and practice. Perhaps as ambitious young 'movers and shakers' they would, in some cases, have challenged the status quo anyway; but they claim that the graduates did view the world differently, did share common assumptions and were able to take critical stances because of their social and educational 'capital'. Of crucial significance, according to one respondent, was that the Essex Police at that time, with Nightingale guiding the process, used its graduates positively and also encouraged them to engage in critical debate.

DISCUSSION

This modest vignette of a handful of police officers going to university some thirty odd years ago is employed here to illuminate one of the sea changes in British policing. This was the decision in the 1960s to send officers to university and to start recruiting graduates into the service with the prospect of rapid promotion. After 130 years, senior officers and policy makers were abandoning the Peelite paradigm of an artisan institution which did not attract the educated, was based on leaders starting at the bottom and exhibited an aversion to lateral entry.

And again, at this moment, British policing is facing monumental change which is fundamentally altering the very architecture of policing (O'Connor, 2005). In recent years, policing in most western societies has been subject to multiple pressures including the effects of globalisation, demographic and population shifts, radical Muslim terrorism, trans-national crime, cross-border policing, militarisation, racial and ethnic diversity in recruitment, a revolution in the use of information, technology and forensic techniques, the impact of NPM and, in Britain, a sustained assault from successive governments who are determined to reform policing.

My personal impression of the contemporary police organisation – going on a range of contacts with senior officers and a number of forces in Britain (and elsewhere), the opinions of colleagues and published material – is that it has become more professional, better resourced, more transparent, more of a learning organisation willing to admit mistakes, more willing to accept dissent and to tolerate diversity of opinion. One significant factor in that shift, I would argue, has been the recruitment of university graduates with some forces now having between 25 and 30% graduates. The economic downturn in the 1980s, allied to substantial increases in police salaries, helped to attract graduates in significant numbers for the first time. This, with increasing research on the police, and for the police, and with an expanding number of specialised programmes at universities, has done a great deal to alter the profile of policing and to break down its institutional isolation (Newburn, 2003). This was illustrated by an interview with a graduate entrant from another force than Essex who joined the police in 1982, took a second degree part-time during his service, and said '*now I have seen the writing on the wall* and am doing a third degree'. In his force about 25% of recruits have a degree on entry and, he claimed, 'we have become more attractive to graduates as policing has become centre stage and is seen as a legitimate profession. In the service, we need conceptual leaps and need to encourage vigorous debate because these are exciting times'. (Respondent 8: my emphasis)

This would appear to represent a changing organisational identity in that the organisation not only actively recruits graduates but has also become attractive to graduates: in Chan's terms (1999), this forms a shift in the 'axiomatic' knowledge of the police. Indeed, Bradley et al. (2006) speak of strategic educational partnerships between the police and universities in some states in Australia both for degree programmes oriented to officers and for partnerships in research projects.

But policing is complex, has many functions and can shift style over time or opportunistically (Bayley & Shearing, 2001; Marks, 2007). Organisational life in general and policing in particular are not always a world of genteel reflection, critical questioning of the leadership, respect for the outspoken, double-loop learning and warm comradeship. Furthermore, organisations are arenas for egos and group dynamics that can be distorting, repressive and even pathological (Punch, 1996). Indeed, one can discern two tendencies that can be viewed as having a narrowing if not retrograde influence on the intellectual emancipation in policing of recent decades.

On the one hand, the overemphasis on 'management' fostered by the governmental push to impose NPM on services has led to restrictive demands to reach quantitative targets (basically old-fashioned 'Management by Objectives' reminiscent of Scientific Management). And it has led also to budget discipline with 'value for money' regimes, whereby forces cut back on many attractive areas of the police occupational community, such as sport and bands, and even say they can no longer justify the expense of sending serving officers to university. This contrasts with the military, which has always had a policy of providing financial support for prospective officers to attend university.

And, on the other hand, the move to 'professionalise' in its restricted sense of certification of standards through gaining qualifications, has led to a highly instrumental emphasis on degree and other courses which are tailor-made for police officers. But this is almost a return to narrow, internally focused vocational education among fellow cops even if it is ostensibly externally taught and validated (Bradley et al., 2006).

What is completely missing currently is the philosophy, backed with resources, of sending serving officers to study non-vocational degrees full-time. The added value was that officers could step outside the police world, could mix with a highly diverse student population and could freely pursue education for its own sake (comparable to the 'liberal arts' concept in the USA: Useem, 1989). Our small sample fervently maintains that this academic experience, rather than the specific knowledge, proved extremely 'practical' in many respects. Interestingly, senior officers on the Strategic Command Course[6] who went on to study at Cambridge, told me that the faculty was leaning over backwards to make things practical when they were more interested in theory. An officer on that course also espoused a liberal arts approach

> I'm still a believer in a liberal-arts approach, it's not fashionable, but it's a good starter as a preparation for life, as opposed to the functional/vocational degree; you're getting an overview of the world and it's encouraging you to think. But everyone should be involved in education in some way; as a learning organization we should have a constant desire to move forward, we need good quality people, with emotional intelligence. I'm for a fairly broad church, it's not what you learn on a course but what you can apply when you get back – in terms of motivation, different ways of looking at the world, being reflective. There should be an underpinning philosophy, aimed at attracting and retaining good people with intellectual horsepower and emotional intelligence because we value learning, we want to improve our performance, and we want learning to be organizationally focused. Everyone here at ACPO level is a graduate and three have masters degrees; *in the pecking order you even ask yourself 'where do we go from here?'* Some people have argued for a totally graduate entry or that all inspectors should be graduates. (Respondent 7: emphasis added)

In essence, our small sample is saying not only that there is no dichotomy between 'theoretical' academic knowledge and practical policing but also that there can be a surprising and valuable synergy. Several of them exemplified this by becoming model 'reflective practitioners' (Schön, 1983).

I would argue, then, that one policy implication is that every police officer should have the right to a one-year paid sabbatical during his or her career. A major orientation should be to providing full-time study at a university in a non-vocational programme. But as one size does not fit all, there should be space for negotiation on other ways of gaining valuable experience such as working in another service industry, NGO or corporation, a period working abroad in a developing country, or a tailor-made course of guided self-study. The key is to be given the opportunity to step out of the police culture, to rub shoulders with a wide range of people and to be given the chance to experience higher education and gain a qualification, or some other valuable experience. Generally, mature students are highly motivated and perform

well, often irrespective of their previous educational background; certainly
our Essex officers, who had never contemplated a university education,
earned good degrees, thoroughly enjoyed the intellectual challenge and
made a valuable contribution to their force. It proved a sound investment

> I think we can look upon ourselves at Essex as a fairly progressive police force. I just
> think we have shown we have been able to adapt and move with change. For me the
> secondment to university came at ideally the right time. If I had come in as a degree
> entrant as PC then the organization at that time would have affected me much more than
> later getting my degree as inspector. I feel I was able to do much more with it than if I
> was a graduate on entry. It continues to give me the confidence to go against the crowd if
> you like, to challenge things. And we need that kind of thinking within the service.
> Certainly I thought prior to university 'well, what's a degree, how does that make you a
> better police officer?' Having been through the system I am now very much aware how
> beneficial the educational process is. That's why I think you don't necessarily need to
> have a vocational degree; it's not the subject matter, it's the process you go through as
> far as I am concerned. (Respondent 3)

One significant benefit could be to break down the social distinction
between top cops and street cops, and certainly between graduates and non-
graduates, within the service.

CONCLUSION

However, we clearly cannot be naïve. Change is never linear and progressive
in organisations but is subject to shifts, reversals, failures and unanticipated
consequences. While progress has been booked in some areas, with
increasing attention paid to ethnic and gender 'diversity', there are persistent
voices maintaining that British police culture and the police institution are
still in some ways racist, homophobic and prejudiced against women (and
currently anti-Muslim).[7] And yet, there has undoubtedly been substantial
structural change in policing and far-reaching proposals for further change.
For example, in the Richard Dimbelby Lecture for the BBC the
Commissioner of the Met (Sir Ian Blair) sketched an organisation that
needed a wide range of expertise at different levels and at different entry
points (Blair, 2005). Effectively, he was saying everyone who is useful is
welcome: and starting at the bottom, working your way up and needing
operational experience for senior positions would no longer be a
requirement but expertise and qualifications would be essential. His
proposals would make lateral entry a fact.

One can only surmise how the police 'serial' in the back of a Transit, waiting to go into action, conducts a discourse on this. Perhaps from their worms-eye view, the nature of the work and their perceptions of that work have altered remarkably little in the last few decades. And a salutary warning comes from the work of Marks (2005). In her study of change in the South African Police Service, she reflects on the fact that substantial socio-political and institutional change, in the massive move from the apartheid regime to a democratic, multi-racial society with positive discrimination policies for government agencies including the police, had not greatly altered the underlying police culture in the unit she studied. This is further argument for the importance of ethnography: we need to know what is really going in response to institutional rhetoric espousing change and optimistically claiming beneficial effects.

In brief, policing is undoubtedly changing and the occupational culture of policing is changing in some respects. The influx of graduates has been one influence, among many, that has fostered greater openness to the media, researchers and external scrutiny, new leadership styles, a willingness to challenge established ways of operating and an ability to ride the waves of change (Blair, 2003). Doubtless there will always remain a resilient residue of the cynicism, solidarity, secrecy, negative stereotypes of outsiders and superiors, emphasis on physical prowess, lauding of practical skills and disparagement of theoretical knowledge that have been the hallmarks of traditional police culture (Waddington, 1999a). But the increasing volume of officers with experience of, and qualifications from, tertiary education has been in my view a significant and positive factor in helping to change the organisation and to alter its culture. Recruiting graduates and stimulating serving officers to attend university from the 1960s onwards ushered in the era of 'smart' cops. But an essential factor, drawing on the Essex experience, is that the police organisation has to learn to use smart cops in smart ways.

NOTES

1. Unless stated otherwise the quotations, with the questions in italics, are from Lee and Punch (2006), which is largely based on interviews with people who joined the Essex Police some 25–40 years ago. In Britain in secondary or further education GCE, 'O' levels means General Educational Certificates at Ordinary Level, usually taken around the age of sixteen; and for those who went on with their education there were 'A' ('Advanced') Level Certificates.

2. Referring to getting free food and services, to techniques of avoiding work and to getting on to sports teams and bands which practised and performed during working hours (Manning, 1977).

3. In 1944 a Post-War Reconstruction Committee recommended a National Police College; this duly opened in 1948 and moved to its present site at Bramshill in 1960. The Police Staff College, as it came to be called, initially provided an occupationally oriented curriculum but went on to offer a range of courses, which were a blend of operational policing and academic activities. Currently, Bramshill is a part of Centrex, which is responsible for police education and training.

4. Later 'Sir John', and also later President of ACPO (Markham, 2002).

5. There had been cases of officers taking degrees at the expense of the service through the Bramshill Scholarship Scheme, particularly in law, only then to leave the service.

6. Both the authors have taught on this course which then started at Bramshill (Police College and part of National Police Training, now 'Centrex') and continued at Cambridge with the possibility of gaining either a diploma or a degree in Applied Criminology.

7. Speech at Black Police Officers' Association by the highest-ranking Asian police officer in the UK: August 2006.

REFERENCES

Ascoli, D. (1979). *The queen's peace*. London: Hamish Hamilton.

Bayley, D. H. (1994). *Police for the future*. New York/Oxford: Oxford University Press.

Bayley, D., & Shearing, C. (2001). *The new structure of policing*. Washington, DC: National Institute of Justice.

Bittner, E. (1967). The police on skid row: A study of peacekeeping. *American Sociological Review, 32*, 699–715.

Blair, I. (2003). Leading towards the future. *Conference on future of policing*. London: London School of Economics.

Blair, I. (2005). *The Richard Dimbleby lecture*. London: BBC.

Bowling, B. (2005). Bobby, Bond or Babylon. Inaugural lecture, King's College London.

Bradley, D., Nixon, C., & Marks, M. (2006). What works, what doesn't work and what looks promising in police research networks? In: J. Fleming & J. Wood (Eds), *Fighting crime together* (pp. 170–194). Sydney: New South Wales University Press.

Brewer, J. D. (1991). *Inside the RUC*. Oxford: Clarendon.

Chan, J. B. L. (1997). *Changing police culture: Policing in a multicultural society*. Cambridge: Cambridge University Press.

Chan, J. B. L. (2003). *Fair cop: Learning the art of policing*. Toronto: University of Toronto Press.

Crank, J. P. (1998). *Understanding police culture*. Cincinnati, OH: Anderson.

Critchley, T. A. (1978). *A history of police in England and Wales*. London: Constable.

Daily Telegraph (17 May, 2000). Bramshill puts the emphasis on corporate management skills rather than old-style thief-catching.

Emsley, C. (1996). *The English Police: A political and social history*. London: Longman.

Ericson, R. V., & Haggerty, K. D. (1997). *Policing the risk society*. Oxford: Oxford University Press.

Etzioni, A. (1969). *Readings on modern organizations*. Englewood Cliffs, NJ: Prentice-Hall.

Foster, J. (2003). Police cultures. In: T. Newburn (Ed.), *The handbook of policing* (pp. 196–227). Cullompton: Willan.

Goode, W. J. (1967). The protection of the inept. *American Sociological Review, 32*(1), 5–19.

Holdaway, S. (1983). *Inside the British Police*. Oxford: Basil Blackwell.

Lee, M., & Punch, M. (2006). *Policing by degrees*. Groningen: Hondsrug Pers.

Leishman, F., Savage, S., & Loveday, B. (Eds). (1996). *Core issues in policing*. London: Longman.

Lipsky, M. (1980). *Street level bureaucrats*. New York: Sage.

Manning, P. K. (1977). *Police work*. Cambridge, MA: MIT Press.

Manning, P. K. (1979). The social control of police work. In: S. Holdaway (Ed.), *The British Police* (pp. 41–65). London: Edward Arnold.

Manning, P. K., & Van Maaanen, J. (Eds). (1978). *Policing: A view from the street*. Santa Monica, CA: Goodyear.

Markham, G. (2002). *Eulogy spoken at funeral of Sir John Cyprian Nightingale* (unpublished).

Marks, M. (2005). *Transforming the Robocops: Changing police in South Africa*. Scotsville, RSA: University of KwaZulu-Natal Press.

Marks, M. (2007). Police unions and their influence: Subculture or counter-culture? In: M. O'Neill & M. Marks (Eds), *Police occupational culture: New debates and directions*. Sociology of crime, law and deviance (Vol. 8), New York: Elsevier (forthcoming).

Martin, S. E. (1980). *Breaking and entering*. Berkeley, CA: University of California Press.

McLaughlin, E., & Murji, K. (1997). The future lasts a long time: Public policework and the managerialist paradox. In: P. Francis, P. Davies & V. Jupp (Eds), *Policing futures: The police, law enforcement and the twentieth-first century*. London: Macmillan.

Muir, W. K. (1977). *Police: Streetcorner politicians*. Chicago: Chicago University Press.

Newburn, T. (Ed.) (2003). *The handbook of policing*. Cullompton: Willan.

Newburn, T. (Ed.) (2005). *Policing: Key readings*. Cullompton: Willan.

O'Connor, D. (2005). *Closing the gap*. London: HMIC.

Punch, M. (1979). *Policing the inner city*. London: Macmillan.

Punch, M. (1985). *Conduct unbecoming*. London: Sage.

Punch, M. (1996). *Dirty business*. London: Sage.

Reiner, R. (1991). *Chief constable: Bobby or bureaucrat?* Oxford: Oxford University Press.

Reiner, R. (1994). A truce in the war between police and academe. *Policing Today, 1*(1), 22–24.

Reiner, R. (2000). *The politics of the police*. Oxford: Oxford University Press.

Reuss-Ianni, E. R., & Ianni, R. (1983). Street cops and management cops: The two cultures of policing. In: M. Punch (Ed.), *Control in the police organization* (pp. 251–274). Cambridge, MA: MIT Press.

Roethlisberger, F. J., & Dickson, W. J. (1939). *Management and the worker*. Boston, MA: Harvard University Press.

Rose, D. (1996). *In the name of the law*. London: Jonathan Cape.

Royal Commission on the Police (1962). *Final report*, Cmnd. 1728. London: HMSO.

Rubinstein, J. (1973). *City police*. New York: Ballantine.

Schein, E. (1996). *Organizational culture and leadership*. San Francisco, CA: Jossey-Bass.

Schön, D. (1983). *The reflective practitioner*. New York: Basic Books.

Scraton, P. (1999). *Hillsborough: The truth*. Edinburgh: Mainstream Publishing Projects Ltd.

Sherman, L. (Ed.) (1964). *Police corruption*. New York: Anchor.

Skolnick, J. (1966). *Justice without trial*. New York: Wiley.

Smith, C. (1978). The Bramshill scholar: An assessment. *Police Journal, XII* (April), 136–170.
Smith, D. J., & Gray, J. (1985). *Police and people in London: The PSI report.* Aldershot: Gower.
Useem, M. (1989). *Liberal education and the corporation: The hiring and advancement of college graduates.* Hawthorne, NY: Aldine de Gruyter.
Waddington, P. A. J. (1999a). *Policing citizens.* London: UCL Press.
Waddington, P. A. J. (1999b). Police (canteen) sub-culture: An appreciation. *British Journal of Criminology, 39*(2), 287–309.
Wall, D. (1998). *The chief constables of England and Wales.* Dartmouth: Ashgate.
Westley, W. (1970). *Violence and the police.* Cambridge, MA: MIT Press.
Young, M. (1991). *An inside job. Policing and police culture in Britain.* Oxford: Clarendon Press.

CHAPTER 5

POLICE STRESS AND OCCUPATIONAL CULTURE

Janet Chan

ABSTRACT

Danger and trauma in police work have long been linked to the development of a suspicious and cynical 'street cop' culture. Nevertheless, there is evidence that stress among police officers in Western democracies is more likely to be produced by organisational pressure and management practices than by actual traumatic experience. This chapter uses data from a follow-up study of police recruits to examine the relationship between police stress and occupational culture. In particular, it analyses the impact of organisational changes on officers' perception of their work and culture. The chapter demonstrates the way changes in the field of policing can modify some aspects of the occupational habitus while reinforcing others.

INTRODUCTION: STRESS AND CULTURE

The notion of 'police stress' has been the subject of many research studies (e.g. Stinchcomb, 2004; Deschamps, Paganon-Badinier, Marchand, & Merle, 2003; Brooks & Piquero, 1998; Brown, Cooper, & Kirkcaldy, 1996), most of which are concerned with identifying sources of stress and ways of reducing

Police Occupational Culture: New Debates and Directions
Sociology of Crime, Law and Deviance, Volume 8, 129–151
Copyright © 2007 by Elsevier Ltd.
ISSN: 1521-6136/doi:10.1016/S1521-6136(07)08005-0

or alleviating stress to prevent burnout or resignation among police officers. The relationship between police stress and the occupational culture has not attracted much research, although a number of early researchers have suggested a direct connection between the demands of police work and the development of the occupational culture. Skolnick (1966), for example, sees the 'working personality' of the police as a response to the danger of police work, the authority of the police constable, and the pressure to be productive and efficient. Reiner (2000, p. 87) similarly suggests that the 'cop culture' develops as a way to help police cope with 'the pressures and tensions confronting the police'. Van Maanen (1978) points out that the nature of police work, the potential for danger, the shift work, the police uniform, the sense of isolation, and the proliferation of rules and regulations within police departments all contribute towards the formation of this culture. For example, police cynicism can be a reaction to their regular exposure to lies and excuses told by citizens who did not wish to be blamed; their hardness a shell police constructed to protect themselves from 'nasty encounters' (Van Maanen, 1978, p. 120).

Yet the danger and unpredictability of police work, as Manning (1997) points out, may not be regarded as a stressful feature of police work by officers themselves; in fact, they may have their peculiar appeal in the 'threat-danger-hero' view of the occupation:

> Doubtless, danger and uncertainty are appealing facets of the work – many officers like the excitement of chases, the danger-filled episode, the life-threatening intervention at a crime scene. The danger and unpredictability allows for a degree of satisfaction and is not a 'negative' feature of the work in the eyes of its practitioners. (Manning, 1997, p. 261)

There is increasing recognition in the literature that stress should neither be regarded simply as 'a stimulus in the environment that creates tension, threat, or anxiety' nor solely as the body's response to stressful stimuli (Stinchcomb, 2004, p. 260). Instead, stress should be conceptualised in terms of the interaction between the individual and the environment: in effect, stress is defined as an '*imbalance* between environmental demands and individual resources' (p. 261). In other words, stress occurs when the demands placed on individuals exceed their capacity to deal with these demands. A more precise way of analysing stress is to distinguish between *stressors*, 'the disrupting conditions which create the need for the readjustment that can potentially produce stress' (p. 261) and *stress*, the strain experienced by individuals as a result of not being able to deal with the demands of the disrupting conditions. Responses to stress can include a variety of physical or physiological symptoms, social and attitudinal changes, as well as dysfunctional or destructive actions (Stinchcomb, 2004; Lord, 1996).

Manning's observation above suggests that whether certain environmental demands are seen as stressful or exciting by officers may depend on how these demands are 'framed' by individuals and their work groups. It is therefore important to examine how police culture[1] can both shape and be shaped by stressors. The relationship between stressors and police culture is a question that can be explored by considering the relationship between *field* and *habitus* in Bourdieu's theory of practice (see Bourdieu & Wacquant, 1992). In simple terms, a field is a social space of conflict and competition, where certain resources (capital) and constraints are at stake, while habitus is a system of dispositions that integrate past experience and enable individuals to cope with a diversity of unforeseen situations. In policing, these dispositions include the skills, cognitions, attitudes, values, and physical attributes officers acquire as part of being in the job (see Chan, with Devery, & Doran, 2003). Using this framework, we can consider stressors as demands in the field of policing. These demands may be physical, psychological, political, social, legal, organisational, or symbolic. Police officers as individuals and as a group can possess varying resources or capacity to cope; they develop the necessary habitus to deal with these demands. According to Bourdieu, the relation between field and habitus operates in two ways: on the one hand, the field conditions the habitus by imposing demands and constraints; on the other, habitus provides the cognitive frame for making sense of the field (Bourdieu & Wacquant, 1992, p. 127). In other words, while occupational or organisational stressors affect aspects of police culture, these stressors are interpreted by officers through the assumptions and shared values embedded in police culture.

Stressors in police work can come in many forms. Recruits who join the police usually experience a 'reality shock' (Hughes, 1958) when they confront a field that they are not familiar with. In order to get on with the job, their habitus needs to adjust to this new field (Chan et al., 2003, Chapter 6). However, new stressors can appear when the field of policing is itself changing – for example, as a result of reform or technological change – officers need to negotiate the field and learn new ways of adapting (Chan, 2001; Chan, 2003; Chan et al., 2003, Chapter 7). Initially, when faced with changes and uncertainties, officers try to make sense of their situation by drawing on the habitus they have acquired through occupational socialisation. However, they do not completely close off alternative interpretations, since they cannot be sure that their 'old' frameworks still apply in the new situation (Chan, 2007). Because of the evolutionary nature of this process of sensemaking (Weick, Sutcliffe, & Obstfeld, 2005), any change in habitus in response to its environment is usually incremental:

Habitus change [sic] constantly in response to new experiences. Dispositions are subject to a kind of permanent revision, but one which is never radical, because it works on the basis of the premises established in the previous state. They are characterized by a combination of constancy and variation which varies according to the individual and his [sic] degree of flexibility or rigidity. (Bourdieu, 2000, p. 161)

In order to explore the relationship between stressors in the field of policing and the occupational habitus, this chapter examines police officers' accounts of the stress they experience in their work. The chapter is organised as follows. The next section describes briefly the sources of data and research methods, and raises some methodological issues. The third section discusses the recent history of organisational changes in New South Wales Police and the stressors brought on by these changes. The next two sections analyse officers' accounts of stressors that operate in the field and how they coped with them: The fourth section deals with episodic stressors, while the fifth is concerned with chronic organisational stressors. The penultimate section examines the connection between stressors and the occupational habitus, and finally the implications of the findings are discussed.

RESEARCH METHODS

Data are drawn from a follow-up study of a class of police recruits in New South Wales, Australia, who originally took part in a longitudinal study of police socialisation from 1995 to 1997 (see Chan et al., 2003). The follow-up study, conducted between 2004 and 2005, revisits the class 9–10 years after they entered the police academy using both a mail-out questionnaire survey and face-to-face interviews. Only 118 of the original 150 recruits were still employed by the police in 2005. These officers were invited to participate in the study. A total of 42 questionnaires were returned and 44 face-to-face interviews conducted. The response rates were 34 and 36 per cent respectively.[2]

The interview sample represents a group of predominantly male (67 per cent) and young (84 per cent under 35) officers, the majority (77 per cent) of whom were at the rank of senior constable, who had had 7–8 years of operational experience and were mostly in general duty (44 per cent) or criminal investigation (33 per cent). The majority (61 per cent) were working in capital cities or metropolitan areas at the time of the interview. Even though the response rates for the follow-up study are low, the survey sample is fairly similar to the population of the remaining cohort in demographics, rank, duty, and current location. Younger officers (28–30 years of age) are over-represented in both the survey and the interview samples by about 10 per cent. Officers located in rural areas and those in criminal investigation are over-represented by 11 and 13 per cent, respectively.[3]

A methodological note is in order here. The main concerns of this chapter – work-related stress, organisational change, and occupational culture – are presented primarily through police officers' accounts. These accounts may be seen as biased, self-serving, or unreliable, given that secrecy and solidarity are well-documented characteristics of police culture. Where possible, I have tried to contextualise officers' accounts with alternative sources of data – for example, official reports or accounts of key informants.[4] There are, however, good reasons to make use of officers' accounts if we are interested in how stress and culture are perceived and constructed by police themselves. Interviews provide a rich source of data for understanding the police habitus – the assumptions, values, ways of seeing and acting embedded in the language, statements and opinions presented. It is also important to note the *silences* in these accounts. Officers were forthcoming about certain types of stressors such as management practices, organisational changes, accountability require-ments, public attitudes, and court decisions perhaps because they were regarded by their culture as legitimate grievances. They may have omitted other stressors that were not seen as stressful. For example, even when gender issues were explicitly raised in interviews, only one of the 15 female officers mentioned 'a bit of bullying' by male colleagues. The stress of sexual harassment, discrimination, or impediments that affect 'women in a man's world' (Foster, 2003, p. 214) was either non-existent among these officers[5] or, more likely, 'misrecognised' (Bourdieu & Wacquant, 1992, pp. 171–172) and accepted as harmless (see Doran & Chan, 2003). By listening closely to officers' accounts, noting their silences and omissions, and contextualising their accounts with other sources of data, we hope to bring a deeper understanding of the interaction between stressors that operate in the field and the occupational habitus of policing.

STRESSORS IN A CHANGING FIELD

Stinchcomb (2004) distinguishes between two types of stressors in the field of policing: *episodic stressors* such as traumatic incidents which rarely occur, and *chronic organisational stressors*, which are routine and pervasive.[6]

Episodic stressors usually 'begin and end quickly' and while they may have long-term effects such as post-traumatic disorder, few officers are affected (pp. 262–263). Chronic organisational stressors, on the other hand, are constant and encountered almost everyday. Stinchcomb (2004, pp. 263–264) cited a body of research that suggests that management practices rather than critical incidents are more likely to produce stress among officers (see also Brooks & Piquero, 1998 for a review of the literature).

Among the sources of organisational stress are management styles, bureaucratic disciplinary procedures, and poor communication (Stinchcomb, 2004, pp. 266–267). Other stressors that have been identified relate to the actual quality of work such as workload, responsibility for others, role conflict and role ambiguity (Lord, 1996, p. 512). The impact of chronic organisational stressors can include the development of physical symptoms, emotional or personal problems, a diminished level of job satisfaction, premature retirement, an increase in illness-related absences, a cynical attitude towards the job, and problems with family life and relationships (Stinchcomb, 2004, p. 265).

Organisational change, one of the main catalysts for changes in work responsibilities and management style, is becoming increasingly important as another source of stressors. For example, the implementation of a new policing philosophy such as community-based policing can produce additional stressors such as lack of recognition for work done, lack of communication between officers and supervisors, and role changes required by the new philosophy (Lord, 1996). The impact of these stressors can range from psychological and physical symptoms, propensity to leave the police force, to the lack of job involvement (*ibid.*). There is some evidence that officers from larger[7] police organisations report a higher level of organisational stress than those from smaller organisations, but force size explains only a very small proportion of the variance in the stress variables (Brooks & Piquero, 1998).

The New South Wales Police Force (NSWPF) provides an excellent case for the study of the relationship between police stress and occupational culture. It is the oldest and largest police force in Australia, with over 14,000 sworn officers (NSW Police, 2005). Apart from being a large police force, it is also a changing organisation. Two major waves of reform took place in the last two decades. In the mid-1980s, following a wide-ranging judicial inquiry, the organisation went through significant and fundamental changes to the philosophy, organisation, and operation of policing (Chan, 1997, pp. 129–136). For members of the cohort in the study, the most significant event that marked the second wave of reforms was the Wood Royal

Commission, which found that a state of 'systemic and entrenched corruption' existed in the Police Service (Wood Report, 1997). In response to the Commission's findings, major reforms were introduced. There was a big shake-up in terms of external scrutiny: the establishment of an independent Police Integrity Commission (PIC) that continued the work of the Royal Commission in relation to serious police misconduct, complementing the Ombudsman's Office which oversees the handling of less serious complaints. Internally, the Commissioner's Confidence provision[8] was introduced in 1998 as a way of streamlining the dismissal process. The organisation has also had two changes in police commissioners and several changes in police ministers. It also underwent two major rounds of restructuring and a total revamp of recruit education. There was a new focus on crime management and a devolved complaint management system was introduced.

Several key informants we interviewed pointed to a more professional culture and less corruption as a result of the Royal Commission and subsequent reforms: evidence of this includes the high rate of police reporting misconduct of other police officers[9] and the fact that recent PIC investigations only found incidents of corruption that were 'isolated' rather than 'systemic or ingrained'. Such a fundamental cultural change was possible, in the view of some informants, because of the Royal Commission, the 'hard work' of bodies like the Ombudsman and the PIC to promote ethics in policing, the change in police education, and the entry of new recruits that have a different attitude to policing. In particular, the Royal Commission had made it possible for 'good cops' to make a difference.

COPING WITH EPISODIC STRESSORS

The extent of physical and psychological trauma experienced by police officers is difficult to measure. Occupational Health and Safety statistics show that during the financial year 2004–2005, 710 new 'hurt on duty' claims were received by the NSW Police, 532 of which were for physical injuries and 178 for psychological injuries (NSW Police, 2005, p. 17). During the same period, the organisation spent nearly $9 million on hospital, medical, and pharmaceutical expenses, while a total of 361 police officers were medically discharged (*ibid.*). These statistics probably underestimate the extent of the problem because some officers may be reluctant to report such traumas unless the incident falls under a mandatory reporting category.

In the follow-up study, we asked interviewees whether they had come across traumatic experience in their work since graduation from the police academy 7 or 8 years ago. The majority of interviewees mentioned one or more incidents that they had found distressing. These include violent crime scenes, such as stabbing or shooting, incidents involving the death of children, fatal car accidents, police deaths (murder or suicide), and other incidents with deceased people.

The personal circumstances of the officer at the time of the incident often aggravated the trauma. For example, a male officer described how a fatal accident encountered a few months after a family member had died in a car accident left a lasting impact on him:

> I still remember the first fatal car accident I went to and that was only about 4 or 5 months after my stepsister went through a car accident ... so I found that really hard at the time, I look back on it now and it took a few years for me to deal with that .... Yeah, that was ... the worst thing I have seen and had to do, I still have nightmares about [it] every now and then.

The murder of a police officer was mentioned by a number of officers as a traumatic experience, partly because he was a friend and mostly because he was a police officer. One male officer explained:

> The most traumatic thing that sticks out in my mind is the death of [name] in [place]. I was a close friend of his ... I was working on the night it happened, you know, and it still, I get a bit teary thinking about it because it's just the nature of how it happened was just – it could have been me ... yeah, that's the most traumatic thing that I can think of ...

The type and level of support traumatised officers received varied. Some told us that they had no support from the police organisation at all (see NSW Ombudsman, 1999 for criticisms of the Police Service responses to critical incidents up to 1999). A male officer described a 'double whammy' some years ago when two traumatic incidents happened within 24 hours of each other. He had gone to a very violent stabbing incident where the victim died while the police were there, and then on the next shift encountered a very gruesome multiple-fatality car accident involving teenagers. He said that he did not get any debriefing or support at the time of the incidents and his partner, a new probationer, resigned a few days later. The way that he dealt with the trauma was to talk to his family, but he felt that there should have been immediate support from the police, although he conceded that support services have improved in recent years.

In spite of the improvement in support services, a male officer pointed out that those who work in remote areas did not have ready access to these services:

> When I first joined [we had] nothing. We just basically talk amongst each other and go down the pub and have a drink. Now they've got the Employee Assistance Branch which is fine on paper but to try and implement when you're in a remote location ... . This is where the whole thing falls down ... well, with a lot of the police stuff, it's all city based ... . Even here at [place] we're a major area category one LAC [Local Area Command] with a heap of major incidents that happen, major traumatics and it's all up and down the highways here, pretty lax in what happens ... you become macabre 'cause you switch off to it.

Officers coped with traumatic incidents in a variety of ways. Talking to family and colleagues was mentioned by a number of officers as one way of dealing with them. A male sergeant who was involved in fatal pursuit of a young person in a stolen car had support from a police psychologist, but he felt it was his wife and colleagues that gave him the most effective support:

> Yeah, I have to admit, like, there was a lot of support networks offered to me which was good ... . Yeah, like the Psychology Branch came out that night ... I mean I had a very good wife and I think that helped me through more than anything else. If I wasn't in a stable relationship I think I would have had ... gone through a lot more stress than I did ... I found talking to my wife easier than talking to psychologists and the like ... I felt like I didn't need it ... and that's where your work mates help you too, because they kind of band together and, like, pull you through and yeah, that's the good side of police culture that people don't hear about ...

One male officer claimed that he had never been traumatised by any incident, probably because he had become hardened:

> I've been to incidents where ... someone's poured petrol over themselves and we've pretty much been asked to clean up, I've been to quite a few fatal accidents where I've been one of the first officers on the scene. In crime scene I've been to murder scenes and ... all sorts of suspicious deaths, things like that. But none of them have really affected me. I mean, you have times where you think about them, but it's more ... in terms of 'Oh wasn't that bloke unlucky?' [laughter] rather ... than have a nightmare or something.

In his view, support services had improved since he joined the police, but police were not always willing to use these services because 'it still tends to be a bit of a macho thing about police: I'm tough, I can handle it'. Another male officer spoke of 'adrenalin junkies' that reflect the 'macho culture' of policing:

> I think the macho culture is certainly part of policing ... you know you get cops who [are] overt adrenalin junkies and they actively seek that adrenalin hit. You know, they will drive fast to jobs that they don't need to. They'll respond to jobs they don't need to so that they can drive fast. They'll actively seek out dangerous situations so they can be involved in them ... . [Q: Is that macho thing then is it male?] No – well predominantly,

I'd have to say like 95 per cent of it – yeah, it's blokes. But I've seen a few chicks suffer
from it and the women seem to suffer from it because they get swept up in it. They want
to be one of the guys, they want to be part of the team or part of the group or part of the
clique and they get sucked up into it and don't know how to deal with it …

Part of the appearance of 'toughness' meant not revealing to others that
one was experiencing stress. While interviewees were quite willing to discuss
their traumatic experiences with the interviewer for this research, not all were
prepared to seek help or even tell their work mates about their inability to
cope. A female officer admitted that she felt she had to keep quiet about her
traumatic experiences because not coping could be considered a weakness:

if you mention … what you're going through and people say, oh, you know, you're a
wuss … you've got to be careful who you speak to about those things … if you're under
those pressures and you're not coping or anything like that and you take time off … I've
never taken time off over anything like that but I know other police that have and they
have copped a bagging [been criticised].

This officer said she had suffered symptoms such as nightmares and sleep-
lessness for a long time without acknowledging that she was under stress. It
was perhaps not coincidental that she also developed a drinking problem for
some years.

The accounts presented in this section suggest that episodic stressors
could have long-lasting psychological effects on police officers, but the level
of support traumatised officers received varied. Some officers preferred to
rely on support from family members, spouses, and work mates rather than
seeking help from organisational sources. Although there was no attempt to
glorify the dangerous and traumatic aspects of the job, some officers gave
the impression that they had become hardened, or they were stronger than
others who needed more help. Only one officer admitted to keeping quiet
about her stressful experience in order not to appear weak. This suggests
that there is an implicit gendered approach ('a macho thing') to coping with
episodic stressors, one that emphasises 'emotional self-management'
(Martin, 1999), including not revealing to fellow officers that one is under
stress or seeking out dangerous situations to appear tough.

COPING WITH ORGANISATIONAL STRESSORS

It is clear that the field of policing in New South Wales has changed
dramatically since the cohort entered the police academy in 1995. We
observed in *Fair Cop* that quite early on in their career, the cohort had

already developed a sense of cynicism about management and the criminal justice system (Chan et al., 2003, pp. 224–231). During the third interview (18 months after entry), they criticised management for not supporting 'frontline' police officers, for being self-serving and ineffective. In particular, interviewees complained about the excessive 'paperwork' and accountability, as well as the constant organisational changes which they regarded as ill-conceived and having created extra work for operational police officers. Some interviewees blamed the Royal Commission for the loss of public respect for police and for low morale among officers. Others thought that the Commission's findings had led to the excessive paperwork and accountability already mentioned. They felt that police had become 'too scared to do their job' for fear of complaints being made against them and management had also become afraid to make decisions or support the lower ranks. The wave of reforms implemented as a result of the Royal Commission had also had considerable impact on the attitudes of the cohort on the reporting of misconduct. The introduction of the Commissioner's Confidence provision was particularly salient in the interviewees' mind when discussing (at the fourth interview, 24 months after entry) the reporting of misconduct. Many saw the risk of being charged or losing one's job as a deterrent against covering-up misconduct. Nevertheless, 'dobbing in' (complaining against) another officer was regarded as an extremely stressful action to take, given that the 'dobbers' would be hated by other officers (pp. 270–272).

In the follow-up survey, respondents were asked their opinion regarding various organisational changes that had occurred since they joined the police (see Chan, 2007 for details). Basically, almost everyone thought that the organisation had changed. Six in ten thought that the change had been substantial. Respondents were quite divided in their perception of the pace of change: half thought the pace of change was about right, about one quarter thought it was far too rapid, while another quarter thought it was far too slow. There was a range of opinions regarding the changes: almost half were indifferent; about one in five were quite satisfied, but 31 per cent were dissatisfied with the changes.

Respondents' degree of satisfaction with the police organisation varied according to the type of issues. A minority were dissatisfied with the police organisation in general (33 per cent) and the current system of performance evaluation (33 per cent), but two out of three respondents (67 per cent) were dissatisfied with the current system of promotion for non-commissioned officers. These results indicate that organisational issues such as performance evaluation and promotion are potential sources of stress for these officers.

Another indication of dissatisfaction with the organisation was the responses to the question whether they had ever considered leaving the NSW Police[10] since the last survey (June 1997). Almost three out of four respondents reported that they had occasionally (52 per cent) or frequently (21 per cent) considered leaving. Among those who considered leaving, 36 per cent considered leaving very seriously and 29 per cent somewhat seriously. In other words, 20 of the 42 respondents were somewhat serious or very serious about leaving their job. In contrast, respondents showed a high degree of satisfaction with their choice of policing as a career: only seven per cent were dissatisfied with their choice (see Chan & Doran, 2006 for details).

The follow-up study provides some indication of the sources of organisational stressors. In relation to the questionnaire item 'How favourable is your experience of the following job conditions?' the majority (73 per cent) of respondents reported having unfavourable experience with regard to stress and pressure in the job (29 per cent had very unfavourable experience). In contrast, only 27 per cent thought that the physical working conditions they had experienced were unfavourable. When asked in interviews what they would regard as 'the worst part of the job', officers nominated a number of organisational issues such as lack of support, lack of positive feedback or recognition, resource constraints, accountability requirements, public complaints, supervisory or management practices, public expectations, and the court systems. A few mentioned shift work and its impact on home life, but no one mentioned danger or traumatic incidents as the worst part of the job, even though, as reported in the last section, the majority of officers had encountered one or more traumatic experience in their work.

Respondents had mixed views about their supervisors and the police organisation. In relation to their supervisors, half (50 per cent) felt that the quality of supervision they received had not met their expectations. About three in 10 (32 per cent) reported that their experience of feedback from supervisors was either very or partly unfavourable, but the majority (66 per cent) reported that their relationship with their supervisor was partly or very favourable. In relation to the police organisation, Table 1 shows that the majority (60 per cent) of respondents agreed that help is available when they have a problem (21 per cent disagreed). However, a substantial proportion of respondents felt that NSW Police does not value their contribution (69 per cent), does not care about their well-being (57 per cent), shows very little concern for them (45 per cent), and does not care about their opinions (52 per cent). Even so, only about 19 per cent felt that they did not have a strong sense of belonging to the organisation, the majority (60 per cent)

Table 1. Attitudes towards Police Organisation (Survey 5, $n = 42$).

Item	Agree/Strongly Agree		Neutral		Disagree/Strongly Disagree	
	Frequency	%	Frequency	%	Frequency	%
NSW Police values my contribution to its well-being	5	12	8	19	29	69
Help is available when I have a problem	25	60	8	19	9	21
NSW Police really cares about my well-being	6	14	12	29	24	57
NSW Police shows very little concern for me	19	45	12	29	11	26
NSW Police cares about my opinions	3	7	17	41	22	52
I do not feel a strong sense of belonging to NSW Police	8	19	9	21	25	60

disagreed. These figures suggest that the majority of officers had good relationships with their supervisors and felt a strong sense of belonging to the organisation, but they felt that the organisation did not value them or their contributions in return.

Interviews with officers provide a rich source of data on organisational stressors they experienced. These include management or supervisory practices, the promotion system, accountability requirements, public expectations, and the court system.

Supervisory or Management Practice

A male officer told us that he had become more cynical towards management because of the way organisational changes were managed:

I think in some respects [I'm] a little bit more cynical ... I think there's a lot of management changes been made and without any consultation and without any forethought and then you see 12, 18 months later the whole decision is reversed and then everything's thrown back to the way it was ...

Resource allocation was mentioned as a point of conflict between some officers and management, but the lack of personal support from management appeared to be a more important issue for some interviewees. As a female officer explained, managers could now refer officers to counselling services without providing the personal support that officers needed in the work environment. She contrasted the management styles in two different stations that she had worked in: one being a warm supportive environment and the other an uncaring one. She felt that she had become hardened by her experience in the latter and believed that without leadership from above, a situation of 'them and us' was created between workers and managers:

> [I felt] I wasn't a valued member and I was shocked and appalled at that attitude, but then I guess that experience in itself has somewhat hardened me not to expect the support and I think now the more junior officers and those that are coming out of the Academy don't expect the support and don't get it and I think that's really disappointing ... well, you see the flow-on effect on camaraderie and mateship. It's not encouraging [from] the top down, therefore it doesn't happen.

The Promotion System

One source of stress mentioned by many officers was the promotion system, which was said to be 'horrible' or 'unfair'. A male sergeant who had a bad experience with appeals believed that the promotion system was abused and police had become 'more focused on promotion than ... on policing'. Promotion criteria were seen to be inconsistent by some officers. A major issue was over whether length of service was a relevant factor in promotion. Complaints that those who were promoted were not necessarily people who could do a good job were raised by a number of interviewees. The promotion system was a major stressor for police officers and those who were left behind could become demoralised and unproductive, as one male officer explained:

> there's too much emphasis on your ability to communicate your achievements on paper rather than your ability to actually carry out the role. It's based on how ... well you can brag is the way I find it ... the big thing is you're finding people that are very capable in positions that aren't getting interviews and it's very demoralising for people and it shuts them off and they become unproducti-ve ... They're bitter with the system and the old TJF syndrome gets passed down through the job – you know, 'The Job's Fucked' syndrome. Yeah, and you've got to be careful because you get caught in the rut yourself and say, what am I doing? I'm treading water here as well.

Accountability Requirements

Another dimension of organisational stressor mentioned was what interviewees regarded as excessive accountability, which was time-consuming and prevented officers from doing 'the job'. As one male officer explained:

> if I send six or seven memos, then I have to come back here and write 'I've just sent six or seven memos in relation to blah, blah, blah' ... that might take me ... an hour or so and they want you to account for every minute of your day in here, so, you know, it's probably 40 minutes a day I'm writing in here where I could be just doing other things.

A common complaint was the presence of multiple watchdogs which could make police afraid to do their job.

Public Expectations

Another stressor mentioned by interviewees was the apparent increase in complaints against the police. According to one female officer, junior police could become intimidated and avoid dealing with people who might complain:

> I think the attitudes of members of the public have totally changed as well ... it's sort of gone downhill ... . A lot more complaints about [police] ... the hierarchy upstairs get a bit more worried about that and they sort of start to freak out ... and I think sometimes, especially the more junior police, they sort of think, oh, I don't want to get complaints, so I'll just leave those people alone ... I think it impacted on a lot of people at this station, yeah, junior ones, whereas the more senior ones just know better than that. They think, well, if they're gonna complain, they're gonna do it anyway, so.

The Courts

Decisions by the criminal courts were cited as another source of frustration. It is in fact a well-known feature of police culture to complain about the leniency of the courts. One male officer saw 'losing at court' after doing a lot of work on the investigation as one of the worst parts of the job. His view was supported by others; for example, this female officer felt that court decisions were getting 'more ludicrous':

> I think decisions in court are getting more and more ludicrous. I don't think it's getting better ... . Like it's gone from one extreme almost to the other, so that part of it I find more frustrating than anything and I feel like a paper tiger sometimes ... . And I'm sure there's a lot of other police and I know I'm not just speaking for myself that just get tired of losing and I don't mean losing because it's not us that lose, it's the victims that lose

but certainly we put in a lot of work and we get nothing, we get costs awarded against us and that sort of thing ... that is a constant frustration for me and I don't think it's getting better at all, it's getting worse.

The picture painted by the survey and interview data in this section is consistent with the findings in the literature that chronic organisational stressors have become an important source of stress for police officers. Although there is nothing new in the views expressed by the interviewees – they reinforce the fundamental division between 'street cop' and 'management cop' culture (Reuss-Ianni & Ianni, 1983) and the traditional attitudes police have about the courts – organisational changes and police reforms in New South Wales had given more oxygen to any dissatisfaction or disenchantment officers had about the organisation and its environment. Interviewees did not discuss how they coped with these organisational stressors other than getting support from fellow officers, hardening themselves against frustration and disappointment, and becoming cynical. The fact that nearly half of the respondents in the follow-up survey had seriously contemplated leaving the police force suggests that leaving the organisation could be another way of dealing with the stressors.

STRESSORS AND POLICE CULTURE

Officers who took part in the follow-up study were asked whether their views and experience of 'police culture'[11] had changed since their last interview in 1997. Although they were not asked to link culture to stress, a clear picture of the relationship came through in the interviews. For example, while most officers thought that police culture had changed since they entered the Academy, many thought that the stressful nature of the job had meant that the cultural characteristic of mutual help and solidarity had not disappeared because it was needed as a support mechanism. One male officer who was particularly reflective explained that officers needed support for mutual protection 'in the street', for alleviating trauma, and for protection against the organisation and its environment:

I think that the police culture has basically developed as a support mechanism and the reason that it has is that we don't trust anybody else to support us. I think that the organisation has recognised that policing is a uniquely stressing – stressful career and it has introduced a whole range of things to sort of alleviate that ... but I don't think any of them are particularly effective because the coppers still don't trust the organisation ... . And that's why they need to stick together because we don't trust any other bugger to do it ...

Many interviewees told us that police reforms and administrative changes over the years had generated organisational stressors that had changed police culture. For example, the same male officer cited in the last paragraph felt that the introduction of the Duty Officer,[12] the competitive promotion system, and the emphasis on fighting corruption since the Royal Commission may have succeeded in destroying a great deal of the trust and solidarity among officers:

> after this Royal Commission, you know, one of those things that they did was they introduced this whole new rank of Duty Officer ... and they created the world's most adversarial promotion system that I've ever seen ... and honestly, the amount of camaraderie that has been destroyed as a result of that process is phenomenal. You know, like, none of those buggers that are in that system trust each other ... my conspiracy theory is if you want to destroy some police culture, you know, like, ... some of the sticking-togetherness, well, make them compete, you know, and ... having some blood on your hands, you know, when you get there to show that you are a corruption fighter, which is important, you know like having dobbed in one or two coppers for doing something wrong, having been the informant a couple of times is just a brilliant thing ... on your CV ... it certainly hasn't bred trust of these people in the lower ranks ... because honestly you feel like these guys would make an example of you so that they could put it on their CV ... . Because there's a lot of money involved in these jobs, you know, they're getting a hundred grand a year these people ... so that's my conspiracy theory as far as ... to tear the fabric of the police culture was to turn them into combatants [laughter].... [Q: And you reckon it succeeded?] Yeah, absolutely.

Cynicism was a common attitude of rank-and-file officers, developed as a result of their lack of trust in the organisation. As this officer pointed out, police often took 'stress leave' as a result of organisational stress, whereas traumatic incidents were dealt with by 'talking to other coppers'. The so-called 'senior constable syndrome' (the negative attitudes displayed by those who had become disillusioned with policing) was regarded by this officer as one strategy to resist the constant cycles of organisational change.

Police reforms brought new laws, regulations, and accountability systems that have generated a new source of stress. Officers felt they were constantly being scrutinised and as a result of the increased sophistication and rigour of surveillance and investigation, the so-called 'code of silence' could no longer operate. As a male officer pointed out, a lot more was at stake in covering-up misconduct:

> Yeah, the days are gone where you have a choice in investigations. You know, they come in the room, they put the tapes in front of you and they say you are directed to answer these questions. Nobody is prepared to put $70,000, a house mortgage and their family on the line for anybody else any more ... . Yeah, if someone stuffs up, they take responsibility for it, because they know full well that these days you can't afford to get

involved in something that's not right ... with the investigation techniques they've got nowadays, you know, the covert surveillance, the listening devices and all that, it's going to come out ... . Realistically, if something goes arse up, your best option is to say. 'Look, yeah, it happened and it was wrong' ... . I make that fairly clear to everybody I work with that I don't put myself on the line for anybody ... I've got a house, mortgage, and you get 70 grand a year to do this job, you get sacked from the coppers, there's not too many other people that are going to employ you.

The tightening of accountability was said to have led to a 'cultural change'. As a female officer observed, 'things have tightened up, checks and balances are in, you're always being checked, you're always being monitored, you've got much more record keeping'. These 'accountability issues' were seen by another female officer as being responsible for the loss of trust and solidarity among police officers, as a result, she felt that 'police culture' had diminished:

> I think there was more of a police culture when I first joined than what there is now. I think that's probably got a lot more to do with the accountability issues and things like that ... people just seemed to look out for ... each other more than what they do now. Yeah, there doesn't seem to be that same sort of closeness as there could be .... [Q: And do you know what brought about that change or why that change might have happened?] I think a lot of people are scared, they're scared of getting into trouble .... Like police don't, like, trust other police and things like that.

Another female officer reported that unethical officers were being 'kicked out of the culture', in effect suggesting that the old culture of corruption and cover-up had been replaced by a new one that no longer tolerated misconduct:

> I think now ... people are slipped out of the culture if they're doing the wrong thing and I think that's a good thing because ... I think years and years ago if something unethical was happening, people just turned a blind eye 'cause they were in the culture, whereas now I'm finding that people are kicked out of the culture and it's being reported.

One well-known element of police culture – self-protection – appears to have been strengthened rather than changed by the new accountability requirements, as a male officer pointed out:

> I think everybody is more concerned about covering their own bottoms as opposed to getting the job done ... . Cover your arse. [laughing] ... basically so you don't get a complaint. So you don't look like you're incompetent ... . Yeah, I think ... the priority for people is covering their arse rather than doing the job, which I think is wrong.

Another male officer agreed; he thought that accountability had become 'ludicrous' – not only did police have to videotape the execution of search warrants, a new protocol specified that there must be a videotape of the person who is videotaping.

The interview excerpts presented in this section suggest that officers themselves saw 'police culture' as a support mechanism that they needed now more than ever because of the stressful nature of the job as a result of organisational changes. The introduction of what was regarded as a competitive and adversarial promotion system, the constant organisational changes, and the tightening of accountability had made it difficult and economically irrational to cover-up misconduct, while at the same time strengthened the need for self-protection.

CONCLUSION

Policing has traditionally been regarded as a stressful occupation. Police officers – especially 'street cops' (general duties police) – have long-lived with and adapted to the potential danger, trauma, and unpredictability of the job. For police working in Western democracies, such stressors tend to be episodic and rare, and have not changed significantly over the years. Part of the adaptive response police take on is denial or some type of emotional hardening ('it doesn't bother me'). Once this has become part of the accepted way of thinking and feeling within the occupation, danger and trauma are seen as stressors that police can cope with, either through talking to family and work mates, or through some kind of workplace support.

As accountability and professionalism are increasingly being demanded of police officers and police forces everywhere (see Goldsmith & Lewis, 2000; Marks, 2005), chronic organisational stressors will become more prominent in the spectrum of occupational pressures faced by police (Stinchcomb, 2004). Some of these stressors are not new: police have always expressed frustration about what they perceived to be the lack of support from management, the general public, and the courts. Officers respond to these stressors by seeking support from each other – they develop the so-called 'us and them' mentality, the street cop/management cop division, and a deep sense of solidarity with each other.

The experience of the police described in this chapter suggests that as a result of reforms introduced after the Wood Royal Commission, the field of policing in New South Wales had changed substantially. Police reforms and organisational changes had brought about new types of stressors: heightened accountability, a more competitive promotion system, and increased pressure (both ethical and financial) to report police misconduct to authorities. These new stressors threatened to disrupt the much-valued solidarity among police officers. Increased accountability and emphasis on integrity had meant that the 'code of silence' was no longer sustainable: officers had too much to lose (their job and the attendant financial security) to protect other officers' misconduct. Instead, police officers' age-old practice of self-protection (covering your arse) had become more salient and entrenched than ever. An adversarial and competitive promotion system also threatened to tear apart the 'fabric' of solidarity – it undermined trust among officers and reinforced police cynicism in relation to managers who were seen to sacrifice lower-rank officers in order to get ahead.

In this chapter, the relationship between police stress and the occupational culture is conceptualised in terms of that between field and habitus. Bourdieu's framework suggests that when the field changes, the habitus will adjust incrementally. Results of this study show that there were changes as well as continuities in the occupational habitus of policing as officers made sense of and reacted to changes in the field. This is consistent with organisational theorists' observation that culture is developed as a group response to problems of 'external adaptations and internal integration' (Schein, 1985, p. 9). Although it may seem ironic that reform measures intended to transform negative aspects of police culture (e.g. code of silence) could result in the further entrenchment of other negative aspects of the culture (e.g. self-protection or cynicism), such consequences are not surprising given that changes in the police habitus happen incrementally rather than radically. Officers' adaptation to organisational stressors will initially be based on the previous state of their habitus, which provides an automatic (some might call 'knee-jerk') response to new experiences. Over time, their adaptation could vary or become entrenched depending on individual officers' 'degree of flexibility or rigidity' (Bourdieu, 2000, p. 161) and the extent to which the field continues to change. The danger of continual change lies not so much in the organisational stressors it creates, but the real possibility of the onset of change 'fatigue' and permanent cynicism.

NOTES

1. Police culture refers to the set of assumptions, values, modes of thinking, and acting that a group of police officers developed as part of their shared understanding. It is not assumed that there is a single culture in any police organisation or unit, although the degree of homogeneity or heterogeneity of culture can vary from group to group. See Chan (1997) for a full discussion.

2. A total of 133 invitations went out because the police also invited officers who did not commence training with the cohort but graduated with them. We included these participants in the study but did not count them in calculating the response rates.

3. For full details see Chan and Doran (2005).

4. To identify changes to policing over the 10-year period, we consulted 11 key informants who were knowledgeable about policing and the history of NSW Police. Six of these came from within the police and five from other government and non-government organisations.

5. Although no recent data are available, an anonymous survey of NSW women officers in 1995 (Sutton, 1996, pp. 11–12) found that among the 822 respondents (55 per cent response rate), various forms of sexual harassment were experienced by 34–80 per cent of respondents. These ranged from 'uninvited teasing, jokes, remarks or questions of a sexual nature' to 'uninvited and deliberate touching, stroking or pinching'. The majority of women officers indicated that they ignored the behaviour, made a joke about it, avoided the person, or told the person to stop (p. 15). Only 17 per cent told someone about the behaviour or reported it as a complaint. The NSW Police had responded to the report by implementing policies to prevent sexual harassment and deal with grievances, although the outcomes of these policies have not been evaluated (Szalajko, 2004). A recent Ombudsman Report reveals that in 2002, 30 NSW police officers were found to have been involved in various sexual misconduct or inappropriate behaviours in relation to students in the Police College, but action taken against these officers 'in many cases has been too little, too late' (NSW Ombudsman, 2006, p. 6).

6. Observations such as Stinchcomb's may be true only in Western democracies. Police in conflict and post-conflict situations may be subjected to danger and trauma on a regular basis. I am grateful to the editors for pointing this out.

7. The largest organisation in the Brooks and Piquero (1998) study had only 1,550 officers. This is typical of US police forces.

8. An amendment of the Police Services Act (s181D) which gave the Commissioner power to remove a police officer 'if the Commissioner does not have confidence in the police officer's ability to continue as a police officer, having regard to the police officer's competence, integrity, performance or conduct'.

9. Complaints against police by police constituted 29 per cent of complaints received by the Ombudsman in 2004–2005, compared with 18 per cent in 2000–2001 (NSW Ombudsman, 2005, p. 43).

10. By 2005, 32 of the original 150 recruits had left the organisation – an attrition rate of 21 per cent over 10 years. The majority (69 per cent) of those who left resigned from their position, one was on medical discharge, while the rest had their employment terminated.

11. Researchers have traditionally derived notions of police culture from their own observation or personal experience, but as demonstrated in the original study, asking serving police to define and describe police culture can be an extremely valuable exercise: it generated some remarkably thoughtful responses and important insights. See Chan et al. (2003, Chapter 7) for details.

12. A senior officer holding the rank of inspector who is in charge of the day-to-day running of a Local Area Command in the Commander's absence.

150   JANET CHAN

ACKNOWLEDGEMENT

The research on which this chapter is based was funded by an Australian Research Council Discovery Grant DP0344753. I would like to thank Sally Doran who assisted with the survey design and conducted nearly all the field interviews and Chris Marel who helped with the qualitative analysis. The cooperation of the NSW Police is gratefully acknowledged. This chapter has benefited from the very helpful comments from the editors.

REFERENCES

Bourdieu, P. (2000). *Pascalian meditations.* Cambridge: Polity Press.
Bourdieu, P., & Wacquant, L. J. D. (1992). *An invitation to reflexive sociology.* Cambridge: Polity Press.
Brooks, L. W., & Piquero, N. L. (1998). Police stress: Does department size matter? *Policing: An International Journal of Police Strategies and Management, 21*(4), 600–617.
Brown, J., Cooper, C., & Kirkcaldy, B. (1996). Occupational stress among senior police officers. *British Journal of Psychology, 87*, 31–41.
Chan, J. (1997). *Changing police culture.* Melbourne: Cambridge University Press.
Chan, J. (2001). Negotiating the field: New observations on the making of police officers. *Australian and New Zealand Journal of Criminology, 34*(2), 114–133.
Chan, J. (2003). Police and new technologies. In: T. Newburn (Ed.), *Handbook of policing* (pp. 655–679). Cullompton: Willan.
Chan, J. (2007). Making sense of police reforms. *Theoretical criminology, 11*(3), Forthcoming.
Chan, J., with Devery, C., & Doran, S. (2003). *Fair cop: Learning the art of policing.* Toronto: University of Toronto Press.
Chan, J., & Doran, S. (2005). Fair cop: Nine years later. Paper presented at the Australian and New Zealand Society of Criminology Conference, 9–11 February, Wellington, New Zealand.
Chan, J., & Doran, S. (2006). *Staying in the job: Commitment and satisfaction among mid-career police officers.* Unpublished paper.
Deschamps, F., Paganon-Badinier, I., Marchand, A. C., & Merle, C. (2003). Sources and assessment of occupational stress in the police. *Journal of Occupational Health, 45*, 358–364.
Doran, S., & Chan, J. (2003). Doing gender. In: J. Chan, with C. Devery & S. Doran (Eds), *Fair cop: Learning the art of policing.* Toronto: University of Toronto Press.
Foster, J. (2003). Police cultures. In: T. Newburn (Ed.), *Handbook of policing* (pp. 196–227). Cullompton: Willan.
Goldsmith, A., & Lewis, C. (Eds). (2000). *Civilian oversight of policing: Governance, democracy and human rights.* Oxford: Hart.
Hughes, E. C. (1958). The study of occupations. In: R. K. Merton, L. Broom & L. Cotrell (Eds), *Sociology today.* New York: Basic Books.
Lord, V. B. (1996). An impact of community policing: Reported stressors, social support, and strain among police officers in a changing police department. *Journal of Criminal Justice, 24*(6), 503–522.

Manning, P. (1997). *Police work: The social organization of policing* (2nd ed.). Prospects Heights, IL: Waveland Press.

Marks, M. (2005). *Transforming the robocops: Changing police in South Africa*. Scotsville: University of KwaZulu-Natal Press.

Martin, S. E. (1999). Police force or police service? Gender and emotional labor. *Annals AAPSS, 561*, 111–126.

NSW Ombudsman (1999). *Officers under stress*.

NSW Ombudsman (2005). *Annual report 2004–05*.

NSW Ombudsman (2006). *Misconduct at the NSW Police College*.

NSW Police (2005). *Annual report 2004–2005*.

Reiner, R. (2000). *The politics of the police* (3rd ed.). Oxford: Oxford University Press.

Reuss-Ianni, E., & Ianni, F. (1983). Street cops and management cops: The two cultures of policing. In: M. Punch (Ed.), *Control in police organization*. Cambridge, MA: MIT Press.

Schein, E. (1985). *Organizational culture and leadership*. San Francisco: Jossey-Bass.

Skolnick, J. H. (1966). *Justice without trial: Law enforcement in a democratic society*. New York: Wiley.

Stinchcomb, J. B. (2004). Searching for stress in all the wrong places: Combating chronic organizational stressors in policing. *Police Practice and Research, 5*(3), 259–277.

Sutton, J. (1996) Keeping the faith: Women in policing – A New South Wales perspective. Paper presented at the first Australasian Women Police Conference, Sydney (available at http://www.aic.gov.au/conferences/policewomen/sutton.pdf).

Szalajko, M. P. (2004). Sex discrimination and sexual harassment within the New South Wales police: Has anything changed? *The Journal for Women and Policing, 15*, 15–25.

Van Maanen, J. (1978). Kinsmen in repose: Occupational perspectives of patrolmen. In: P. Manning & J. Van Maanen (Eds), *Policing: A view from the street* (pp. 115–128). Santa Monica, CA: Goodyear.

Weick, K. E., Sutcliffe, K. M., & Obstfeld, D. (2005). Organizing and the process of sensemaking. *Organization Science, 16*(4), 409–421.

Wood Report. (1997). *Royal Commission into the NSW Police Service: Final report*. Sydney: NSW Government.

CHAPTER 6

POLICE REFORM, GOVERNANCE, AND DEMOCRACY

Mark Bevir and Ben Krupicka

ABSTRACT

If we are to understand police reform in the United Kingdom and United States during the latter half of the twentieth century, we have to explore the various narratives that have inspired it. Many of these narratives are elite ones. Yet, the reforms are implemented and enacted in part by local police officers. Rank and file officers will necessarily interpret and extend the elite-inspired reforms through their own local beliefs. Several problems with the reforms reflect the inability of the elite narratives properly to recognize the impact of local cultures. A better understanding of this process of reform, and its implications for democratic governance, might orientate reformers and scholars toward more bottom-up approaches to police reform.

INTRODUCTION

In this chapter, we argue that police reform – the formal and informal changing of policing strategies and practices of public and private sector institutions and agents – can be understood as the outcome of diverse actions inspired by various competing narratives and cultures of reform.

Police Occupational Culture: New Debates and Directions
Sociology of Crime, Law and Deviance, Volume 8, 153–179
Copyright © 2007 by Elsevier Ltd.
All rights of reproduction in any form reserved
ISSN: 1521-6136/doi:10.1016/S1521-6136(07)08006-2

We draw attention to the differences between the elite narratives, which inspire the reforms themselves, and the local narratives or cultures of rank and file officers, who are intimately involved in implementing the reforms. Recognition of these different narratives highlights, and also begins to explain, the incomplete and continuing nature of police reform by drawing attention to the importance of local cultures and local reasoning. We would suggest, in addition, that an appreciation of local reasoning might point the way toward more bottom-up and participatory approaches to police reform. In some ways, the recent reforms have made policing more efficient, and they might also have managed to increase the extent to which individuals and civic associations are able to participate in policing. Nonetheless, their neglect of local cultures appears in a series of unintended consequences that are now barriers to the democratization of policing.

The first part of this chapter explains our approach, introducing key ideas such as an anti-essentialist concept of culture. The second part outlines the main elite narratives of police reform in the UK and the US. It traces a history from a progressive narrative tied to bureaucratic modes of governance, to a neoliberal narrative that championed markets and new managerial practices, and a new narrative of community policing that promotes partnerships and networks. The third part of the chapter turns to ethnographic evidence of the local cultures and reasoning through which rank and file officers have responded to the reforms. It shows how the reforms have been incomplete and how they have posed dilemmas for serving officers. This ethnographic evidence points, moreover, to what we call the 'fallacy of expertise;' the gap between the reformers' intentions and the local police cultures is less an example of the intransigence of serving officers than one of the hubris of social science and policy expertise. Finally, in the last part of the chapter, we offer a democratic assessment of the different narratives of reform and their impact on policing.

CULTURE AND REFORM

Calls for the study of cultures of police reform should perhaps be clear about how they conceive of policing, police reform, and especially culture. Policing includes 'all explicit efforts to create visible agents of crime control, whether by government or by nongovernmental institutions' (Bayley & Shearing, 1996, p. 586). Over the past 50 years, policing practices have undergone significant reform. The attempts to reform the police during this time have had much in common with broader trends in public sector reform.

In both the UK and the US, there has been a shift from bureaucratic modes of governance to a greater emphasis on markets, partnerships, and networks. Much of the twentieth century was characterized by the rise and the consolidation of policing bureaucracies and police professionalism (Sklansky, 2005). In the UK and the US, policing became the exclusive purview of centralized and state-sponsored police departments. In the 1970s and 1980s, however, the rise of neoliberal ideas and other social changes brought both a proliferation of private security forces and the outsourcing of some government services related to law and order (Bayley & Shearing, 1996). Recently, the creation and maintenance of quasi-markets has given way to new approaches to community policing. While community policing has been a slogan for reformers since at least the 1960s, it has now, since the 1990s, taken on a distinctive concern with organizational forms such as networks and partnerships. In short, then, policing, like much of the public sector, has been subject to reforms that have attempted to bring about a shift from bureaucratic to market- and network-oriented governance.

The broad contours of police reform are widely recognized. But there is less recognition of the conflicts between elite narratives of reform and the local cultures of policing in which the reforms are enacted. The agency and resistance of local police means not only that the reforms have been incomplete but also that the reforms have led to a series of unintended consequences. If we want to develop a thicker account of the process of reform, we need to examine not just elite cultures and their narratives of reform but also the ways in which these narratives have been understood and enacted on the ground within various local cultures.

Culture is, of course, a widely used term that can have many meanings. We understand cultures to be aggregate concepts based on the inter-subjective beliefs and the routine actions and practices of a group of individuals. So, in our view, far from being constitutive of an individual's beliefs and actions, cultures are aggregate descriptions of beliefs and actions. The beliefs and actions comprising local cultures can best be explained historically. People adopt the beliefs they do against the background of an inherited tradition, and they modify these traditions in response to various dilemmas.

Tradition, and so culture, is to be understood here as a pragmatic concept, not an essentialist one (Bevir, 1999, pp. 187–220). Traditions of policing and police cultures are not monolithic; they are defined not by fixed cores but by the ways in which we distinguish them from each other in accord with the particular topics that interest us. Likewise, traditions of policing and police cultures are not static; they are constantly changing as people respond to various dilemmas, altering their beliefs and practices to accommodate new experiences and new ideas. Our anti-essentialist concept of culture suggests that police cultures are contingent and contested.

Among the intersubjective beliefs that make up a culture, we usually will find various narratives about human actions and the social world. These narratives make sense of human life by connecting people, actions, and beliefs to one another (Bevir, 1999, pp. 298–306). In what follows, we will be concerned with narratives of police reform. These narratives concern police, their attitudes, their behavior, their interactions with criminals and citizens, and the problems they face. They thereby suggest particular sets of policies and strategies as ways of making policing more efficient, more just, or more democratic. Reform narratives provide a general orientation, a vocabulary, and a history for tackling and answering questions regarding the appropriate ways in which to prevent crime and enforce the law.

We ourselves are offering, of course, a narrative about policing. We are providing a narrative of narratives; we are telling a story about the various elite beliefs that have informed successive attempts to reform policing, and about the ways in which local police cultures have affected these reforms, a story that thus highlights the gap between the elite narratives of reform and the reality of their implementation. Yet, our narrative of narratives is not just a review. To the contrary, the whole point of exploring narratives or cultures lies in their impact upon actions – the police reforms and their unintended consequences.

Where many social scientists think of governing structures as formal institutions, we conceive of institutions as practices composed of actions, beliefs, and the narratives in which they are embedded. Our narrative of narratives is, in other words, an attempt to identify and explain the beliefs and actions that, to a greater or lesser degree, have taken policing from bureaucratic hierarchies to markets and networks. We explain police reform precisely by explicating the beliefs and narratives of the relevant policy-makers and local officers. Indeed, by taking on beliefs and narratives as objects of analysis, we are better able to explain why current policing is an amalgam of competing practices and why the reforms have failed to create the world their advocates envisage.

NARRATIVES OF REFORM

Police reform has generally consisted of a program of initiatives developed by political and administrative elites, often with advice from social scientists or management specialists, and then imposed on local departments and rank and file officers. Yet, while policy experts, public officials, and politicians formulate narratives against a background of particular traditions that point to ways of making policing more efficient or effective, they do not always agree among themselves. Rival elites drawing on rival ideologies or traditions propose quite distinct sets of reforms. Hence police reform is contested, and there are multiple narratives of reform co-existing with one another.

Three reform narratives have had a profound impact on policing during the latter half of the twentieth century. We provide a summary account of these three narratives in Table 1. Each narrative arose out of a particular elite culture with a distinct intellectual ethos. Each narrative also privileged a particular mode of governance; indeed, the successive waves of police reform and public sector reform more generally, can be understood in terms of a decline of the progressive narrative and the rise of neoliberal and community-orientated alternatives. Each narrative also has, even if only implicitly, a characteristic vision of democracy, accountability, and choice in the public sector.

The progressive, neoliberal, and community narratives are all fairly familiar in policing and the public sector more generally. We do not provide

Table 1. Reform Narratives.

Narrative	Intellectual Ethos	Mode of Governance	Democratic Ideal
Progressive *Examples:* US – Blue-ribbon crime commissions	Empiricist, technocratic	Bureaucratic	Electoral representative, Democratic pluralism
Neoliberal a) New public management b) Private police/security c) Outsourcing/privatization *Examples:* UK – Police and Magistrates' Courts Act (1994)	Rationalist, deductive	Market-oriented	Electoral representative, Empowered consumers
Community-oriented *Examples:* UK – Police Reform Act (2002) US – Violent Crime and Control Act of (1994)	Empirical social theory (e.g. Communitarianism, Organization theory, new institutionalism)	Networks and partnerships	State-sponsored networks, Electoral representative

a full history of the nature and impact of each narrative in the UK and US. We simply identify the main themes of each narrative – its intellectual ethos, its preferred mode of governance, and its democratic ideal – illustrating them by reference to one exemplary policy initiative.

The Progressive Narrative

The intellectual ethos of the progressive narrative relies on empiricism and technocratic expertise. This ethos influences both who makes policy decisions and what constitutes an appropriate response to a given policy problem. Decisions are made by elected officials but on the advice of social scientists and other experts. Suitable advice responds to a problem by analyzing empirical data, discovering correlations and trends, and recommending policies based on such knowledge.

A bureaucratic mode of governance appeals to advocates of the progressive narrative in part because bureaucracies provide organizations in which expert advice can easily be relayed up to elected politicians and down to subordinate groups. Indeed, the top-down, hierarchic nature of bureaucracy mirrors the elitist and specialist approach to knowledge that is found in the progressive narrative. Advocates of the progressive narrative also favor bureaucracies on the grounds that they are especially effective at implementing the policies that experts recommend. In this view, bureaucracy insulates policy-making from community leaders and political pressures, leaving it to impartial specialists who possess the appropriate methodological training.

The dominant traditions of progressive politics in the UK and US, such as Fabianism, have usually accepted a liberal, representative vision of democracy. Democracy consists, in this view, mainly of periodic elections by which citizens hold politicians accountable together with a system of government within which these elected politicians are able to hold public officials accountable. In addition, the rise of behavioral topics led, especially in the US, to some accounts of an elite pluralism. Elite pluralism allows for major interest groups as well as public officials influencing the policy-making process, but with the responsibility for decision-making still residing with elected politicians who can be held accountable by the electorate. Typically, elite pluralists remain profoundly distrustful of citizens, who are thought to lack the training and expertise needed for the impartial collection and analysis of empirical data. Hence, they restrict mass participation to elections. Experts develop policy, political elites make policy decisions, and citizens periodically use the ballot to pass judgment on politicians and policies.

Police forces in the UK have never been under direct control by political operatives (Johnston, 1992). The Police Act 1964 established a tripartite system in which the governance of police forces is shared among the home secretary, chief constables, and local police authorities, the last of these comprised of two-third elected councilors and one-third unelected magistrates. This tripartite arrangement reflects the progressive narrative's emphasis on insulating the police from political pressure. The tripartite system typically left chief constables in charge of the operational policy of the police forces, with the home secretary in charge of promoting greater efficiency, and with the local police authorities being given the role of maintaining an adequate and efficient police force. Hence, the policies followed by rank and file officers generally arose not from political consultation with local authorities (much less ordinary citizens) but from in-house decisions by the chief constables with occasional interference from the Home Office. Indeed, the progressive narrative sustained tendencies toward centralization and professionalism. Within the UK, the Police Act of 1946, and later the Local Government Act of 1972 and the Police and Magistrates' Courts Act of 1994, decreased the number of provincial departments and insulated police forces from political and social influence (Jones & Newburg, 2002).

In the US, the progressive narrative was even more closely entwined with what is often labeled 'second wave' professionalism. This second wave of police professionalism sought to increase efficiency through a range of technical measures, including 'streamlining operations, strengthening lines of command, raising the quality of personnel, leveraging personnel with technology, clarifying the organizational mission, and building public support' (Sklansky, 2005, p. 1743). As late as the 1960s and 1970s, the blue ribbon crime commissions created in the US continued to take their inspiration from the progressive narrative. These commissions arose when cities, states, and the federal government responded to urban riots and campus protests by bringing together collections of experts to examine the available evidence and propose reforms. The Commission on the Los Angeles Riots, the National Advisory Commission on Civil Disorders, and the President's Commission on Campus Unrest were all composed of members with an alleged expertise based not just on practice but more often still on the scientific study of crime and civil disorders. The commissions proposed various reforms that were then adopted, somewhat selectively, by the relevant policing agencies. An alleged scientific expertise lay behind a host of regulations and rules that were implemented through and on rank and file officers. The progressive narrative thus led simultaneously to a top-down bureaucracy and to rules and procedures to limit the discretion of field agents.

The Neoliberal Narrative

The neoliberal narrative arose as people responded to dilemmas such as state overload by drawing on themes from traditions such as neoclassical economics. Often it also drew on, or at least overlapped with, specific concerns about law and order. In the UK, industrial strife, associated with the Winter of Discontent and later the Miner's Strike of 1984–1985, brought policing issues to forefront of public debate, and, for many, revealed the inefficiencies of the tripartite system established by the Police Act of 1964. In the US, urban riots, campus protests and the (sometimes excessive) use of force on the part of police officers led to a re-examination of how policing was practiced.

Whereas the progressive narrative relies on inductive empiricism, the neoliberal one draws on neoclassical economics with its more rationalist and deductive ethos. Neoliberals characteristically rely on deductive models based on assumptions about the rational nature of individual action. Their assumptions lead neoliberals to favor markets over bureaucracy; in their view individuals are far better able to determine their needs and to meet these needs by operating in markets than is big government acting on their behalf. So, the neoliberal reforms of the Reagan and Thatcher governments were primarily attempts to promote efficiency through market reforms. Neoliberals believed that the state was inherently inefficient especially when compared to the free market. They promoted a range of market-oriented reforms and market-mechanisms in the public sector. They also tried to spread various private sector management techniques through the public sector.

While the neoliberal narrative typically emphasized the goals of effectiveness and efficiency, it also contained a normative strand about choice and participation in public services. Many neoliberals argued that markets and quasi-markets provide greater scope for personal choice than the one-size-fits-all solutions of large bureaucracies. Similarly, they argued that markets enabled people to hold service providers accountable since they could simply withdraw their custom from any service provider with whom they were not satisfied. By turning citizens into consumers of public services, neoliberals hoped both to expand opportunities for choice and ensure that public officials were accountable to those they served. The values of democracy are better served, they implied, by the spread of markets than by bureaucratic hierarchies.

Commentators have well documented the dramatic rise of marketization and even private police in the UK and US over the past three decades (Bayley & Shearing, 1996; Johnston, 1999). They have traced the influence that market-oriented reforms have had on the role of the public police and the relationship between public and private providers of security services. The privatization of security forces and public safety has taken place in several ways. There has been an increase in the presence of for-hire private security firms. The state increasingly provides official certification to some public safety agents. In the UK, for example, police now certify private-sector bouncers working at clubs and pubs. Finally, police forces increasingly employ civilians to perform activities that used to be the role of officers. In the UK, for example, there are now a plethora of accredited community safety officers and community support officers; these officers are usually part of community action teams that provide a visible uniformed presence to offer reassurance to the public, but their tasks are restricted to those that do not require the experience or powers of police officers. Such redefining, or even contracting-out, of public services is, of course, an increasingly popular way to maintain or increase levels of service while decreasing costs. Policing is no exception to the trend.

Neoliberals also sought to spread private sector managerial techniques to policing. Like many public sector organizations, police departments have seen the spread of what is often called the new public management (NPM). The imposition of NPM into police departments has led to the publishing of performance targets and the evaluation of programs in relationship to these targets, charging of fees for services that may or may not have been provided otherwise, decentralized administrative structures, and performance budgeting (Jones & Newburg, 2002).

In the UK, the neoliberal concern with 'effective' management techniques, market-oriented governance structures, and a strong emphasis on the role of expertise were all being pressed forward by a range of Inquiries and Acts in the mid-1990s. In 1992, the Inquiry into Police Responsibilities and Rewards (the Sheehy Inquiry) focused on the internal management of police forces (UK Home Office, 1993a). Patrick Sheehy, a prominent businessman, made 272 recommendations for reform, many of which reflected the ideas of NPM and other corporatist management techniques. The reforms met heavy resistance from police unions, with the most contentious proposals being those that were 'driven by market forces: lower starting salaries and allowances, performance related pay, and fixed-term appointments' (Leishman, Cope, & Starie, 1995).

Soon after the Sheehy Inquiry, the government published a White Paper on Police Reform (UK Home Office, 1993b). The White Paper focused on the wider governance of policing within the UK. It suggested that policing was being damaged by overlapping and confusing lines of responsibility and accountability; the tripartite structure of policing had led to police forces becoming inflexible, resistant to change, fiscally unaccountable, and ineffective. Like the Sheehy Inquiry, the White Paper recommended imposing private sector management techniques, and also devolving decision-making responsibility to local police commanders in order to provide autonomy and choice to localities in setting priorities and funding programs (Cope, Leishman, & Starie, 1997).

Many of the White Paper's recommendations were incorporated into the version of the Police and Magistrates' Courts Act (PMCA) of 1994 that was introduced into the House of Lords. Although, following stiff resistance from police officers and unions, many of the more controversial reforms were cut from the final draft of the legislation; the Act still introduced a number of neoliberal reforms. The Act gave police authorities the duty of establishing an 'efficient and effective' police force for its designated area, and it associated efficiency with the creation of local policing plans and the implementation of performance targets (Police and Magistrates' Courts Act, 1994). At the beginning of each fiscal year, the policy authority had to establish a set of local policing objectives, taking into account national and local goals. Then, at the end of the financial year, it had to compile an annual report showing how the local policing plan had been carried out to what degree of success. In general, the Act gave a legal basis to the neoliberal concern with corporate management strategies based on financial planning, performance targets, evaluation, and managing by results. In the words of one set of observers

> Despite a parliamentary mauling, the PMCA further centralised the 'steering', while decentralising the 'rowing' of the police. Though chief constables have more managerial control over their police forces, Home Office hands are firmly placed on the rudder in its attempt to steer the police in the 'right' direction. (Cope et al., 1997)

Finally, the Home Office Review of Police Core and Ancillary Tasks, more commonly known as the Posen Inquiry, examined the services being delivered by public police forces (UK Home Office, 1995). The Posen Inquiry's findings, published in 1995, divided the services being performed by public police into two categories: core and ancillary. It recommended that police promote cost-efficiency by changing their delivery systems for their core tasks and by transferring responsibility for many of their ancillary tasks to other public or private agencies (Cope et al., 1997).

Taken together, these inquiries, reports and Acts exemplify the policies and governance of neoliberal reform: experts, from private industry or executive agencies, reviewed the internal management and governance of public police forces and argued for reforms based on market principles and private-sector management styles to cut costs and improve performance.

The neoliberal reforms went some way toward turning police departments into providers of services in competition with other agencies for resources and customers. They also introduced fragmentation within police departments, creating teams and groups who are in competition with one another for scarce resources. Both within departments and between departments and other providers of security services, the police are under greater pressure to demonstrate their effectiveness in deterring crime, enforcing the law, and using resources appropriately. Nonetheless, we should not overestimate the extent to which the reforms have their intended effects. For a start, NPM and related reforms have often turned out to depend on just the kind of top-down managerial authority that they purportedly set out to overcome; the new managerialism often strengthens the oversight and control of administrators and managers over rank and file officers even if it shifts the mode of control from formal rules to financial audits. In addition, we should be wary of the assumption that the reforms have transformed the practices of rank and file in the ways that neoliberals hoped.

The Community Narrative

Intellectually, the community-oriented narrative of police reform renews a belief in empirical social theory. Although it eschews the positivism and top-down ethos that characterized much of the progressive narrative, it draws on theories of governance that arose out of similar strands of empirical social science. Like the more general shift to networks and partnerships, it draws heavily on theories such as the new institutionalism, communitarianism, and organization theory (Bevir, 2005). These theories all reject the deductive ethos of neoclassical economics; they defend empirical studies of social facts against deductive conclusions based on micro-level assumptions. Yet, these theories also share a loose concern to broaden the concept of an institution or organization to cover informal ones based on norms as well as more formal ones defined by laws or rules; they focus as much on networks as on hierarchies. The community narrative draws on such theories to portray networks and partnerships as preferable to both bureaucracies and markets. The proliferation of networks and partnerships across the public sector in the UK, US, and elsewhere is well documented. Networks are integral to the increasingly popular appeals to holistic governance or 'whole of government' strategies. The proponents of network governance argue that it combines the flexibility of markets with the long-term stable relationships of hierarchies. They also argue that it is peculiarly conducive to the kind of innovation needed in a globalizing world. In policing, the community narrative has inspired both networked approaches to security and a new version of the concern with partnerships between police, community, and public (Fleming & Wood, 2006). It is fast becoming a commonplace that police, whether they like it or not, now have to operate in and through local, national, and international networks.

Advocates of community-oriented approaches argue that the police fight crime more effectively, if they involve communities as co-producers in the attempt to promote public safety. The argument is that, at least in contemporary society, a comprehensive strategy toward crime prevention must combine the resources of many different public, voluntary, and private sector groups. Policing, thus, appears to require the formation and management of networks based on partnerships between the police, other public agencies, community groups, and citizens.

Like neoliberal reformers, community-oriented reformers often seem to be mainly concerned to promote efficiency. Yet, the community narrative also incorporates more normative, democratic themes. Networks and partnerships are advocated as means of increasing public participation and promoting social inclusion. Indeed, the community narrative often comes across as a reassertion of social democratic ideals against the more individualistic and market vision of neoliberals. It argues for increased participation by community members in policy-making and suggests that such participation can serve, in particular, as a way of including socially marginal groups. Certainly, policy documents often laud community policing for being sensitive and responsive to the needs and fears of citizens. The UK National Policing Plan for 2005–2008 suggests, for example, a 'citizen-focused police service which responds to the needs of communities and individuals, especially victims and witnesses, and inspires public confidence in the police, particularly among minority ethnic communities' (UK Home Office, 2004a).

Community policing arose in the 1960s and 1970s as something of a grassroots movement by rank and file officers who felt powerless in the face of rising crime rates and increasing social unrest. In the US, it was developed and sustained at the local level in cities such as Detroit, New York, Madison, and Portland. But, more recently, a new type of community policing, often arising in part from the evaluation research of the 1970s and 1980s, has given a heavy emphasis to partnerships and networks, and it is this type of community policing that is now being championed as a reform program by members of the political and administrative elite.

The new type of community policing became increasingly visible in the US following an Executive Session on the Police at Harvard University from 1985 to 1990. This Executive Session was funded by the National Institute of Justice, part of the Department of Justice. It brought together social scientists and police chiefs with the explicit aim of developing a new approach to policing and crime prevention (Bayley, 1998). Today then, although 'community policing' can refer to widely different visions, it is typically associated with increased consultation with members of the community, increased flexibility through decentralization, increased partnerships with other agencies and community organizations, and a problem-oriented approach to crime prevention (Bayley, 1998).

The new type of community policing has already had an impact on legislation in the United States and the UK. The Federal government now funds community policing through the Office of Community Oriented Policing Services (COPS), which was established by the Violent Crime Control and Law Enforcement Act of 1994. The COPS office has handed out more than $11 billion in grants to local communities to implement more community oriented policing strategies, including the hiring of extra officers to patrol neighborhoods (US Department of Justice, 2006). In the UK, the Police Reform Act of 2002 expanded not only the powers of the Secretary of State but also the role of the local community in the police force. Part 4 of the act allows for the creation of 'community safety accreditation schemes' (Police Reform Act, 2002) that are supposed to combat crime and increase safety by having civilian officers patrol the streets. These community schemes allow for law enforcement powers (those granted to official constables) being given to civilian employees provided that they identify themselves by means of some sort of uniform badge, and provided that they work within guidelines established by the chief officer overseeing the scheme. The government aims to provide support for 25,000 Community Support Officers by 2008 (UK Home Office, 2004b). Other aspects of the community narrative have received an airing in a recent UK Home Office Green Paper (UK Home Office, 2004c). This Green Paper, 'Policing: Building Safer Communities Together,' emphasizes the importance of 'joint working' and 'policing by cooperation,' and it identifies the private sector as a key 'partner' in tackling crime.

LOCAL PERSPECTIVES ON REFORM

Policing has been subject to a host of reforms based on neoliberal and community narratives. Yet, the mere fact that elites enact reforms does not mean that those affected by the reforms respond as expected. To properly understand the effects of the reforms, we have to examine the ways in which local officers and others have responded to them from within their own local cultures. The suspicion must surely be that the reform narratives have relied on deductive models or sweeping social theories that do not allow sufficiently for such local cultures and so have generated false expectations about the consequences they are likely to have. All too often reform initiatives simply do not fit with the day to day experiences of rank and file officers at least as they understand those experiences. Hence, serving officers necessarily adapt and modify the reform strategies in an attempt to respond to the dilemmas thrown up by their experiences. The actual practice of policing, like other occupations and identities, is a 'constant process of adaptation, subversion and re-inscription' of meanings and practices (Davies & Thomas, 2003). In short, far from the narratives of reform remaking policing in their own image, they have created dilemmas for police officers, and policing has then been remade by the diverse ways in which the officers have responded to these dilemmas.

An Ethnographic Taster

To give a taste of how police officers have responded to the reforms, we offer a set of quotations from two major ethnographic studies.[1] We then go on to cite a number of themes from these studies. While these are all over-simplified generalizations, we would suggest, in part to make the contrast with the idea that the reforms have remade policing that (a) bureaucracy still exists, (b) markets are resisted, (c) community reforms are neglected, and (d) constant reform has become self-defeating.

On bureaucracy

* 'There is still a command and control mentality within the service and [a sense] that the police have no ownership of what goes on.'
* 'They pay a lot of lip service to the notion that we have a corporate mentality – no rank distinction – everyone can say what they want, but believe you me when you step out of line, the military line comes right back and if you want to get on you are not going to be part of a frank discussion.'

On neoliberal reforms

- 'When I arrived, in the order of 110 performance measures were being proposed! We got it down to 75 in the end but it was difficult. I couldn't believe it when I saw the rising crime figures and this ongoing preoccupation with things like how many forensic tests we might perform in any one year. There didn't seem to be a concern about crime at all at this point.'
- 'I think we shouldn't sort of minimise just how serious it is and I keep saying to officers, you know "to actually arrest somebody and take somebody's liberty away is a very, very major event" and so to see them if you like, in consumerism terms, it sort of wears a little bit thin, probably for them more than us.'
- 'I think the thing is, for me, that the public actually as a rule have to take the service that they get, they can't actually go out and say, "I don't actually like the way X Police do this so I'm going to see if I can phone through and get Y Police to come and do it, because on such and such scales they deal with my type of incident in a far better way."'

On community policing

- 'I think your biggest problem will be the culture. It's still isolated, a "boy's own" club – community policing means beat policing to them [rank and file officers] and they don't do that well. They don't like all this touchy feely stuff.'

On continuous reform

- '[The force] is change weary. Since 1990, it has been one major upheaval after another. The [last Commissioner] had big ideas, and [so did] the Commissioner before him. They would go around telling it how it was but every time there was a change of management, there was another reorganization. Police are so fed up with this, that the [current] Commissioner has decreed that any further change must be incremental.'

Bureaucracy Still Exists

As the first two quotations suggest, bureaucratic modes of governance are still pervasive within policing. Command and control continue to be, in many ways, the guiding principles of police departments even after decades of reforms aimed at breaking down the walls of bureaucracy and eliminating red tape. Many police officers do not think that markets or networks are appropriate to what they still regard as core parts of the job. At least parts of policing involve a kind of danger that, in their view, is best dealt with by having clear lines of command and clear decision-makers. Hence, when police officers perceive themselves as facing a dilemma between the dictates of the job and the rhetoric of markets and networks, they are likely to fall back to the kind of command and control bureaucracy that they know and often also think is appropriate. It might seem that our interpretation lends credence to complaints about police conservatism and their resistance to change; yet such complaints ignore the lived experience of the police. For them, the question is not whether or not to embrace change; it is how to make a proposed change work given the nature of their life-world and job. Bureaucracy still exists because it has a number of very clear advantages. Perhaps the main advantage of bureaucracy is that it imposes order in a world composed of seemingly incompatible demands.

Markets are Resisted

Many reform narratives, when first implemented, create seemingly impossible demands of rank and file officers. Yet, officers seem especially resistant to neoliberal reforms. They are skeptical of the relevance of corporate governance mechanisms to crime prevention. Some believe that the neoliberal reforms question not only how police officers go about their business, but also the very identity of police officers (Davies & Thomas, 2003). Hence, while performance indicators and outcome measurements have been introduced to policing, many officers treat them as words without meaning or a type of rhetoric to which they need to pay lip service without modifying their practices. The third quotation highlights police skepticism of corporate management techniques. The officer clearly takes the high-level discussions of performance measures to be more or less irrelevant to law enforcement. Some officers believe that the neoliberal reforms have simply taken resources and time away from the battle against crime. They do not necessarily deny that performance measurement is important. But they do typically believe that the neoliberal reforms have introduced performance measurements that simply do not provide an adequate picture of crime prevention programs; productivity (filings and fingerprinting operations), fiscal status (per capita costs of service), and performance (crime rates in the Uniform Crime Report) may be easy to quantify but they are not adequate measures of police effectiveness or efficiency (Wadman & Bailey, 1993).

Such skepticism means that NPM is unlikely to be effectively implemented; perhaps it is doomed to fail.

Neoliberals clearly need to make the case to officers that managerial reforms are linked to crime prevention. Alternatively, they need to make the case that officers should conceive their job in terms that pay less attention to crime prevention. Part of the issue here is, as the fourth and fifth quotes suggest, that most officers perceive a clear tension between the need to ensure public safety and the neoliberal ideal of promoting choice for consumers. They are far from convinced by attempts to redefine the police as service providers and citizens as their consumers. At the very least this redefinition ignores the authority and power that are built into the law, and at times it also seems to ignore or at least neglect the idea that security and law and order constitute public, not just private goods. Policing is, at least to those engaged in it, not a commodity but a public service vital to a functioning society. Once again, then, we have a gap between the narratives that inspire the reforms and the local police cultures in which the reforms have to be made to operate.

Community Reforms are Neglected

While community-policing efforts have not faced as much resistance from rank and file officers as have neoliberal reforms, this is in part because serving officers see themselves as already involved in partnerships and networks where appropriate. One problem here is perhaps the vagueness of the concepts of partnership and network. If a police officer talks regularly with local businesses, does that constitute a network? Do visits to local schools count as partnerships? The community reforms have tended to encourage the police to work through networks and partnerships while being perilously thin on concrete proposals for such working and how to put it into effect. It is all too easy for police officers to define their existing activities in terms of the reforms. If they do so, they domesticate the reforms, removing from them any real sense of a need for dramatic changes to existing practices.

Resistance to community reforms arises when police officers perceive them as placing additional emphasis on parts of the job with which they are unsympathetic. As the sixth quotation suggests, community-oriented policing is associated with routine patrols and the personal touch. Yet, many police officers consider such activities to be unexciting and, in many case, as simply ineffective in combating crime. It is perhaps worth adding that many social scientists would argue that the evaluation research of the 1970s and 1980s showed that these police officers are right: having a lot of highly visible officers on the streets is not necessarily an effective way of reducing crime, and may even be inappropriate in some situations (Bayley, 1998). Hence, police officers can be faced with a dilemma in trying simultaneously to meet the demands of the community-orientated reforms and the neoliberal ones. Once again, the reformers need to make the case that community activities are an effective way to combat crime, or to convince officers to rethink their job in terms of, say, promoting a sense of personal security among the public. When neither case is made, the rank and file does not buy into the reforms, so they remain top-down initiatives that are ignored if not actively resisted.

Constant Reform is Self-Defeating

Studies of the ways police officers have responded to the reform narratives help to explain the limited success of the reforms. The reforms have been constructed out of forms of expertise that rely on form models and social theories rather than dialog with those they will affect. They embody a top-down approach that has failed to secure buy-in from rank and file officers or even to explore whether the requirements of the reforms have a suitable fit with the lived experience of the officers. Hence, police officers have found themselves having to negotiate dilemmas that arise from the tensions between the reforms and their local cultures. They have had to interpret the reforms to try to make them fit with their experience. Crucially, when the police interpret the reforms, they transform them, resisting them or domesticating them in ways that have consequences unforeseen and certain unintended by the advocates of the reforms. All too often, moreover, this whole process becomes reiterative. The reforms meet with police skepticism, the way the police respond to them generates unintended consequences, the negative consequences then inspire another set of reforms that again meets with local skepticism, and so on.

The continuous process of reform soon will reach, if it has not already reached, a point where police are so weary of reform that they become increasingly immovable. Constant reform undermines morale and breeds ever-greater skepticism about reform. Declining morale and growing skepticism, especially if combined with confusion among officers about what is required of them and how that translates into their daily practice, erodes the ability of the police to enforce the law and to protect the public.

It would be foolish to ignore the extent to which police forces need to change. But, equally, the quote suggests that too many different waves of reform following to quickly upon one another might produce not change but an exhausted inertia.

THE FALLACY OF EXPERTISE

We have found a gap between elite narratives of reform and local police cultures, a gap that helps explain the limited impact of the reforms, their unintended consequences, and the continuous nature of reform. This gap clearly bears some resemblance to what is often described as the 'implementation gap' (Dunsire, 1978). Equally, however, our approach and also our account of local police practices, suggests that the concept 'implementation gap' can miss key issues. There is nothing amiss with the broad concept of an implementation gap that arises from a lack of understanding between top-level strategists and the mid-level and street-level managers or bureaucrats who independently implement the strategy. But all too often this broad concept carries narrower connotations that explain the gap in terms of the failings, intransigence, conservatism, or self-interest of those working at the mid-level and street-level. To dramatize our doubts about these narrower connotations, we might say that whereas an 'implementation gap' points to failings at the local level, we are pointing at least as much to failings in the elite narratives of reform. Perhaps, we should talk less of an 'implementation gap' and more of 'the fallacy of expertise.'

Narrower concepts of the 'implementation gap' locate the problem as a lack of follow through by street-level bureaucrats. The implication is that policies are poorly implemented due to the intransigence or vested interests of lower level public officials. The practicality of elite policy-making based on expert knowledge, thus, goes more or less unquestioned. Indeed the solution appears, in this view, to be to limit the discretion, i.e. give to field agents, binding their actions with more rules and procedural requirements, and thereby ensuring that they do as the elites and experts intended. Yet our perspective suggests, to the contrary, that the problems arise not because of the unreasonable or self-interested nature of street-level bureaucrats but because of the limitations of elite policy-making based primarily on the formal models or abstract theories of social scientists.

The fallacy of expertise consists of the assumption that discretion could be avoided, or, to put it differently, that public policy could be comprehensive, clear, and self-defining. People generally adopt the fallacy of expertise whenever they ignore the contingent and contestable nature of action, and, consequently, the open-ended diversity of the cases to which street-level bureaucrats might have to respond. The fallacy arises here because people assume, as much social science encourages them to, that contingency and contest can be tamed, and action predicted, by means of knowledge of, say, formal models, statistical correlations, and social laws. They assume that expertise gives them generalizable knowledge of human action, institutions and their effects, and they apply this generalizable knowledge to construct policies that are supposed to be applicable and have certain effects more or less irrespective of local cultures and local circumstances. So, for example, police reform has often been defined by narratives that purport to tell us how expertise, bureaucracy, markets, or networks will operate, and the benefits they will bring, largely irrespective of things such as particular policy fields, diverse traditions of citizenship and local economic cultures.

In the case of police reform, the fallacy of expertise neglects (a) competition among elite narratives, (b) the limited buy-in to elite narratives, and (c) the impossibility of narratives fixing their application to particular cases. All too often the reformers have not recognized the particularity of their own narrative, the importance of including actual police officers in the policy development process, or the variable and open-ended nature of the cultures and actions within which and to which the reforms will have to apply.

Consider, first, competition among elite narratives. Reformers often overlook the particularity of their own reform narrative. They forget that other reformers, policy actors, and citizens have different narratives about the nature of policing, its failings, and how to improve it. Yet, as we have shown, police reform has come as down in various, often incompatible measures inspired by competing narratives. Given competing narratives and reforms, police officers simply are not confronted by a consistent and coherent agenda. To the contrary, they are confronted with conflicting elite narratives and demands. Hence, they have to interpret and negotiate among these narratives to try to forge a single perspective that is consistent enough for them to act upon it. What is more, police officers have, as we have also shown, their own narrative, and they necessarily deploy their understanding of their job and what it requires in attempting to make sense of the demands of the competing reform narratives. Rank and file officers interpret the often conflicting policy guidance that is passed down from the elite in a way that reflects their own culture and their own experiences. Police officers resist or reinterpret reforms because they are struggling to make sense of conflicting demands in a way that will enable them to act in the way that they believe their job requires.

Let us turn now to the limited buy-in to elite narratives. The top-down view of the policy process held by many reformers means that local police departments and rank and file officers are often only cursorily consulted about reform programs. On the one hand, this can indeed create resistance from rank and file officers. The rank and file does not appreciate being told what to do by outsiders, especially outsiders whom they perceive as unacquainted, or at least out of touch, with the daily demands of their job. No doubt reforms imposed by outsiders are likely to spawn resistance in almost any occupation. Such resistance is especially likely, moreover, in areas like policing in which there is often a long-established and deeply entrenched culture of in-group preference and out-group hostility. Local police culture often encourages the view that reforms have been developed by individuals who have never 'worn the badge' and do not understand the daily challenges facing officers. Reformers need to do more to secure prior buy-in from rank and file officers, or the professional organizations that represent them, if they want the rank and file to have a sense of ownership over the reforms.

Consider, finally, the impossibility of narratives fixing their application to cases. How reforms operate depends on how people interpret them within local cultures, and how people interpret them is not fixed in advance but is rather the result of a creative, if situated, agency. Hence, the reformers simply cannot know in advance what kinds of circumstances rank and file police will confront. They cannot specify a complete set of rules telling officers how they should act in all possible circumstances. What is more, the rules they do provide are necessarily rather abstract, so the application of these rules or guidelines to any given police force or situation necessarily involves something like a creative act of interpretation. Police officers are, in other words, bound to interpret the reforms if only in an attempt to apply them to particular contexts.

The narrow concept of an implementation gap embodies an over-simplified account of the policy process that leads, in turn, to a largely negative view of local discretion. We have suggested, in contrast, that the policy process is contested, incomplete, and open-ended, so local discretion is inevitable. Police officers have no option but to act creatively in attempts to address the dilemmas thrown up by the gap between policies and their experiences (Lipsky, 1980). What is more, we would add, they are no more bound to be conservative and self-interested in their discretionary acts than they are to be radical and other-regarding. We should no more demonize them than romanticize them.

DEMOCRACY, CITIZENSHIP, AND PARTICIPATION

The fallacy of expertise encourages policy-makers to underestimate the importance of involving the targets of a policy in its formulation. The participation of street-level bureaucrats and citizens in the policy-making process might increase the effectiveness of policy-making. It is also, of course, a democratic issue. It is, moreover, a democratic issue that most of the reform narratives play down in part because of their over-riding concern with effectiveness and efficiency and in part because they are tied to a representative concept of democracy rather than a more participatory one.

It is true, of course, as we saw earlier, that the reform narratives are linked to somewhat different views of democracy. Nonetheless, they all share a commitment to representative democracy as a primary way of holding accountable a policy-making process that is largely left to experts with little space for popular participation. The clearest example is no doubt the progressive narrative; within the progressive narrative, citizens are voters who assess politicians and their policies through periodic elections – the democratic endorsement of reform proposals is sustained through regular, free, and fair elections. Yet, while the neoliberal and community narratives rethought the citizen, they did not thereby endorse notably greater participation in the policy-making process.

The neoliberal narrative redefined the citizen as being also a consumer. It implied that we could exercise choice and held others accountable by acting as consumers within market-like settings at least as adequately as we could by voting. Citizens choose or buy the services they prefer, and they punish those who behave badly by withdrawing their custom. Yet, while the neoliberal narrative offers a different vision of citizenship, it still leaves it up to others to construct policies; others produce the policies and services that citizens then choose whether or not to buy. Indeed, neoliberals relied on expert assertions of the benefits of the market to the extent that they were more than willing to impose markets upon citizens apparently for their own good even if the citizens vehemently objected.

The community narrative stresses partnerships and networks to increase public involvement in the policy process. Citizen review boards, task forces, and community support officers have formed partnerships that involve rank and file officers and the public. Citizens are meant to be active. They provide democratic input and endorsement to policing activities by meeting and talking – directly airing grievances or giving support – to their beat officer or their local department. Performance measurements now often include ones designed to assess how the local community feels the police are doing. Yet, the community narrative is still one that calls for more widespread participation in policy implementation precisely because policy experts now argue that such participation leads to more efficient and effective public policy. The formulation of public policies is still based on expert discourses about networks, partnerships, and inclusion. There is, after all, a difference between engaging in dialog with community members and granting citizens actual powers of policy-making or policy-oversight.

We do not mean to deny that the neoliberal and, more especially, the community narrative can lead to significantly greater public choice and involvement in policing. We do want to point out, however, that the extent and moment of choice and involvement are restrained by the fallacy of expertise. Typically, choice and involvement act as ways of endorsing or evaluating reform programs, rather than formulating them. Likewise, choice and involvement typically apply to how local police forces are doing in the context of a national agenda based on relatively fixed assumptions about the importance of markets or, alternatively, networks and partnerships. Hence, although each reform narrative has its own view of how police reform might be endorsed by the affected community, they gave similarly limited roles to rank and file officers and to citizens in the process of policy-formation. They relied on technocratic expertise to craft reforms that were then imposed on local police cultures.

We would suggest that the restrictions that the reform narratives place on choice and involvement help to explain the skepticism with which they have often been met. Skeptics view community-oriented policing reforms, for example, as little more than exercises in public relations. They argue that community policing neglects a genuine concern to integrate police departments into their communities in favor of a concern to secure public support for policing activities; community policing has become little more than an exercise to improve the public image of policing (Loader, 1997).

We would also suggest, more generally, that the reform narrative's privileging of expertise, effectiveness, and efficiency has led to inadequate thought being given to the impact of the reforms on democratic practices. Consider the relationship of the neoliberal reforms to ideals of account-ability and equity. Private police are not under the same legal and constitutional restrictions as public police forces. Often they are neither directly accountable to voters nor indirectly accountable by way of politicians. Sometimes the only way they can be held accountable is by having a license or contract cancelled. Moreover, citizen-consumers enter the market for policing with very different levels of wealth and power. The current distribution of wealth in advanced democracies means that well-to-do citizens, neighborhoods, and commercial interests are far more able to afford private security than are poorer ones, but it is typically the latter who suffer the worst effects of crime. Consider now the relationship of community-orientated reforms to ideals of accountability and equity. A proliferation of networks and partnerships generally blurs the clear lines of authority and responsibility that sustained older notions of accountability. Moreover, police officers and citizens are likely to have different resources (time, money, knowledge) that influence the likelihood of their becoming members of commissions, task forces, and citizen boards, let alone having a decisive impact upon them.

The fallacy of expertise has lead to reforms that neglect both local police cultures and democratic ideals. Perhaps, it is time we turned instead to more participatory forms of policy-making, allowing citizens, and rank and file officers a far greater role. Perhaps a more bottom-up approach to police reform will bring greater success in implementing reforms. Perhaps, it also will provide a participatory solution to some of the problems that now confront attempts to reconcile increasingly complex policing networks with concepts of accountability associated with representative democracy.

Workplace democracy in particular remains, of course, an alien practice to most police forces. Nonetheless, a few police departments, mainly in the US, have begun to reorganize their leadership structures so as to increase the opportunities for participatory decision-making. In Madison, Wisconsin, the police have replaced their old top-down management structure with a 'Quality Policing' approach. The new approach involved organizational decentralization, greater employee participation in policy discussions and decisions, and the promotion of a healthy working environment in which employees were viewed as 'internal customers' (Wycoff & Skogan, 1994). The Broken Arrow Police Department in a suburban area of Oklahoma has similarly introduced what appears to be a successful expansion of participatory management techniques. The Broken Arrow Chief of Police gave rank and file officers a say in departmental procedure, including extensive decision-making powers, and the result seems to have been increased morale and efficiency as well as a greater willingness to engage in community-oriented policing (Wuestewald, Steinheider, & Bayerl, 2006).

CONCLUSION

To conclude, we have argued that to explain changes in policing over the past 50 years in the UK and the US, we must look to the three main narratives that have inspired successive reform agendas – the progressive, neoliberal, and community narrative. These narratives draw upon different approaches to social science to advocate different modes of governance associated with different democratic ideals. The apparent transition from bureaucratic modes of organization toward markets and networks has arisen, in other words, as the neoliberal and community narratives rose to dominance in place of the older progressive narrative.

We also have emphasized that these narratives were typically elite ones. They inspired elite programs of reform. But they did not necessarily have much impact upon local police cultures. To the contrary, the reforms have often failed to have anything like the consequences that the elites anticipated precisely because they have not meshed with local police cultures. At a local level, we have suggested that we find that bureaucracy still persists, markets are resisted, community reforms are neglected, and the constant waves of reform have sapped the morale of police officers, at times producing a kind of tired and cynical sclerosis. The failure of reformers to allow for local police cultures reflects the dominance of a mistaken belief in the value of expertise in policy-making.

Finally, we have suggested that this emphasis on expertise means that while recent reforms may have striven to increase choice and involvement in policing, they still place severe restraints on participation in decision-making by rank and file officers and by citizens. If reformers more fully expanded internal democratic practices, using police officers as agents of change, then they might have more success in the implementation of their reform programs. Moreover, the neoliberal and community-orientated reforms have had a number of unintended consequences, including resource scarcity and problems of accountability and equity, all of which arguably pose dilemmas for policy-makers that might indeed prompt them to adopt more participatory approaches to policing.

A more participatory approach to policing might resolve problems of public policy and democracy. It also might have a salutary impact on our national identities. Certainly, some scholars have argued that policing has special salience in shaping shared identities. The symbolic link between police and the state 'is capable of framing a deep commitment to the idea of the nation as a community of attachment, to a political community whose members can legitimately lay claim to certain rights, and acknowledge certain mutual responsibilities, simply on account of being members of that community' (Loader & Walker, 2001, p. 24). Police officers play important roles in the construction of national imaginaries whether as 'New York's finest' or as 'bobbies on the beat' (Loader, 1997). For many critics, neoliberalism undermined just these kinds of national identities; it emphasized a selfish individualism that eroded community. Yet, the attempt to forge a new type of community-orientated policing sometimes projects a homogeneous national identity based on shared values. Is it possible that a more participatory approach to the governance of policing, one that involved local officers and local citizens, might help to foster both a broad commitment to democratic values and a greater awareness of the plural, overlapping, contingent, and contestable nature of the identities that make up many modern societies?

NOTE

1. One study by Jenny Fleming was based on interviews with senior officer and focus group meetings with officers of all ranks in the UK and Australia in 2003. For details see Fleming and Rhodes (2005), and Fleming (2006). The other, led by John Clarke and Janet Newman, was based on interviews and other ethnographic techniques involving all kinds of public service providers and citizens in the UK. For details see Clarke, Newman, Smith, Vidler, and Westmarland (2006), and Clarke (2007). We are grateful for permission to draw on them.

REFERENCES

Bayley, D. (1998). *What works in policing*. Oxford: Oxford University Press.
Bayley, D., & Shearing, C. (1996). The future of policing. *Law and Society Review, 30*, 585–606.
Bevir, M. (1999). *The logic of the history of ideas*. Cambridge: Cambridge University Press.
Bevir, M. (2005). *New labour: A critique*. London: Routledge.
Clarke, J. (2007). 'It's not like shopping': Citizens, consumers and the reform of public services. In: M. Bevir & F. Trentmann (Eds), *Governance, citizens, and consumers: Agency and resistance in contemporary politics*. Basingstoke: Palgrave Macmillan.
Clarke, J., Newman, J., Smith, N., Vidler, E., & Westmarland, L. (2006). *Creating citizen-consumers: Changing publics and changing public services*. London: Sage.
Cope, S., Leishman, F., & Starie, P. (1997). Globalisation, new public management and the enabling state. *International Journal of Public Sector Management, 10*, 444–460.
Davies, A., & Thomas, R. (2003). Talking cop: Discourses of change and policing identities. *Public Administration, 81*, 681–699.
Dunsire, A. (1978). *Implementation in a bureaucracy*. Oxford: Martin Robertson.

Fleming, J. (2006). Working through networks: The challenge of partnership policing. In: J. Fleming & J. Wood (Eds), *Fighting crime together: The challenges of policing and security networks* (pp. 87–115). Sydney: University of New South Wales Press.

Fleming, J., & Rhodes, R. (2005). Bureaucracy, contracts and networks: The unholy Trinity and the police. *Australian and New Zealand Journal of Criminology, 38*.

Fleming, J., & Wood, J. (Eds). (2006). *Fighting crime together: The challenges of policing and security networks*. Sydney: University of New South Wales Press.

Johnston, L. (1992). British policing in the nineties: Free market and strong state? *International Criminal Justice Review, 2*, 1–18.

Johnston, L. (1999). Private policing in context. *European Journal on Criminal Policy and Research, 7*, 175–196.

Jones, T., & Newburg, T. (2002). The transformation of policing? *British Journal of Criminology, 42*, 129–146.

Leishman, F., Cope, S., & Starie, P. (1995). Reforming the police in Britain. *International Journal of Public Sector Management, 8*, 26–37.

Lipsky, M. (1980). *Street level bureaucracy: Dilemmas of the individual in public services*. New York: Sage.

Loader, I. (1997). Policing and the social: Questions of symbolic power. *British Journal of Sociology, 48*, 1–18.

Loader, I., & Walker, N. (2001). Policing as a public good: Reconstituting the connection between policing and the state. *Theoretical Criminology, 5*, 9–35.

Police and Magistrates' Courts Act. (1994). London, UK: Her Majesty's Stationery Office.

Police Reform Act. (2002). London, UK: Her Majesty's Stationery Office.

Sklansky, D. (2005). Police and democracy. *Michigan Law Review, 103*, 1699–1830.

UK Home Office. (1993a). *Inquiry into police responsibilities and rewards, Cm. 2280*. London: Stationery Office.

UK Home Office. (1993b). *Police reform: A police service for the 21st century, Cm. 2281*. London: Stationery Office.

UK Home Office. (1995). *Review of police core and ancillary tasks*. London: Stationery Office.

UK Home Office. (2004a). *National policing plan 2005–08: Safer, stronger communities*. London: Stationery Office.

UK Home Office. (2004b). *Building communities, beating crime: A better police service for the 21st century*. London: Stationery Office.

UK Home Office. (2004c). *Policing: Building safer communities together*. London: Stationery Office.

US Department of Justice (2006). Office of community oriented policing services website. *About Us*. http://www.cops.usdoj.gov

Wadman, R., & Bailey, S. (1993). *Community policing and crime prevention in America and England*. Chicago: Office of International Criminal Justice.

Wuestewald, T., Steinheider, B., & Bayerl, P. S. (2006). From the bottom up: Sharing leadership in a police agency. In: M. Marks & D. Sklansky (Conf. Org.), *Police reform from the bottom up* (pp. 313–355). Berkeley, CA: University of California, Berkeley.

Wycoff, M. A., & Skogan, W. G. (1994). Community policing in Madison: An analysis of implementation and impact. In: D. Bayley (Ed.), *What works in policing*. Oxford: Oxford University Press.

CHAPTER 7

POLICING THE 'IRRELEVANT': CLASS, DIVERSITY AND CONTEMPORARY POLICE CULTURE

Bethan Loftus

ABSTRACT

Using ethnographic material derived from an in-depth study of contemporary police culture, this chapter explores a contradiction which emerged between the police's organisational emphasis on diversity and axes of class. While efforts aimed at changing police culture both within and beyond the organisation focused on notions of equity, discrimination and diversity, it was predominantly poor and low-status white males who occupied a central position in the police's practical workload, and in their occupational consciousness. Taking class contempt as a relatively unexamined aspect of police culture, this chapter raises questions about the place of class in current 'policing diversity' debates.

The incremental slide away from [class] is marked as more than an economic retreat, it is also a retreat from regarding the white poor as 'people like us' – the white moral majority population. (Haylett, 2001, p. 358)

Police Occupational Culture: New Debates and Directions
Sociology of Crime, Law and Deviance, Volume 8, 181–204
Copyright © 2007 by Elsevier Ltd.
All rights of reproduction in any form reserved
ISSN: 1521-6136/doi:10.1016/S1521-6136(07)08007-4

INTRODUCTION

It is widely accepted that the characteristics of police culture[1] are not divorced from the wider organisational and societal context; rather, they both reflect and exacerbate the prevailing social structure (Reiner, 2000). Police culture, with its variants, thus illustrates the 'isomorphic relationship' (Reiner, 2000, p. 136) between the police and the wider arrangements of social disadvantage. A number of commentators have recently argued that late modern societies are increasingly characterised by widespread fragmentation, inequality and exclusion, in which a structurally marginal 'underclass' features prominently (Taylor, 1999; Young, 1999; Wacquant, 2000). In this new landscape Reiner (2000, p. 216) suggests that 'police property'[2] is 'far larger than ever before and more fundamentally alienated'. The issue of class, notwithstanding the widening of economic inequality, is of declining interest in current social thought and political practice, and one of the reasons for this is the sharp ascendance of culture and identity politics in recent decades, where culturally defined groups have emerged to defend their identities and seek recognition of their social differences (Fraser, 1997). While the general shift of attention from political economy to culture has served to de-centre class from discussions of social justice, it has also positioned the white poor in particular as 'illegitimate subjects' (Haylett, 2001). Residual from notions of recognition, multiculturalism and 'progress', this group is perceived as culturally burdensome and is subjected to a range of disparaging discourses (Charlesworth, 2000). Gender may also be a pertinent issue here, for as McDowell (2003) illustrates, it is the young white, working class male who is currently constructed as the embodiment of disorder and distaste.

The official concern with the promotion of 'diversity' has become increasingly relevant to the internal and external character of contemporary police organisations – not least in the post-Macpherson setting.[3] Yet, as I shall illustrate, the retreat of class from contemporary thinking and political practice is problematic as it permits class contempt and other forms of symbolic domination to persist largely unobserved and unchallenged (Sayer, 2005). Drawing on ethnographic material collected from a provincial English police force, this chapter accordingly aims to illustrate how aspects of class pervade the daily narratives and interactions of officers. What emerges is an apparent contradiction between axes of class and the highly concentrated police organisational emphasis on questions of diversity. While efforts aimed at changing police culture, both within and beyond the organisation, focus on the promotion of equality of service to its culturally diverse 'publics' and the eradication of racism and other forms of discriminatory language and behaviour along the lines of gender and sexuality, it is predominantly poor and low-status white males who continue to occupy centre field both in the practical workload of the police and in their occupational consciousness. In this setting, a prominent aspect of police culture has been the class contempt displayed towards this (class) grouping. And even if disparagement of the poor was only rarely articulated in explicitly class terms, the classed component of the contempt exhibited towards such targets was plain enough. In reflecting a relatively unexamined aspect of police culture, this chapter accordingly also raises some questions about the place of class in current 'policing diversity' debates.

The field notes reproduced here relate to the policing of what I shall refer to as Northville – an urban centre which has undergone dramatic de-industrialisation in recent years.[4] In attempting to uncover and explore their informal norms, values and assumptions, I spent 18 months accompanying officers of what I shall call 'Northshire' Police from a range of shifts and units as they went about their ordinary duties both on and off the streets.[5] Employing an ethnographic method based primarily on participant observation, I also conducted a number of focus group discussions and interviews with officers.[6] These constituted the more structured elements of the research and the aim was to capture officers' perceptions and attitudes towards their job and the immediate policing environment and also their understandings of recent national and local reform efforts. Following Norris (1994), I distinguished two types of data as particularly relevant in researching the occupational culture of officers: firstly, the way officers engaged in spontaneous *talk* with their colleagues, and secondly, descriptions of officers *doing* police work. As I did not wish to disrupt the setting, field notes were collected relatively inconspicuously and thus intermittently, during the shift. However, a full set of field notes was always reconstructed at the end of each shift, and as far as possible in all circumstances I aimed to record people, places, events and conversations.[7]

RETHINKING POLICE CULTURE AND THE OMNIPRESENCE OF CLASS CONTEMPT

Police ethnographies now span a number of decades and continue to be widely debated in contemporary discussions of policing and police culture (Banton, 1964; Skolnick, 1966; Westley, 1970; Cain, 1973; Punch, 1979;

Ericson, 1982; Holdaway, 1983; Smith & Gray, 1985; Young, 1991). The main focus has been the way in which the informal cultural norms and values of the police influenced police perceptions of, and conduct towards, those with whom they principally come into contact. A recurring theme in these ethnographies is the way in which low-status groups featured prominently in the occupational consciousness of police officers, and the idea that the police overwhelmingly deal with the least powerful and marginal groups in society is now something of an academic orthodoxy. While the common denominator among these perennial police targets is their social, economic and political powerlessness, the class-natured aspects of this have become obscured in recent years.

Contemporary understandings of police culture have been shaped by the findings of these classic ethnographies but it is also the case that, in present-day perspective, they reflect police environments and culture of an earlier and different social, economic and political context. Many of the studies were conducted over twenty years ago and more recent contributions have examined police culture in circumstances of social and political turmoil (Glaeser, 2000). We are left, therefore, with an account of police culture which largely predates many of the significant changes which have since taken place in police organisations and in newly identified social fields of policing. Changes in the internal and external policing landscape have altered both the composition of police organisations, and the character of the differing 'publics' that the police come into contact with. The classic 'police culture' paradigm which has been much invoked to describe and explain a range of police attributes is by now somewhat exhausted, and new lines of research and reflection are needed to track the shifts in the wider field of policing – a field which, as I illustrate, is increasingly characterised by widespread social, political and economic exclusion. Against such a background, I wish to appeal for a rethinking of police culture that recognises how class continues to permeate cultural knowledge and everyday practices.

Recent debates around police culture have, quite rightly, been concerned with police perceptions and treatment of differing groups along axes of ethnicity (Chan, 1997), gender (Westmarland, 2001) and sexuality (Burke, 1993), both within and beyond the policing organisation. However, while there has been a great deal of public and professional debate concerning the policing of these social divisions, police perceptions of the poor and their treatment of them have been largely ignored. This is especially the case with the white poor. Most studies acknowledge that the police have always controlled the lower strata, and indeed that their 'working rules' delineate such groups as problematic, but the issue of class receives explicit attention chiefly in the context of 'high' policing such as 'spectacular', and (in most Western democracies) relatively rare, occurrences of industrial conflict (see e.g. Scraton, 1985; Green, 1991). And even if we do find recognition in these circumstances of the classed dimension of relationships between the police and those policed, dramatic moments of this kind inevitably tend to be presented as somehow 'set apart' from ordinary life. But class is not just an occasional condition. Class is something that people live in and experience through their bodies and through their minds. And in equal measure to gender, ethnicity and sexuality, infusing as it does all daily human interactions, class has the latent potential to be a significant source of injury (Sennett & Cobb, 1972; see also Charlesworth, 2000).

My purpose in this chapter is to foreground the importance of class in a 'low'-policing context: class as it is policed in the *ordinary*, the routine and mundane dimensions of police work. What I hope to illustrate is that matters of class are highly relevant in understanding contemporary police culture. And the focus on the ordinary has crucial significance in the general retreat from class in current discussions of social justice (Fraser, 1997). A defining feature of symbolic domination is its capacity to persuade a subordinate group – through ideology and everyday practices and institutions – that certain moral, political and cultural occurrences are the 'natural order' of things. In the absence of a clear focus on aspects of class in current policing discussions, it is the ordinary and mundane disposition of police culture in regard to the poor which needs to claim our attention.

There has been no shortage of testimony to the ubiquity in British society of both blatant and subtle manifestations of class contempt towards the working class. Class contempt, as Sayer observes,

> like other kinds of 'othering', ranges from visceral revulsion, disgust and sneering, through to the tendency not to see or hear others as people, to the subtlest form of aversion. (Sayer, 2005, p. 163; see also Skeggs, 2004)

Not necessarily expressed verbally, it can reveal itself through subtle and 'theatrical' facial expressions – 'from the raising of the upper lip into a sneer' or 'from slightly grimaced smiles to aggressive sneers' (Sayer, 2005, p. 163). Class contempt is a potent force of 'othering', and as it preserves the myth that the lower strata are deficient in virtues that appertain to the majority, it also has an important role in reifying class relations. Although primarily experienced as an emotion, class contempt does have a tangible dimension which manifests itself through a person's response to visual and moral 'markers' including appearance, accent, language, demeanour, values, actions, possessions and lifestyle (Sayer, 2005). What is important here is that such signifiers of class serve as prompts for judgements of worth – or perhaps more to the point, of moral worth*lessness*. Describing someone as 'rough' or 'dirty' is a code for their perceived class and carries powerful moral connotations. At this most basic level, class contempt colours the way people are perceived and treated, and can profoundly affect someone's life chances (Sayer, 2005).

The police act as an important carrier and authoriser of class contempt. At an implicit level, the value choices reflected in their cultural knowledge (Chan, 1997), along with the routine attention devoted by the police to working-class crime and localities, serve to reinforce the more widely diffused disregard for the poor in society at large. More explicitly, the impunity with which officers focus on, and talk about (predominantly) the white poor also reiterates, or 'confirms', their status as legitimated targets of contempt.

As I shall illustrate, class contempt goes largely unchallenged in present-day policing organisations. Indeed, the official emphasis on respect for 'diversity' would appear to have the effect of delivering up young powerless white males as uncontentiously legitimate terrain for unchallenged exercise of police discretion and authority. This is not a politicised group, and police action against the 'roughs' has furthermore always had the support of the 'respectable' majority (Reiner, 2000).[8] Equally, as we shall see, in the post-Fordist economic arrangements of Northville, white male youth occupy large areas of public space where they are all the more likely to come into contact with the police.

In the new policing discourse – the contemporary organisational and operational policing context – of respect for diversity and recognition of cultural and gendered identities, the (enduring) dimension of class tends, I suggest, to disappear from view. I see this as further confirmation of the degree to which class issues – including outright class contempt – remain simply taken for granted and unheeded in policing practice.

CHANGING POLICE CULTURE IN NORTHSHIRE

The recent history of Northshire Police has seen its involvement in a top down drive to produce cultural change both within and beyond the organisation. The change initiative has focused both on improving the working conditions of personnel *inside* the organisation and on the delivery of an effective and equitable service to the various 'publics' *outside* the organisation – with a particular emphasis on equitable policing of ethnic minorities. In the wake of the Macpherson Report (1999), the Northshire initiative closely tracks corresponding approaches in recent years by other British police forces (Holdaway & O'Neill, 2004). Diversity issues feature prominently on the agenda of external inspecting bodies, and internally can be crucially significant in assessment ratings for individual career success – not just for senior personnel but increasingly for front-line officers too.

Attempts to change culture have many dimensions. Changes in policy and training, alterations in the composition of the workforce, introduction of internal cultural associations, reformulations of the organisation's guiding principles – specifically through 'community policing' philosophies – all represent ways in which change may be implemented (O'Neill & Holdaway, 2007; Holdaway & O'Neill, 2004; Cashmore, 2001, 2002). Harnessing together various such approaches, the change process in the Northshire force was driven principally through the vehicle of a 'Diversity Agenda'.

A core policy focus was the explicit official interdiction of discriminatory conduct. Expressions of racism were especially deplored and a strong disciplinary line was taken against racist comments or utterances within and outside the organisation. The message was communicated chiefly through internal channels in a campaign which also had recourse to an interesting range of organisational props extending to the physical architecture of the workplace – from posters promoting 'celebration of cultural difference' to anti-discrimination messages on police mouse pads and coffee cups. Officially at least, the organisation was saturated with notions of diversity and its 'recognition'. And while it is clearly possible that officers may now just choose their spaces or audiences more carefully when they express racist, sexist or homophobic sentiments, it was nonetheless unequivocally the case that a heightened awareness of the official hard-line against 'discrimination' permeated the organisation. At the very least, the present generation of Northshire officers *manage* their talk and behaviour somewhat differently from their predecessors.[9]

Externally, the recasting of diversity as a central policing concern focused particularly on equitable delivery to the community which the force was charged to serve. Equitable policing of ethnic minorities, gay and lesbian communities and (mainly female) victims of domestic violence was put high on the agenda – a more pro-active policing strategy towards their victimisation, better consultation with marginalised populations and improved community and race relations (CRR) training were just some of the ways in which the organisation linked questions of equality to new policing agendas. In short, the diversity agenda emphasised, and on some issues, *demanded* that officers afford just and fair regard and treatment to groups which have previously not been equitably served by policing.

Yet a fundamental contradiction emerged in the course of my study between the 'diversity' emphasis and axes of class. In the practicalities of routine police work, the policing of 'diversity' featured only minimally. Rather, officers overwhelmingly gave their attention to policing sections of the local 'underclass' – of which a large proportion were young white men. This was the group that occupied an overridingly prominent position in officers' occupational consciousness as socially defiling, problematic and in need of control. And to understand how and why such groups so regularly turned up as 'property' of Northville officers, we need to consider the occupational culture of these officers, along with their 'property', in the wider environmental context that shaped them both. In the observations that follow, it is not my intention to 'condemn' individual police officers (see Waddington, 1999) but rather to locate their dispositions within broader organisational, socio-economic and political currents.

DIRTY WORK IN 'BEIRUT' – POLICING THE 'IRRELEVANT'

For the Northshire officers, Northville presents a particularly disorganised and chaotic policing locality, a battlefield even – as their nickname for it, 'Beirut', implies – where they see themselves locked in a constant battle with marginal groups who would otherwise 'infest' the town. Mostly, it was the 'scrotes' who symbolised trouble in their minds. I will deal later with the etymology of this term, but it chiefly denoted poor and low-status white males. If policing has been described as a genus of 'dirty work' (Hughes, 1962, cited in Waddington, 1999, p. 299) then in 'Beirut' the police are essentially street cleaners. Their work is intrinsically linked to people who are profoundly disadvantaged and stripped of personal dignity: the homeless, drug addicts, alcoholics, prostitutes and those generally condemned to living in poverty. Northville officers saw themselves as the proverbial 'thin blue line' protecting the moral majority from those at the bottom of the social strata, and policing the 'scrotes' was their heroic and even exciting responsibilty. Their vision of themselves as bold venturers into the 'seedier' side of the world fed into their sense of solidarity, their moral conservatism, and also confirmed the demarcation of a common adversary.

For all the rich history of its heyday in heavy industry, coal mining and export manufactures, present-day Northville is now a place of severe and uniform social and economic decline with numerous factory closures and systematic withdrawals and relocations on the part of key employers. Economically, this is a zone of long-term and inter-generational unemployment, low income and wealth, low educational attainment and poor health. Spatially, the dramatic de-industrialisation has left a landscape of boarded up buildings, empty factories and derelict land with pockets of chronic poverty in large housing estates and run-down terraced streets. While local in consequence, these are symptoms of wider processes in which exclusion, fragmentation and inequality pervade the broad social structure.

In the marginal 'underclass' created (in contemporary Western and liberal democracies) where whole spheres of work are removed or disappear, there are distinctly gendered dimensions that we can observe. Increasingly, poor young men are the ones who predominantly constitute the 'never-employed' (Young, 1999), and are propelled in turn to live out more and more of their daily lives in public spaces. And Box (1994) reminds us how male unemployment is invariably flagged as a danger signal for its perceived association with crime and disorder. Against the backdrop of their social, political and economic marginalisation, present generations of young men struggle to construct some semblance of a masculine identity. Arrested masculinity manifests, in turn, in the contradictions of what Connell (1995) calls 'protest masculinity' – a term that usefully captures the way in which populations of young men come to occupy public street space and subsequently become implicated in certain types of street crime.[10]

In Northville, young men are particularly liable to be thus displaced. Compelled through lack of employment to occupy public, and thus *police*, space, they are a highly visible emblem of the post-Fordist paradigm – and, for the police, stand as the direct and evident embodiment of local 'disorder'. The manifest concentration of 'whiteness' in Northville means that the police frequently come into actual contact with young white men,[11] who then also stand forth as problematic in the occupational consciousness of these officers. And to understand just how they come to be targeted for denigration it is useful to reflect briefly on the significance of this 'whiteness'. Like any other skin 'colour', whiteness is a product of socio-cultural, historical, economic and psychological processes (Bonnett, 1998). Yet frequently it is assumed to be simply and purely a category of privilege: an assumption which is to obscure the complex history and contradictory socio-economic and political character of its ascription to this or that person

or group (Bonnett, 1998). In nineteenth-century Britain when racial purity
was emphasised, the urban white working class were excluded from any such
mark of privilege – they were not white *enough* (Bonnett, 1998). Today, in
contrast, in the current project of multiculturalism when the accent is on
cultural diversity, difference and recognition, it would seem that the white
poor are *too* white – 'offensively and embarrassingly white' (Haylett, 2001,
p. 355); that, indeed, their emblematic whiteness is what marks them out for
abuse and denigration.[12]

Concentrated populations of poor white people are liable to expose a
fundamental tension in the dominant systems of class and race-based
privilege. As Haylett (2001) suggests, for these dominant systems to
maintain their credibility, it is necessary to stigmatise aspects of working
class culture while at the same time segregating the working class into
groups along discourses of 'deservedness' – with the 'roughs' being set apart
from the aspiring 'respectable' working classes (Haylett, 2001). The police
perceive themselves as falling into the latter (Reiner, 2000) and in their work
discern between those they do things *for* and those they do things *to*
(Shearing, 1981). Yet in the context of the current study, this is seemingly
contradictory when the majority of front-line officers were overwhelmingly
white themselves. Despite being close in terms of ethnicity (white) and
gender (male) to their 'property', the police in the Northville study were not
sympathetic to this subject group and treated them with active disdain.

One explanation for this hinges directly on class in what Taylor (1999,
p. 17) identifies as the 'fear of falling'. In circumstances of economic
precariousness a fear of slipping in status permeates the social structure as a
'metaphorical displacement' of a wider set of fears about position in the
economic order. This kind of uncertainty breeds intolerance of the poor,
and manifests itself in the drawing of moral boundaries between those at the
bottom of the social strata and those who, for time being, are secure.
Officers in the Northville study came for the most part from (in general
parlance) a 'respectable' working class background; they also displayed a
strong adherence to strands of working class authoritarianism, and as
I illustrate, sought to distance themselves from social groups below them.
Ethnicity and gender afford privileges to white men in some spheres; in
others, their class position renders them subordinate (McDowell, 2003).
Stigmatisation of white poor males in police cultural knowledge as socially
impure and disruptive stands out in especially sharp relief when set against
the backdrop of the explicit police policy emphasis on acknowledging
diversity.

CLASSED PLACES, CLASSED PEOPLE

In the straitened social and economic context of Northville police officers constructed their cultural knowledge of the landscape and its populace according to some familiar themes in traditional police culture. They cast themselves as crime-fighters in ongoing adversarial competition with the roughs 'out there'. On 'the ground' (Holdaway, 1983) certain places stood out in the contingencies of their cultural knowledge about the *who* and *where* of 'trouble': impoverished public housing estates, terraced streets, derelict buildings and other areas to which the most marginalised are relegated.

While illustrating a typical interaction between the police and their 'property', the following field note demonstrates the way in which officers typically viewed lower working class areas as places to routinely target and gather intelligence – localities in which a *crime control* model of policing invariably took precedence over a *service* model. The extract records a night shift where I accompanied Scott and Andy, two young immediate response officers with whom I had been out on a number of occasions. The radio had been quiet and like many officers whom I observed they took the opportunity to do some 'pro-active' police work: in other words, not just random patrolling but actively seeking out places where they thought there was a chance of running across criminal activity and 'troublesome' individuals:

Scott and Andy decided it was time for some 'sneaky policing'. They drove to the Barracks council estate which was especially impoverished and known among some officers as 'scrote city'. They didn't like the layout of the estate because it has too many roads going in and out of it – 'the estate is like a rabbit warren, they can hide anywhere', Andy theorised. Switching the car lights off so we would not be seen, Andy drove slowly round and round the same run-down streets paying particular attention to public walkways and addresses of those 'known' to them. ... After half an hour they saw 4 young men sitting on a wall next to a street lamp, said 'right, here's some shit' and pulled up next to them. They were local men who were white, approximately aged between 17 and 22 and were smoking and drinking cans of beer. Andy asked them what they were doing out at this time of the night. They sheepishly murmured that they were just hanging around because there was nothing else to do. After making some small talk, Scott asked the group for their names, addresses and dates of birth and said 'will any of you be known to me'? They nervously said no and compliantly consented to the questioning. ... None of them were 'known' and we left. Once back in the car, Scott and Andy were pleased that they had gathered some more intelligence from the 'scrotes' off the Barracks estate – and were particularly pleased that the young men would go back and tell their associates about the encounter. For Scott and Andy, their presence would indicate to the rest of the 'scrotes' on the estate that the police 'were watching them'.

The Barracks is a large council estate with high levels of unemployment and general deprivation. For Northville police, this was a 'problem' locality with socially contaminating 'problem' people. 'Shit', as the collective here for young white lower working class males, is grammar that plainly enough captures the officers' disdain for the estate and its inhabitants. Nor were they necessarily out to make arrests. In the style of policing observed by Choongh (1998), they were content to 'informally discipline' and subordinate this section of the community – putting out the message that 'scrotes' on the estate were under surveillance.

The next instance is another illustration of how class is inscribed in police culture. Although rarely employing specific class *terminology*, officers routinely draw upon powerful class imagery and this featured heavily in their daily narratives:

> Tom asked me, 'has anyone told you what a scrote is yet'? After replying that no-one had, he offered me the following picture: 'scrotes' are 'the dregs of society', the 'lazy', 'unemployed scum' who reside on 'shit estates that should have walls built around them to stop them from leaving'. And just like their council houses, 'scrotes' are 'dirty', 'smelly' – and proximate towards being 'like animals'. Tom assured me that I would meet a lot of 'scrotes' over the coming 18 months – particularly in 'Beirut' where the policing of the high number of 'scrotes' in the area was like 'shovelling shit uphill'.

This field note was written after the first police shift I attended, and Tom's comments were made as he drove me around to acquaint me with the patrol area. I recall being surprised at the matter-of-fact disparagement of lower working class mores since this officer had otherwise presented himself as 'politically correct' – subscribing, at face value anyway, to the language and spirit of the force's diversity agenda. Indeed, moments earlier he had shown me where members of 'our local ethnic minority community' and 'our itinerant population' live. A number of important issues can be further unpacked from this field note.

First there is the term 'scrote' itself. In the company of Northville police this was a word that was constantly bandied about. Originating as a shortened version of 'scrotum', 'scrote'[13] was their specific descriptor, strongly loaded with meaning, for an identifiable section of the local community; for low-status groups who would be considered socially, economically and politically impoverished: drug addicts, the homeless, residents from run-down streets and estates, the unemployed hanging around in public space, and particular groups already 'known'[14] to the police. On the face of it the usage appears 'race' and gender neutral, but unequivocally this was an epithet to advertise, revile and implicitly define the low social, political and economic position of the person to whom it is being applied. And in practice, for the police, 'scrote' predominantly denoted 'young, poor, white male'. If we consider that the institution of privacy has in any case a class dimension (Stinchcombe, 1996), in an area where males of the community, predominantly 'white', have been especially displaced and thus relegated to living their lives in street space, the assigning of the term 'scrote' to this group may not be wholly surprising.

'Scrote' is a peculiarly derogatory epithet in the judgement it makes on the social, economic and cultural character of the local poor and powerless, and even without the explicit invocation of class, the implicit class dimension of the disparagement was clear. It symbolises police disdain at both the lack of material possessions, *and* the associated deficit of moral and cultural virtues of the poor at the bottom of the social 'scrapheap'. 'Scrotes' are assumed, moreover, to have a 'natural' propensity to crime because, as the police see it, they are 'too lazy to get a job' or because 'their scrote families are the same'. As the episode may have suggested, 'scrotes' stand as the omnipresent adversary of the police – most notably in the remark that policing them was like 'shovelling shit uphill'. 'Scrote' is a convenient blanket term for a range of prejudicial meanings, and served the Northshire officers as a handy, quick-recognition shorthand for a preconceived population category. As we shall see, it also shaped the way officers interacted with the individuals so identified.

First, though, it is worth pausing for a moment to reflect on some of the issues that the currency of a term like this in the occupational milieu raises about the role of language in an occupational culture. 'Scrote' is clearly yet another incarnation of the epithets used by the police to describe their 'property' in differing settings – from 'pukes' (Ericson, 1982) in Canada to 'slag' (Smith & Gray, 1985) in London. An in-depth examination of the tacit meanings and stigmatisation processes behind police labelling has been provided by Van Maanen (1978) who recognised the importance of assigning epithets to 'assholes'. One of the functions this kind of labelling serves is to establish social distance from those who are routinely policed. Northville officers thought this was desirable; as one officer put it to me, 'if all the scrotes around here liked us we wouldn't be doing our job properly'. It also adds meaning to their role as protectors and crime-fighters. 'Scrotes' represent not only their main adversaries but also what is wrong with the world 'out there'. And the general currency of the expression throughout the organisation 'solidifies police organisations around at least one common function' (Van Maanen, 1978, p. 235). This latter point comes out in the way Northville officers handled photographs of suspects and persons 'known' to the police. The official term for the mainly young, white males whose images were pinned up around the parade room walls was 'nominals'; yet scrawled next to the photographs on one wall was, 'scrotes'.

Going back to the previous field note, some further points are worth mentioning. Tom's comments were made in the context of his role as a police officer. He was extremely open to me about his contempt for the poor and impoverished and, notably, felt no need to *manage* his talk in relation to this group. While senior officers would no doubt frown on such overtly explicit language,[15] Tom's articulation of class contempt was both quite unabashed and in no way out of the ordinary. Indeed, one of the striking features of the ethnography was how common this kind of expression of class contempt was among front-line officers. What is more, these sentiments did not attract any rebuke either from peer officers or, in instances I observed, from superiors – as illustrated on the following occasion where there was a conversation between a sergeant and a group of community and immediate response officers:

> Duncan, Scott and Chris came into the parade room where Nick, Matt, Sergeant Jones and I were sitting. They seemed excited and were laughing as they began to recount an earlier incident between themselves and Shaun – a 'known scrote' who, by all accounts is homeless. The officers had initially suspected Shaun of having some drugs on him but, in the beginning, he would not let them search him. The conversation was very animated, full of bravado and laughter, and revolved around their disgust at Shaun's personal poverty and lack of dignity:
>
> *Duncan*: The little scrote definitely had some on him but he was being an arsehole
>
> *Scott*: Yeah, wouldn't let us touch him though – as if I wanted to. Honestly, if you could swap smack [heroin] for soap our job would be easier.
>
> *Nick*: You should have done a section 5 [Public Order Act] on him, brought him in [to the cells] and stripped searched the dirty shit.
>
> *Chris*: Fuck that – that's what he probably wanted. Dirty bastard gets a nice clean bed, cup of tea and a roof for the night
>
> *Sergeant Jones* (laughing): You wouldn't make it [tea] though! Did you take him in then?
>
> *Duncan*: No – he let us search him in the end but we found nothing, probably swallowed it.

This pervasive and apparently tolerated kind of 'talk' about the poor runs directly counter to the current hardline disciplinary policy towards expressions of racism, sexism and homophobia whether within the working environment or outside it. 'Police talk', of which this is an instance, has itself been the subject of some debate recently, and one argument questions whether it should be taken as a legitimate indicator of police culture, with a fundamental distinction being made between talk and action (Waddington, 1999). On the other hand, with the distinction between words and behaviour pointing to a more general problematic in the social sciences, some critical linguists argue that language itself is a form of practice (Edley, 2001). And connecting this debate to the current topic, Shearing and Ericson (1991) resuscitate language as the primary aspect in the production and reproduction of police culture. Without wanting to further debate this issue here, what does remain clear is that language and practice are intimately linked – and as several of the field notes excerpted here illustrate, the classed nature of officers' cultural knowledge also manifested itself in their routine policing of the poor.

CLASSED BODIES: A VISUAL REGISTER

Class contempt is highly sensitive to indicators of appearance, accent, clothing and possessions – and such markers extend into judgements of moral worth (Sayer, 2005). In 'Beirut' the poor were highly visible and recognisable since they displayed important signifiers. Put simply, the police could *see* scrotes 'a mile off'. Consider the following field note recorded during the routine policing of a local football match:

John and I went over to stand with two of the sergeants and their officers who were located by the parking bay. The stadium gate had now been opened and a number of fans started to get out of their buses and cars and make their way towards the entrance. Those coming through the gates were predominantly young [age around 18–30] white men with short or shaven hair. As they started to walk past us the police stopped talking amongst themselves and stared intently at the group. Although some of the men stared back, many of them dropped their eyes to the floor and continued to walk towards the stadium. As they were doing so the following conversation ensued:

Richard (looking them up and down with a stern frown): Look at them – they're like a bunch of animals

Phillip: I know. Why is it you can tell a scrote a mile off? I'm telling you, if you see anyone in shell suit [tracksuit] bottoms, cheap bling [jewellery], T-shirts with a waft of stale cigarettes and shit trailing behind them – a guaranteed scrote

Shaun: What gets me though is that they have started to wear Stone Ivory jumpers, £200 a piece, yet they can't be arsed to work and live in shit holes

Richard (sniggering): They're probably nicked – they can't buy them with their giros [state benefits] can they!

... Phillip then approached some of the young men and told them that there was a lot of bobbies about tonight and if there was any 'agro' they would all be 'coming in for the night'. There were some compliant murmurings from the group of lads, but no conflict on their part

Yet another encounter in which sections of the poor are seen in a framework of class, this episode also illustrates how the bodies of the poor are implicated in the occupational consciousness of police officers. Marking of lower working class bodies as defiling and socially deficient comes to be associated with a visual register lodged in the occupational culture (Young, 1991) and officers readily recognise and delineate their 'property' through the associated markers. Signs of class lifestyle are emblemised in the flesh; or as Bourdieu (1984, p. 190) puts it, 'the body is the most indisputable materialisation of class taste'. Material circumstance shapes the outward appearance of our bodies and also acts as the basis for the formation of habitus and development of taste: a conscious manifestation of habitus.

For Northville officers, clothes, bodily comportment, articulation and even smell (actual or imagined) all betrayed the class origins of 'scrotes'. The identification of 'scrotes' according to the officers' cultural dictionary sets the rationale for policing interaction, as we can see played out in the cited incident: indexing the group as 'scrotes' prompted a reflex of suspicion and predetermined what the police interaction would be. And even though this kind of recognition is something that operates at the deeper level of cultural knowledge, it can also be overtly acknowledged and used to the advantage of the organisation. Officers on covert operations targeted at certain forms of street crime – operations inevitably aimed at those with least resources (Box, 1994) – often adopted the dress, manners and speech associated with 'scrotes' in order to pass as 'one of them'.

The bodily appearance of the poor comes to be associated not just with a perceived 'innate criminality' but with the whole of their intrinsic moral worth. The following extract records a shift in which I attended a court session with Matthew, a community beat officer, who was giving evidence against two 18-year old males charged with affray and criminal damage:

Jim and Dave [the defendants] were outside the courthouse with Jim's dad having a cigarette when Matthew and I arrived. ... We were sitting in the witness room when Jim and Dave came back up the stairs and walked past us. Matthew scowled and said angrily to me – 'It's disgusting that people think they can turn up to court dressed like that, it makes me sick. Have they no respect for anything?' Jim and Dave were pale and thin. They were wearing t-shirts, jeans, trainers and chunky gold jewellery. They both had skinheads with tram lines [the current trend among youth sub-cultures] cut into the back of their hair. Matthew said that he couldn't wait to see them get 'potted' [sent to prison] as there would be 'two less scrotes to worry about' on his patch.

As we have noted, a person's class deeply affects how others value and respond to him or her. The injuries of class are inflicted not only in economic disadvantage but also, crucially, in experiences of class contempt and symbolic domination – such as a withholding of recognition. So it is not surprising that a frequent complaint made against the police is that they are impolite in their dealings with certain members of the public – with the unemployed feeling particularly disrespected (Choongh, 1998). Equally (and thinking back to what I have said about the emotional force of class contempt) the facial expressions of the officers in the incidents I have described made very plain the repulsion and disgust provoked in them by the poor.

'Scrotes' occupied a prominent place in officers' practical daily workload – in both reactive and proactive encounters. It is particularly important to focus on the latter type of encounter as the choices officers make regarding the *who* and *where* of crime conveys a great deal about their priorities, values and commitments in controlling their 'patch'. As the incident relating to Andy's and Scott's policing of the Barracks estate illustrates, attitudes of rejection towards the poor extended to certain geographical areas – most notably run-down streets and housing estates. These areas were frequently targeted and held significance in the police occupational culture insofar as they were perceived as harbouring problematic populations, ranging from the 'disorderly' and 'criminal' to 'benefit scroungers'. And just as the bodies of the poor were coded in terms of dirt and filth, so too their homes represented sites of disorder and uncleanness – as the following exchange during a focus group with front-line officers illustrates:

Simon: It was a big culture shock for me joining the job because I have walked into a house in West Street. [interruption (all laughing): ahhh that one]

Carl: name and shame them, I would ...

Simon: I walked into the house and my feet were sticking to the carpet it was that dirty. I actually couldn't breathe, the smell of piss – I had to say to the guy can you come and sit in the car ...

Gareth [laughing]: Your shift sent you there on purpose

Mark [quite aggressively]: People seem to not have a grasp of how to live their life. Their idea of a life is finally getting your house off the council, and then being able get your benefits to sit in, drink beer, smoke and watch television – and that's their life, their lifestyle.

Police disapproval of lower working class predicaments – such as being on state benefits and relegated to living in poor public housing – appears to be bound up with notions of cleanliness, dirt and 'respectable' notions of morality. For Young (1991) the police are particularly adverse to the poor because they stand in opposition to what the police themselves represent as enforcers of respectability. The organisational emphasis on discipline and uniformity accentuates police disdain for persons regarded as falling short of such standards. Sibley (1995) argues that allusions to bodily waste, disease and impurity are an important factor in the exclusion of marginal groups. Furthermore, exclusionary discourses in respect of the poor have always centred on notions of filth, disease and the animal brutishness of the impoverished. Much of this is borne out in the field notes I have cited, but preoccupation with the dirt and disease of impoverishment also manifested itself in a directly physical aspect of police procedure – namely, putting on surgical gloves before touching anyone who was the subject of a policing operation.

UNEMPLOYMENT – THE EROSION OF WORTH

Unemployment was an issue that loomed large throughout the research and presents another instance of the way that the class factor permeates contemporary police culture. It had a practical dimension where the employment status of an individual needed to be established for some bureaucratic requirement – like taking a formal statement or collating the file of a person brought into custody. But it was also plain that 'unemployment' was in itself a category saturated with meaning, taken to signal the moral worth of a person. Officers routinely asked their 'property' for his (very seldom *her*) employment status – mainly, indeed, in the absence of *any* bureaucratic need. Most of the time 'Are you working?' was just a loaded question aimed at exposing the moral worth (or deficiency) of that person.

The following field note captures the way in which notions of worth played out in the course of everyday interactions. Will was a young immediate response officer (24 years old) who had been in the job for just over two years having previously been in the army. He was extremely crime-control oriented, known affectionately among his colleagues as the 'shift terrier' for his high arrest rates. Will and I had been driving around on patrol when an immediate response (IR) came in concerning an accident in one of the more impoverished streets in the policing area:

A young boy had been hit by a car in Lower Lane – a narrow terraced street which is pretty run down and dilapidated. Will and I were at the other side of the Local Policing Unit and arrived there just after the rest of the shift and the ambulance crew. ... Residents had come out of their houses to see what was going on and were standing around and watching all of the commotion. Will was approaching some of them and asking whether anybody had seen anything. He saw Jamie sitting on a kerb – a white male who was in his 20 s. He was wearing an unkempt white vest, tracksuit bottoms with holes in it and had a muddy face and hands. Will said, 'come on Beth lets go and check out this scrote while we are here'. He walked over, stood over the lad and said 'I know you don't I'? Jamie uncomfortably shuffled and replied 'don't know'. Will then asked him 'are you still on the bad stuff [drugs] or the good stuff now'? The lad said he was being good and staying out of trouble. Finally Will asked, 'are you working?' and when Jamie answered that he wasn't, Will turned to me, rolled his eyes and gave me a knowing smirk. ... Walking away, Will commented that: 'if he can't be arsed getting a job he is never going to sort his shit out'.

More generally, and in more private spaces such as the police car, officers would routinely give moral lectures to (what they called) 'prisoners' in which the frequent refrain would be admonishment to 'get themselves a job'. For the police, getting a job was the ultimate answer to being respectable and staying out of trouble. Ironically, the very geography of the area, in which inter-generational unemployment was high, meant that officers *did* frequently come into contact with people who had no legitimate employment and so it was just a short step for them to associate unemployment with crime and disorderliness. We could add that police officers tend in any case to put a high value on having a strong work ethic, being conditioned by the intrinsically quite labour-intensive nature of the police role itself.

In sum, young unemployed males were perceived as problematic because work is believed to be the main way in which males acquire discipline and gain their major source of identity (Box, 1994). These cultural meanings of work found support in the occupational consciousness of officers. For the police, the unemployed are more likely both to commit *economic* forms of crime such as burglary and theft and to occupy public street space – space which is the police's function to keep orderly (Ericson, 1982). Notions of 'respectability' infuse the police's cultural knowledge. Police view themselves as guardians of public morality, and it is worth re-emphasising that in so doing, they juxtapose the 'rough' lower working classes with the 'respectable' *working* classes – and seem to support the interests of the latter in discourse and practice (Shearing, 1981; Reiner, 2000).

CONCLUSION: POLICE CULTURE AND THE CONTINUING SIGNIFICANCE OF CLASS

As this ethnography demonstrates, class contempt was a pervasive and seemingly acceptable feature of the occupational culture of officers in

Northville, and issues of class permeated daily narratives and interactions. While 'class' did not necessarily operate at the surface level of officers' discourse and interactions, the class iconography often drawn upon by officers implies that it did exist at the deeper level. Officers' informal cultural knowledge was infused with class themes and orientated them towards those whose bodily appearances and comportment 'betrayed' their class origins. While relating primarily to Northville, a policing area which has experienced dramatic de-industrialisation in recent years, the themes discussed here arguably have wider implications for other police forces across the United Kingdom. Northville is not alone in experiencing the adverse effects of post-Fordist restructuring in which inter-generational unemployment among young men is commonplace (see Taylor & Jamieson, 1997; Charlesworth, 2000). Furthermore, the overarching and official accent on diversity and recognition has served to eclipse discussions about class and redistribution (Fraser, 1997) – with the spaces of representation for the *white* working class also becoming increasingly subordinated (Haylett, 2001; McDowell, 2003). Contemporary police organisations are under increasing pressure to understand, and indeed project themselves, as sites of diversity and as providers of an equitable policing service for those groups which have previously fallen outside of fair policing. This principle does not, however, extend to the policing of the poor – and especially the white poor.

Exacerbated by the current emphasis on 'performance', the main focus of street policing continues to be on working class crimes and areas. In focusing un-problematically on axes of class, the police continue to reproduce the exclusion and domination of the poorest sections of the working class. While not wishing to present class as standing free from other axes of disadvantage, these issues nonetheless raise important questions about the place of class, explored here in relation to the white poor, in current 'policing diversity' discussions. Yet in many circumstances the displacement of class also has important implications for other axes of difference. While ethnicity, gender and sexuality complexly intertwine with one another to produce *different* experiences of discrimination, the marginalisation of class is problematic because deprivation often *co-exists* with the adverse policing of the many social divisions which currently abound our social structure.

NOTES

1. While not wishing to portray police culture as homogenous and fixed – the increasing recognition of the need to refer in the plural to police cultures

(Foster, 2003) to aptly reflect the important layers of differences being acknowledged here – I wish to retain its singular use in order to emphasise the commonalities around the classed nature of the findings presented here.

2. As characterised by Lee (1981, pp. 53–54). The term is used to describe those powerless, low-status groups whom the majority see as problematic and offensive – and who are subsequently left for the police to deal with and control.

3. Following the assertion that failure to properly investigate the murder of black teenager Stephen Lawrence was a consequence of 'institutional racism', the Macpherson Report (1999) has been seen as transforming the political debate about the policing of ethnic minorities – at least at the level of formal policy and discourse.

4. In order to preserve the anonymity of the police force in question, the names of localities and of individual officers have likewise been altered.

5. Although I observed a number of specialist units, I mainly accompanied those officers whose function was to respond to immediate-response calls and also community beat officers who dealt with community oriented issues.

6. These were recorded.

7. While a number of conversations were written verbatim, the majority represent a précis of what was said.

8. Paradoxically, engagement about the predicament of the white working class has originated from the far Right – most notably through the articulations of the British National Party. This kind of association has arguably dampened the likelihood of sympathetic debate about their plight.

9. I particularly have in mind the study by Smith and Gray (1985) in which ostentatiously racist, sexist and homophobic 'talk' featured as an acceptable aspect of the occupational cultures.

10. See also Taylor and Jamieson (1997).

11. Recent statistics for the area confirms that the dominant composition of the area is mainly white at 94 per cent – a composition not unlike the rest of the United Kingdom (McDowell, 2003).

12. It is important to note, however, that the disparagement of ethnic minorities does not disappear within this framework, but rather, appears alongside the denigration of the white poor. Commenting on disparaging representations of white poor males in political and popular spheres, Cloward (1994 cited in McDowell, 2003, p. 63) does nonetheless suggest that such representations would 'cause outcry' if used to refer to ethnic minorities or women.

13. According to a number of dictionaries the meaning of 'scrote' ranges from 'a term of abuse' to a 'despicable person'. One dictionary refers to a newspaper article which features a man from West Belfast recounting his treatment by British paratroopers during the 'troubles'. He reported, 'they had a name for us – it was scrotes – they were young guys and aggressive' (*The Sunday Times*, 29 Jan 2005, cited in Dictionary of Contemporary Slang. (3rd ed.), A & C Black: London).

14. There were both formal and informal aspects to being 'known' by the police. Firstly, an individual could be officially 'known' – having gone through the system and thus being formally inscribed with a criminal record. Secondly, officers got to 'know' who on their patch were 'scrotes' and, as it were, fed the co-ordinates of these individuals into their cognitive map. In both cases the surname of the individual was the key marker for identifying them.

15. Although I doubt whether they would explicitly focus on the class component of these slurs.

ACKNOWLEDGEMENTS

Many thanks to the editors, and to Bill Dixon, Philip Stenning and Ian Loader for their helpful and constructive comments on earlier drafts of this chapter.

REFERENCES

Banton, M. (1964). *The policeman in the community*. London: Tavistock.
Bonnett, A. (1998). How the British working class became white: The symbolic (re)formation of racialised capitalism. *Journal of Historical Sociology, 11*(3), 316–340.
Bourdieu, P. (1984). *Distinction: A social critique of the judgement of taste*. London: Routledge.
Box, S. (1994). The criminal justice system and 'problem populations'. In: N. Lacey (Ed.), *A reader on criminal justice*. Oxford: Oxford University Press.
Burke, M. E. (1993). *Coming out of the blue*. London: Cassell.
Cain, M. (1973). *Society and the policeman's role*. London: Routledge.
Cashmore, E. (2001). The experiences of ethnic minority police officers in Britain: Under-recruitment and racial profiling in a performance culture. *Ethnic and Racial Studies, 24*(4), 642–659.
Cashmore, E. (2002). Behind the window dressing: Minority ethnic police perspectives on cultural diversity. *Journal of Ethnic and Migration Studies, 28*(2), 327–341.
Chan, J. (1997). *Changing police culture: Policing in a multicultural society*. Cambridge: Cambridge University Press.
Charlesworth, S. (2000). *A phenomenology of working class experience*. Cambridge: Cambridge University Press.
Choongh, S. (1998). Policing the dross: A social disciplinary model of policing. *British Journal of Criminology, 38*(4), 623–635.
Cloward, R. (1994). Whipping boys. *Guardian Weekend*, 3 September 1994.
Connell, R. W. (1995). *Masculinities*. Cambridge: Polity Press.
Edley, N. (2001). Analysing masculinity: Interpretive repertoires, ideological dilemmas and subject positions'. In: M. Wetherell, S. Taylor & S. Yates (Eds), *Discourse as data*. London: Sage Publications.
Ericson, R. V. (1982). *Reproducing order: A study of patrol work*. Toronto: University of Toronto Press.
Foster, J. (2003). Police cultures. In: T. Newburn (Ed.), *Handbook of policing*. Devon: Willan.
Fraser, N. (1997). *Justice interruptus: Critical reflections on the 'postsocialist' condition*. London: Routledge.
Glaeser, A. (2000). *Divided in unity: Identity, Germany and the Berlin police*. Chicago: Chicago University Press.

Green, P. (1991). *The enemy without: Policing and class consciousness in the miner's strike.* Milton Keynes: Open University Press.

Haylett, C. (2001). Illegitimate subjects: Abject whites, neoliberal modernisation and middle-class multiculturalism. *Environment and Planning D: Society and Space, 19,* 351–370.

Holdaway, S. (1983). *Inside the British police force: A force at work.* Oxford: Blackwell.

Holdaway, S., & O'Neill, M. (2004). The development of black police associations: Changing articulations of race within the police. *British Journal of Criminology, 44,* 854–865.

Hughes, E. C. (1962). Good people and dirty work. *Social Problems, 10*(1), 3–11.

Lee, J. A. (1981). Some structural aspects of police deviance in relations with minority groups. In: C. Shearing (Ed.), *Organisational police deviance.* Toronto: Butterworth.

Macpherson, Sir, W. (1999). *Report of the Stephen Lawrence inquiry.* London: HMSO.

McDowell, L. (2003). *Redundant masculinites: Employment change and white working class youth.* Oxford: Blackwell.

Norris, C. (1994). Some ethical considerations on fieldwork with the police. In: D. Hobbs & T. May (Eds), *Interpreting the field: Accounts of ethnography.* Oxford: Clarendon Press.

O'Neill, M., & Holdaway, S. (2007). Examining window-dressing: The views of Black Police Associations on recruitment and training. *Journal of Ethnic and Migration Studies, 33*(3), 483–500.

Punch, M. (1979). *Policing the inner city.* London: Macmillan.

Reiner, R. (2000). *The politics of the police* (3rd ed.). Oxford: Oxford University Press.

Sayer, A. (2005). *The moral significance of class.* Cambridge: Cambridge University Press.

Scraton, P. (1985). *The state of the police.* London: Pluto.

Sennett, R., & Cobb, J. (1972). *The hidden injuries of class.* London: W. W. Norton.

Shearing, C. (1981). Subterranean processes in the maintenance of power. *Canadian Review of Sociology and Anthropology, 18*(3), 283–298.

Shearing, C., & Ericson, R. V. (1991). Culture as figurative action. *British Journal of Sociology, 42*(4), 481–506.

Sibley, D. (1995). *Geographies of exclusion.* London: Routledge.

Skeggs, B. (2004). *Class, self, culture.* London: Routledge.

Skolnick, J. H. (1966). *Justice without trial: Law enforcement in democratic society.* New York: Macmillan.

Smith, D. J., & Gray, J. (1985). *Police and people in London: The PSI report.* London: Policy Studies Institute.

Stinchcombe, A. L. (1996). Institutions of privacy in the determination of police administrative practice. In: R. Reiner (Ed.), *Policing* (Vol. 2, pp. 65–77). Aldershot: Dartmouth.

Taylor, I. (1999). *Crime in context: A critical criminology of market societies.* Cambridge: Polity Press.

Taylor, I., & Jamieson, R. (1997). Proper little mesters: Nostalgia and protest masculinity in de-industrialised Sheffield. In: S. Westwood & J. William (Eds), *Imagining cities: Scripts, signs, memory.* London: Routledge.

Van Maanen, J. (1978). The asshole. In: P. K. Manning & J. Van Maanen (Eds), *Policing: A view from the street.* California: Goodyear.

Wacquant, L. (2000). Logics of urban polarisation: The view from below. In: R. Crompton, F. Devine, M. Savage & J. Scott (Eds), *Renewing class analysis.* Oxford: Blackwell.

Waddington, P. A. J. (1999). Police (canteen) sub-culture: An appreciation. *British Journal of Criminology*, *39*(2), 287–309.
Westley, W. (1970). *Violence and the police: A sociological study of law, custom and morality*. Massachusetts: MIT.
Westmarland, L. (2001). *Gender and policing*. Cullompton: Willan.
Young, J. (1999). *The exclusive society*. London: Sage.
Young, M. (1991). *An inside job: Policing and police culture in Britain*. Oxford: Oxford University Press.

CHAPTER 8

FROM CULT OF MASCULINITY TO SMART MACHO: GENDER PERSPECTIVES ON POLICE OCCUPATIONAL CULTURE

Jennifer Brown

ABSTRACT

This chapter's discussion of the concept of occupational culture proposes that whilst operational policing and its management may have changed, the masculine ethos of police officers has not. The introduction of equality legislation, new managerialism in the public sector and initiatives in community policing presaged a potential transformation of policing by adoption of more co-operative and collaborative styles that might be held to be more feminine in orientation. Recent research suggests that attention to gender issues has not only slipped but has been eclipsed by demands of other diversity agenda. The claim is made that police occupational identity was and still is privileged by a masculine orientation.

Police Occupational Culture: New Debates and Directions
Sociology of Crime, Law and Deviance, Volume 8, 205–226
ISSN: 1521-6136/doi:10.1016/S1521-6136(07)08008-6

INTRODUCTION: THE CULT OF MASCULINITY

The notion of a 'cult of masculinity' being one of the defining characteristics, or indeed *the* defining characteristic, of the police occupational culture has been attributed to Smith and Gray (1985) in their study on the people and police in London: the phrase represents police occupational culture as one within which men define themselves in terms of physical and sexual prowess and women find themselves trapped in an ambient environment of sex discrimination and sexual harassment. Smith and Gray concluded that the structural inhibitions they observed – such as unofficial quotas limiting the numbers of women in more prestigious departments or deployments and a debilitating working ethos depriving women of informal social support or mentoring – restricted policewomen's career aspirations and options. Much research since has confirmed such findings (e.g. Heidensohn, 1992; Brown & Heidensohn, 2000; Foster, 2003). This chapter will demonstrate that there have been substantial changes in operational policing and its management in the last several decades, but questions whether the occupational cultural resources used to construct a masculine occupational identity of officers have also changed. The concept of 'smart macho' (Maddock & Parkin, 1993) is invoked to describe the version of masculinity that has survived in this period of change. Smart macho managers are driven by their own competitiveness and give short shrift to employees less eager to work excessive hours or unable to deliver to tight schedules.

Two psychological concepts (identity construction and organisational attention) will be described that explain the central thesis of the chapter, namely that the masculinised ethos underpinning policing has been sustained and that its adverse manifestations remain detrimental to women officers. The work of Breakwell (1986) is used to conceptualise identity construction processes and get a sharper focus on the persistence of policing's masculine ethos, following which we consider how Ocasio's (1993) notion of organisational selectivity of attention under conditions of adversity can help explain the resistance to change of this ethos.

OPERATIONAL CHANGES IN POLICING: THREATS TO MASCULINITY

Edwards (2005) details seismic changes in the conduct of policing brought about by science and technology, legislative and constitutional changes, mass communication, greater accountability and increased specialisation. Notions of intelligence-led policing provide a specific example of the use of new information technologies to direct police activity. Cope (2004) argues that 'in many respects analysis represents the antithesis of traditional action-oriented police work, which police officers have long valued over more mundane paper work tasks .... As intelligence has become increasingly important in policing, officers' roles have shifted in emphasis towards knowledge work' (p. 197). Cope goes on to argue that street level officers continue to have considerable control over intelligence acquisition and in applying the analytic outputs of intelligence. Cope concluded from a qualitative analysis of two British police forces that the failure to feed and utilise the analytic cycle was influenced by 'the gendered nature of policing' because the less desirable police task of analysis 'became associated with feminine traits and these were regularly sidelined by police officers in pursuit of masculine crime fighting roles' (p. 198).

Edwards (2005, p. 79) suggests that high tech strategies have had little effect on crime rates in America and that stretching of resources due to the volume of public calls for assistance has contributed to declining public satisfaction. Underlying the loss of public confidence, Edwards argues, is concern about police objectivity and perception of police behaving in a racist, sexist and homophobic manner. Barton (2003, p. 347), in reference to British policing, supposes that the various operational changes have yet to impact the way front line officers go about their daily duties. Such research suggests that the collective and individual persona of the police officer has indeed been resistant to change and therefore retain its masculine ethos.

Perhaps more challenging to the masculine ethos of policing have been influences implicit in the public's demand for services that are more relevant and responsive (Miller, 1999; Vanstone, 2001). Vanstone, from an Australian perspective, argues that rather less attention is now paid to detecting crime and more to the causes of crime, and that associated with this has been a reduced emphasis on the physical attributes of law enforcement culture and greater reliance on emotional strength. Australian policing, she proposes, has re-aligned itself to more in-depth community interaction requiring greater communication and interpersonal skills from officers. In her view, this represents recognition of feminine skills such as effective communication, especially in mediation and conflict resolution. This analysis is echoed in the United States by Miller (1999) and the United Kingdom by Heidensohn (2003). The 'reassurance programme' was one strand of the version of community policing adopted in England and Wales, in which police officers were to become more visible, accessible and familiar to provide a reassuring presence and involve the community in tackling local problems that were identified as the drivers of crime and insecurity (Innes, 2006).

Other research contests the Vanstone position. Westmarland (2001), for example, argues that the use of physical force is still a key activity and a core value of policing. Miller (1999) demonstrates that women officers in her study often seemed to derive satisfaction from 'doing' masculinity through their work whilst Heidensohn (2003) concludes that 'police and policing remain gendered in the twenty-first century. The macho culture is still alive in some forces even now, although it is a source of embarrassment' (p. 574). Thus, it seems overly optimistic to suggest as Miller (1999) does that community policing will help 'police departments [to] ease the change from being [a] masculinist crime fighting organization' (p. 224) to one that draws on feminine resources and engages quality of life.

MANAGERIAL CHANGES IN POLICING: THREATS TO MASCULINITY

Of related significance have been the shifts in management as a consequence of progressive reforms of the public sector, in the United Kingdom and elsewhere, which have included the police service (Leishman, Loveday, & Savage, 2003; Fleming & Lafferty, 2002; Barton, 2003). This has seen the introduction of performance indicators along with best value and value for money regimes. As has been previously argued (Brown, 2003), these managerial changes did offer the opportunity of a paradigm shift in policing through a re-orientation of masculine/feminine working practices. Such a paradigm shift, according to Maddock (1999, p. 131), challenges command and control models of management with a perspective that is more sympathetic to collaborative-style working and femocratic practices. Fleming and Lafferty (2002) take the position that new managerialism within Australian policing 'should have led ... to at least some erosion of the insular character of police recruitment, training and promotion' (p. 3). Maddock (1999) argues that this project failed in the public sector and that women 'were overwhelmed by pressures to avoid reality and hide behind old practices' (p. 166). Worse, their innovations were ignored or met with resistance, and new practices such as contracting out, rather than heralding new collaborative ways of working, intensified competition and reinvented the blame culture. With respect to policing, Brown (2003) reaches much the same conclusions as Maddock does in relation to the public sector. Brown's review of research evidence demonstrates that there has been remarkably little change in the old order – 'cult of masculinity' – which valorised danger, excitement and 'good' arrests; what we find now is that the same underlying values have been seamlessly mapped directly onto the 'new' order – the 'smart macho' management regimes, which rate achievement of performance targets. In the kind of smart macho performance culture that Maddock and Parkin identify, police targets and 'comstat' protocols pressurise the workplace to such a degree that filing a routine report of command unit statistical returns is made almost as fraught with competitive masculinity (like that described by Smith & Gray, 1985) as an operational exercise would be. Fleming and Lafferty (2002) are more optimistic about changes being wrought in the Australian public sector by the new managerialism, but they also note that police organisations and the police unions successfully resisted and insulated the police service from the changes occurring elsewhere.

CHANGE THROUGH EQUALITY LEGISLATION: THREATS TO MASCULINITY

Structurally, police organisations remain male dominated, with the United Kingdom, the United States and Australia being the jurisdictions with the highest percentage of women officers at about 20% (Fleming & Lafferty, 2002; Van der Lapp, Graumans, Sevenhuijsen, 2004). The limited numbers of women also impact the occupancy of supervisory ranks. Fig. 1 (raw data taken from Her Majesty's Inspectorate of Constabulary annual reports[1])

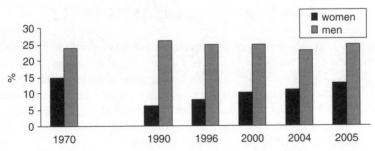

Fig. 1. Percentage Share of Supervisory Rank as a Function of the Total Numbers of Men and Women, Respectively.

presents a calculation of percentage share of women senior officers in England and Wales.

Sex discrimination legislation in the UK was passed in 1975. As the figures given here illustrate, before that date the proportion of women having senior rank was about 15% (with 25% being the comparable percentage for men). At that time women were employed in a separate policewomen's department. Whilst the UK's Sex Discrimination Act resulted in an integration of women into mainstream policing, it can be demonstrated that their proportionate share of rank has not yet caught up with pre equality legislation levels. Fiske (1991) argues that structural imbalance in the numbers of women and low proportionate share of seniority, in an environment in which sexual matters (such as rape and vice investigations) are made explicit, are a predictor for the occurrence of sexual harassment. In an international survey, Brown and Heidensohn (2000) present evidence of the presence and persistence of sexual harassment in two dozen police jurisdictions they investigated. In their analysis of the situation in Australia, Fleming and Lafferty (2002) conclude likewise that equity and anti-discrimination initiatives have had limited effect on changing police organisations. As they put it, 'the capacity of police organisations [in Australia] to evade equity legislation has been remarkable, based on their conservatism, male dominance ... and the close relationship that police organisations have had historically with state governments (derived largely from the political importance of 'law and order' issues)'(p. 4).

The occupational identity of police officers seems to have withstood three decades of equality legislation and policies and changing operational and managerial practices. That occupational identity resides in and is supported by the organisational culture and it is to this concept we now turn.

POLICE OCCUPATIONAL CULTURE

Trice (1993, p. 46) proposes that occupations have their own ideologies, which are conveyed through cultural forms such as stories, rituals and ceremonies. Johnson and Scholes (2002) suggest that underpinning these are taken for granted assumptions that work to define, guide and constrain what is seen as appropriate behaviour. The taken-for-grantedness, moreover, is handed down over time and becomes institutionalised to a degree that makes it difficult to challenge and question.

Several observers of the police occupational culture note the potency of this taken for granted element. Foster (2003) exemplifies it in the implicit assumptions of politicians and media who speak of 'policemen' rather than the gender neutral 'police officers'. This may be typified by Oliver Letwin who as the UK shadow Home Secretary stated in his speech to the 2003 Conservative Party Conference that 'over the years from 1997 to 2003, the Labour Government has provided an average of 1,500 extra policemen a year. We will provide 5,000 extra policemen each year until we reach our 40,000' (*Guardian*, 2003). Gendered assumptions are not restricted to politicians. A recent illustration can be found in the Cardiff University prospectus for an Institute of Police Science in which all the pictures of police officers were male. So, says Foster, despite changes in policy and recruitment the police service remains a largely male white and heterosexual organisation where those who are perceived to be different by virtue of their race, gender or sexuality have reported significant problems in gaining acceptance – and in some cases recognition or legitimacy – for their experiences. She concludes that sexual discrimination is firmly institutionalised in policing (p. 215). Cashmore (2001) provides a further powerful example of the institutionalisation of taken-for-granted assumptions, in this case about race. He put the following question to an Asian officer: 'An Asian or African Caribbean bobby is hardly likely to be motivated by racism when he or she is going to pull over a black kid driving an expensive car, right?' The officer's answer was 'You'd be surprised. If I'm being honest with myself I've done it. It's hard to understand the pressure you're under. If you are in a particular situation and things are slow, then you almost subconsciously find yourself targeting blacks' (p. 652).

The police occupational culture has been variously defined but is often taken to mean the accepted practices and underlying attitudes and values that construct and transmit norms of how to be a police officer and how to do policing (Paoline, 2003, p. 200). Paoline points to the twin aspects of policing that contribute to its distinctive occupational culture: danger and use of coercive authority. Thus, values derive from the mission associated with preserving law and order (Reiner, 1985) and the hazards of doing so (Brown, 1988). Ethnographic research by Westmarland (2001) indicates that demonstrations of physical courage are still deemed to be critical elements of police work and remain important features in the construction of a police officer's identity. Interestingly, Heidensohn (1992) found in her grounded theory analysis of both American and British policewomen that they were just as likely as their male counterparts to tell 'war' stories of physical encounters. Such stories represented 'transformational scenes' whereby women demonstrate courage in the face of physical danger that contributed to their acceptance by male colleagues. Physicality of this kind represents one way of *doing* (male) gender in the pursuit of the policing task and constitutes what Westmarland (2001) calls identity construction work.

Paoline (2003, p. 199) reviews the considerable volume of research devoted to police culture and a growing critique of the concept. Chan (2005), for example, argues that not only is police culture loosely defined, if defined at all, but also the concept is neither monolithic, universal, unchanging nor insulated from social, legal, political and organisational contexts, nor do officers simply absorb its tenets in a passive acculturation process. Chan (1996) developed a sophisticated analysis of police culture through an ethno-methodological approach focused on how police officers 'do' their social lives, utilising Bourdieu's 'field' and 'habitus' concepts. Fielding (1997) says in his review of her book 'such accounts prod at the more facile understandings endlessly informed by the gruesome bonhomie of 'canteen culture' and missing the undercurrents, inconsistencies and quirks which make of any working culture a far more subtle thing'. Similar critique underscoring the obsolescence of an essentialist construction of police occupational culture will be found elsewhere in the present volume. Prokos and Padacic (2002) show how the presence of women in policing can further the 'masculine project' when they serve as a foils to permit masculinity to be defined by what it is not, and when they invite elevation of men's status through devaluation of the status of women.

Prenzler (1997) argues that the term police culture has become a cipher for a critique (of male) police behaviour. This is usually taken to indicate a gap between formal and informal practices and a disregard or disdain for rules and procedures. The police role, or task environment, is the primary explanation given for the development of police culture and its preservation of the myth of dangerousness. In the police culture thesis, the effect of the task environment on police is reinforced through occupational socialisation. Traditional recruitment and training and promotion practices contribute to the creation of homogeneity and insularity. The deterioration of trainee ideals and values is well attested and the general conclusion has been that it is the result of police socialisation. In this context, there is an inevitably gendered dimension to critique of police misconduct (Lersch, 1998; Palmer, 1999; Terrill, Paoline, & Manning, 2003). Palmer, for example, notes that in the Australian case (male) police culture has been invoked as an explanatory variable for excessive use of force and corrupt practice by both the Fitzgerald and the Wood inquiries into, respectively, the Queensland and the New South Wales Police. Prenzler (1997) is more critical of the assumption that police culture is the cause of learnt aggressive behaviour by police officers and proposes that changes in attitude by probationer officers and their acquisition of combative behaviour may have more to do with the pragmatic reality of direct experience of crime and criminals and hostile public reactions to officers rather than acculturation through rule bending or breaking. He concludes, 'there is insufficient evidence from research and inquiries ... that police services have been characterised by many of the undesirable qualities captured in the term police culture' (p. 52).

Observers of police culture have also linked the concept to other negative repercussions, such as the inhibiting of female officers' deployment options and of their chances of promotion to higher rank (Holdaway & Parker, 1998; Dick & Jankowicz, 2001; Westmarland, 2001; Dick & Cassell, 2004). The argument is expressed in terms of there being a degree of complicity by women in which they respond to preferences either as self limited by broader societal stereotyping or adapting to the demands of the police occupational culture. Thus, Westmarland (2001) proposes that 'women are not being coerced to deal with children or enter these departments any more than the men who apply for traditionally 'macho' specialities such as the CID are being controlled' (p. 45). Holdaway and Parker (1998) found that women officers in the British force, they studied, were generally less interested than men in police work concerned with traffic, motoring offences and vehicle accidents and more interested in intervening in domestic disputes and working with juveniles. They conclude that whilst they observed many features of the occupational culture of the rank and file that were shown to be discriminatory to women 'we have nevertheless found women officers sustaining key features of the culture, mostly by placing and retaining aspects of crime work in the ascendancy' (p. 58). Dick and Cassell (2004) explore why this may be so. Their research task was to examine why women seem to accept, or at least not oppose, police working practices that appear to marginalise them. In effect, women articulate a discourse of police/parent incompatibility in which parenting is problematic for policewomen as mothers but not for policemen as fathers. The presumption of a mother's greater commitment to child rearing was seen as compromising her commitment to long hours, dangerous assignments and career advancement. Dick and Cassell argue that women attempt to offset this by constructing the police role in the same way as men in order to be accepted by their colleagues.

A different position is taken by Fielding (1999) who used the opportunity of the Macpherson inquiry into the murder of black teenager Stephen Lawrence[2] to examine whether aspects of the police culture have been reformed. He considered both race and gender dimensions but it is his observations on the latter, which are considered here. In the light of the kind of failures on the part of (London) Metropolitan Police officers that were uncovered in the Macpherson report, Fielding identifies a masculine/feminine dichotomy where femininity has a reforming potential in that 'women may actually possess qualities which can improve on the delivery of policing services'. Heidensohn (1992) points out that policewomen's characteristics have been defined as a series of deficits (lack of physical presence, tough physique and, above all, masculinity). Fielding argues that very little police work actually requires brute strength, even in potentially violent encounters. More critical to successful intervention in conflict reduction is talk. Women's talk, he contends, tends to be co-operative, mutually re-enforcing, turn taking, and which makes it more difficult to identify dominance. Men's talk, however, is declamatory, assertive, abrupt and where dominance is asserted. As men still numerically dominate it is men's talk that still has the loudest voice (and style).

Foster, Newburn, and Souhami (2005) reviewed the longer-term outcomes of the Macpherson report and took the opportunity to likewise examine gender aspects of policing. They noted that the urgency in tackling racist language was not mirrored in the response to other forms of discriminatory language and behaviour. In all their research sites (four qualitative studies, three national surveys, as well as a series of in-depth interviews) they found that a greater tolerance of sexist and homophobic language was apparent and that sexist language and behaviour was widespread in all sites. The experiences of women and minority staff suggest that the excision of explicitly racist language in the service has not lead to broader changes in the internal culture of the police organisation. Women report feeling excluded by the predominantly male heterosexual culture. Women officers frequently felt undermined and undervalued; strong feelings of exclusion and discrimination went unrecognised and unaddressed. In these authors' quantitative survey results, only a third of all officers questioned agreed with the statement that 'we need more women in this force' (compared to over 90% who agreed that forces need more Black and ethnic minority officers). Fewer than 30% agreed with the statement that there is very little sexism in the force. Decline in the use of exclusory language appeared strongly related to heightened awareness of a potential disciplinary response rather than reflecting a change in officers' attitudes towards or understanding of racist language.

Foster, Newburn and Souhami conclude that desistance from racist language and behaviour occurred because it would not be tolerated within the discipline regime rather than because such behaviour was unacceptable. Nor has the excision of explicitly racist language in the service led to broader changes in the internal culture of the police organisation. Women, minority and gay officers reported a climate where, in their view, less overt forms of discrimination were widespread, and in which they felt excluded, isolated and uncomfortable. Women felt ignored and excluded in their teams and restricted in the roles and tasks made available to them, and they also felt they had to work harder than male officers to prove themselves. In one research site, women officers reported an atmosphere of all-consuming sexism.

Sir William Morris's inquiry into the Metropolitan Police (Morris, 2004) likewise found that concerns about race and ethnicity had eclipsed those relating to gender, and it concludes (paragraph 5, p. 27) that gender had been neglected in recent years. The Metropolitan Police's Association of Senior Women Officers is cited in the Morris report as contending 'that gender has not featured significantly in diversity training. This may in part be responsible for the apparent willingness in parts of the MPS to condone or at the very best ignore sexist banter and language' (paragraph 5.28).

Foster (2003, p. 203) sees training as a mechanism that perpetuates this. Fledgling officers may begin with ideals about serving the community, but it does not take long before they find themselves reassessing their idealised motives of helping people and abandoning an outward-looking public service orientation for a more inwardly focused crime control approach. Training school provides a rehearsal of the way the occupational culture can nurture and protect its members, along with the message that being accepted by the group has primacy over individual needs; the training environment serves to reinforce rather than challenge prevailing received police wisdom. In their participant observation study in an American policing academy, Prokos and Padacic (2002) articulate a process – 'the hidden curriculum' – through which this reinforcement occurs. Whilst the explicit curriculum and policy manual was gender neutral and designed to produce professional and competent officers regardless of gender, the informal curriculum was 'riddled' with gender lessons. This was accomplished by treating women as outsiders, such as eliminating them from classroom examples and excluding them from bonding experiences. There was an exaggeration of the physical differences between men and women rookies in the self defence classes; instructors treated women with less courtesy and respect. Prokos and Padacic conclude from their data that 'men learnt masculinity by seeing it contrasted with a caricature of femininity' (p. 450) whilst 'women learned that the expected role of women in the criminal justice system is as victims and the objects of male workers' fantasies and ridicule' (p. 452).

So much, then for an overview of the persistence of physical and symbolic aspects of masculinity as a critical feature of the police culture and from which the stories and the routines help to define parameters of accepted and acceptable behaviour. But as a response to Fielding's (1997) critique of ethnomethodological approaches, in which he argued that they fail to provide a satisfactory account of motives, this chapter invokes some psychological conceptualisations to address this question. Much previous research tackles the question of *how* cultural actors do gender but not *why* they do it. As Waddington (1999, p. 302) reiterates, 'the normative orientation to the police sub-culture tells us little about why the police in so many jurisdictions express the beliefs and values they do'. The psychological orientation proposed in this chapter attempts to explore this 'why' territory through the concepts of Identity Process Theory (IPT) (Breakwell, 1986) and organisational attention (Ocasio, 1993).

DOING MASCULINITY

The approach considered in this chapter is to treat occupational culture as emerging from social interaction, in other words as socially producing and reproducing behaviours that reinforce a police identity. Dick and Cassell (2004) present an account of how the nature of policing is itself constructed during interactions involving 'identity work'. The resources available in the environment are the symbols, rituals and stories that re-enforce the constructed identity. Various studies (Holdaway & Parker, 1998; Westmarland, 2001) show how physical attributes of masculinity are preserved as core features of worth that define an officer. But identity construction is a dynamic process. Shifts in policing practices such as the focus on community engagement and reassurance – which emphasise skill sets like empathy and mediation and are construed as more feminine – might be expected to dislodge the occupational identity founded so heavily upon physical resources. Yet, police occupational culture is still imbued with masculine images of physique, guns and crime fighting and its cultural resources (stories, rituals symbols) are the means for not only doing but also preserving masculinity. Martin (1996) contends that 'men create an idealized image of policing as action-orientated, violent and uncertain' (p. 15). They define themselves through these images which are closely associated with the masculine side of contrasting pairs of gender-linked symbols: street/station house; crime fighting/service; public/domestic; dirty/clean (Hunt, 1984, p. 294). Real (male) police work – crime fighting – takes place on the street, celebrates physical prowess and demands emotional control in the face of danger and injury. Station house work, in contrast, is inside work involving administrative or interpersonal skills. Martin and Jurik (1996) argue that men and women do gender identity through their social interactions in the workplace and that male work cultures often advance unsavoury images that effectively subordinates women: interactional devices for constructing men's dominance include undermining and invalidating women's skills (p. 41). The analysis by Prokos and Padacic (2002) gives evidence that this is still the case. As Martin (1996) had previously suggested, the presence of women elicits fears in men of exposure of their racist and sexist behaviour and language because of a belief that women's presence sets a higher norm of moral conduct. Prokos and Padacic (2002) found examples of concessions to this higher order morality in comments like 'we can't talk about this now because there are ladies in the room' (p. 447). In their study policemen remain fearful of such exposure and protect themselves by retaining strategies that entrench women's outsider status: harsh treatment and harassment, segregation, and using women's presence as confirmation of the masculine nature of the job.

IDENTITY PROCESS THEORY

Breakwell's Identity Process Theory (IPT – see Breakwell, 1986) provides a model which can help explain why policemen might seek to preserve their occupational identity. Individuals whose identities are threatened will seek to re-establish *continuity* with traditional gender roles, re-create *distinctions* between themselves and those who threaten their identity construction and re-establish *self-esteem* and job satisfaction by denigrating the interlopers. A further psychological process is *self-efficacy,* which is defined as people's beliefs about their capabilities to perform at a level where they can exercise influence over events that affect their lives. Self-efficacy beliefs determine how people feel, think, motivate themselves and behave. This is an important process in the maintenance of identity. The reality of slighter, less physically strong women managing the police tasks competently challenges the norm that these tasks require physical strength and men's monopoly for undertaking them effectively.

The application of IPT to policing posits that the traditional stereotype of police as male, rough and tough, exerting coercive authority with minimal levels of street supervision, was adopted as the archetypal occupational identity. The rituals supporting such an identity are created through the occupational culture. Examples can be found in the masculine uniform (trousers, collar and tie, about which women still complain) personal protection equipment (long-handled batons, etc.) and forms of address ('sir', which is sometimes mischievously applied to women senior officers). But threats to this masculine identity appeared, firstly in the shape of sex discrimination legislation, which integrated women into policing. A series of ritual arguments were then deployed to preserve the distinctiveness, self-esteem, self-efficacy and gender continuity of male officers – arguments that assumed women were physically less capable, emotionally labile, uneconomic because they would leave prematurely through child care commitments (see Jones, 1986). Informal quotas, harassment and segregated deployment were the means to maintain the dominance of a male-constructed police identity.

The raft of reforms in managerial and operational practice has occasioned a second threat to a male model of police officers. The encouragement of new working styles that emphasise negotiation and collaboration rather than strict command and control, has produced some corresponding shifts in the ritual arguments employed to preserve distinctiveness, continuity, self-esteem and self-efficacy – now encapsulated in a loss of standards discourse in which the presence of women in policing is no longer contested per se, but where instead their presence is said to reduce the efficiency and effectiveness of policing. (Scant evidence has materialised to support this contention. See Steel & Lovrich, 1987; Brown, Hegarty, & O'Neill, 2006.) Thus, we find cultural practices which aimed to restrict women's entry into the police during the 1975 debate on the implications of the Sex Discrimination Act on policing being resuscitated in the 1980s and 1990s with the introduction of performance management in policing, and latterly yet again in response to the more feminised practices discernable in contemporary community and reassurance policing.

Previously, the argument was that women were uneconomical because marriage and child bearing and rearing would lead them to resign. Equal opportunities have subsequently introduced more family friendly policies that support the retention of policewomen and the ritual argument is now re-framed in terms of conflict between being a fit mother and a professional police officer, with the implication that doing one role well compromises the other role. Holdaway and Parker (1998) undertook a survey of police officers in one British force and found a third of male officers in their sample (compared to 6% of women) agreeing that a woman who stays at home all the time with her children is a better mother than a woman who works outside the home at least half of the time. Similarly, a third of policemen (compared to 8% of women) agreed with the statement that women officers who leave to have children should not expect a job to be waiting for them if they come back to work. And finally 19% of policemen (4% of women) agreed that women officers who want to be mothers should not expect to have a serious police career. The obverse, that a police officer father suffers the same conflicts, is not apparent. These results show differences in attitudes towards women and motherhood on the part of policemen and policewomen and appear to contradict the arguments offered by Dick and Cassell (2004) in which women in their study constructed their role in similar ways to policemen to be accepted – Dick and Cassell's point being that women appear to be blamed for their own discrimination and that their women participants were attempting to explain that the problems for women were located not in discriminatory practices but in aspects of the job itself. To be accepted they consent to the idea that a police career and motherhood are incompatible, because policing itself is seen as harsh activity requiring tough interactional styles where child care requires nurturing and emotional labour.

Silvestri (2000) interviewed both men and women officers to reveal that policing is still constructed as dangerous, physically and emotionally demanding, unpredictable and potentially violent. When policewomen have children, shift work makes looking after them difficult. Conflicts between home and family may mean that women cannot respond to the unpredictability of policing tasks or the demand of breakfast meetings or lunar hours. The logic goes something like this: Good coppers put the job before anything else, women put children first; ergo, women with children do not make good coppers. Another example of the conflict in being a mother and a woman police officer is represented as follows: kids whose mothers work get into trouble, women working fulltime as police officers are not at home looking after the kids; ergo, women officers are creating problem children. A young Afro-Caribbean woman officer interviewed as part of another research study (Brown & Harleston, 2003) recounted how she had shown colleagues a picture of her recent pregnancy scan; the response it evoked from a male officer was, 'Where's the CRO number?' [criminal record office marker of convicted offenders].

Thus, women's commitments to policing are alleged to be incomplete if they have domestic care obligations. Tuffin and Baladi (2001) note that women part-time officers were regarded as not fitting in with a working culture because they 'could [not] be handed their jackets any time and told to get out there at any time' (p. 44). This was seen as diminishing the effectiveness of their contribution and potentially the efficacy of service. Silvestri (2000) contends that the imagery of policing as a career option tends to define it as one intrinsically at odds with domestic responsibilities.

As a result career progression in policing appeals primarily to single people – men and women – who can devote themselves single-mindedly to their work. If women limit their working hours they do so in the knowledge that they may also be limiting their career opportunities. Men, for their part, insist on the importance for one's career prospects in the police of always being available for breakfast meetings and ready to accept long working hours.

Elements of IPT can also be tracked in regard to the physical requirements of policing – where the standards debate again crops up. Cohn (2000) shows how differentiated physical training (PT) criteria in the military are seen as lowering standards. Male soldiers in her sample articulated their feelings about the perceived injustice of gender-norming the physical fitness standards in statements like, 'They say they want equal rights, well they should be held to the same fitness standards as we are'. The PT protest accordingly becomes an acceptable way of reasserting gender differences and saying that women are physically inferior, and offers an avenue for expressing anger about the expansion of women's role within the military. It is a means of constructing and reinforcing gender difference, a way of asserting male superiority and signalling rage and grief at the loss of the military as a male sanctum.

A similar discourse can be found in the police service in regard to use of equipment and physical fitness standards. Prenzler (1997) discusses these issues as they are related to the situation in Australia. He notes that a major ideological source of opposition to women officers is that policing involves physical confrontation. Physical fitness tests, in which women fail at a greater rate than men are an area of potential discrimination. Monkhouse (personal communication, 2002) discussed the problem (in British policing) of parity in fitness tests for men and women that disadvantages women to the degree that the un-normed test (in other words, a test normed only to a male standard) resulted in 40% of female recruits failing compared to over 90% of men passing, with the failing women being excluded from the service. The problem elements in the test were the upper-body strength 'push-pull' testing, a grip test, and the shuttle run, ostensibly measuring lung capacity, in which recruits had to do return runs between two fixed points with a metronome synchronised to diminish the time interval between runs. The stated purpose of the tests is to ensure a level of fitness whereby officers can meet the requirements of their day to day work, manage shift working, minimise sickness absences and, when necessary, physically restrain and/or run after people. A UK Home Office Circular (2003) tabled changes to the job-related fitness test (JRFT) which discontinued the grip strength test and reduced the endurance element of the shuttle runs. Subsequently, 99% of men and 76% of women recruits passed. The reduction of the physical testing requirement has created a debate about standards reminiscent of the military examples cited above. Thus, a police trainer is quoted in a Police Review article by Roystone Martis as commenting that

> No right minded individual expects all police officers to have the speed of Linford Christie, the stamina of Paula Radcliffe or the strength of Geoff Capes. But I do think the public would be genuinely surprised – if not a little concerned – if they knew the low fitness standard people have to meet when they join the police service and how easy it is for someone to pass the fitness test to become a sworn constable. The endurance element of the JRFT can be passed at not much more than walking pace and those people who can comfortably carry some packed shopping bags from the supermarket should have no worries over making the grade when it comes to the dynamic strength test. Obviously the pass levels are only minimum amounts designed to encourage a more inclusive and representative workforce. (Martis, 2006, p. 18)

This comment may be interpreted as an example of men indirectly claiming greater natural suitability for the policing task, the implication being that when gender norming leads to recalibration of fitness tests, the lower requirements for physical fitness will mean reduced capacity to restrain or pursue suspects – not to mention more time lost to sick leave. Disavowal of gold medallist expectations (for men or women officers) still urges the point about falling standards: by this logic it is all very well to promote diversity and boost the representation of women and ethnic minorities, but the price to pay will be fewer officers with real (meaning physical) capacity for the job.

ORGANISATIONAL ATTENTION

Elements of social IPT can be helpful in understanding the reactions of individuals when their identity is under threat, and this line of analysis has been extended by Ocasio (1993) to explain how organisations seek to protect themselves under conditions of adversity. In particular, the concept of organisational attention may be useful to invoke in situations where the police service concentrates on an immediate criticism (internal or external) at the expense of the attention equally demanded by other continuing issues. When an organisation is facing a threat (for example, operational failure such as the death of Stephen Lawrence, or corruption inquiries such as the Warren or Fitzgerald Commissions) impending risk can result in restriction in information used by decision makers and constriction in control (Ocasio, 1993, p. 2).

Organisations facing performance failures have been found to limit the number of information sources consulted and reduce the attention senior executives give to potential solutions (D'Aveni & MacMillan, 1990). Ocasio's proposition is that threats are categorised as loss rather than opportunity and that response to adversity is regulated by the institutional logic embedded in the organisation's cultural systems. Senior decision makers in the organisation place greater reliance on readily available hypotheses, decrease their tolerance of ambiguity and increase their tendency to emit well-learned dominant responses. Ocasio goes on to argue that the decision making is shaped not only by narrow self interest but also by the dominant group identification. Group identification invokes schemas (goals, interests, norms, categorisations) for attending, interpreting and responding to diverse situations and dictating which to focus on. These are stored in the organisational memory (through standard operating procedures, organisational programmes and routines, formal systems and control, structures and roles, stories and myths) whence they are in turn brought to bear on present crises. The implicit rules for deciding which problems get attended to and which solutions are considered are reflective of the organisation's culture. Identification of threats increases reliance on available repertoires stored in the organisational memory.

Ocasio (1993) provides evidence that failure-induced organisational change is of this nature. He also suggests that to the extent that the dominant organisational identity is cohesive and stable and its power well established, the interests and beliefs of the core dominant group will predominate and reliance on core cultural assumptions will increase. This kind of hypothesis seems highly plausible for a police organisation, where the occupational culture literature argues there is strong internal cohesiveness – and certainly a strong hierarchical organisational structure in which men dominate. Criticisms of the police are often couched in terms of failure: poor performance in investigating a high profile crime, corrupt practices not rooted out. In this chapter, we have considered the eclipsing of gender-related reform and a reconstitution of masculine identity. So when the police occupational identity is threatened by external criticism – such as that contained in the Macpherson Inquiry which both called in question, the operational competency of the police and criticised the organisation itself as institutionally racist – there is a narrowing of focus. As Rycroft, Brown, and Innes (2007) put it, the Metropolitan Police failed to pick up 'errors, omissions and mistakes [observed by Macpherson in] systems and processes that are part of the standard operating procedures of police homicide investigations' (p. 148); reformation of gendered operational practices and procedures had to yield priority to ethnicity as the focus for organisational attention. Much of the ethnicity agenda, too, is male dominated (Brown & Harleston, 2003; Morris, 2004), meaning that taken for granted male cultural assumptions are more likely to be invoked when considering and adopting solutions and also more likely to limit forms of organisational change less consistent with those core assumptions.

CONCLUSION

The argument presented here posits a tension between the changes that have undeniably occurred in policing practices and management and the reluctance of police officers to repudiate deleterious masculine attributes of the police occupational identity. Identity construction is a dynamic process in which self-esteem and self-efficacy are critically tied into content. The occupational culture provides the resources to create and maintain identity. Under threat, the organisation draws on repertoires grounded in the occupational culture to focus responses that will preserve the dominant identity. These prove to be versatile and resourceful in perpetuating the image and likeness of male model of police in which women may collude. Reviewing the position of women in the police, they appear still to be viewed oppositionally in terms of what they are not rather than of what they are. Psychologically, changes in police identity construction must find ways in which efficacy and self-esteem are grounded in both feminine and masculine attributes.

There is little doubt that the police-working environment generates a sense of internal solidarity and coherence and that there is also a physical requirement in policing tasks such as public order duties. These become problematic when attempts to preserve continuity in the dimension of masculinity lay stress on the distinctiveness of male and female character-istics and attributes. When this happens, aspects of masculinity become exclusory and domineering. Notions of the 'moral' woman give rise to assumptions that her presence in policing will change the problematic aspects of the culture. Indeed there is currently debate within the British police service that positive discrimination, presently unlawful, should be introduced to increase the numerical representation of women (Brown et al., 2006). The implications from IPT and organisational attention theory suggest that numbers alone will not produce the desired differences and that rather more radical dismantling of the cultural resources is required.

NOTES

1. Annual reports can be found at http://inspectorates.homeoffice.gov.uk/hmic/
2. Stephen Lawrence, a black teenager, was murdered by white racists and the Metropolitan Police failed to bring the perpetrators to court. A political campaign resulted in the setting up of the Macpherson Inquiry into the police management of the murder investigation resulting in the charge of 'institutional' racism in the ensuing report.

REFERENCES

Barton, H. (2003). Understanding occupational (sub)culture – a precursor for reform: The case of the police service in England and Wales. *International Journal of Public Sector Management, 16*, 346–358.

Breakwell, G. (1986). *Threatened identities*. London: Methuen.

Brown, J. (2003). Women leaders: A catalyst for change. In: R. Adlam & P. Villiers (Eds), *Police leadership in the twenty-first century*. Winchester: Waterside Press.

Brown, J., & Heidensohn, F. M. (2000). *Gender and policing*. Basingstoke: Palgrave Macmillan.

Brown, J., Hegarty, P., & O'Neill, D. (2006). *Playing with numbers: A discussion paper on positive discrimination as a means for achieving gender equality in the police service in England and Wales*. Guildford: Department of Psychology University of Surrey.

Brown, J. M., & Harleston, D. (2003). Being black or Asian and a woman in the police service. *Policing Futures, 1*, 19–32.

Brown, M. K. (1988). *Working the streets: Police discretion and the dilemmas of reform* (2nd ed.). New York: Sage.

Cashmore, E. (2001). The experiences of ethnic minority police officers in Britain: Under-recruitment and racial profiling in a performance culture. *Ethnic and Racial Studies, 24*, 642–659.

Chan, J. (1996). Changing police culture. *British Journal of Criminology, 36*, 109–134.

Chan, J. (2005). Changing police culture. In: T. Newburn (Ed.), *Policing: Key readings*. Cullompton: Willan.

Cohn, C. (2000). 'How can she claim equal rights when she doesn't have to do as many push-ups as I do?' The framing of men's opposition to women's equality in the military. *Men and Masculinities, 3*, 131–151.

Cope, N. (2004). Intelligence led policing or policing led intelligence? *British Journal of Criminology, 44*, 188–203.

D'Aveni, R., & MacMillan, I. (1990). Crisis and the content of managerial communication: A study of top managers in surviving and failing firms. *Administrative Science Quarterly, 35*, 634–657.

Dick, P., & Cassell, C. (2004). The position of policewomen: A discourse analytic study. *Work Employment and Society, 18*, 51–72.

Dick, P., & Jankowicz, D. (2001). A social constructionist account of police culture and its influence on the representation and progression of female officers: A repertory grid analysis in a UK police force. *Policing: An International Journal of Police Strategies and Management, 24*, 181–199.

Edwards, C. (2005). *Changing policing theories for 21st century societies* (2nd ed.). Sydney: The Federation Press.

Fielding, N. (1997). *Changing police culture: Policing in a multicultural society, review.* www.socresonline.org.uk/2/2fielding.html

Fielding, N. (1999). Policing's dark secret: The career paths of ethnic minority officers. *Sociological Research Online, 4*(1), www.socreonline.org.uk/socresonline/4/lawrence/fielding.html

Fiske, S. (1991). Expert testimony presented in Robinson v. Jacksonville Shipyards, US District Court, Florida Division, 482 US 301.

Fleming, J., & Lafferty, G. (2002). Equity confounded? New managerialism, organisational restructuring and women in Australian police service. Paper presented to the 3rd Australian women and policing conference Canberra, 20–23 October.

Foster, J. (2003). Police cultures. In: T. Newburn (Ed.), *Handbook of policing*. Cullompton: Willan.

Foster, J., Newburn, T., & Souhami, A. (2005). *Assessing the impact of the Stephen Lawrence Inquiry*. HO Research Study 294 HO Research Development and Statistics Directorate.

Guardian. (2003). Speech by the shadow home secretary, Oliver Letwin, to the Conservative party conference. http://politics.guardian.co.uk/tories2003/story/0,1057994,00.html

Heidensohn, F. (2003). Gender and policing. In: T. Newburn (Ed.), *Handbook of policing*. Cullompton: Willan.

Heidensohn, F. M. (1992). *Women in control*. Oxford: Clarendon.

Holdaway, S., & Parker, S. K. (1998). Policing women police: Uniform patrol, promotion and representation in the CID. *British Journal of Criminology, 38*, 40–60.

Home Office Circular (2003). 51/2003 National recruitment standards – eligibility criteria for police recruitment and consistent recruitment practices. London: Home Office, Police Personnel Unit.

Hunt, J. (1984). Logic of sexism amongst police. *Women and Criminal Justice, 1*, 3–30.

Innes, M. (2006). The public face of policing. *Criminal Justice Matters, 63*, 14–15.

Johnson, G., & Scholes, K. (2002). *Exploring corporate strategy* (6th ed.). London: Pearson Education.

Jones, S. (1986). *Policewomen and equality*. London: Macmillan.

Leishman, F., Loveday, B., & Savage, S. (2003). *Core issues in policing* (2nd ed.). London: Pearson Educational.

Lersch, K. M. (1998). Predicting citizen race in allegations of misconduct against police – understanding and controlling police abuse of force. *Journal of Criminal Justice, 26*, 87–97.

Maddock, S. (1999). *Challenging women: Gender culture and organisation*. London: Sage.

Maddock, S., & Parkin, D. (1993). Gender cultures: Women's choices and strategies at work. *Women in Management Review, 8*, 3–10.

Martin, S. (1996). Doing gender, doing police work: An examination of the barriers to the integration of women officers. Paper presented to the first Australasian women police conference Sydney, 29–31 July.

Martin, S., & Jurik, N. (1996). *Doing justice, doing gender: Women in law and criminal justice occupations*. Thousand Oaks, CA: Sage.

Martis, R. (2006). Let's get physical. *Police Review, 114*(5879), 16–18.

Miller, S. L. (1999). *Gender and community policing*. Boston, MA: Northeastern University Press.

Morris, Sir William. (2004). The case for change: People in the Metropolitan police service. Results of an independent inquiry. www.morrisinquiry.gov.com

Ocasio, W. (1993). *The structuring of organisational attention and the enactment of economic adversity: A reconciliation of theories of failure-induced change and threat rigidity.* Working Paper 3577–93, MIT Sloan School of Management, Cambridge, MA.

Palmer, D. (1999). Confronting police culture or is the force still with you. *International Journal of Police Science and Management, 1,* 333–346.

Paoline, E. A. (2003). Taking stock: Towards a richer understanding of police culture. *Journal of Criminal Justice, 31,* 199–214.

Prenzler, T. (1997). Is there a police culture. *Australian Journal of Public Administration, 56,* 47–56.

Prokos, A., & Padacic, I. (2002). There oughtta be a law against bitches: Masculinity lessons in police training. *Gender Work and Organisation, 9,* 439–459.

Reiner, R. (1985). *The politics of the police.* Brighton: Wheatsheaf.

Rycroft, M., Brown, J., & Innes, M. (2007). Reform by crisis: The murder of Stephen Lawrence and a socio-historical analysis of developments in the conduct of major crime investigations. In: M. Rowe (Ed.), *Policing beyond Macpherson.* Cullompton: Willan.

Silvestri M. (2000). *Visions of the future.* Ph.D. thesis, University of London, London, Goldsmiths.

Smith, D., & Gray, J. (1985). *Police and people of London.* London: The Policy Studies Institute.

Steel, B., & Lovrich, N. P. (1987). Equality and efficiency tradeoffs in affirmative action, real or imagined? The case of women in policing. *Social Science Journal, 24,* 53–70.

Terrill, W., Paoline, E. A., & Manning, P. (2003). Police culture and coercion. *Criminology, 41,* 1003–1034.

Trice, H. M. (1993). *Occupational sub cultures in the workplace.* Ithaca, NY: ILR Press.

Tuffin, R., & Baladi, Y. (2001). *Flexible working practices in the police service.* Home Office Police Research Paper 147.

Van der Lapp, T., Graumans, A., & Sevenhuijsen, S. (2004). Gender policies and position of women in the police forces in European countries. *Journal of European Social Policy, 14,* 391–405.

Vanstone, A. (2001). No longer lady policemen: The changing role of women in law enforcement in Australia. *Forum on Crime and Society, 1,* 119–123.

Waddington, P. A. J. (1999). Police (canteen) sub culture: An appreciation. *British Journal of Criminology, 39,* 287–308.

Westmarland, L. (2001). *Gender and policing: Sex, power and police culture.* Cullompton: Willan.

PART III:
POLICE AS CHANGE AGENTS

CHAPTER 9

POLICE UNIONS AND THEIR INFLUENCE: SUBCULTURE OR COUNTER-CULTURE?

Monique Marks

ABSTRACT

This chapter examines the concept of 'subculture' in the context of police organisations and considers whether police unions present an alternative cultural influence. While the unions certainly challenge hierarchical cultural practices, they tend to defend established notions of police professionalism and ways of doing things. However, evidence suggests that police unions have the capacity and desire to shape new directions in policing. Nor are police unions always backward looking, and their (expected) preoccupation with defending the traditional role and identity of the public police could be interpreted as a 'left' agenda. Ultimately, the cultural influence of the police unions is in no way fixed. Much depends on union leaders' willingness to engage with the new directions in policing and on the extent to which they are prepared to push the thinking of their membership base.

As late as the mid-1960s police chiefs had virtually unlimited power to run their departments. Today police chiefs are seriously constrained. Not only are many important issues subject to collective bargaining, but police unions exert enormous informal influence both within the department and in the community at large. Police

Police Occupational Culture: New Debates and Directions
Sociology of Crime, Law and Deviance, Volume 8, 229–251
Copyright © 2007 by Elsevier Ltd.
All rights of reproduction in any form reserved
ISSN: 1521-6136/doi:10.1016/S1521-6136(07)08009-8

unions are here to stay. We cannot ignore them. (William O. Douglas Institute, 1984,
cited in Magenau & Hunt, 1996, p. 1315)

Police unions are today very much part of the landscape of policing in
most liberal democracies. Their very existence has been a signal to police
leaders and managers that decision-making in the police is a zone of sharp
contestation, banishing any notion that policing can be rolled out like some
kind of smoothly oiled bureaucratic machine. But do police unions really
set forward alternative agendas in policing or do they block change programmes? Are they influential in reshaping fundamental police organisational
culture? Do they present as a specific 'culture' of their own, and, if so,
should this be understood as a *sub*culture or as a *counter*-culture?

These are elusive questions, not least because before we can locate the
presence or influence of police union 'culture' we are faced with the initial
difficulty of trying to get in focus the continuously evolving 'parent culture'
or dominant culture of public policing agencies, in which there have been
substantial shifts in management discourse and practice over the past two
decades. Taking a lead from the work done by Davies and Thomas (2001)
on managerial identities in the UK public sector, my initial premise in this
chapter is that public police agencies now exhibit a varied matrix of
management discourses and practices, and I shall be examining the way that
this matrix, in turn, provides space for both resistance and acculturation
'from below' from groups such as police unions. As things stand, and as this
chapter argues, police unions are more likely to acculturate than to resist,
and to defend what is known rather than pioneer new directions.

The questions I have indicated are fundamentally empirical questions and
would therefore be most suitably approached through case studies that focus
on the culture of police unions and the impact that the union culture has on
parent police occupational culture. So it is somewhat against my better
judgement that, for the purposes of this chapter, I have opted instead for a
rather more speculative approach, surveying the existing knowledge
internationally about police unionism and offering some reflections on my
own engagement with police unionists from five different countries. The
chapter draws on mixed sources of empirical data: interviews with key police
unionists from America, Canada, Australia and New Zealand, and South
Africa; official police union documents; papers presented by police unionists
at recent conferences and newspaper reports about police unions. A more
case study-based approach would no doubt provide for greater empirical
depth, but I think it may also be useful to explore some broader observations
about police unions and their cultural influence as subcultural groupings.

Students of subcultures within the police will recognise a familiar set of subgroup cleavage lines that analysis commonly homes in on: exposure to danger (Van Maanen, 1974); gender (Sherman, 1973); race and ethnicity education (Holdaway & O'Neill, 2004); street and management cops (Reuss-Ianni & Ianni, 1983); rank (Punch, 1983); occupation or subunit (Rubenstein, 1973; Manning, 1977); shift assignment (Jermier & Berkes, 1979); organisational tenure (Jermier, Slocum, Fry, & Gaines, 1991); organisational loyalty (Reuss-Ianni & Ianni, 1983); work performance (Reuss-Ianni & Ianni, 1983; Jermier et al., 1991, p. 174). Police unions, on the other hand, seldom feature as a subcultural element in this picture. Indeed, considering the influence that police unions have within police organisations (Marks & Fleming, 2006), scholarly work on police unions remains scant (Walker, 2006).

There was, to be sure, a flurry of academic interest in police unions in the 1970s (particularly in the United States) when it began to be evident that the unions would change the way that police managers do business. There was a general consensus at that time that police unions (for better or worse) directly challenged both the hierarchical framework of police agencies and the prerogatives of management in those agencies. Interest then seemed to tail off, and in the past two decades or so relatively little has been written about police unions (Walker, 2006). Those who have attended to this topic have been concerned with the politicisation of the unions (Finnane, 2002); the importance of police labour rights (Marks & Fleming, 2006; Sklansky, 2005) and the role of unions in building participatory management practices (Wuestewald et al., 2006). But, with one recent exception, there has been little or no attention paid to the cultural influence of police unions.

The exception is a forthcoming piece by Pat O'Malley and Steven Hutchinson to be published in forthcoming a special edition of *Police Practice and Research* on 'reshaping policing', in which these authors look at the corporate management culture in policing and the ways in which police unions are responding to and shaping this corporate culture. O'Malley and Hutchinson (2007, forthcoming) conclude that 'police unionism should perhaps be moved to the forefront of our analysis of contemporary transformations in policing'. This chapter is an attempt to bring police unionism into the foreground of our understanding of contemporary tendencies in police culture.

Police force members and police unionists in particular are inclined to take their bearings, both structurally and culturally, from within the police organisation. Buying into the normative orders of the agency, there may be moments of dissidence but these are not often sustained. Not surprisingly, the primary identity of a police union member continues to be that of police officer, not unionist or social activist. All this means that the cultures that evolve in police unions tend to be very insular, with the unions inclined to keep their distance from external influences which could shift union self-identities and strategies. Although it is now not uncommon for unilateral decision-making to be challenged by police unions, it is rather seldom that union objections are targeted at any kind of strategically progressive reshaping of the organisation. Put another way, we do not commonly find that the subculture of police unions is appreciably at odds with the predominant and established culture of the policing organisations within which they subsist.

This chapter begins by examining the concept of 'subculture' in the context of police organisations. It then turns to a discussion about contemporary 'management cop' culture (the presently dominant culture) as a way of illustrating both that police managers are innovators within police organisations but also that changing the fundamentals of police organisational culture is extremely difficult. Of course there is no one way of capturing police management culture – many different ones exist, even within individual police organisations – and what I write here is about a general trend within police management circles. Similarly, when I talk about police unions I am pointing to general characterisations which gloss over the differences between police unions across the world.

The chapter then turns to consider the kinds of subcultures that police unions generate, showing that while the unions certainly challenge hierarchical cultural practices, they have not (for the most part) actively shaped an alternative police occupational culture. To the contrary, rather than partnering with police managers in promoting new ways of organising, they defend established notions of police professionalism and identity. However, as Samuel Walker (2006) recently pointed out, police unions are complex and constantly changing. They have the capacity to impact both positively and negatively on change. Much depends on the circumstances in which they find themselves and the alliances they make with other societal groupings. In the final section of the paper, then, I explore evidence of progressive tendencies within police illustrating that the cultural influence of the unions is in no way fixed.

SUBCULTURE AND COUNTER-CULTURE
IN POLICE ORGANISATIONS

The informal dimension (the 'organisational culture') of policing is just as important as the more formal dimensions, if not more so, in shaping police behaviour and the broader evolution of policing organisations (Winslow, 1998).[1] Organisational culture is now seen as perhaps *the* key factor in understanding how police organisations function, inasmuch as it provides organisational members with a 'set of common understandings around which action is oriented' (Becker & Geer, 1960, p. 305). More deeply, organisational culture is the set of basic assumptions and beliefs that operate unconsciously within an organisation and function as learned responses to a group's survival (Schein, 1996).

Organisational leaders are the key source of an organisation's ideology. They generate organisational norms and values which stand as the official or dominant culture of the organisation, expressed in formal statements of mission and standards of conduct intended to legitimate the organisation in the eyes of the outside world (Jermier et al., 1991). But this does not mean that an organisation hosts a single and uniform organisational culture: co-existing within it will inevitably be sub-groupings with their own characteristics and identities, each creating its own networks of meanings, while remaining, for the most part, tied into the ideologies and values of the organisation's leadership. When the tenets of the subculture are at odds with those of the dominant (or official) culture, a counter-culture has been forged. And a counter-culture is one that we would generally understand to be promoting some kind of acting outside of the usual conventions of an organisation.

Jermier et al. (1991) argue that top management in police agencies is often unable to impose organisation-wide conformance. This is not a new point. Reiner (1992) in his highly influential account of 'cop culture', pointed out that police culture, while constituted by a set of 'core characteristics', is 'neither monolithic, universal or unchanging' (p. 137). Police culture is shaped by the kind of people who make up a particular police organisation, the types of situations and problems that are confronted, the philosophies of individual police agencies and the wider cultural beliefs that are held in society (Chan, 1996). Within any single agency 'lines of fissure' in the occupational culture can be detected between different sub-groups of police based on rank, race, function, religion and gender (Brewer, 1991). As individuals and as sub-groups police officers may accommodate or resist police culture (Fielding, 1989).

Individual officers will be influenced by official cop culture each according to their individual experience of their work, their individual motivations and commitments and whatever individual affiliations they may have internally within the organisation (such as to identity-based associations or police unions). And in every police agency the internal cultural diversity this creates will exhibit various lines of cleavage – rank, race, function, etc. – according to the composition of the particular force. Officers create a diversity of cultural response as they actively configure their understanding of the organisation and its environment (Chan, 1996; Harrison, 1988; Waddington, 1999). They are active decision-makers but they are guided by the existing organisational and symbolic framework of the organisation (Fielding, 1989).

Organisational theorist Randall Rose (1988) argues that multiple cultures within an organisation can take on a variety of forms along a continuum between full acquiescence and outright resistance to the core values of the dominant culture. Rose points out that there are two ways of understanding the notion of 'multiple cultures' here: 'On the one hand, the phrase might refer to a loose constellation of unique cultures (in terms of meanings, values and structures or linkages between meanings/values) not connected to an overall core culture. On the other hand, the phrase could be defined as an array of distinct subcultures that exist in relationship to a core or umbrella culture' (p. 143).

In a similar vein, Jermier et al. (1991) argue that police managers have to concede (however reluctantly) that it is beyond their capacity to enforce conformance to the official, dominant, parent culture. While there may well be sub-groups that do unreservedly embrace the official culture (paramilitary unit members, perhaps), there are also 'resistance subcultures' within the police. In these authors' view, organisational subcultures emerge as groups of employees challenge, modify or even replace official culture. But even as these sub-cultural groupings may resist the official police culture, degrees of resistance are limited by shared stated and unstated norms.

Herbert (1998) uses the term 'normative order' to explain what holds police organisations together across internal subcultures. He defines these normative orders as 'a set of generalised rules and common practices oriented around a common value' (p. 347). Herbert identifies six such normative orders as generally shared by all police actors: law, bureaucratic control, adventure/machismo, safety, competence and morality. Each furnishes a possible channel of understanding and response in one or another policing situation. While any police organisation will inevitably be beset with ongoing conflicts and disputes, the sharing of these normative orders has the effect of containing and setting bounds to internal friction. Police officers regularly enact internalised rules and values, 'but they consciously adapt and transform them in the process of defining and engaging ongoing situations' (p. 364). This individual adaptation and transformation of normative orders can be (and often is) shared with other individuals with similar experiences and dispositions leading to 'multiple cultures, subcultures and countercultures' (Jermier et al., 1991).

Those who write about subcultures in policing often foreground the distinction between management cops and street cops (Holdaway, 1983; Reuss-Ianni & Ianni, 1983). Management cops are seen as aligned chiefly with the formal and bureaucratic dimensions of policing, with street cops as the ones who innovate in the face of the bureaucratic ethos (Herbert, 1998). Similarly, Adlam (2002) writes about the 'culture gap' that exists between the language of management and the discourse of the front-line service deliverers.

While there are abundant studies about policing subcultures that evolve in clusters of personnel aligned with divisions, departments, groups and work teams, there is no substantial account of employee-representative organisa-tions (unions, associations, lodges) as sites of alternative police culture. Police unions are the surest manifestation that police are direct social actors, tangibly and immediately shaping their world and responsive to broader societal currents. Police leaders, on the other hand, are innovators within police organisations and while they may wish to work collaboratively with the unions, their main objective is to direct efficient and effective organi-sations. This may well lead them into confrontations with the police unions – running counter to formal commitments to collegiality and team building as framed, particularly, in new police managerial discourses.

BUREAUCRACY, MANAGERIALISM AND THE 'NEW' POLICE MANAGEMENT CULTURE

Over the past few decades there have been big changes in the organisational machinery of state policing. In advanced liberal democracies reform has been 'fuelled variously by demands for efficiency and effectiveness, a concern about the relationship between the police and the community they serve, and organisational corruption' (Fleming & Rhodes, 2005, p. 192). Bureaucratic ways of organising are now viewed as expensive and lacking market incentives (Bevir & Krupicka, this volume). Policing scholars now write about the shift from hierarchical bureaucracy to markets and networks as the new governing framework for the police (den Boer, 2004; Skelcher, Mathur, & Smith, 2004; Shaw & Shearing, 1998; Fleming & Rhodes, 2005). 'Managerialism' or 'new public management' is flavour of the month as public police agencies, sometimes under political orders, follow the lead of the private sector in reinventing their administrative philosophy and practice.

The extent of this convergence between private and public management systems is still under debate and Poole, Mansfield, and Gould-Williams (2006, p. 1051) argue it is 'most evident in rhetoric rather than in attitude and behaviour let alone organisational or institutional change'.

Absolute convergence between private sector management models and police management practices is limited by the persistence of bureaucratic ways, public service ethics and the fact that shareholder interests have no real meaning in the public sector (Poole, et al., 2006). Still, police managers have been forced by their ever changing environment to be more open in policy and decision-making, more responsive to the needs of communities and also more flexible and creative in their management practices (Steinheider & Wuestewald, 2007, forthcoming). Neo-liberal reform agendas in public policy prioritise efficiency and accountability and have 'fostered the inclusion of corporate governance strategies such as performance indicators into police departments' (Bevir & Krupicka, this volume). In their pursuit of efficiency and effectiveness, police managers are also experimenting with new service delivery plans and this has led to a 'blurring of the frontiers between public, market and voluntary sectors' (Pool et al., 2006, p. 1052). New experiments include the contracting out of police services to non-governmental actors and the crafting of competitive 'self-directed' teams within police organisations (Bevir & Krupicka, this volume). These innovations in service delivery and management practices, as a package, challenge in very fundamental ways traditional notions of police professionalism and established ideas about what the police do.

In the past three decades, police managers have adopted managerial discourse and practice from other service sectors (Kiely & Peek, 2002) and from the language of networked governance. Murphy (2004), writing about the Canadian police executive community concludes that police executives have changed from being senior police officers into modern organisational managers. The new police manager discourse is about value for money, business planning and efficiency (Murphy, 2004). Public sector managerialism and corporate business models emphasise 'managerial rather than legal or public interest standards, favour external oversight combined with self-regulation rather than centralised control and promote risk management rather than rule control' (Chan, 1999, p. 251).

Police leaders, particularly in the English-speaking world, now repudiate as outmoded the legacy of military structuring. Australian officials, for example, have for some years been proclaiming a 'new era' in policing management – vide John Murray (2002) confirming at a recent leadership conference that police leaders across the developed world have been forced to examine the appropriateness and efficacy of [the] traditional model for at least two reasons. The first is its inflexibility and consequently inability to meet the demands of efficiency and effectiveness in an environment described as volatile as any competitive market. ... The second is the experience of many police leaders that the autocratic style of leadership and the strict enforcement of rules associated with the traditional model is at odds with the expectations of a modern workforce. (2002, p. 1)

Murray continues that 'the challenge to modern policing, it seems to me is to provide a leadership and managerial system which recognises the value of a more democratic style and at the same time provides a disciplinary process not built on blame but on values that the organisation seeks to promote' (2004, p. 15). The Australian Federal Police has shifted towards a 'democratic' managerial structure, and in 1995 a National Teams Model was introduced into the organisation, 'resulting in the flattening of the hierarchical structure of the AFP ... . It was envisaged that the concept of empowerment would extend to all areas of the organisation and in practical terms this would increase the authority and decision making power of members from the lowest level up' (p. 17).

A growing number of police agencies in places like Canada, the United Kingdom and Australia are now signing up (sometimes literally so) to neo-liberal business models and values. They project themselves as organisations 'doing business' (O'Malley & Hutchinson, 2007, forthcoming). The old bureaucratic terminology has been displaced by private sector jargon: police managers now speak about offering products and services, creating strategic visions and mission statements, and organising police stations as budgeting units (Vickers & Kouzmin, 2001). Going hand in hand with notions of self-regulation is a preoccupation with increased 'professionalism'. The favoured new managerial mechanisms of building police professionalism are stepped-up training, micro performance management and certification (Evetts, 2006). These new disciplinary technologies are, not surprisingly, sharply contested, especially by police unions who are not generally disposed to abandon more traditional models of police 'professionalism' that emphasise notions of autonomy, discretion and legitimacy (Davies & Thomas, 2001).

Agencies such as the Victoria Police in Australia and the Suffolk Police in the United Kingdom are now led by corporate governance committees tasked with formulating policy, performance targets and budget priorities, and also with monitoring and auditing the performance of the police individually and as an organisation (Victoria Police, 2004, 2005). The new official public police management discourse insists on the need for harnessing the capacity and knowledge of all police service members at all levels as well as those of the community groupings in the business of policing. Prioritising of 'people potential' has seen the introduction in several police agencies of team leadership programmes designed to provide employees with a channel for sharing their experiences and discussing ways of improving the workplace environment (O'Malley, 2005; see also Steinheider & Wuestewald, 2007, forthcoming).[2]

Does this new direction in police management mean that there are shifts, too, in the dominant police culture, so that it no longer has quite the same bureaucratic centre of gravity as formerly? It's probably too early to judge; the reinvented police officer may be a more tolerant and managerially disposed operative, but in policing generally the traditional reliance on codes of discipline is still very much in place as the foundation for efficiency and accountability (Davies & Thomas, 2001). Vickers and Kouzmin (2001, p. 19) in their examination of Australian police agencies conclude that managerialism 'remains a front for centralised control ... a debilitating charade'. For Davis and Thomas (2001, p. 18), the discourse and practice of the new managerialism are 'neither coherent nor unified'. In a work environment where scandals and charges of inequity are never far beneath the surface, police administrators see the paramilitary model as the one that will preserve accountability and control (Wuestewald & Steinheider, 2006). None of this offers much inducement for officers in the lower ranks to learn from their mistakes, take responsibility for their actions or share in decision-making.

Despite the spoken commitment to flattened managerial systems as part of the corporate management turn, Adlam (2002) argues that what has really occurred is an increased gap 'between the different dramaturgical worlds of the "street cops" and the "management cops"' (p. 33). This is perhaps, in part, because more traditional ways of managing persist while radically new management practices are being introduced. Commenting on the British police, Kiely and Peek (2002) suggest that the worst of both management systems are combined – close performance management alongside poor downward communication in a still strongly hierarchical ethos.

The introduction of police reform, even when this involves more inclusive management practices, is 'implemented in a top-down fashion that fails to secure buy-in and support from rank-and-file officers' (Bevir & Krupicka, this volume). And so, while shifts in management discourse and style may have created the space for more collaborative decision-making, a preoccupation with efficiency, target setting and monetary accountability also create tendencies towards enhanced micro-management. This creates the fertile ground for union defensiveness and a looking backward towards more established practices and identifications. But there is also now greater space than ever before for unions to rethink and to reshape the way that police organisations 'do business'.

POLICE UNIONS AND THEIR CULTURAL INFLUENCE

While there is certainly discordance between the vision of police managers and the daily experiences of rank-and-file offices working within police organisations, public policing is increasingly beginning to look like one more example of corporate enterprise. But lip-service to mutual enterprise and employee participation has done little to close the divide between management and rank-and-file, and the police unions have noticeably strengthened their presence (see O'Malley & Hutchinson, 2007, forthcoming).

The police unions have always presented a cultural challenge to police organisations by insisting on giving the rank-and-file a collective voice in decisions around a range of issues related to management of police organisations. If we are to assume that bureaucratic traditions and practices die hard in police organisations, then the unions have and continue to present a counter-cultural influence. But new cultural shifts require us to reappraise the cultural contribution of the police unions and look ahead at their possible influence on the occupation of police work, taking particular note of how the unions are situated and what their mandate is.

Counter-Cultural Dispositions

For the most part, police unions have positioned themselves vis-à-vis managers as contestant rather than partner organisations. Walker (2006) puts it well when he states that the advent of police unions was a 'rude shock' to police managers who had never had to seriously consider the contributory voice of the rank-and-file. What the unions have contested most strongly is unilateral decision-making, particularly when police organisations are, or were, organised (nominally at least) on conventionally down-the-line bureaucratic principles. The police union challenge to hierarchical decision-making practices and notions of 'discipline' within police organisations has been an abiding source of anxiety on the part of police managers everywhere (Grimes, 1975).

Police unions have fundamentally reshaped the way in which police organisations work internally by constraining police leader authority and introducing a 'rights regime' into police organisations (Finnane, 1999, p. 11). The idea of police asserting their 'rights' (as workers and as citizens) has always been unsettling for police managers and employers (Marks & Fleming, 2006).

Where police unions do exist, they generally represent the overwhelming majority of the members of the police organisation – a real achievement given the decline of trade union membership internationally (Fleming & Peetz, 2005; Finnane, 2002; Farber, 2005; Marks & Fleming, 2006). It is in large part due to this high degree of representation that police unions are viewed as a force to be reckoned with. They have become influential 'insider groupings' (Fleming, Marks, & Wood, 2006) and police managers and employers are eager not to 'upset' the unions (Punch, Huberts, & Lamboo, 2000). Police unionists are well aware of their power and influence. As a police unionist from New South Wales in Australia recalls:

> We don't flaunt our power as a union and we try to use it responsibly. But, I always remember when they tried to take away the appeal rights for discharges under Commissioner Ryan. They only managed to do this for a very short period of time because we got 3000 cops marching down Macquarie Street. That scared the devil out of the government and police management because they knew we could bring them down. (Telephone interview, October 2003)

Most police unions, like other industrial unions, have fought for collective bargaining rights. Through collective bargaining, employees can address fundamental concerns such as training and professional development, as well as organisational resources and basic workplace conditions. They have also been able to expand the rights of police officers in regard to accountability procedures, transfers, promotions, assignments, participation in political organisations and even the use of weapons (Halpern, 1974). The ambit for collective bargaining is potentially very wide and police unions, while mostly focused on narrow workplace bread and butter issues, would ideally like to be partners in a range of other key decisions related to police planning and policy making (Fleming et al., 2006).

Given that police unions see themselves as representing the collective voice from below, we might expect them to support, even promote, corporate management agendas, especially those that speak of police employees as entrepreneurs and as partners (O'Malley & Hutchinson, 2007, forthcoming). Yet, police unionists have opposed new managerial reform programmes (Fleming & Lafferty, 2000; McLaughlin & Murji, 1998; O'Malley & Hutchinson, 2007, forthcoming). They have not been actively involved in finding avenues for more direct participation, and this contrasts with their general position that it should be 'automatic' that the rank-and-file are actively involved in police reform and planning initiatives (Kinnear, 2006).

Instead of looking at how corporate management approaches could potentially enhance rank-and-file participation, the unions have contested what they view as a police management preoccupation with performance indicators and national target setting. In the union view, this preoccupation has produced police organisations that focus on what can be quantified and measured rather than on the daily dilemmas faced by individual officers in providing policing services (Berry, 2006; Kinnear, 2006).

The unions' recent critical stance towards management reform agendas comes from a desire to protect the welfare interests of police officers, their professional status and their 'career' prospects. In defending officers' career prospects, the unions have tended to invoke established notions of seniority and have not generally favoured the introduction of merit as the key promotion criterion. Finnane (2006) argues that this defensive and even backward looking stance is hardly surprising given both the majoritarian democratic culture of unions and their mandate in protecting the working conditions of their members.

In striving to bolster the professional image of the police, the unions have demonstrated 'a cultural orientation toward a historically defined kind of police work, and a fundamental material investment in the continuity of that work' (Finnane, 2006, p. 12). By way of example, at an international police union network meeting held in Texas (which I attended) in September 2006 police unionists expressed their deep reservations about the opening up of policing tasks to non-sworn police. In recent years, and in the face of the multilateralisation of policing (Wood & Dupont, 2006), police unions have defended their 'professional' autonomy and their monopoly over policing functions.

The police unions' self-perceived role in the 'new' policing era is to defend the 'unique status of the constable in law' (Berry, 2006, p. 8) and to safeguard their core role as protectors of the public against crime and disorder. There may be some defensiveness in this kind of standpoint and it does hark back to a more Keynesian time when those who monopolised policing activities (more or less) were the public police. Ironically, this conservative reaffirmation of public policing values could position the unions once more as counter-cultural organisations with a left (rather than neo-liberal) perspective on where policing should be heading.

Policing scholars do not generally credit police unions with having a progressive or innovative bent. More commonly they are seen as obstructive in change agendas, clinging to traditional orthodoxies of public policing culture. It is to this view of the unions that we now turn before briefly considering an alternative perspective of police unions.

Bastions of Conservative Normative Order

What, then, should we make of the frequent categorisation of police unions as occupationally protective, inclined to reinforce inward-looking traditional occupational culture and set constraints on managerial initiation of organisational or operational change (Murphy, 2004, p. 4)? Certainly, as we have noted, police unions may well challenge management hierarchies but they also actively impede progressive management initiatives when they fall back on conservative police cultural dogma. So it is no surprise when police managers and policing scholars see police unions as 'natural enemies of change and as committed to protecting hard earned gains reflected in the status quo' (Goldstein, 1979, p. 312).

Police unions in places like the United States continue to emphasise a law enforcement agenda rather than an order maintenance and service delivery agenda (Magenau & Hunt, 1996, p. 1318). By clinging to the idea of police as experts in law and order the unions fortify an isolationist tendency in police culture marked by general distrust of non-police values and attitudes. Unsurprisingly, a recent Human Rights Watch report notes that police unions obstructed a commission into police corruption in New York in the early 1990s, using their influence to 'fuel the insularity that characterises police culture' (Human Rights Watch, 1998).

But why is this conservative instinct, this looking backward rather than forward, so typical of the cultural make-up of police unions? I would like to suggest a number of possible answers.

Police unions are made up of police workers whose identities are very powerfully shaped by their occupation, which, despite organisational overhauls, is still steeped in entrenched traditional police cultural norms (Bevir & Krupicka, this volume). Police union members identify primarily as police rather than as unionists, let alone as rights-based activists. It is their policing credentials not their labour credentials that have propelled union leaders into their leadership roles. This is best put by the president of the New Zealand police union:

> All police unionists in Australia and New Zealand, and probably elsewhere, have good credibility as cops. We are elected because we have status as functional cops. We have cut our teeth in policing. (Informal interview. Canberra, February 2006)

Remarkably, some police union leaders have held the same executive positions for decades. The President of the Combined Law Enforcement Association of Texas, Ron de Lord, for example, is currently serving his 10th three-year appointment. The police unionist just quoted finds it no surprise that police unionists hold onto their positions rather than returning to active police service:

> Don't forget that most people involved in police unions were bored by police work. We were all looking for something else. ... So, once you get into power, we hold onto it. This means knowing what your members want and defending their interests. We don't want to go back into the police. Not having to go back to the police organisation is very liberating. (Informal interview, Canberra. February 2006)

Oligarchic tendencies are strong in police unions and union leaders know that to hold onto their positions they have to retain the support of their members. This often translates into defending members against reforms (workplace, operational, governance) that make police officers feel uncomfortable or vulnerable.

In many ways police unions themselves mirror the bureaucratic and oligarchic characteristics of their 'parent' police organisations The Chief Executive Officer of the Police Federation of Australian, Mark Burgess, described to me the cultural and structural synergy between these organisations:

> Police unions replicate police departments more closely than we often think we do. The challenge is not to replicate the dominant culture. We need to be sure that if we are critical of command and control in the police that we are the same in our own organisations, for example. We need to see ourselves as part of the community, not separate from them. ... Ultimately what we need to be doing is pushing police organisations and ourselves into a more peer driven culture. (Interview. Canberra, January 2006)

Police unions and police managers may clash over the nature and pace of reform, but their shared normative orders mean that both sides remain in agreement on the fundamentals of policing (Halpern, 1974). Even if they disagree about how to achieve organisational goals both still want to promote the idea of police as 'professionals'. What they think this 'professionalism' means may likewise differ, particularly with recent management changes, but police managers and unions both want to protect 'their own market position through controlling the licence to practice and protecting their elite positions' (Evetts, 2006, p. 136). Police unions are likely to use the discourse of professionalism 'as a way to close markets in order to be able to endorse and guarantee the education, training, experience and tacit knowledge of licensed practitioners' (Evetts, p. 137). The professional values they invoke include notions of discretion and autonomy, occupational control of work and collegial authority (Fleming & Marks 2004). For police leaders and managers who buy into the corporatist agenda, on the other hand, professionalism is linked to a concern with 'improving complex and discretionary services' (p. 136). Nevertheless, while police managers and employers complain that unions use the rhetoric of professionalism as a disingenuous pretext to win concessions from management and support from the public (Harrison, 1998), there still tends to be more convergence than disagreement on notions of professionalism (see, for example, the Australasian Police Professional Standards Council, http://www.appsc.com.au/index2.php; also see Wood & Dupont, 2006).

The close identification of police unions and unionists with the police occupation and the perceived obligation to defend their members against internal and external threats has meant that they have not made great headway in leading reform or change initiatives. Police managers (with help from academics and experts) remain the innovators within police organisations (Bayley, 2006). In no small way this is because they interface with a range of other organisations and have little option but to function simultaneously as leaders of police organisations, as public sector managers and as heads of corporations; there is constant political pressure for them to deliver better policing in continuously changing circumstances. But there are certainly also instances where police unions can and do take a leading role in reorienting police culture – and without abandoning their traditional defence of their members' welfare or their commitment to the traditional verities of public policing .

POLICE UNIONS AS PARTNERS IN INNOVATION

Despite 'common-sense' notions of police unions as reform bashers and innovation blockers, there are examples of police unions subscribing to forward-looking cultural change. Maurice Punch (2006) has identified Dutch police unions as 'progressive and generally supportive of change' (p. 6) – unions that have argued for changing the organisation to 'make it more open, more responsive to "the troops" and more accountable for better and safer working conditions' (Punch, 2006, p. 8).

In the USA there is evidence of police unions working together with police managers and administrators to create alternative workplace arrangements focused on teamwork and dispersed leadership. The Broken Arrow Police Department (BAPD) in north-eastern Oklahoma is a good example. The BAPD has for the past three years experimented with management through a cross-functional employee steering committee called a Leadership Team with 'authority to make binding reform decisions on a wide range of policy issues, working conditions and strategic matters' (Wuestewald, Steinheider, & Bayerl, 2006, p. 10). The police union has been an active partner in designing the Leadership Team. In 2003, at the start of the project, the union initiated a survey to find out about attitudes among sworn officers towards the administration of the police department. This survey was repeated in 2005, two years after the Leadership Team was established. Unionised police members surveyed felt there had been a dramatic improvement in labour–management relations and in police officer commitment since the introduction of the collaborative management initiative. This is an interesting example of police executives and police unions together forging a new workplace culture that actively seeks to mobilise rank-and-file capacity and knowledge.

Police union leaders are even beginning to consider ways in which the unions could incorporate non-sworn officers into existing police representative associations and into the police profession. This possibility was presented by the General Secretary of the Scottish Police Federation, Joe Grant, at the recent international police union network meeting held in Texas. Even more surprisingly he suggests that the unions reconsider their opposition to the extension of police duties to a second tier of police and that the overriding priority in union responses should be commitment to a cohesive and well co-ordinated police service.

Changes in the fundamental organisation of policing, in Grant's (2006) opinion, should be siezed upon as opportunities rather than threats – as spaces for the unions to actively contribute to new directions in policing. Here we have the leader of a police union insisting on the importance of taking stock, looking forward – and of unions taking their position as co-producers of new policing arrangements. Perhaps we shall have to wait and see whether Grant is able to bring his members onboard: shedding some of their instinctive defensiveness and letting go of more traditional police cultural identifications. Whether he is able to continue urging alternative agendas (to 'play devils advocate' as he puts it) may depend on how willing he is to put at risk his own position in the union.

The Police and Prisons Civil Rights Union (POPCRU) in South Africa is perhaps the most exceptional case of a police union that has catalysed fundamental cultural change within a police department. POPCRU was launched in 1989 when a group of black police officers in the Eastern Cape came together to denounce the brutality and racism of apartheid policing

(Hopkins, 2004). They campaigned for more community oriented policing and for a complete transformation of the police 'force' into a police 'service' (see Brogden & Shearing, 1993; Marks, 2000).

Over the years, and particularly since the transition to democracy in 1994, POPCRU has become much more like police unions in other countries, increasingly focused on industrial issues and on building their membership base. But they still persist in their founding commitment to democratic police reform. At the POPCRU 2004 General Conference, for example, a number of key resolutions were articulated that reflect their concern with both the internal democratisation of the South African Police Service and the furtherance of democratic policing within communities. There were commitments to press for additional resources to speed up transformation in the criminal justice system, to work towards more equitable redistribution of police resources, to embark on a campaign to eradicate police corruption, to push for the targeting of women for leadership positions in the police service, and to challenge unilateral action on the part of police employers and managers (POPCRU, 2004).

POPCRU has undeniably been a force for significant cultural change. No doubt the possibility exists that POPCRU could become more narrowly focused on defending hard won labour rights and improved workplace conditions and less concerned with pushing debate on what police professionalism should mean in a changing policing environment or investigating the democratic credentials of new management paradigms. But the fact remains that POPCRU has radically and irreversibly changed the face of the public police in South Africa.

What can we conclude from these examples of forward-thinking police unions and unionists? Finnane (2006) cautions us that not too much should be expected of the police unions' role as change agents given their conservative membership base, their mandate to protect the welfare of their members and the oligarchic tendencies often present in their structures. Even so, it would be wrong to assume that police union identities and agendas are simply set in stone.

Clearly, it is possible for police unions to actively shape new directions in policing or at very least be partners in innovation, and their ongoing, classically unionist (and counter-cultural) challenge to the bureaucratic inertia of police organisations is itself a reminder of their potential. Whenever they do pressure corporate management in an employee friendly direction, whenever, in this pluralised policing era, they do return the debate to issues of abiding concern such as the professional identity of the public police, it would be a great mistake to detect in this nothing but knee-jerk defensiveness or intransigent clinging to tradition.

CONCLUSION

As significant repositories and transmitters of policing culture and subculture, the unions have the potential to preserve or refashion police culture to the benefit of policing or to its detriment. With their own cultural characteristics, shaped by their occupational location, they are, for the most part, fiercely protective of officers' rights and of the professional distinctiveness of the public police, which makes them, often, insular and defensive upholders of the more traditional characteristics of police culture (Reiner, 1978, 1992).

   This cultural influence has undergone inevitable shifts over time. Initially the unions presented a strong counter-cultural challenge to heavily bureaucratic police organisations; as policing, and the parent culture, became more inclusive and consultative, the shift was reflected to at least some degree in the union culture. Police unions will always present a challenge from below, but since union members identify themselves primarily as police officers so too their union culture will always have a strong affinity with the umbrella culture of the police organisation. Admittedly, changes can be slow to emerge. Managers may experiment with new ways of governing police organisations and indeed security in general (Wood & Dupont, 2006) but police union leadership has been much less inclined to step into the vanguard of reform. Even so, there is nothing inevitable about the cultural influence of police unions and simply branding them as 'conservative' is a good deal too simplistic, not least when we consider their steady resistance to orthodox hierarchies. And when they stand up for the integrity of public policing and indeed of public service, their voice is one that often resonates with progressive critique emanating from public service trade unions more generally and from wider civil society.

   But police unions need to recognise the importance of critical and political self-reflection. Police organisations themselves are currently in a phase of considerable self-examination and re-invention at many different levels. With their inherent internal solidarity the police unions can deploy considerable impetus for progressive transformation and the time is ripe for them to do so. But they will need to both open themselves to external influences and also create the space internally to think freshly and creatively about police professionalism and what this can mean for the structuring of the police workplace.

NOTES

1. In broad terms, occupational culture is seen as providing organisational members with a sense of identity and as facilitating commitment to the organisation. Such an identity helps in the reduction of uncertainty, and as a result, organisational cultures are enduring. As Scot and Lane (2000) put it, occupational culture is 'inherently sticky', it binds people to an organisation and creates a 'community' of members.
2. It should be noted, however, that concerns with participatory management predate shifts towards managerialism. Indeed, as Broderick (1977, p. 206) points out, forward-thinking managers in the 1970s were well aware that real knowledge resides at the bottom of the organisations and that building professionalism would have to involve a greater stress on participation by lower-ranking officers.

ACKNOWLEDGEMENT

I would like to thank Mark Burgess, Ron de Lord, Joe Grant, Abbey Witbooi, Dale Kinnear and Greg O'Connor for their very useful feedback on this paper and for openly engaging with me about police union issues over the years.

REFERENCES

Adlam, R. (2002). Governmental rationalities in police leadership: An essay exploring some of the 'deep structure' in police leadership practice. *Policing and Society, 12*(1), 15–36.
Australian Institute of Police Management. (2003). Corporate Plan 2003–2007, Sydney. Australasian Police Professional Standards Council, http://www.appsc.com.au/index2.php
Bayley, D. (2006). Police reform: Who done it? Paper presented at the conference on police reform from the bottom-up, University of California, 12–13 October, Berkeley.
Becker, H., & Geer, B. (1960). Latent culture: A note on the theory of latent social roles. *Administrative Science Quarterly, 5*(2), 304–313.
Berry, J. (2006). Police reform from the bottom-up. Paper presented at the police reform from the bottom-up conference, University of California, 12–13 October, Berkeley.
Brewer, J. (1991). *Inside the RUC: Routine policing in a divided society*. Oxford: Clarendon Press.
Broderick, M. (1977). *Police in a time of change*. Morristown, NJ: General Learning Press.
Brogden, M., & Shearing, C. (1993). *Policing for a new South Africa*. London: Routledge.
Chan, J. (1996). Changing police culture. *British Journal of Criminology, 36*(1), 109–133.
Chan, J. (1999). Governing police practice: Limits of the new accountability. *British Journal of Sociology, 50*(2), 249–268.
Davies, A., & Thomas, R. (2001). From passive to active subjects: Gender, restructuring and professional/managerial identities in the UK public sector. Paper presented at the second international conference on critical management studies, 11–13 July, Manchester, UK.

den Boer, M. (2004). *Plural governance and EU internal security: Chances and limitations of enhanced cooperation in the area of freedom of security and justice.* Working Paper no. 3/04 for ARENA, 25 May, Oslo.

Evetts, J. (2006). The sociology of professional groups: New directions. *Current Sociology, 54*(1), 133–143.

Farber, H. (2005). *Union membership in the United States: The divergence between the public and the private sectors.* Working Paper no. 503, Industrial Relations Section, Princeton University, September.

Fielding, N. (1989). Police culture and police practice. In: M. Weatheritt (Ed.), *Police research: Some future prospects.* Sydney: Avebury Press.

Finnane, M. (1999). Police unions in Australia: A history of the present. Paper presented at the history of crime, policing and punishment conference convened by the Australian Institute of Criminology, December, Canberra.

Finnane, M. (2002). *When police unionise: The politics of law and order in Australia.* Sydney: Institute of Criminology, University of Sydney.

Finnane, M. (2006). No longer a 'workingman's paradise'? Australian police unions and political action in a changing industrial environment. Paper presented at the police reform from the bottom-up conference, University of California, 12–13 October, Berkeley.

Fleming, J., & Lafferty, G. (2000). New management techniques and restructuring for accountability in Australian police organisations. *Policing: An International Journal of Police Strategies and Management, 23*, 154–168.

Fleming, J., & Marks, M. (2004). Reformers or resisters: The state of police unionism in Australia. *Employment Relations Record, 4*(1), 1–14.

Fleming, J., Marks, M., & Wood, J. (2006). Standing on the inside looking out: The significance of police unions in networks of police governance. *Australian and New Zealand Journal of Criminology, 39*(1), 71–90.

Fleming, J., & Peetz, D. (2005). Essential service unionism and the new police industrial relations. *Journal of Collective Negotiations, 30*(4), 283–305.

Fleming, J., & Rhodes, R. (2005). Bureaucracy, contracts and networks: The unholy trinity and the police. *Australian and New Zealand Journal of Criminology, 38*(2), 192–205.

Goldstein, H. (1979). *Policing a free society.* Ballinger: Cambridge University Press.

Grant, J. (2006). Speaking note on second tier policing. Presented at the international law enforcement council biannual conference, October.

Grimes, J. (1975). The police, the union and the productivity imperative. In: J. Wolfle & J. Heaphy (Eds), *Readings on productivity in policing.* Toronto: Lexington Books.

Halpern, S. (1974). Police employee organizations and accountability procedures in three cities: Some reflections on police policy-making. *Law and Society Review, 8*(4), 561–582.

Harrison, S. J. (1988). Police organizational culture: Using ingrained values to build positive organizational improvement. Electronic Version from www.pamij.com/harrison.html

Herbert, S. (1998). Police subculture reconsidered. *Criminology, 36*(2), 343–369.

Holdaway, S. (1983). *Inside the British police.* Oxford: Basil Blackwell.

Holdaway, S., & O' Neill, M. (2004). The development of Black Police Associations. *British Journal of Criminology, 44*, 854–865.

Hopkins, P. (2004). *Justice for all: The first 15 years of POPCRU.* Johannesburg: POPCRU.

Human Rights Watch. (1998). Shielded from justice: Police accountability and brutality in the United States, http://www.hrw.org/reports98/police/uspo99.htm

Jermier, J., & Berkes, L. (1979). Leader behaviour in a police command bureaucracy: A closer look at the quasi-military model. *Administrative Science Quarterly, 24,* 1–23.

Jermier, J., Slocum, J., Fry, L., & Gaines, J. (1991). Organisational subcultures in a soft bureaucracy: Resistance behind the myth and façade of an official culture. *Organizational Science, 2*(2), 170–194.

Kiely, J., & Peek, G. (2002). The culture of the British police: Views of police officers. *The Service Industries Journal, 22*(1), 167–183.

Kinnear, D. (2006). Police unions and police reform. Paper presented at the police reform from the bottom-up conference, University of California, 12–13 October, Berkeley.

Magenau, J., & Hunt, R. (1996). Police unions and the police role. *Human Relations, 49*(19), 1315–1342.

Manning, P. (1977). *Police work.* MIT Press: Cambridge, MA.

Marks, M. (2000). Labour relations in the South African Police Service. In: G. Adler (Ed.), *Public service labour relations in a democratic South Africa.* Johannesburg: University of Witwatersrand Press.

Marks, M., & Fleming, J. (2006). The untold story: The regulation of police labour rights and the quest for police democratisation. *Police Practice and Research, 7*(4), 309–322.

McLaughlin, E., & Murji, K. (1998). Resistance through representation: Storylines, advertising and police federation campaigns. *Policing and Society, 8,* 367–399.

Murphy, C. (2004). The rationalisation of Canadian public policing: A study of the impact and implications of resource limits and market strategies, *The Canadian Review of Policing Research,* http://crpr.icaap.org/issue1/cmurphy.html

Murray, J. (2002). Leaders and integrity in policing: The march away from militarism. Presentation at the third police leadership conference on managing change through principled leadership, 10–12 April, Vancouver, Canada.

Murray, T. (2004). The Canadian police executive community and its pressures. *The Canadian Review of Policing Research,* 1, http://crpr.icaap.org/index.php/crpr/article/viewArticle/6/6

O'Malley, P. (2005). Converging corporatisation? Police management, police unionism, and the transfer of business principles. Paper presented at the centre for market and public organisation, University of Bristol, September.

O'Malley, P., & Hutchinson, S. (2007, forthcoming). Converging corporatisation? Police management, police unionism and the transfer of business principles. *Police Practice and Research: An International Journal.*

Poole, M., Mansfield, R., & Gould-Williams, J. (2006). Public and private sector managers over 20 years: A test of the 'convergence thesis'. *Public Administration, 84*(4), 1051–1067.

POPCRU. (2004). Constitutional amendments, resolutions and programme of action, Book 4, 5th National Congress, June.

Punch, M. (1983). Officers and men: Occupational culture, inter-rank antagonism and the investigation of corruption. In: M. Punch (Ed.), *Control in the police organisation.* Cambridge: MIT Press.

Punch, M. (2006). Shaping an agenda for research and activism. Paper presented at the police reform from the bottom-up conference, University of California, 12–13 October, Berkeley.

Punch, M., Huberts, L., & Lamboo, T. (2000). Perceptions on integrity of Dutch police officers in comparative perspective. Paper presented at the IIPE conference on ethics in the new millenium, September, Ottawa, Canada.

Reiner, R. (1978). *The blue coated worker: A sociological study of police unionism.* London: Cambridge University Press.

Reiner, R. (1992). *The politics of the police.* London: Harvester Wheatsheaf.

Reuss-Ianni, E., & Ianni, F. (1983). Street cops and management cops: The two cultures of policing. In: M. Punch (Ed.), *Control in the police organisation.* Cambridge: MIT Press.

Rose, R. (1988). Organisations as multiple cultures: A rules theory analysis. *Human Relations, 41,* 139–170.

Rubenstein, J. (1973). *City police.* New York: Straus and Giroux.

Schein, E. (1996). Culture: The missing concept in organisational studies. *Administrative Science Quarterly, 412,* 229–240.

Scot, S., & Lane, V. (2000). A stakeholder approach to organisational identity. *Academy of Management Review, 25,* 43–67.

Shaw, M., & Shearing, C. (1998). Reshaping security: An examination of the governance of security in South Africa. *African Security Review, 7*(3), 3–12.

Sherman, L. (1973). A psychological review of women in policing. In: J. Kinton (Ed.), *Police roles in the seventies: Professionalization in America.* Anne Arbor: Edwards Brothers.

Skelcher, C., Mathur, N., & Smith, M. (2004). Negotiating the institutional void: Discursive alignments, collaborative institutions and democratic governance. Paper presented at the political studies association annual conference, April, University of Lincoln.

Sklansky, D. L. (2005). Police and democracy. *Michigan Law Review, 4,* 1699–1830.

Steinheider, B., & Wuestewald, T. (2007, forthcoming). From the bottom-up: Sharing leadership in a police agency. *Police Practice and Research: An International Journal.*

Van Maanen, J. (1974). Working the street: A developmental view of police behaviour. In: H. Jacobs (Ed.), *Annual review of criminology: The potential for reform* (Vol. III, pp. 83–117). Beverly Hills: Sage.

Vickers, M., & Kouzmin, A. (2001). New managerialism and Australian police organisations. *International Journal of Public Sector Management, 14*(1), 7–26.

Victoria Police. (2004). *Annual report 2004/2005,* Melbourne.

Victoria Police. (2005). *Delivering a safer Victoria all day every day: Business plan 2005–2006,* Melbourne.

Waddington, P. A. J. (1999). Police canteen (sub) culture. *British Journal of Criminology, 39,* 287–309.

Walker, S. (2006). Why the neglect of police unions? Exploring one of the most important areas of American policing. Paper presented at the police reform from the bottom-up conference, University of California, 12–13 October, Berkeley.

Winslow, D. (1998). Misplaced loyalties: The role of military culture in the breakdown of peace operations. *Canadian Review of Sociology and Anthropology, 33*(3), 344–367.

Wood, J., & Dupont, B. (2006). Introduction: Understanding the governance of security. In: J. Wood & B. Dupont (Eds), *Democracy, society and the governance of security.* New York: Cambridge University Press.

Wuestewald, T., & Steinheider, B. (2006). Shared leadership: Can empowerment work in police organisations? *The Police Chief, 73*(1), http://www.policechiefmagazine.org/magazine/index.cfm?fuseaction = archivecontents&issue_id = 12006

Wuestewald, T., Steinheider, B., & Bayerl, P. (2006). From the bottom-up: Sharing leadership in a police agency. Paper presented at the police reform from the bottom-up conference, University of California, 12–13 October, Berkeley.

CHAPTER 10

BLACK POLICE ASSOCIATIONS AND THE POLICE OCCUPATIONAL CULTURE

Megan O'Neill and Simon Holdaway

ABSTRACT

In recent years, Black Police Associations (BPAs) have become key forces of change within the police service, involved in minority ethnic recruitment and retention initiatives, working closely with senior management, and also serving as mechanisms of support minority ethnic constabulary members and recruits. Most police services in England and Wales now have an officially recognised BPA, making it essential to consider the effect these groups have on the police occupational culture. Using data from our recent research project on BPAs, we explore issues such as the decreasing importance of rank and grading in the police culture; whether a parallel, 'black' occupational culture is emerging alongside the traditional 'white' one; the indirect influence BPAs have had as part of a wider process of change and the interplay between changing individuals and changing the institution as a whole.

Police Occupational Culture: New Debates and Directions
Sociology of Crime, Law and Deviance, Volume 8, 253–274
ISSN: 1521-6136/doi:10.1016/S1521-6136(07)08010-4

INTRODUCTION

Research and debate on the issue of racism in the police are hardly new topics. Racist canteen 'banter', for example, was identified as an aspect of the police occupational culture many years ago (see Smith & Gray, 1985) and disproportionate policing of minority ethnic groups[1] is also well documented and researched (see Bowling & Phillips, 2003). Minority ethnic police officers have also discussed their experiences of prejudice and discrimination in the police service (Holdaway & Barron, 1997; Cashmore, 2001). Holdaway (1996, 1999) has written about the prevalence of stereotypes in police work, both racial and otherwise, and how the framing (or lack of framing) of an event as racially significant is a part of the police occupational culture. His work is based upon the concept of *racialisation*, indicating that race is constructed socially and, within the context of constabularies, negatively for many minority ethnic police staff.

The Lawrence Report (Macpherson, 1999 – also referred to, elsewhere in this volume, as the Macpherson Report) is often cited as a pivotal moment in the history of the police and race relations. Its finding of 'institutional racism' within the Metropolitan Police Service (and, by implication, all police forces in the UK) in light of its botched investigation of the murder of black teenager Stephen Lawrence was expected to lead to widespread changes in the quality of service offered to minority ethnic communities and police staff. One of Macpherson's recommendations was for all police constabularies to establish a local Black Police Association (BPA).

Over the past 10 years, and especially since the publication of the Lawrence Report, BPAs have been gaining influence and prominence in police constabularies throughout the UK. With a National Black Police Association (NBPA) established in London and a local BPA group[2] in almost every constabulary in England and Wales (and a growing number in Scotland and Northern Ireland), these groups cannot be ignored when it comes to the consideration of ethnicity and diversity in police work within and outside the police service. The BPAs are voluntary groups of minority ethnic police officers and support staff. They first started forming in the UK in the mid-1990s (Holdaway & O'Neill, 2004), stemming largely from informal (and sometimes secret) support groups that had existed previously for minority ethnic officers and staff in several constabularies.

The objectives of BPA groups are multifarious, but paramount among them is the desire to support police minority ethnic employees through any hardship or discrimination they may suffer by virtue of their ethnicity. This can range from lending an occasional sympathetic ear, to emotional or even legal support in an employment tribunal. They also aim to work with chief officers to address matters of ethnicity and diversity to bring about a police service that is beyond reproach in these matters. This is pursued through membership of formal policy and advisory boards, informal consultation with senior management, involvement in recruitment and training, as well as mentoring services for new recruits (O'Neill & Holdaway, 2007). Further, BPAs are often involved in local communities, especially those with a high minority ethnic population, to improve relationships between them and their police service.

All of these efforts are related to addressing what Lord Macpherson (1999) defined as institutional racism in police forces. The BPA members and chief police officers alike tend to agree that institutional racism existed or still exists in the police service (Rowe, 2004) but opinions differ as to what it means and how it can be identified. This can include outcomes of policy, lack of awareness of specific cultural issues or neglecting the general 'black perspective'. We have discussed the implications of BPAs for the institutional racism discourse at length elsewhere (see Holdaway & O'Neill, 2006). It seems fair to say, though, that there is not a clear understanding of the term in police constabularies and, that being so, adequately addressing the matter will be difficult (Foster, Newburn, & Souhami, 2005). In particular, many rank-and-file police officers remain unconvinced that the 'institutional racism' accusation was accurate or helpful for the police service.[3]

The notion of institutional racism infers a related occupational culture with features that discriminate openly or covertly to the disadvantage of minority ethnic groups, including police staff. This can include negative racialised stereotypes, through jokes, banter, and exclusion from the police team. We use the term 'occupational culture' here to refer to not only the ideas and related informal practices and procedures that develop in the course of doing and discussing police work, but also the particular sense of self that develops throughout one's career in the police service. There are many other definitions for this concept (see Cockcroft, 2007) but the one we have indicated will suffice for the purposes of this chapter. The BPAs have identified the institutional racism within police culture as a key issue for their group. However, it is not the only issue with which they concern themselves. Other aspects of police culture are also affected by their work, intentionally or not. It is these other cultural changes that we will consider here.

We will begin with a brief description of the research project from which this chapter is drawn. We then describe some subtle changes in the police occupational culture brought about by BPAs, such as the resistance to using rank and grade designations among the BPA membership. This leads on to the question of whether a distinct, parallel, police occupational culture can be detected among BPA members. What we argue in this paper is that, regardless whether or not a parallel BPA police culture has been forged, BPA members as well as chief officers view the BPA as playing a significant, although embedded, part in a wider process of change in the police service (especially in light of the 1999 Lawrence Report). It is these indirect influences and the relationships between BPAs and chief officers that are considered next. The final two sections of the chapter consider more cognitive aspects of changing police occupational culture. We demonstrate how some BPA members are willing to accept a change in colleagues' actions in relation to ethnicity and diversity, even if this falls short of a more fundamental change in their attitudes. These BPA members regard behavioural change of this nature as a minimal indicator of the positive impact of the BPA on the police organisation as a whole.

THE RESEARCH

This chapter is based on data gathered from a two-year study of BPAs in England and Wales.[4] The research was conducted from October 2001 to September 2003, and was largely based on in-depth, structured interviews with BPA chairs, deputy chairs, assistant/deputy chief constables (with a personnel portfolio), human resources directors (if in post) and the local Police Federation Joint Branch Board chair. Interviews were tape-recorded and ranged from 45 min to 3 h. At the time of the research, 33 BPAs were in existence, so we contacted 22 of these and their respective chief officers for interviews to provide a sufficient sample[5] for the research. All interviewees were assured complete confidentiality, which is respected in this chapter.

Prior to our project, no specific research had been done on BPAs in the UK. Such previous research as had been conducted on minority ethnic police officers chiefly highlighted their extensive experiences of discrimination and isolation (Wilson, Holdaway, & Spencer, 1984; Holdaway, 1991; Holdaway & Barron, 1997). Minority ethnic officers were subjected to joking and banter that they found offensive, excluded from full acceptance in their operational teams, and often lacked support from senior officers in dealing with the situation. They adopted various ways of coping. Some just accepted that this is a part of police organizational life; some regarded the joking and banter as harmless because their colleagues did not really mean it; some resigned their posts and a small number took a confrontational approach by telling jokes about white people or offering a rebuke. All of these were individualistic responses. Before the formation of the London Metropolitan Police BPA in 1994, no formal support groups existed to assist aggrieved colleagues. Since many constabularies had a relatively small number of minority ethnic officers and staff, these officers often found themselves stationed at great distances from one another, making it even more difficult to offer mutual support. A few officers did manage to set up mostly informal support groups but, to avoid questions and confrontation from colleagues, they would usually meet off-site and out of working hours (Holdaway & Barron, 1997, p. 106).

Prior to the launch of the first BPA, minority ethnic officers would tend to describe themselves as 'police officers who happen to be black', but felt that their white colleagues would see them as 'black people who happen to be police officers' (Wilson et al., 1984; Holdaway & Barron, 1997). In this respect, the minority ethnic officers were trying to minimise the centrality of their ethnic identity and status for their job, whereas their colleagues would accentuate ethnicity and use it (deliberately or not) as a basis for exclusion from full membership in the police team. This is important to note as our research on BPAs reveals that the opposite is now the case for many minority ethnic officers: they tend to see themselves as 'black police officers' in that their ethnicity is a source of pride and central to their self-identities (Holdaway & O'Neill, 2004). However, this is not the case for all minority ethnic officers in the UK, as the work of Cashmore (2001, 2002) has revealed. Many are not members of BPAs, and even for those who are, instances of discrimination or isolation can still be experienced. Nevertheless, BPAs are becoming significant forces for change in the occupational culture.

SMALL STEPS FOR CULTURAL CHANGE – CHALLENGING HIERARCHY

We will now consider the subtle developments that the BPAs have effected, at least within their own groups, and the implications these may have for the police occupational culture as a whole. While there is certainly no single, monolithic, police occupational culture (Fielding, 1988; Chan, 1996; Waddington, 1999), common attributes can be found in police cultures both in Britain and elsewhere (Reiner, 2000; Foster, 2003). One of these is the importance placed on a hierarchical rank structure. While rank itself is a feature of the organisation and not the occupational culture, the importance of rank in the ethos of the rank-and-file can be seen, for example, in their attitudes towards their university educated peers, as Maurice Punch (2007) points out in the present volume.

Unlike the police organisation itself, the vast majority of the BPA members we interviewed did not attach any importance to rank during their meetings and other ventures. This was reflected in the ways that the BPAs organised themselves internally. The chair and deputy chair of each BPA were not necessarily the highest-ranking police officers with full membership. Any full member could run for any post within the executive committee; high rank was not a requirement. In addition, when BPA members encountered each other, either in group meetings or elsewhere, most would refer to each other by first names only. The BPA principles of unity and mutual support in the face of a generalised experience of prejudice and discrimination would dictate that the group should not self-segregate by rank or position. The institutionalised and hierarchical rank structure had no place in a BPA group. As one BPA chair put it:

> It is first names ... because (rank) completely defies the ethos of the BPA where we are challenging and tackling discrimination and unfairness per se. And if we were the perpetrators why are we there?

It would seem that an unofficial edict has developed within the BPA that rank should be replaced with ethnicity and that its use is inverted. For example, only those of minority ethnic status are allowed to be full members of the BPA and hence eligible to vote and run for executive committee places. Majority ethnic members are thus subsidiary members, without voting privileges or executive committee seats. One's ethnicity becomes the deciding factor in one's place in the BPA, not rank.

The problem, of course, is that once the BPA members are back in their police jobs and roles, the usual rank structure comes into play. They acknowledge that they must respect the rank of other officers, regardless of ethnicity. This is perhaps especially so for minority ethnic officers of high rank – the fact that they have managed to progress far in the organisation is something many BPA members want to honour:

> In formal areas I will refer to him as Sir ... and that is out of respect to his position, because I am acutely aware of the fact that there are very few minority ethnic senior managers. And the last thing I want to do is see other people see him or her being treated in a familiar way, because that gives them the excuse that they need to undermine them. (BPA chair)

So while rank is seen as a barrier within the BPA group, it gets very explicit acknowledgement in interactions with those outside of the group, especially in the case of high-ranking minority ethnic officers.[6] As will be discussed in more detail below, there is some ambivalence among BPA members as to how much they should challenge the way the organisation works.

Another non-traditional aspect of the BPA group is the presence of support staff. Any person of minority ethnic origin directly employed by the police service can join a BPA as a full member.[7] While police officers and support staff often work together, they are usually regarded as separate groups within the police service. They have different unions, training, uniforms, contracts and hours of working and different kinds of encounters with the public. One BPA chair put it this way:

> They are second-class citizens, and even if they are not, they perceive themselves to be because we don't do enough to shatter that perception. You know, you are our support staff basically, you know, civilian staff. You are something different, you are not just an employee, you are a support to me, a policeman. So you are less important than me obviously.

The BPAs have a very different practice in regard to support staff.[8] As with rank, all ties to role within the police are dropped when it comes to the BPA. In their view, to maintain the differentiation between police officers and support staff would be to perpetuate a discriminatory system. Once again, self-segregation based on the formal police structure of employment is avoided. Consequently, many of the BPAs we interviewed had support staff among the members of their executive committees.

Considering the non-traditional internal arrangements BPAs have, and their consultative role with senior management (another contrast to the usual rank boundaries) on matters both internal and external to the organisation, is it possible to see the BPA as a model for police reform? We posed this question to one BPA chair. He responded:

> [LAUGHS] No comment. I think we definitely have some good practices which the organisation could adopt and the – Project, I think is showing the new models of consultation and empowerment.

While BPAs are adopting non-traditional working practices internally, a constabulary-wide overhaul is not on their agenda. There seems to be no direct attempt to translate successful internal BPA practices to a review of practices within the police organisation more broadly. This is not surprising, in that many BPAs have to struggle continuously to prove to their ethnic majority colleagues that the group is not attempting to take over the police service in a total cultural and organisational revolution. They want to work within the system, to earn their rightful places throughout the ranks and to change the system for the better in partnership with senior management. But should the service come to see the BPA as an example of good practice to emulate, so much the better.

PARALLEL CULTURE?

If BPAs work differently from the rest of the police service in relation to rank and grades, could it be argued that a distinct, or parallel, police occupational culture is emerging for minority ethnic staff? As many recent writers on police culture have noted, it is more appropriate to refer to police *cultures*, rather than one homogenous police culture (Foster, 2003; Chan, 1996; Sklansky, 2007). We use the word 'parallel' here to refer to a distinct police culture where ethnicity is an issue of such primary importance that it influences how the officers and staff work in certain respects (such as in relationships with the community or with senior management). However, in other respects, these officers will follow similar paths to their white majority colleagues (such as in the preference for action-orientated police work). It is still a *police* occupational culture, in that they do not deviate from majority culture and practice in every respect, just one where ethnicity plays a very different role. We will discuss this in more detail later.

In exploring this issue of a parallel culture for minority ethnic staff, let us look at the BPA of the Metropolitan Police Service in London. This was the first BPA to be formed, in 1994 amid great controversy. It was the end product of several years' work among its members, and evolved from a more informal support and networking group. This group would meet annually for formal social events that were characterised by attributes that 'members of the Afro-Caribbean communities within the police liked' (Holdaway & O'Neill, 2004, p. 859). This included things such as formal attire, strict rules of decorum and a prohibition of racist jokes and banter. It was felt that social events organised by white police officers did not always share these characteristics; the black events were, in this respect, culturally distinct and 'safe' for those attending (Holdaway & O'Neill, 2004, p. 860). It is from these roots that the Metropolitan BPA was formed. The legacy of these early gatherings can still be felt in NBPA Annual General Meetings. The first evening of each conference is a formal dinner with Asian and Afro-Caribbean food and music – attendees are required to wear either traditional or formal attire and the celebrations carry on into the early hours.

Can the cultural markers in these formal police events be seen as evidence of a parallel police occupational culture emerging? The Metropolitan BPA is the largest of all the regional BPAs and is certainly an active group – both within the community and within the police service itself. It has an extensive range of activities and projects with which it is involved,[9] and has served as a catalyst for black and Asian colleagues in other police forces to start up their own groups. As one BPA chair commented in describing the launch of the Metropolitan BPA,

> when we went there we listened to some of the problems that some of the Met officers were having ... . The problems in (our force) were very small in comparison to the Met. Having said that, the Met on that particular day was quite inspirational for those of us who went down in terms of, sort of inspired us to do something more forward ... we felt that we should do something as well.

The Metropolitan BPA emerges as a strong force in the history of BPAs in the UK, culturally and organisationally distinct from other members of its police service. It was a force to be reckoned with at the time and remains so. This is not to suggest, however, that BPA members perform their police duties entirely differently from their ethnic majority colleagues. The BPA members are still police officers and staff, and their parallel culture will still be a *police* occupational culture, just one that takes a different perspective on a number of identified subjects related to race and ethnicity, and engenders a distinct sense of self in its members. However in other respects, such as in their routine work outside the organisation, their occupational culture may not be distinguishable from that of their colleagues.

When considering if this pattern has been repeated in other BPAs, difficulties emerge. The first problem is that many of these groupings are struggling to get off the ground. One BPA chair from a rural police service commented:

> There isn't very many of us. I think that a lot of black staff feel as if, you know, if I start joining things like the Black Police Association and I'm on a shift with sixteen white officers, they are going to think what's going here then? You know, why does he need to join that? ... . And a lot of people embarrassed about being a member of the BPA. They don't want to be sort of be going to BPA meetings and be looked upon as a BPA member. That's the situation here ... . It's totally different in London and places where you are surrounded by black officers, and there are plenty of black officers.

This feeling was repeated in many interviews – the sheer number of minority ethnic officers in the Metropolitan Police means that they will find it much easier to make their presence felt and work within the service as a united group. A BPA general secretary talked about the isolation that minority ethnic people in general can experience in rural areas:

> If you look externally in the police service, if you look at the 'shire forces, there's rural isolation, rural racism. And that's the probably the biggest effect on discrimination is that people live in isolation, they don't actually meet anyone who's similar to themselves or have empathy. So they end up acquiescing to the majority or basically keeping quiet. Well that's going to be reflected identically if not compounded in the police service. So the desire to keep one's head down and be the same as everyone else would be even greater.

Small numbers and the subsequent isolation and pressure to conform for minority ethnic people in rural areas as well as in rural police forces makes creating a parallel and culturally distinct organisation very difficult. Similar difficulties appear to confront BPAs in urban areas as well. One BPA chair of an urban police service commented that

> The problem with the police service is that sometimes officers are very narrow-minded, and we've had cases of harassment, we've had cases of bullying. Bear in mind that when you are in a group you are by and large in the minority and you are working with, as I said the dominant culture is white Anglo-Saxon males who look after their own .... I suppose that is the worry. And I suppose it means that one or two of our essential members would prefer to acquiesce than to actually stand up and be counted. So they will go along for the easy ride, get by and be seen to be one of the boys if that's a phrase I can use.

Even when there are relatively large numbers of minority ethnic staff in an organisation the pressure to conform is still present, and will prevent some people from joining the BPA. Thus, the experiences of the Metropolitan BPA in respect of a parallel culture cannot be generalised. Other experiences are of course shared across the country, such as in a common history of racist language and discrimination in their organisations, but the notion of an embryonic culture seems to be unique to the Metropolitan BPA.

INDIRECT INFLUENCES

The discussion so far may seem rather negative in regard to the influence of BPAs on the culture of their organisations outside of the Metropolitan Police. However, there are more indirect challenges that the BPAs throughout the UK have presented. Many of our respondents discussed subtle influences that BPAs have had, or the role the BPA has played in the police service *alongside* other key developments in the broader field of police ethnic relations. Chief officers seem to support this perspective. In the words of one of the several assistant/deputy chief constables and human resource directors who made this kind of point,

> There's certainly greater awareness that people aren't inappropriate and it's not banter and you can't carry on like this and it's not a joke. Especially you know, not just the BPA, but the grievances and the tribunal cases around things like that. They've become more aware. Whether it was, you know, fear that did it or awareness or whatever, but [the BPA] did have an impact.

The HR director quoted here points to a general appreciation among staff as to what is and is not acceptable behaviour and language, even though the exact catalyst for this increased awareness is not clear. The ACC quoted next also identifies a range of factors, one of which is the BPA:

> I don't think it is the BPA. I think is it about ... not compartmentalising. It is not saying 'well because of the BPA this is happening'. It is because the BPA is part of a whole suite of things that the force has used and because of that whole suite of things relations are much stronger because, I mean part of it is down to the BPA bringing a change in the culture.

This ACC seemed reluctant to single out one group or event for credit in the perceived change of culture. An HR director who took a similar line emphasised the role of police officers themselves in changing their culture:

> I think that the BPAs played a role in as much as ... they're part of that whole, you know, this is where we used to be and this is how it's changed. You know, police officers are not stupid, they can see all of that and so they do recognise that there are issues for Black officers ... the establishment of the BPA would be in another layer in their sort of, for them in terms of thinking yeah 'well life has moved on and this isn't acceptable' ... the establishment of the BPA would have been another factor in making that shift.

It is not just chief officers who made these observations. One BPA general secretary spoke of the well-publicised events in the recent history of the police as also significant contributors to change:

> I won't put that down to just the BPA. I'll put that down to the fact that, as I said, once you start getting, once you got the Macpherson report and all the rest of this type of stuff and police officers and Chief Constables being hauled up in court and what's-his-name highlighting that there was institutionalised racism and they felt that they were opening themselves up for litigation which was going to cost them a lot of money, then all of a sudden things had to start being done ... I think the BPA was just an added avenue.

One BPA deputy chair was a little more cynical in his analysis of the role of the BPA in changing the police culture, and described the dynamic this way:

> Nobody who makes decisions that influence everybody else's life in [this constabulary] ever comes back and says that the BPA has made a difference. Put it this way, a lot of people know the BPA exists so from that point of view the BPA must be doing something ... . Police officers are very, very interesting by nature. They will take an idea, plagiarise it and say it is their own. No one is going to say 'well the reason why policy changed was because the BPA did it.' They'll say it was a joint effort; it was a joint coming together of minds. So I like to think that because we get involved in the joint coming together of minds, the BPA has at least made a difference somewhere.

So while this officer may not expect the BPA to get much of the credit for organisational and cultural change, he does acknowledge that the BPA has had an impact.

Although some of our BPA respondents spoke of the impact of the BPA on the occupational culture as being indirect, most of the comments made to us in this vein came from chief officers. This is not unsurprising, considering that their perspective on this issue will include detailed knowledge of the full range of equal opportunities legislation, tribunal cases, the impact of Lawrence and other inquiries, the internal plans and policies to address issues of diversity and ethnicity, and the pressure they face from external organisations. The BPA is one influence in a wider organisational field of change (Chan, 1996). The BPAs are of course aware of these issues, too, especially through their past and current involvement in tribunal cases. However, chief officers will see all these issues from a management perspective that enviably packages them together under the banner of their diversity portfolio; to them the BPA is one of a number of variables.

CHIEF OFFICERS' VIEWS

The fact that BPAs now seem to be a taken-for-granted organisational entity for chief officers is in itself a signifier of cultural change. As our previous work has indicated (Holdaway & O'Neill, 2004), the first BPA (as well as the next few) encountered many difficulties in establishing itself. Chief officers were by no means eager for it to be formed. Other BPAs have encountered very different receptions, however, and today most have some kind of consultative relationship with senior management, either informally through open-door policies with the chief constable (or ACC/ DCC) or on formal committees (Holdaway & O'Neill, 2004) such as policy advisory boards.[10] Chief officers have not only welcomed the most recently formed BPAs, but were in some cases actively involved in helping the groups to launch. This makes for a marked change in chief officers' views from those of a decade ago; today BPAs are no longer resisted, they are openly embraced.

Thus, it would seem that the occupational culture of senior management has indeed experienced a significant change – one that welcomes the influence and input of the BPA, as noted by this BPA chair:

We're pushing on an open door now. It might change in a couple of months when we get a new Chief Constable but at the moment we are pushing on an open door. So in terms of change, change in terms of policy the Chief is prepared to listen to his ACC, this union is very, very supportive.

Another BPA chair recalled an earlier experience where chief officers welcomed a direct challenge from minority ethnic officers on the racist aspects of the occupational culture of the 1980s and 1990s:

> And then we started to challenge the Chief Officers, and in fair play to them, they put on a forum where all the Superintendents, you know the top of the organisation, had a two-day diversity seminar. We had (names several prominent figures in the police and National BPA at the time) there and it was a real top-notch crowd and I said 'brilliant, absolutely superb this. It's about time the organisation did something about diversity'.

This groundbreaking event was not quite as radical as had been hoped, however. It took a bit of work on the part of this BPA chair to get the highest-ranking minority ethnic officer in the force to be invited, as he was not of Superintendent rank at the time. But it was in some part a result of minority ethnic involvement that the event happened in the first place.

Some BPA officers expressed doubt to us as to whether their senior managements' current enthusiasm and support of the BPA is deep-rooted. They argued that because of the exterior pressures on police forces to address racism the executive management knows how to 'talk the talk' (as one BPA deputy chair put it), but whether or not they also 'walk the walk' is a different matter. This BPA general secretary agreed when asked if the views of chief officers need to be changed:

> Yes, in the fact that support is more than rhetoric. And support has to be real, tangible and they have to be, have the confidence to be able to answer to the rest of the service when they ask the question 'why is this group here?' So they have to have the confidence in order to be able to say 'well, these are the reasons' .... Acknowledging a thing like institutional racism would help.

In our interviews with chief officers, nearly all agreed that there was a place for the BPA in terms of consultation on policies and procedures, and as we have noted elsewhere (Holdaway & O'Neill, 2004) this is an integral part of a new, collective approach to addressing institutional racism. Regardless of the extent to which this might be just rhetoric, the way in which BPAs are welcomed in arenas that used to be the sole preserve of the most senior of police officers is indicative of a very telling cultural shift, and one which BPA members were involved in bringing about.[11]

ATTITUDES VERSUS ACTIONS

There was some doubt among BPA members about whether or not chief officers' rhetoric about diversity matched their action. Our respondents also felt that the cultural shift detected in senior ranks has not been fully replicated at the lower ends of the police hierarchy. Part of this is seen to be a result of 'race' issues being interpreted as separate to the daily experiences of police officers, as this BPA chair noted:

> I think people are quite happy to sort of say well there is the BPA, let them get on with race. Just let them do it, you know, so there is no problem changing things that way. But I think probably changing attitudes is different. You know, getting people to see it as a serious burning issue is more difficult. You know, right ok, we're legally bound to see this as a serious issues. But do we actually see it as serious issue? Now a lot of well meaning people do, but quite a sizeable minority probably don't see it as relevant. It doesn't impact on their day-to-day policing so they don't see it as a relevant issue.

One BPA general secretary laid the blame on the kind of training police officers receive, which inadvertently presents diversity as a *problem* to be addressed in a particular way:

> I mean Community Race Relations Training is churned out. And I think it is just stereotypical and inherently causes the problem. Because it just perpetuates Black people .... I mean you have to understand their religion, their diet. You know, it's all technical isn't it? I mean it's all very important stuff... but ultimately, we should be doing that for everyone. It's dealing with people's differences as a problem, rather than 'we're all different.

While some of our respondents were indeed concerned about an ongoing lack of understanding about issues of ethnicity and diversity, others inclined towards a more pragmatic approach:

> I mean if people want to be racist then so be it, but it's just I think you need ... the only thing you can ask for is for people to have a neutral value at work. 'Cause if people want to be complete and utter sort of like Nazi's/racists in their home lives then so be it. You can't be the thought police can you? It's just like keeping a neutrality at work. That's the only thing you can ... 'cause you can't stop freedom of thinking can you? It doesn't matter if you're prejudiced against people really does it? As long as you don't discriminate against them by treating them differently. (BPA general secretary)

Another saw the matter in terms of professionalism:

> They can have their views ... it's a democratic society, people are entitled to their views. But there are standards of behaviour they that they are getting paid for as professionals. If I do something wrong and it is shown that I have done something wrong out of bad disrespect or whatever, I expect to be punished for it .... There are too many examples within this organisation of where they have ... brought their own private views of people, of colour, and brought it into the organisation and criminalised ordinary citizens, because of their bigoted views outside. (BPA chair)

In this respect, some BPA members feel that changing the actions of police officers alone is preferable to having no impact at all. Although the ideal for BPA members is to have police services entirely free from more deep level discriminatory assumptions and values, achieving a service that is free from racist *action* is a first and important step. This separation of action from thought has also appeared in the police culture literature in the past (see for example, Smith & Gray, 1985), but as Holdaway (1996) points out, this view neglects the interrelated nature of police thought about 'race' and police work and culture in general. This will be explored in more detail below.

Numerous official policies and procedures about ethnicity and diversity have been put in place by senior management, along with training, to ensure that officers and staff are well aware of the behaviour that is expected of them. Greater Manchester Police, for example, has gone so far as to institute an acceptable-language policy to make sure that its employees never use certain racist terms, under penalty of termination. For many BPA members and chief officers with whom we spoke, altered actions are the most that can be expected in terms of change at the moment.[12]

INDIVIDUALS AND THE INSTITUTION

What we have been considering so far is the connection between what individual police officers think or say and what they do in the context of the police occupational culture. This has of course been debated before (see for example, Waddington, 1999). However, there is also a further relationship to consider, and that is the relationship between individuals and the institutions in which they work. Holdaway (1999), drawing on the work of Jenkins (1996), has argued that institutions are in fact the product of the taken-for-granted action of their members. If the actions of the individuals change, then so does the nature of the institution. The police occupational culture is the primary context in which these processes are articulated.

The comments of our BPA respondents about the tension between thought and action are pertinent here. Holdaway (1996) has noted that police action is *racialised*, in that routine police work and mundane relationships attribute a racial framing (Goffman, 1974) to an event that could be defined in a different, non-racial, way. In order for the institution to change, the actions of its members also need to change. If we follow the logic of our respondents then we can argue that if police officers, through their individual experiences of the BPA along with the overall policy changes in the institution (such as the 'zero tolerance' approach to racist language) which the BPA helped to bring about, modify their actions to the extent that some of these racialised processes are stopped or altered, then a significant shift in the police occupational culture could perhaps be possible. The taken-for-granted action of the officers would not be racialised (or, perhaps more practically, would be less so) and the resulting nature of the institution itself would also be less or not racialised.

However, as some BPA members have noted, their impact on the way officers *think* may only be detected in a few individual officers. For example:

M.O. Do you think the BPA will be able to help change their views?

Oh, I think individuals would be able to influence individuals, yeah.

M.O. But not like the BPA as a group?

No. No. (BPA general secretary)

One BPA chair discussed the following intervention with a single white officer which, while successful, did not have a significant impact in the organisation as a whole:

I was on a discipline panel, where there's a young white officer who was there, who had been, I'd been involved in the recruitment process with him. But he was under the discipline scenario for alleged racist comments … and he went through the process and at the end of the process, he was having some difficulties with regards to understanding where the force was coming from, how he himself was gonna take it forward, and I said 'give us a call.' He came back in here, and we sat down and we had about, ooh, a good half an hour or so. Talked things through and notwithstanding that, he has now gone back into the work environment, very positive. Understands the issues, where we're coming from. He hasn't gone back on the BPA. I see that officer on a regular basis, and we have a good working relationship. So I think that there is an educational process, there's an awareness process that goes on.

The BPA work in the police service has certainly made an impact on police actions, but their impact on officers' ideas and attitudes is less consistent when it comes to rank-and-file officers. What needs to be considered here is the extent to which one must also change the way police officers *think* as well as how they *act* in order to engender long-term change in the police occupational culture. According to many of the BPA officers and chief officers we interviewed, changing actions alone is sufficient (or the most one can expect).

Can altered action alone address issues of institutional racism and the racialised nature of police work? Previous research in this area (Holdaway, 1999) has described police thought processes and police action as congruous. Some of our respondents, however, would describe them as separate and would not see this separation as problematic (as does Waddington, 1999). Brubaker, Loveman, and Stamatov (2004) have argued that cognitive processes (such as stereotyping, categorisation and schemas) are vital in the act of social construction, especially in relation to issues of race or ethnicity. They argue that 'it is only in and through cognitive processes and mechanisms that the social construction of race, ethnicity and nation can plausibly be understood to occur' (Brubaker et al., 2004, p. 52). Therefore, if we take Holdaway's (1996) notion of racialisation in police work, which is in fact the social construction of a situation as being a race-related one (which then informs subsequent acts), then cognition is vital to this process and cannot be entirely separated from police action. Looking back at Macpherson's (1999) definition of 'institutional racism', we see that he allows for 'unwitting' prejudice within this (para. 6.34). The idea of 'unwitting' prejudice implies that racist behaviour (or, the racist outcomes of collective action) can happen without the actors intending it. The work of Brubaker and colleagues would support this in that they argue these cognitive processes are without conscious effort (Brubaker et al., 2004, p. 39).

Considering these arguments, it would seem that our respondents' view of there being racist 'thought' alongside non-racist action is not an entirely accurate assessment of these ongoing processes. The BPAs have helped to create an uncertainty in what used to be certain – the old way of doing things in the police is no longer an option, methods must change. However, this process is more complex than a simple decision to 'hide' one's racist feelings or methods. The cognitive processes that inform police cultural knowledge involve more than just racist thoughts and feelings (there are schemas and categories as well as the officer's own lifetime of personal and occupational socialisation). This cultural knowledge must be mediated by the police actor and cannot be simply ignored. Therefore, each actor may respond to this tension in a different way (Chan, Devery, & Doran, 2003), but perhaps this is a tension that some of these officers can manage.[13] The recent documentary 'The Secret Policeman'[14] has shown that this now covert (rather than overt) racism is indeed present for some officers, but the film's aftermath demonstrated that discovery of this covert racism can have devastating consequences.

CONCLUSION

Is there a possibility that BPAs can effect a significant change in the police occupational culture? As BPA members have pointed out, much of their impact is in their individual relationships and interactions with colleagues, rather than at the constabulary-wide level. As we have noted in this chapter, some of the challenges that BPAs have presented to traditional police culture and practice have been subtle, like ignoring rank or support staff grade demarcations at BPA meetings and events. The BPA is one of very few police groups where support staff are welcomed and treated on an equal footing to police officers. The BPA executive committee members, regardless of their rank or grade, are welcome in many senior management consulting arenas. The official separation of the top of the police service from the lower ranks is disregarded in the case of the BPA, in either formal or informal mechanisms. These aspects of the police service (rank and role) are anathema to the ethos of the BPA, which is all about breaking down barriers that separate colleagues in the service. Thus, this group can be seen as an example of how the police could operate in a more egalitarian way across the board.

While most BPAs may be too small or overall numbers of minority ethnic members of the police service too few to bring about a parallel police occupational culture, the Metropolitan BPA does possibly seem to be in a position to offer a challenge of this nature. This group is very large, active and powerful and has a wide base of minority ethnic police officers and staff. This development is probably not generalisable to all police services, but in the case of the Met significant cultural changes could be possible because of the BPA. At the very least this reinforces the argument that not all constabularies have the same occupational culture (Reiner, 2000) (for example, some have working definitions of racialised groups; others might be less wide-ranging). In other constabularies, the impact of the BPA may be embedded within a wider range of events. The Lawrence Report (Macpherson, 1999) was published at a time when many BPAs were starting to gain prominence. It may, therefore, not be possible to entirely tease apart which organisational and cultural changes were due to which developments, but it is clear that BPAs are part of a fabric of events from which has grown a significant shift in organisational policies, practices and police relationships.

Our research on BPAs indicates that the impact of a BPA on the police occupational culture takes place within the context of a wider series of events and actions and in individual interactions with white colleagues. In relation to the 'field' and 'habitus' of policing as analysed by Chan (1996), the BPA has a role to play in altering both of these. BPAs are a part of the historical events that have shaped the British policing field in the past decade, their power located in their being a recommendation of the Lawrence Report and in the symbolic capital they hold as vocal and politically active minority ethnic members of a police service. They are of course not the only factor that makes up this field – wider social processes of ethnicity as well as other aspects of policing history are relevant here – but they are a definite part of it.

The BPAs particularly influence what Chan defines as the habitus (referred to earlier in the chapter as police cultural knowledge). This term describes 'a set of historical relations "deposited" within individual bodies in the form of mental and corporeal schemata of perception, appreciation and action' (Wacquant, 1992, p. 16). The BPAs have to some extent influenced the perceptions and actions of individual police officers through their encounters with them as described in this chapter. Some of these encounters, especially the more individualistic ones, have left a deep impact on the officers concerned in that ways of thinking about ethnicity have been altered. For other officers, only a surface-level change in behaviour has been affected.

Chan (1997) has argued that changes in police officers' habitus can be sustained only if there is supportive change in the policing field. However, BPAs and issues of ethnicity are not always at the forefront of officers' minds, nor always at the top of the wider political agenda. On their own and with the non-radical stance they have adopted within their constabularies (as they tend to work with senior management rather than directly against it), BPAs will probably not have a dramatic influence on policing at this moment. But BPAs are still relatively new to the internal police world and so their impact may not yet be fully realised. There are no easy answers to the question as to how the BPA is changing the police occupational culture, but it is fair to say that the influence is there, and will perhaps make a deeper impression in line with further developments in the broader field of police and minority ethnic relations.

NOTES

1. The phrase 'minority ethnic' is used intentionally here for two reasons. First, it is done out of respect to our respondents who preferred this terminology over 'ethnic minority'. Second, it supports the assertion that we all have an ethnicity. It is more helpful to focus on 'ethnicity' as the noun and refer to 'majority' and 'minority' ethnicities, rather than to refer to 'minorities'. The latter risks obscuring the universality of ethnicity.

2. Not all local groups have adopted the name 'Black Police Association'. Some are called the 'Black and Asian Police Association' and others have entirely different names such as 'Black and Asian Staff Support Group'. The reasons behind these variations in name are beyond the scope of the current paper, as they involve differing interpretations of ethnic categorisation and organisational relationships

with police senior management. For simplicity's sake, only the term 'Black Police Association' or 'BPA' will be used here.

3. See the forthcoming book edited by Michael Rowe (2007), Policing Beyond Macpherson, for more on this issue.

4. This research was funded by the Economic and Social Research Council, Award number: R000239360.

5. As there were such a small number of groups, the sampling could not be done randomly. Therefore, we selected constabularies that would best present a balance between rural and urban areas, different types of minority ethnic populations, and number of minority ethnic staff employed.

6. Rank is a feature of police culture that may be changing generally. Many of our respondents indicated that referring to others by rank or as 'Sir/Ma'am' is a custom that is losing its force throughout the police service. The growing influence of a managerial culture among chief police officers (see Marks, 2007) may be related to this trend. It is impossible to say how far this change in the wider organisation of the police and in the police culture is due to the BPA, but it is certainly clear that the strict observance of rank is an aspect of the police that is changing, in one way or another.

7. Some BPAs allow all employees of a police service to be eligible for full membership, regardless of ethnicity, but this is not the norm.

8. The British Association for Women in Policing (BAWP) is another organisation within the police service that observes no distinction between support staff and police officers.

9. See the Metropolitan BPA website for more detail on their activities: http://www.metbpa.com.

10. The exact relationship between BPAs and senior management will vary depending on the constabulary in question. In most, the BPA has no more than a consultative role, and does not have power to directly affect force policy. In some forces, however, this consultative role has become ingrained in policy-making procedures in that the BPA is contacted as a matter of course on all related issues.

11. In some respects, the BPA now takes the place of the Police Federation when it comes to representing the interests of minority ethnic members of the service. This is significant in cultural terms in that for rank-and-file police officers, the Police Federation was formerly their only voice and tended to enshrine the occupational culture. Even though BPAs are not trade unions, they do often appear at the same tables as the Police Federation and signify a significant challenge to its ability to speak on behalf of all lower-ranking police officers and defend their way of doing things.

12. These policies and hard-line approaches to racism in the police service have had the unintended consequence of making it covert, according to some of our respondents. Officers know what not to do in front of superiors and/or minority ethnic colleagues, but will still find ways of expressing their racism elsewhere that are hard to detect or to prove. We explore the idea of covert racism more fully in a forthcoming publication (Holdaway & O'Neill, 2007).

13. Of course, not all police officers and staff reject Macpherson's (1999) findings about institutional racism (Foster et al., 2005). This discussion thus only concerns those who do and who see the 'new' way of doing things as unnecessary.

14. 'The Secret Policeman' was a BBC documentary by journalist Mark Daly in 2003. He went undercover as a new recruit for Greater Manchester Police and discovered deep-seated racist feelings among a number of his fellow recruits. These feelings were not detected by their trainers and only came to light when the documentary aired. All were removed from duty immediately afterwards, either through their own resignations or by suspension (Daly, 2003; BBC News, 2003).

ACKNOWLEDGEMENTS

The authors wish to thank Monique Marks and Janet Chan for their helpful comments on previous drafts of this chapter.

REFERENCES

BBC News (2003). *Fifth officer resigns over racism film.* BBC News online, 22 October 2003, URL: http://news.bbc.co.uk/1/hi/uk/3203287.stm

Bowling, B., & Phillips, C. (2003). Policing ethnic minority communities. In: T. Newburn (Ed.), *Handbook of policing.* Cullompton: Willan Publishing.

Brubaker, R., Loveman, M., & Stamatov, P. (2004). Ethnicity as cognition. *Theory and Society, 33,* 31–64.

Cashmore, E. (2001). The experiences of ethnic minority police officers in Britain: Under-recruitment and racial profiling in a performance culture. *Ethnic and Racial Studies, 24*(4), 642–659.

Cashmore, E. (2002). Behind the window dressing: Minority ethnic police perspectives on cultural diversity. *Journal of Ethnic and Migration Studies, 28*(2), 327–341.

Chan, J. (1996). Changing police culture. *British Journal of Criminology, 36*(1), 109–134.

Chan, J. (1997). *Changing police culture: Policing in a multicultural society.* Cambridge: Cambridge University Press.

Chan, J., Devery, C., & Doran, S. (2003). *Fair cop: Learning the art of policing.* Toronto: University of Toronto Press.

Cockcroft, T. (2007). Police culture(s): Some definitional, methodological and analytical considerations. In: M. O'Neil, M. Marks & A.-M. Singh (Eds), *Police occupational culture: New debates and directions.* Oxford: Elsevier Press.

Daly, M. (2003). *My life as a secret policeman.* BBC News Magazine online, 21 October. news.bbc.co.uk/1/hi/magazine/3210614.stm

Fielding, N. G. (1988). *Joining forces: Police training, socialization, and occupational competence.* London: Routledge.

Foster, J. (2003). Police cultures. In: T. Newburn (Ed.), *Handbook of policing.* Cullompton: Willan.

Foster, J., Newburn, T., & Souhami, A. (2005). *Assessing the impact of the Stephen Lawrence inquiry.* London: Home Office Research, Development and Statistics Directorate.

Goffman, E. (1974). *Frame analysis: An essay on the organization of experience.* New York: Harper & Row.

Holdaway, S. (1991). *Recruiting a multi-racial police force*. London: HMSO.

Holdaway, S. (1996). *The racialisation of British policing*. Basingstoke: Macmillan.

Holdaway, S. (1999). Understanding the police investigation of the murder of Stephen Lawrence: A 'mundane sociological analysis'. *Sociological Research Online, 4*(1). www.socresonline.org.uk/socresonline/4/lawrence/holdaway.html

Holdaway, S., & Barron, A. M. (1997). *Resigners? The experience of Black and Asian police officers*. Basingstoke: Macmillan.

Holdaway, S., & O'Neill, M. (2004). The development of black police associations: Changing articulations of race within the police. *British Journal of Criminology, 44*, 854–865.

Holdaway, S., & O'Neill, M. (2006). Institutional racism after Macpherson: An analysis of police views. *Policing and Society, 16*(4), 349–369.

Holdaway, S., & O'Neill, M. (2007). Where has all the racism gone? Views of racism within constabularies after Macpherson. *Ethnic and Racial Studies, 30*(3), 397–415.

Jenkins, R. (1996). *Social identity*. London: Routledge.

Macpherson, W. (1999). *The Stephen Lawrence inquiry: Report of an Inquiry by Sir William Macpherson of Cluny*. Cm 4262-I. London: HMSO.

Marks, M. (2007). Police unions and their influence: Subculture or counter-culture? In: M. O'Neil, M. Marks & A.-M. Singh (Eds), *Police occupational culture: New debates and directions*. Oxford: Elsevier Press.

O'Neill, M., & Holdaway, S. (2007). Examining "Window Dressing": The views of Black Police Associations on recruitment and training. *Journal of Ethnic and Migration Studies, 33*(3), 483–500.

Punch, M. (2007). Cops with honours: University education and police culture. In: M. O'Neil, M. Marks & A.-M. Singh (Eds), *Police occupational culture: New debates and directions*. Oxford: Elsevier Press.

Reiner, R. (2000). *The politics of the police* (3rd ed.). Oxford: Oxford University Press.

Rowe, M. (2004). *Policing: Race and racism*. Cullompton: Willan Publishing.

Rowe, M. (Ed.) (2007). *Policing beyond Macpherson*. Cullompton: Willan Publishing.

Sklansky, D. (2007). Seeing blue: Police reform, occupational culture, and cognitive burn-in. In: M. O'Neil, M. Marks & A.-M. Singh (Eds), *Police occupational culture: New debates and directions*. Oxford: Elsevier Press.

Smith, D. J., & Gray, J. (1985). *Police and people in London: The PSI report*. Aldershot: Gower.

Wacquant, L. J. D. (1992). Toward a social praxeology: The structure and logic of Bourdieu's sociology. In: P. Bourdieu & L. Waquant (Eds), *An invitation to reflexive sociology*. Cambridge: Polity Press, cited in J. Chan (1996), Changing police culture, *British Journal of Criminology, 36*(1), 109–134.

Waddington, P. A. J. (1999). Police (canteen) sub-culture: An appreciation. *British Journal of Criminology, 39*(2), 287–309.

Wilson, D., Holdaway, S., & Spencer, C. (1984). Black police in the United Kingdom. *Policing, 1/1*, 20–30.

CHAPTER 11

CULTURAL CHANGE THROUGH 'NEXUS' POLICING

Jennifer Wood and Monique Marks

ABSTRACT

Policing reform often assumes that new sensibilities are difficult to inculcate globally in an organisation, rather than targeting a specific level, like senior management, charged with developing new visions. This chapter contends that police culture change is highly possible when officers as individuals are enabled to remake working practice in active engagement with changing circumstances. Cultural change is best understood as small, incremental shifts in perception and response, in the tiny pockets of activity that constitute the social operations of the police. The challenge is to foster these incremental influences, both within and beyond the police organisation. This micro-level process is explored in the context of the Nexus Policing Project in Victoria, Australia, focusing on how Nexus emphasises collaborations between police and academia in the generation of knowledge and ideas to shape policing practice.

INTRODUCTION

In the study of organisations[1] the concept of culture is often invoked with little sense of nuance or specificity (see chapter by Sklansky in this

Police Occupational Culture: New Debates and Directions
Sociology of Crime, Law and Deviance, Volume 8, 275–294
Copyright © 2007 by Elsevier Ltd.
ISSN: 1521-6136/doi:10.1016/S1521-6136(07)08011-6

collection) – wielded as a brush to paint in broad social patterns, rather than illuminate the tiny practices of social actors as they derive meaning from, and ascribe meaning to, the immediate, everyday situations in which they find themselves. In the field of policing studies, several commentators (see Chan, 1997; Reiner, 1992) have insisted that it is a mistake to regard culture as some kind of pre-determinative universal, but what Reiner calls the 'monolithic' view of culture (1992, p. 109) still retains its foothold. This can create a conceptual barrier to innovation (such as in police operational practice) when it obscures the importance of small but significant shifts in thinking that need to be cultivated within a social field (Billet, 2006). Planners too often forget that individuals within an organisation – at every level – are active participants in actually making and transforming its culture.

In policing, as in other organisational fields, there seems to be a consensus that inculcating new sensibilities will be very difficult, perhaps impossible, to attempt across an entire organisation; easier to push new worldviews in a specific part of a structure like senior management – where developing new visions is an intrinsic leadership responsibility – and overlook the creative capacity of a young constable figuring how to solve problems out on the streets.

But is cultural change simply about finding new ways of integrating the sensibilities of 'street cops' and 'management cops' (in the parlance of Reuss-Ianni & Ianni, 1983)? Yes, culture can be analysed as a 'patterned set of understandings' (Reiner, 1992, p. 109), but in its mundane, everyday expressions it is inevitably de-centred and fragmented and the 'patterns' can mask ambivalence, tension and contestation on the part of thinking, and in many cases, highly reflective social actors.

Our point of departure in this chapter is that police cultural change is eminently possible if practitioners (police officers), as individuals, are able to 'engage with, deploy, and remake their work practice in changing circumstances' (Billet, 2006, p. 54). But while it is true that cultural transformation is realised through individual agency and subjectivity, the constant relationship between individual agents and their social world can never be overlooked. Individual agents are actively situated in social contexts that both hinder and facilitate new ways of thinking and responding. This role of individual agents in changing culture is highlighted by Australian educationalist Stephen Billet:

> Individuals transform culture as they appropriate practices and carry it forward to the next generation in an altered form, as their creativity builds upon technological

transformations and through resolutions to problems they encounter in new times and novel circumstances ... . Vocational practices are not merely reproduced by individuals, they are elaborated, refined, and remade as their agency and intentionality engages and interacts with socially determined tasks and initiatives. (2006, p. 59)

From this perspective, cultural change results from interchanges between individual actors and their social world as they interpret new knowledge and negotiate new practices. Change, as a negotiated outcome, needs to be understood not as some kind of overall cataclysm but as a series of little shifts in ways of seeing and acting: not as a process sweeping across the whole spectrum of an organisation, but as one that resides in the tiny pockets of activity that constitute its social operations. Our contention is that the challenge in realising cultural change *writ large* is one of how best to allow these local, incremental pockets of change to grow in their influence, both across organisational units and beyond organisational boundaries.

In this chapter, we develop this micro-level understanding of opportunities for cultural change in the context of the Nexus Policing Project in the state of Victoria, Australia and in which the present authors have both been participants. Nexus places emphasis on collaborative relationships between police and academic organisations in the generation of knowledges and ideas that can shape ways of seeing and doing in policing practice and in policing research. Based on its collaborative philosophy, Nexus is devoted to cultural change not only within police organisations, but in academic institutions that have an expressed commitment to improving policy and practice. With this in mind, this chapter limits its focus to the creation of spaces and processes of thinking and reflection for police officers within a collaborative research context. We suggest that these spaces give rise to new policing cultures as individual police officers generate new ways of resolving practical problems that they encounter in the ever-changing field of policing. The importance of cultural change within academic institutions doing collaborative research is equally important and deserving of rigorous debate. We suggest some cultural challenges academic institutions are presented with if they wish to engage in collaborative research with practitioner organisations. Although space does not permit us to give this subject the attention it deserves, we hope the analytical perspective offered here will inform future analyses.

CULTURE, AGENCY AND CHANGE

Definitions of culture vary. Shearing and Ericson describe it as 'a sensibility, a way of being out of which action will flow' (Shearing & Ericson, 1991, p. 491).

In a similar vein, Bevir and Rhodes (2006) focus on 'meaning in action' (p. 1) which is revealed in the everyday life of political actors and public sector bureaucrats. Although 'culture' is not their core analytical concept, they stress the importance of exploring the mutually constitutive relationship between people's actions and the meanings that surround them. Beliefs inform practices, and practices reinforce and re-work beliefs. 'To explain an action', they say, 'we cannot merely correlate it with an isolated attitude. Rather, we must interpret it as part of a web of beliefs and desires' (p. 3).

This kind of interpretation supports a conception of culture as something fragmented, de-centred, expressed through tiny practices and the webs of meaning that surround them:

> No abstract concept, such as a class or an institution, can properly explain people's beliefs, interests or actions. Such a concept can represent only proxy for the multiple and complex beliefs and actions of all those individuals we classify under it. An interpretive approach often concludes, for such reasons, that practices require bottom-up studies of the actions and beliefs out of which they emerge. They explore the ways in which social practices are created, sustained and transformed through the interplay and contest of the beliefs or meanings embedded in human activity. (p. 3)

Bevir and Rhodes make it clear that the everyday practices of individuals may indeed be informed by wider webs of meanings but this is not to say they are pre-determined by the wider context. People have the capacity to reflect on the beliefs that shape their behaviour and also to adjust those beliefs in relation to the ideas that circulate around them and to the accumulated insights of their own personal histories and their own negotiated meanings. It is true that no individual exists outside of a particular social context (or multiple contexts) and, notwithstanding that they are 'conscious thinking subjects' (Weedon, 1987, p. 26), all individuals are inevitably 'situated' rather than fully autonomous (Bevir & Rhodes, 2006, p. 4). Individual actions derive from an existing social basis; as Weedon puts it, 'Social meanings are produced within social institutions and practices in which individuals, who are shaped by these institutions, are *agents of change*, rather than its authors' (Weedon, 1987, p. 25, italics added). Even so, while individuals are always subjected to social suggestion, they retain the capacity to respond innovatively to new ideas, problems, or dilemmas. As Bevir and Rhodes (2006) explain, 'A dilemma arises for an individual or group when a new idea stands in opposition to existing beliefs or practices and so forces a reconsideration of the existing beliefs and associated tradition' (p. 9). Equally, as dilemmas are resolved, social backgrounds are themselves transformed, even if only at the most local of levels.

Within police organisations, as with all other organisations, cultural change is vitally contingent on agency, and more specifically on the capacity – and opportunities – for individual police members to exercise this agency. If we adopt the view that all police members – across all ranks – are change agents in their own right, it would seem that the challenge for cultural change projects is to both identify and create the conditions that nourish and build this capacity for agency through all layers of the police hierarchy.

Bradley, Nixon and Marks begin to pursue this normative line of inquiry by identifying some of the conditions required for police organisations and for police members in particular to become 'reflective', that is, be capable of assessing their daily practices against the contemporary values, sensibilities and knowledges that inform and shape their world (Bradley, Nixon, & Marks, 2006, p. 171). For these authors, a central condition for having reflective people and reflective organisations is a robust and sustained process and structure for generating new knowledge and ideas. Police members must have both access to knowledge and capacity (and available resources) to use that knowledge to guide better practice. But accessing knowledge is much more than just a passive process. Bradley and colleagues' bigger point is that police must also be 'knowledge workers' in their own right (p. 171). Furthermore, this built-in knowledge work must be supported by a 'sustained interface between researchers and practitioners throughout all the phases required to ensure that change occurs: knowledge generation, validation, diffusion and adoption' (p. 185).

For the remainder of this chapter, we will explore this theme of 'interface', knowledge building and cultural change through a discussion of the project known as 'Nexus Policing'. Nexus is co-managed by Victoria Police and the Australian National University (ANU) and is supported by the Australian Research Council (ARC) through their Linkage Program. The word 'nexus' has much the same connotation as 'interface': a binding or linking together. Applying this term emphasises the linking together of different forms of knowledge and capacity in thinking reflectively about police practice and in developing the capacity for problem-oriented policing innovations. Nexus reflects the linkages not only between police and other agencies and groupings in thinking through common problems of safety and order, but also the linkages between police organisations and academia in joint reflection and innovation.

CREATING REFLECTIVE SPACES

Victoria Police has a policy of active collaboration with academic researchers on a range of policing issues, in the Nexus initiative and in other projects (see Bradley et al., 2006). Projects of this kind seldom have an easy ride; scholarly interventions in the work of the police frequently fall short of expectations, and one scholar (Bradley, 2005) attributes the failures at least in part to the kind of intellectual relationships between police and academics that narrowly traditional social science methodologies tend to produce. Bradley's analysis implies that the field of policing research and scholarship is in need of cultural transformation. But there are signs that academic researchers are beginning to alter their disposition towards the police. In some of the most recent research it is notable that police agencies feature less as experimental spaces for research, and more as zones of learning (Bayley, 2006). Nexus, too, operates from the perspective that police organisations are places for learning and knowledge building and that police have been for too long excluded from the 'thinking process' that informs the production of knowledge and ideas. Nexus takes this one step further, suggesting that academics must enter jointly with police into a relationship of reciprocal learning and reflection. Through this process, ways of seeing and doing on both sides of the partnership become subject to change.

The Nexus project was initiated and planned collaboratively – in the form of a proposal to the ARC – by Victoria Police and the ANU. The two Chief Investigators (CI's) from the ANU had a long history of intellectual engagement with the Chief Commissioner of Victoria Police, in both her current capacity and in her previous roles in Australian Policing. Having agreed in principle to jointly pursue an ARC grant – and to match the proposed funds with direct and in-kind contributions from the police – the CIs assembled a team to write a grant proposal. The final proposal emerged through multiple iterations and deliberations, central to which was the role of David Bradley (referenced in this chapter), a Senior Research Fellow for Victoria Police located within the Chief Commissioner's office. An expert on police education (in a career devoted to bridging the fields of theory and practice) part of Bradley's role is to initiate and support collaborative research and innovation projects, with diverse Australian academic institutions, in a wide array of operational and strategic areas.

Having in place this position of Research Fellow has done much to entrench and institutionalise long-term collaboration between Victoria Police and academia, spanning well beyond the Nexus project which represents only a fraction of the research and innovation projects that Victoria Police is involved in (see Bradley et al., 2006). Victoria Police has also undergone internal governance changes that signify a move, as Bradley describes it, 'from deference-based conversation and change to evidence-informed conversation and change' (personal communication). For example, their Organisational Development Standing Committee was created as a deliberative structure that monitors and supports organisational innovations and projects. Its establishment has formed part of a wider agenda aimed at discarding elements of command-and-control management that stifle reflection and creativity amongst police officers.

From the outset, the Nexus initiative has been based on the premise that, in a pluralised social context, building the capacity of police as knowledge workers and generators of ideas requires something more than just honing the research skills of the police themselves or, on the other hand, giving academic researchers closer access to the 'coal face'. Nexus seeks to create opportunity for self-reflection and re-examination by police members, at all levels, of their own ways of thinking and at the same time to foster interaction with outsiders – public and private agencies involved in safety generation – who can contribute different perspectives, different expertise and experience, different kinds of problem solving and may well also see different challenges.

At the local level Nexus has the police engaging, for example, with school children and youth service agencies to discuss school safety. Together they have identified specific safety problems, constructed scenarios around these problems and enacted role-plays around possible solutions to these problems. These scenarios were based on real life situations that have occurred, or may occur, in their everyday lives. They included issues such as bullying due to sexual orientation and young people's engagement in self-harm. Interestingly, these situations identified by young people did not reflect the problems that police imagined were foremost in their minds: the police were surprised to learn, for example, that self-harm is a key safety issue for school-going youth. Role play exercises have given police a way to put across their own view of how to tackle problems like petty theft or drug abuse at schools and at the same time given young people a chance to question police approaches.

The Nexus Policing Project tries to work with small groups and individuals in the context of specific policing problems, in this way creating spaces for reflection and for new ideas to 'bubble up' (see Braithwaite, 2006) through dialogue. The cultural change this process fosters may be incremental and slow but it centres on real engagement by police as social actors who have a stake in doing policing differently.

Central to the Nexus methodology is this creation of reflective spaces in which researchers and practical actors can come together to reconsider their everyday working assumptions about policing in general and about specific safety and order problems that have to be tackled. This way Nexus does certainly provide opportunities for academics to ground and to test their theories through engagement with the lived realities of police members but more significantly it emphasises continual dialogue between academics and police practitioners based an equal exchange of knowledge and worldviews. Nexus is at pains to avoid what Fox calls the traditional 'hierarchy of knowledge which situates research evidence in a position superior to other forms of knowing'; its agenda is to 're-privilege the role of the 'practitioner' in generating useful knowledge, without rejecting the skills and perspectives of the 'academic' researcher' (Fox, 2003, p. 82).

In its principle of collaborative reflection and innovation, the Nexus Project draws inspiration from the concept of Participatory Action Research (PAR) which has evolved in contexts largely outside of policing such as development agencies, business and agriculture (see Foote Whyte, Greenwood, & Lazes, 1991) but has also been experimented with by some other police forces, for example the Israeli Police in the mid 1990s (Geva & Shem-Tov, 2002). The Israeli research project formed part of a programme aimed at decentralising Israeli policing services. A police officer from the Community Policing Unit worked together with a researcher and they jointly decided what methods and tools were needed to set up a new community policing centre. Focus groups were used as an inclusive mechanism for both collecting data and also then analysing the data when transcription was completed. In their review of the project Geva and Shem-Tov argue that

> the participatory research technique prevented any alienation of the research subject group ... from the researchers. By not presenting themselves as authority figures, the researchers allowed the CPOs [Community Policing Officers] to take an active role in the research enterprise, to have input into the research questions, the research design and, of course, the research outputs ... . The research methodology completely matched the partnership and flexibility of community policing philosophy and strategy under study. Just as participatory research sees its subjects as partners in the research process and adapts itself to their needs, so community policing makes for cooperation and collaboration with local residents, as well as the flexible adaptation of policing services to their changing needs and governing principles. (p. 196)

Geva and Shem-Tov offer the collaborative thinking process described here as an example of acquiring experience in partnership building that can be subsequently carried through to further police partnership situations. They also highlight the importance of aligning the research methodology with the outcomes of the research.

The Nexus Project similarly espouses a PAR approach to generating new thinking for partnership-based solutions to community safety. Problem issues that have been identified include youth safety, management of family violence cases at the 'front end' (pre-trial phase) of the criminal justice system, safety on the transit system and case management of sex offenders post-release.

The reflective spaces that Victoria Police and their academic partners attempt to create in the context of such problems come in a variety of organisational and intellectual forms (see Foote Whyte et al., 1991). Organisational spaces involve a physical coming together of police members of various ranks together with researchers and safety partners involved in Nexus. All participants in these conversations share concerns about particular safety problems. Safety partners include local authorities, non-government organisations, voluntary groupings, private security agencies and school children. Different safety partners engage in conversations about such problems and the ways in which they can more effectively link their knowledge and capacities in addressing them. The wide range of actors participating in these forums counters tendencies, particularly on the part of government bureaucracies, to view problems and their solutions with silo vision.

The 'nexus' in Nexus between the academic and practitioner members of the team is meant to be based on trust, reciprocity and mutual respect for one another's point of view. The management structure for the project was designed so that it could be jointly steered by team members from Victoria Police and the ANU: a Central Coordination Team is led jointly by a Victoria Police Inspector and a senior researcher from ANU and the team membership is made up of other police officers from Victoria Police Centre (head office) and researchers from ANU. The Central Coordination Team oversees the operations of local teams set up in each of seven pilot areas. Each local team is led by a senior manager at the Inspector or Superintendent rank and this manager is in turn tasked with selecting team members from his or her particular station or police area who are considered to have the requisite enthusiasm and capacity to be 'agency champions'. This local police team then combines with 'champions' from other local agencies such as the city council, resident groups, service organisations and private security companies to steer and shape the local project.

The message that central Nexus team members stress to police colleagues working in the pilot site teams puts more emphasis on the *thinking process* that Nexus can offer, applicable across a range of concerns, than on any particular input on substantive issues that the local pilot partnerships may be working on. The message rather is that Nexus offers a methodological approach that can be applied across issue areas. Put another way, the essence of Nexus is its reflection methodology which embraces a phased approach to reflection and innovation. There are four key phases that structure thinking and problem-solving (Wood and Marks describe these phases elsewhere: Marks & Wood, 2007; Wood & Marks, 2006). These are: (a) 'mapping' existing forms of knowledge and capacity around specific problems, (b) conducting an in-depth research module on particular issues, strategies or partnerships identified in the mapping exercise, (c) designing a nexus arrangement (partnership model) to be piloted, and (d) implementing and refining the nexus arrangement.

The mapping process aims to ascertain who the various agencies and groupings are that have a role in addressing a particular safety and order problem. For example, in the youth safety pilot, academic members of the Nexus team developed an inventory of the agencies in the relevant local government area with involvement in youth service delivery in areas ranging from mental health to education. Interested, as we were, in a better understanding of policing cultures, we also sought to get a more in-depth view of how police members thought about youth safety. We wanted to know how their worldviews shaped their understanding of youth issues, and how underlying beliefs influenced the way they set about tackling these issues in practice. Together with researchers from the ANU, police members from the Nexus Team drew up a set of questions for submission to focus groups. Police members facilitated focus groups with local police and the data from the focus groups was jointly analysed by police and academics. Qualitative research with the young people and police supplemented the initial map of safety partners by providing us with a richer perspective on how security was 'imagined' and governed beyond the immediate realm of the police and the criminal justice system (Marks & Wood, 2007).

The mapping and research phases generated a document which in turn informed the design of a new nexus model to be piloted by police in conjunction with their safety partners. In the context of a separate Nexus project on case management of sex offenders post-release, this document will inform a workshop with representatives from agencies from the criminal justice and health sectors along with representatives of other relevant community-based organisations that play a role in one form or another in the monitoring, care and supervision of sex offenders in community settings. The research undertaken in this project to date has consisted of individual and group interviews, carried out jointly by academic and police members of Nexus, with representatives of the above safety partners. To date this research has revealed distinct worldviews surrounding respondents' conceptualisations of sex offenders and how best they should be managed in reintegrating them into the community. This has provided both police and academic researchers with new sets of thinking about post-release management by spelling out the complex social implications of populist public policies centred on enhanced monitoring.

As with the other Nexus projects, the pilot design workshop will be devoted to aligning these differing worldviews through identifying a shared language and shared meanings that can serve to connect sex offender case management practices in new and more effective ways. In order for this alignment process to occur, however, it will be necessary for all safety partners to reflect upon the beliefs of the other partners and to understand the unique dilemmas each faces on a daily basis.

Implementing, reviewing and tweaking the pilots is also collaborative and similarly yields theoretical returns. Upon initiation of a pilot, all safety partners involved in managing a particular nexus pilot are committed to monitoring progress, taking stock of what works and what doesn't, and doing 'evaluative de-bugging' (Thacher, 2007) to improve the chances of a pilot's success. This gets all safety partners, and the police in particular, to re-think traditional performance evaluation and accountability arrange-ments. In the case of the youth safety project, for example, 'success' will be measured in part by the extent to which school-going youth are able to identify and solve their own safety problems by, if necessary, drawing on the capacities of youth service agencies.

Another way in which reflective space for police members is created has been through awareness of the Nexus project being spread in concrete interaction with safety partners and broader constituencies (such as other police organisations or academic conferences). In creating this awareness, police and academic members of the Nexus team present themselves in a variety of public forums as intellectual partners bound together in a joint endeavour to improve policing practice. In presenting themselves as intellectual partners in this way, both academic and practitioner members of Nexus symbolically challenge the research/practice and researcher/subject dichotomies inherent in traditional research paradigms (see Fox, 2003).

THE 'RIPPLING OUT' OF CULTURAL CHANGE

The research undertaken in Nexus is designed as an open process, where both theories and practices are reworked. It is meant to be reflective in nature, aimed at exploring possible answers and assessing the plausibility of those answers through dialogue. One vital element of such dialogue is its embrace of difference (of worldviews, legacies and traditions, problem-solving capacities). What this means is that the spaces for reflection that Nexus endeavours to create are not organisation-wide, but occur rather in tiny organisational pockets, in specific settings associated with particular problem areas. The intention is thus to open up small spaces of thinking and action that ideally 'ripple outwards' (see Braithwaite, 2006) into other parts of the organisation.

Very often it is middle management that turns out to be the crucial organisational level in this rippling out process. Drawing middle management into the reflective process and the generating of new ideas is very important if lower ranks are going to feel comfortable about challenging both themselves and established practices. More than that, middle managers function as the basic units of organisational learning, responding on the one hand to organisational directives from the top and providing guidance in the daily enactment of organisational requirements to those below.

Middle managers have been key players in all the phases of Nexus. They are in many ways the focal point of the pilots. Often they are the first point of contact in local police organisations for academic researchers and for other safety network partners. They have been extremely instrumental in the initial identification of local policing quandaries and they are generally responsible for identifying local police 'agency champions' (mostly rank-and-file) who will participate in every phase of the project and promote the project in a range of forums.

In working through the phased thinking process of Nexus, police members hone their capacity to apply this process (of mapping, problem solving and evaluative debugging) across a range of problem areas – a capacity that is often decisive for both vertical and lateral career advancement in the police hierarchy. One might go so far as to suggest that mastery of any particular substantive area in policing is less important than mastery of the capacity to reflect – to identify, analyse and act upon a wide range of problems. From this perspective, Nexus aims to build capacity for 'problem-oriented policing' in a world of plural policing, and it attempts to do so one person at a time.

In our experience to date, past and current police members of the team have applied the aptitude for phased thinking that they have acquired through their Nexus participation to new substantive problems they have become responsible for through lateral or vertical shifts in their roles. As one example, early on in the project, when the substantive focus of each Nexus pilot was being negotiated with senior management, an Assistant

Commissioner collaborated with ANU members of the Nexus team to undertake a review of the existing organised crime strategy of Victoria Police. This led to the establishment of a team of practitioners and researchers, including a police member who spent time at the ANU to conduct an intense research module on cutting-edge analyses of organised crime. The Nexus thinking process that underpinned this research directly was jointly presented at a high-level workshop on organised crime hosted by Victoria Police and directly influenced the design of a new Organised Crime Strategy. When the same police member who conducted the research module at ANU later moved to the police Transit Safety Division he applied the Nexus mapping approach in assisting with the development of a new Victoria Police Road Policing Strategy. Nor has his application of Nexus thinking ended there. He also played a pivotal role in the design of a public perceptions survey on the transit system as part of a research module for one of the Nexus pilots on transit safety. Examples like this demonstrate how organisational learning can happen incrementally through individual actors, as small but significant vehicles of learning, as they move about to different pockets of the organisation.

The 'rippling out' can also occur when other change agents who may have no connection with Nexus approach members of the team for inspiration, either hoping for fresh ideas to address substantive problems or interested more generally in the kind of thinking process Nexus offers. For example, an Inspector from a local government area in Victoria recently approached a police member from the central Nexus team for suggestions about managing youth safety issues. Finding out this way about the youth safety model developed as part of Nexus in another jurisdiction, the Inspector is now mobilizing local organisations to help tailor the model for implementation in his own area. This example illustrates how Nexus team members serve as 'brokers' to the kind of ideas being developed in the pilot sites and propagate the Nexus thinking process by introducing others to its methods.

Our argument here is that cultural change can and does happen one person at a time. In Nexus, individual police members can and do apply the Nexus thinking process to new operational areas as they take on different strategic challenges or move within the organisation. Alternatively, they function as 'ideas brokers', linking their colleagues to new ways of thinking that could be relevant to other challenges. In both cases, particular forms of 'story-telling' have occurred (see Shearing & Ericson, 1991 on the importance of stories). The stories may be about the value of Nexus thinking in illuminating complex policing problems. The stories may consist of a simple empirical description of what has occurred in a particular pilot project, including what the Nexus approach has meant for police members in addressing their concrete operational priorities. In both cases, it matters who the story-teller is. The stories that police members tell to other police members are laden with particular sources of legitimacy and authority that derive from bases of knowledge and experience that they share with their colleagues.

Maybe it is *shared* story-telling, the collaborative diffusion of new forms of thinking, which sits less comfortably with academics and practitioners in their respective institutional contexts. In any event the Nexus emphasis on breaking down the theory–practice divide through collaborative research and innovation comes replete with challenges. In the next section, we will review some of these challenges and provide modest suggestions for addressing them.

CHALLENGES

With the organisational support of Victoria Police, the Nexus Project has successfully created more space for police members to display their identities and roles as knowledge workers, and ultimately also as agents of cultural change. There are, however, several challenges associated with the Nexus methodology, and in particular the PAR approach that it advocates. Some of these challenges stem from structural or procedural issues, both of which can be related to differences in the traditional interests and missions of police and academic organisations (Canter, 2004). The success of this kind of academic–police partnership can also be highly contingent on timing and on the current vision of police leadership.

The openness of the police to collaborative research and innovation depends, in large part, on what is happening within the police organisation itself. A police service could be undergoing a learning phase or a period of defensiveness, resulting from a host of internal and external dynamics. Academics who want to work in partnership with the police need to time their interventions to coincide with a period of change and learning in the police organisation. In the case of Nexus, the appointment of Commissioner Nixon presented a key moment of opportunity for pursuing this kind of collaborative relationship. Under her leadership a number of collaborative partnerships between Victoria Police and universities have been established with the support of the ARC (Bradley et al., 2006), including the Nexus Project. Whether partnerships like this, backed by substantial monetary and in-kind contributions, would have been pursued without the presence of Commissioner Nixon is an open question. Nor is it certain whether they will continue when she is no longer in office. But what we do know is that the support and involvement of key police organisational leaders is absolutely critical to the success of these partnerships, particularly given the habitual scepticism of police and police representative organisations (such as police unions) towards academic knowledge workers.

Good timing and assurances of benefits to the police are not the only requisites for partnerships like this to work. Police are likely to remain sceptical of outside thinking even once projects are up and running. That makes it very important for academics and police to jointly negotiate the styles and tools most appropriate for mutual engagement and reflection. There are a host of different methods that can be used, for example, in 'democratising' the research process. Police and academic researchers have had long discussions about methods to be used in particular Nexus pilot sites and in some of these pilot sites the police are the lead researchers with academic researchers in the background providing technical support when called upon. Police who are part of the Nexus Team have facilitated focus groups with police officers on youth safety and with other police responsible for policing domestic violence, and (together with local academics) have drawn up survey questionnaires for train commuters to find out about sources of insecurity and how these could be ameliorated. Police from the Nexus Team regularly lead discussions in local police forums about research findings and analysis and around approaches for dealing with practical problems that have been identified.

Police officers, whether management or rank-and-file, do not script changes on their own. They are situated actors who have constraints that limit their capacity to be visionaries, innovators, and more generally agents of cultural change. The organisations in which they work remain highly bureaucratised and pragmatic. Moving beyond the organisational constraints requires collaboration with others who can bring fresh perspectives to issues of safety. It is thus important for collaborative projects like Nexus to ensure that police emerge with positive experiences of being in a partnership and with a commitment to thinking outside of the police box as designers and participators (though not necessarily as primary agents) in new public safety institutions and networks. For this to happen, there must be ways of promoting 'mutual and reciprocating recognitions' between police, academic researchers and other safety partners (Marenin, 2004, p. 299).

In this vein, we offer some recommendations about what kinds of shifts are required to foster more equal partnerships between police and academic researchers, including some fundamental reconsideration of established cultural traditions in the institutions within which police and academic researchers work. In the first place, universities need to pay more than lip service to the importance of outreach-based programmes. Academic institutions looking to set up collaborative relationships with practitioners such as the police need to rethink their narrow rewarding of academic researchers who publish in high-rated peer reviewed journals. Unquestionably these journals are important for knowledge sharing among scholars and between scholars and police practitioners, and it is also the case that as police increasingly interface with tertiary education institutions they themselves are beginning more and more to read these journals. Nevertheless, if academic knowledge is really going to impinge on police practice then universities need to give greater credit, for example, to publishing in journals that are accessible to the police in terms of distribution and the style of writing. In-house police agency journals are one option, and indeed the one published by Victoria Police has featured articles on two of the pilot projects to date. There are also journals produced by police unions/associations, not to mention the impact of writing up interesting findings in the mainstream press.

Conference funding should also be more easily available for researchers who wish to bring practitioners and academics together. A recent example of this is a conference that took place in October 2006 at the University of California, Berkeley (UCB) funded by the UCB Law School and the Research Office at the Australian National University. Themed 'Police Reform from the Bottom-Up', this conference took the form of a round table discussion bringing together policing scholars, police leaders and police unionists to talk about how rank-and-file police can be more actively involved in reform processes. As part of the round table, a Police Chief (from the Broken Arrow Police Department in the USA) and his academic collaborator gave a joint presentation on their shared project in creating team management structures and processes. Like the Nexus Project, the conference was conceived as a forum for practitioners and academic researchers from across the world to learn from each other's experiences, frustrations and opportunities. Yet it remains the case that participation from police and other practitioners at events such as these is still more the exception than the rule.

Academic researchers and the broader research community need to be better informed about the involvement of practitioners in research and innovation projects. There is room for more frequent joint authorship of papers and conference presentations. Joint academic/practitioner authorship and presentation is one option which the Nexus Project has pursued on several occasions. But police also need to be motivated to get involved in this kind of joint endeavour. Authorship does not presently get much credit as 'important police work', let alone any formal recognition in police organisational appraisal systems. Nor, in general, does this kind of collaborative endeavour flourish when starved of funds, and funding (internal or external) often needs to be more actively pursued.

Unsurprisingly then, what has emerged in the Nexus Project is that local police officers are happy to lend support to the project but this is usually limited to promoting the project within the organisation, attending joint workshops and participating in focus groups. There has been some resistance from both the middle managers and from rank-and-file to 'just' talking through ideas which do not appear to lead to immediate solutions or action. To get beyond this there has to be a rethinking on police performance measurement in the context of new roles, new endeavours and new self-identities.

Police reluctance to search out possibilities of more networked approaches to safety issues also comes from their lived reality of being, as the public police, the only 24/7 on-call agency. As they see things, whatever the promise that collaboration and partnerships may hold out for police not just to do things differently but also get on with their 'core business' with less interruption, they remain acutely aware that they are constantly on call to handle just about any kind of social crisis, and most especially between 5 p.m. and 8 a.m. when the office doors of nearly all their 'partners' are shut. So when police participate in projects like Nexus they almost inevitably do so with a certain reserve of cynicism, not wholly uninformed, about the limits of non-police actors and the 'unreality' of academic theorising, however well-intended.

We offer these comments as no more than introductory thoughts about the challenges associated with partnerships between police and academics to create the kind of reflective spaces that are crucial for cultural and practical change. Suffice it to say that it is likely such partnerships will continue to be uncomfortable for some time. Building relations founded on reciprocity and trust between these two partners requires serious rethinking of professional identity and unravelling of familiar ways of doing things. Both partners will need to get their hands dirty – researchers by crawling out of the safety of academic fortresses and police by peeling off their armour of pragmatism and standing somewhat naked in educational institutions and forums. Both partners will need to leave behind the safety of their professional havens when they relate to one another and to other network agencies as equal contributors to new thinking and new practices.

From our perspective, partnerships like this can nonetheless play a significant role in cultivating the capacity of police members, regardless of rank, to exercise agency in cultural change. For changes to evolve within and across different pockets of the organisation, *all* police members need to be seen as knowledge workers capable of reflecting on what they believe and do, and on the way they mutually inform and influence one another. The Nexus Project is one modest attempt at establishing a new thinking process that taps the situated knowledges and capacities of police members, academics and a range of other organisations with a contribution to make to practical innovation in policing.

CONCLUSION

Culture is often made out to be the culprit for failures in reform, but we have tried to suggest a more optimistic view of police culture in which the emphasis, conceptually and in practical terms, is on the potential for *all* police members to be change agents. The practices of police officers, like those of any other social actor, may indeed be shaped by their worldviews, but they are not determined by them. Individual officers do have the capacity (or at least the potential) to reflect on the relationships between their beliefs and knowledges and practices and to direct these to innovation and problem-response. Unfortunately, little attention has been paid, either by academics or by police, to the conditions that enable police of whatever rank to bring fresh thinking to the work they do. In short, police organisations – together with their academic partners – should pay more attention to building the capacity of police officers to be, in the full sense of the word, knowledge workers. By taking on this identity, each officer can contribute to cultural change, and to police reform generally in their own tiny, but significant corner of the organisation. If this nurturing and capacity building reaches sufficient numbers of individual officers in different parts of the organisation, their aggregated contributions would seem to hold out considerable promise of forward-looking innovation.

This chapter argues in particular that collaborative spaces and processes (nexus arrangements) for thinking, reflection and innovation must become more central to the field of policing reform. Research partnerships between police and academic researchers need to be established on an equal footing, sharing knowledges, capacities and resources. For this to occur, academics have to become more inclusive, more practical, and less abstract in their working modes. Police need to shed their defensive gear and open themselves up to innovative knowledge generation with 'outsiders'. The model of PAR, with its array of techniques available to democratise the research process, challenges the bureaucratic tendencies of both academic researchers and the police and provide, we believe, a strong intellectual foundation for reflection and innovation in policing. Rhodes suggests that the role of academics can be to 'offer narratives that enable policy-makers to see things differently'(Rhodes, 2006, p. 31). But it is not simply academics that do have, or should have, this role. In the field of policing, cultural change is dependent on engagement with multiple narratives within and across diverse organisational and intellectual settings. Change will only occur if practical actors have both the capacity and opportunity to reflect on their existing worldviews, to get a better sense of the perspectives of other actors and alter their own ways of thinking if they see a better way.

NOTE

1. We are grateful to David Bradley, Megan O'Neill, Anne-Marie Singh and Tess Walsh for their insights and suggestions.

ACKNOWLEDGMENTS

We wish to acknowledge the financial support of the Australian Research Council (Grant LP0348682).

REFERENCES

Bayley, D. H. (2006). Police reform: Who done it? Paper presented at the Conference on Police Reform from the Bottom Up, University of California, Berkeley, 12–13 October.

Bevir, M., & Rhodes, R. A. W. (2006). *Governance Stories*. London: Routledge.

Billet, S. (2006). Relational interdependence between social and individual agency in work and working life. *Mind, Culture and Activity, 13*(1), 53–69.

Bradley, D. (2005). Crime reduction and problem-oriented policing. *Police Research and Practice: An International Journal, 6*(4), 391–394.

Bradley, D., Nixon, C., & Marks, M. (2006). What works, what doesn't work and what looks promising in police research networks. In: J. Fleming & J. Wood (Eds), *Fighting crime together: The challenges of policing and security networks* (pp. 170–194). Sydney: University of New South Wales Press.

Braithwaite, J. (2006). Peacemaking networks and restorative justice. In: J. Fleming & J. Wood (Eds), *Fighting crime together: The challenges of policing and security networks*. Sydney: University of New South Wales Press.

Canter, D. (2004). A tale of two cultures: Comparing the police and academia. In: P. Villiers & R. Adlam (Eds), *Policing a safe, just and tolerant society* (pp. 109–121). Winchester: Waterside Press.

Chan, J. (1997). *Changing police culture: Policing in a multicultural society*. Melbourne: Cambridge University Press.

Foote Whyte, W., Greenwood, D. J., & Lazes, P. (1991). Participatory action research: Through practice to science in social research. In: W. Foote Whyte (Ed.), *Participatory action research*. Newbury Park: Sage.

Fox, N. J. (2003). Practice-based Evidence: Towards Collaborative and Transgressive Research. *Sociology, 37*(1), 81–102.

Geva, R., & Shem-Tov, O. (2002). Setting up community policing centres: Participatory action research in decentralised policing services. *Police Practice and Research, 3*(3), 189–200.

Marenin, O. (2004). Guest editor's Introduction. *Police Practice and Research, 4*(4/5), 299–300.

Marks, M., & Wood, J. (2007). Generating youth safety from below: Situating young people at the centre of knowledge-based policing. In: T. Williamson (Ed.), *Handbook of knowledge based policing: Current conceptions and future direcitions*. West Sussex: Wiley.

Reiner, R. (1992). *The politics of the police* (2nd ed.). New York: Harvester Wheatsheaf.

Reuss-Ianni, E., & Ianni, F. (1983). Street cops and management cops: The two cultures of policing. In: M. Punch (Ed.), *Control in police organizations*. Newbury Park: Sage.

Rhodes, R. A. W. (2006). The sour laws of network governance. In: J. Fleming & J. Wood (Eds), *Fighting crime together: The challenges of policing and security networks*. Sydney: University of New South Wales Press.

Shearing, C., & Ericson, R. (1991). Culture as figurative action. *British Journal of Sociology, 42*(4), 481–506.

Thacher, D. (2007). Police research for the front lines. *Policing and Society*.

Weedon, C. (1987). *Feminist practice and poststructuralist theory*. Oxford: Blackwell.

Wood, J., & Marks, M. (2006). Nexus governance: Building new ideas for security and justice. In: C. Slakmon, M. Rocha Machado & P. Cruz Bottini (Eds), *New directions in the governance of justice and security* (pp. 719–738). Brasilia: Ministry of Justice of Brazil; United Nations Development Programme; School of Law of the Getulio Vargas Foundation.

PART IV:
NEW POLICING CULTURES IN
A PLURAL POLICING FIELD

CHAPTER 12

REFLECTIONS ON THE STUDY OF PRIVATE POLICING CULTURES: EARLY LEADS AND KEY THEMES

Anne-Marie Singh and Michael Kempa

ABSTRACT

Almost all the functions of the public police are also performed, in some manner, by private security agents, but the cultures of private policing agents have been far less fully studied than those of public police officers. With the private security industry employing a wide array of coercive techniques and in many cases operating punitive strategies for controlling crime and maintaining public order, this chapter suggests that sectors of this industry exhibit a reactive and punitive organisational culture. It also explores similarities between private and public police cultures; the focus is upon the relevance for private policing cultures of concerns traditionally raised in analyses of public police cultures. The chapter concludes with some questions about what the surprising culture and practices of the private security industry may signal about the emergent political economy of human security.

Police Occupational Culture: New Debates and Directions
Sociology of Crime, Law and Deviance, Volume 8, 297–320
Copyright © 2007 by Elsevier Ltd.
All rights of reproduction in any form reserved
ISSN: 1521-6136/doi:10.1016/S1521-6136(07)08012-8

INTRODUCTION

Over the past three decades private security has expanded exponentially in both the 'established' democracies of the West and the fledgling democracies of the 'post-authoritarian' and more generally 'developing' world. Pioneering research in the 1970s and 1980s that first drew scholarly attention to this trend (e.g. Shearing & Stenning, 1981, 1983; Spitzer & Scull, 1977) gave a lead that has been taken up with increasing vigour in academic policing studies over the past few years. Particular focal points in empirical analysis have been the overall size of the private security industry (in overview, see: Johnston, 1992; Kempa, Carrier, Wood, & Shearing, 1999), the range of functions the industry seeks to engage (see, for example, Johnston, 1992, 2006; Shearing & Stenning, 1981) and the forms of authority and other modalities of power the industry relies upon to effect these purposes (Stenning, 2000; Walker, 2000). Taken together, these empirical issues have been used as data for broader discussion of what the emergence of private security signals about wider trends in politics and governance generally (see especially Johnston & Shearing, 2003; Rigakos, 2002; Singh, 2005a).

Less studied have been related questions about the practice and culture of private policing on the ground (for notable exceptions see Manzo, 2004; Micucci, 1998; Rigakos, 2002; Wakefield, 2003). Much more is known about the culture and actual practices of public policing organisations than about those of private policing organisations of various stripes. Where scholars have commented on private policing culture, they have tended, moreover, to infer that these organisations emphasise the same risk management/harm minimisation/loss prevention logics that are prioritised by their corporate paymasters (Shearing & Stenning, 1981, 1983). This may seem on the face of it a reasonable enough assumption, but it does not to date have much empirical validation.

In this chapter, we use first-hand data to discuss the nature and the underlying drivers of the culture of the private security industry in South Africa (see further Singh, 2000, 2005a, 2005b) and we go on from there to explore connections both with issues that have been taken up in the limited literature that does exist on the culture of the private security industry elsewhere around the globe, and with certain more commonly debated issues relating to the culture of public policing agencies. Our purpose is to describe the empirically dominant forms of private policing culture and 'theorise' this culture in terms of the factors that enable and drive particular forms of private policing culture while suppressing alternative forms. Our findings indicate that, contrary to many expectations, private security corporations exhibit a reactive and punitive culture that is in some important ways akin to the dominant culture of public policing organisations of the 'professionalised era' of the middle decades of the 20th Century. We argue that these counter-intuitive findings make perfect sense in light of (1) the individual characteristics and professional aspirations of more recent recruits to these agencies, (2) the current organisational structure and legal environment of the private security industry, (3) the institutional origins of the private security industry, and (4) broader transformations in the field of policing and/or the governance of human security. In developing these arguments, we note the utility of classic studies of public policing culture in providing starting points for research into private policing culture, but we also detail a number of points of conceptual departure from these classic studies for the future of policing culture studies, both private and public. We also indicate some further concerns which these surprising findings signal about the emergent political economy of human security (and which will be taken up in a separate piece for later publication).

PRIVATE SECURITY CULTURE

Previous commentators have tended to assume that private security promotes the client's interest first, ahead of more broadly public interests, with the emphasis on preventing and reducing loss at private sites rather than on apprehending and punishing those who violate the law (see, for example, Shearing & Stenning, 1981, 1983). Private policing agents are thus thought to exhibit the 'future-oriented' thinking and behaviour associated with the logics of risk minimisation/profit maximisation pursued by their employers.

Some years ago, and from a more theoretical than empirical perspective, Johnston (1992) criticised the distinction that scholars have commonly made between 'loss minimisation' and 'crime control' security functions, on the grounds that this obscured the extent to which these objectives had become complementary in an increasingly marketised (i.e. neo-liberal) political economy. Indeed, the complementarity of these objectives is often spelled out quite explicitly by private security agencies in their own public representations: these businesses frequently market themselves as 'Security *and* Loss Control' providers (emphasis added; see Singh, 2000), which implies that they do not see security as purely a matter of loss control. Yet academic discussion still tends to assume that private security focuses primarily, if not exclusively, on loss prevention. Only quite recently has a small body of empirical research begun to detail the crime control and other coercive responsibilities that the industry also takes on, leading to suggestions, notably by South (1997), that punitive measures are now at the forefront of private security activities. Very recently Johnston (2006) has noted that risk-based and coercive technologies are also combined in the organisational philosophies and practices not just of transnational commercial providers of criminal justice services but also, more recently, of contracted military operational services. But it remains the case that grounded field research on the transnational contract security market is in its infancy; ethnographies are very much needed, and as yet none have been undertaken.

Indeed, empirical studies of the private security industry still mostly focus on official representations by the industry itself of its purposes, functions and practices, rather than on the actual cultures of the industry and, more particularly, the way security managers and line officers think about and act on the world around them. Thus, for example, Huey, Ericson, and Haggerty (2005) examine security guard deployment on urban streets in two Vancouver neighbourhoods, empirically grounding their research on the electronic and paper records of the private security companies they investigate, in combination with distanced observation of the execution of security officers' duties, and face-to-face interviews. Among their observations they note how the homeless, panhandlers, and other 'disorderly' folk (read non-consumers) are 'moved on', sometimes forcefully, by private security guards. In addition, shoplifters and vandals are arrested and turned over to the public police. The authors' concern is chiefly with the perceptions that the police, shopkeepers, business associations and area residents have of the activities of the private security companies; the views of security managers or of the guards themselves on their assigned tasks remain largely, though not entirely, unexplored. Setting out to illuminate the meaning and significance of the roles and functions of the private security agencies, Huey et al. end up implicitly borrowing the familiar 'crime control/order maintenance/service provision' template from public policing research: according to these authors, private security agents perform crime control and service functions in furtherance of a preventive order maintenance mandate. They explain that private security extends the 'broken windows' approach, with varying degrees of coercion used to create and preserve a commercialised order. However, while it may indeed be logical to infer that private security agents embody and reflect the preventive and profit maximising logics of their retail paymasters, we cannot be certain that they do indeed reflect these logics without more empirical research.

Taking us a step further in this regard is the recent work of George Rigakos (2002) in his innovative study of Intelligarde, a Toronto-based contract private security company. This is one of the few studies we know of that does address the issue of private security operational practices and occupational subculture, doing so through ground-level research based upon ethnography-inspired methods that include participant observation and interviews with frontline private security agents. Rigakos finds that Intelligarde agents assume 'parapolicing' responsibilities, identities and attitudes at the level both of rhetoric and of actual practice. At the level of practice, Intelligarde's private parapolicing functions extend to 'clearing crack houses, processing evictions, and even disrupting the business of "drug gangs"' in Toronto's inner city neighbourhoods, through such means as surveillance and making full arrests of perpetrators 'caught in the act' (p. 27). From interviews with ground-level private security agents, Rigakos characterises this parapolicing mission as 'crime fighting within a "wannabe" culture': private agents who identify with, and aspire to engage in, romanticised notions of 'exciting' careers in public policing (p. 30). We get a company crime fighting model in which the working environment and cultural context includes elements, noted by Rigakos, such as the need to look busy; isolation or a siege mentality; fear/danger; solidarity and mutual assistance; status frustration; perceived lack of respect from the public and the police; and hyper-masculinity. Rigakos observes that this dominant culture permeates the private policing organisation in a very similar fashion to matching tendencies in public policing organisations: aggressive sub-cultural mores were communicated and reinforced among front-line officers through informal 'on-the-job' socialisation, with 'storytelling' between private security agents being one of the primary mechanisms of this socialisation (on similar cultural diffusion processes within the public police, see especially Shearing & Ericson, 1991).

Building upon this emergent picture of private policing culture, grounded empirical studies of private security services by both Micucci (1998) and Manzo (2004), again in the North American context, underline the point that security forces are not necessarily harmonious wholes (see also Wakefield, 2003). As in the case of public policing agencies (see, for example, Bayley, 1994; Reuss-Ianni & Ianni, 1983), private security organisations may also be segmented into groups that engage and promote distinct worldviews and work styles not always consistent with the preferred objectives and goals either of the security firm or of the security client. These authors take the further helpful step of compiling their data into typologies of private security agents, in which they trace categories of agents that mirror familiar stratifications in public policing organisations. Thus, in the domain of private security, there are the 'crime fighters', the 'guards' (the service providers) and the 'bureaucratic cops', corresponding to the public policing labels of, respectively, 'new centurions', 'bobbies' and 'uniform carriers' (on these categories, see Reiner, 2000). Following on from these observations, we can begin to discern possible differences too in the cultures of 'in-house' and 'contract' private security agents. In our own research, and staying for the present within the focus of the existing literature, we have, however, restricted our comments to the culture of the 'contract' security industry, though we flag the point that the cultures of in-house security may or may not be distinct. We turn now to examine the culture of private security in South Africa.

THE CASE OF SOUTH AFRICA[1]

Private security has a long and rather ignoble history in South Africa. The initial period of large-scale growth in this industry occurred during the mid-1970s through to the mid-1980s, at the height of political resistance to the apartheid regime. In this epoch, private security growth and expansion was actively encouraged by the state. With public police capacity spread thin by counter-insurgency functions in the huge, densely populated black townships and along South Africa's wide borders, the apartheid state promoted private security as an acceptable policing force to meet the immediate security needs of white South Africans: a complementary role which private security readily took up and promoted (Grant, 1989). Employed at commercial, industrial and residential sites, private security protected the interests of white property owners. The apartheid government also made more direct 'national' use of private security through the *National Key Points Act* (102 of 1980). This Act required the employment of private security at 'crucial infrastuctural sites' – including railway stations, water treatment and electric energy generation plants – the 'loss, damage, disruption or immobilisation' of which would prove prejudicial to the Republic. The Act brought these 'Key Point' guards under the direct control of the Minister of Defence – standing as a classic historical illustration of the mobilisation of non-state security providers under public auspices (on the auspice/provider distinction, see Bayley & Shearing, 2001). In this case, government action through private proxy was undertaken with the odious intention of increasing the repressive capacity of the apartheid state and, in some cases, blurring the lines of accountability for human rights abuses between government programmers and private providers. One of the most sinister and most covert links between the apartheid regime and private security involved the establishment, by the state security forces, of private security firms as fronts for the illegal trade in weapons, ivory and diamonds – all to help shore up the embargoed and crumbling pariah state (on contemporary Western incarnations of inappropriate 'public/national security' policy being conducted 'at-a-distance' through private providers, see O'Reilly & Ellison, 2006). Many of these companies have survived as legitimate businesses and retain aspects of their paramilitary and covert institutional character. One example reported by the Network of Independent Monitors is Shield Security, originally a front company for the South African Defence Force. Today it has a reputation for employing mainly former Rhodesian special forces and security branch members, capitalising on their counter-insurgency training and experience (NIM, 1996).

During the 1990s the private security industry underwent significant change in the context of transition to a fully inclusive democracy. Most notable was the massive expansion of the industry in both size and overall activity: private security grew rapidly in the context of the high (and rising) levels of recorded crime and fear of crime that accompanied the demise of apartheid. Significantly, the ranks of the private security industry swelled with recruitment of former combatants on both sides of the apartheid struggle, with ex-members of the state security apparatus tending to occupy higher rungs in the operational and management ladder. But crime was more than simply the 'natural' environment within which private security organisations operated and flourished. Rather, it emerged as the principle *object* of private security regulatory strategies and practices: crime was targeted as a marketable resource for an industry of control, offering considerable potential for expansion (Singh, 2005a).

The upshot has been that private security is now the primary performer in the socio-political field of crime control in South Africa: it is well known that private security agents outnumber public policing agents by ratios estimated to be as high as 7 to 1 (see Berg, 2004; Irish, 1999; Kempa & Shearing, 2002). There are literally no functions performed by the public police in South Africa that are not also performed by non-state security agencies – sometimes with state support and other times contrary to the desires of the state (on problematic relationships between public and private policing agencies in the South African context, see especially Berg, 2004). Thus, as in North America and parts of Western Europe, private security guards routinely police new forms of 'communal space' that are privately owned yet open to various degrees of public access (on the range of these forms of property, see Kempa, Stenning, & Wood, 2004; Von Hirsch & Shearing, 2000). These spaces include classic forms of 'mass private property' such as shopping centres and leisure complexes frequented by the wealthy, as well as more unconventional forms such as fully enclosed gated communities – or 'gated villages' as they are often called in South Africa. One of the most fantastical examples of these is 'Heritage Park' – a 200 hectare space (roughly the size of the principality of Monaco) in the wine regions surrounding Cape Town, designed to be a self-sufficient 'city state' explicitly modelled (according to the developer's promotional materials) on the fortified towns of medieval Europe (see the Heritage Park website at: http://www.heritageprk.com; Carrol, 2006; Kempa & Shearing, 2002). Inside the electrified boundary (which, though lethal to the touch, is in an 'attractive palisade style' – according to the web site) that encircles the residents of this atavistic mode of collectivity, security and crime control are almost entirely matters for a fully privatised police service (Kempa fieldnotes 12 January 2000).

Lately the private security industry in South Africa has also been assuming a more active presence in fully public forms of space, including beachfronts and 'ordinary' street thoroughfares.[2] In particular, the greatest expansion to date has occurred in domestic (residential) patrol and armed reaction sector. All of these developments suggest that private security increasingly plays a role reminiscent of the state's conventional 'professionalised' reactive response/law enforcement function in all manner of both gated and more ordinary residential collectivities and confirm that is no longer sufficient for analysis of the private security industry to focus simply on the dimension of loss and crime prevention through risk management. It is plainly the case that in South Africa private police organisations are now increasingly involved in preventing and responding to property and violent crime through applications of the law and coercive technologies (more on this below). Nor, as the literature indicates, are these trends unique to South Africa; they are evident, too, in Canada (Rigakos, 2002) and in the transnational context of the war on terrorism (Johnston, 2006). Private security thus in many cases operates reactive strategies for controlling crime and disorder, to the extent that – in South Africa, and perhaps elsewhere too – these are saleable services in rising demand.

This leads to the question of whether these 'traditional' reactive policing functions translate into the emergence within private policing organisations of a culture corresponding to the empirically dominant punitive and author-itarian occupational culture and strategic orientation of the public police that reached its high point in the 'professionalised era' of policing. It is well known that while public police organisations are comprised of several different 'types' of officers, the dominant culture of the public police through the middle decades of the twentieth century (the period in which this institution evolved into the highly self-contained agency it is today with specialised structures for carrying out the business of reactive law-enforcement) was insular, punitive, authoritarian, politically conservative and hyper-masculine (see especially Bittner, 1990; Bouza, 1990; Reiner, 2000). As we have already implied, this 'classic' dominant public policing culture has often been contrasted in the literature with the ostensibly more forward-looking and risk-orientated outlook of the private security industry, assumed to be aligned with the interests of its (frequently corporate) employers (see especially Shearing & Stenning, 1981, 1983). This future-oriented, risk management culture was read into the rhetoric and preventive strategies deployed by the private security agencies being studied, such as enrolling ordinary staff and passers-by to participate in the maintenance of order and safety by censoring their own behaviour: classic 'responsibilisation' strategies (Rose, 1996). Our data, consisting of the observation of the daily activities of front-line private security agents in South Africa together with interviews with senior management, offers a counter-perspective indicating that the dominant culture of the certain sectors of this industry does indeed approximate to that of classic public policing – albeit with some distinctive nuances on which we shall elaborate.

A note to add here is that refocusing the discussion as we propose – to emphasise private sector involvement in conventional crime control and order maintenance that relies on traditional applications of law and other symbolic means of physical intimidation – raises questions about earlier observations made by Shearing (1997) and others (for example Ericson & Haggerty, 1998; O'Malley, 1997) that in the climate of a marketised neoliberal political economy the public police have of late become more like private security in turning to preventative future-focused risk management orientations. Rather, we suggest, it would seem that both sets of agencies are in many cases becoming increasingly punitive and militarised. It is indeed appropriate that so many pages of academic and practitioner commentary should have been devoted to the 'community policing' revolution that now runs three decades deep in public policing and extends even further to developments such as the 'restorative policing' practices inspired by indigenous peoples in South Africa, Australia and Canada. But at least as much needs to be said about the parallel trend of the militarisation (or remilitarisation) of public policing organisations. Community involvement and partnership approaches may still be the buzzwords in public policing but a serious case can be made that September 11th put the lid on many of these changes, supplanting them – in the actual substance if not the rhetoric of public policing reform – with intelligence gathering, order maintenance, weaponisation and other aspects of 'high policing' (Brodeur, 1983; O'Reilly & Ellison, 2006). And if the historical trend of acclimatisation to ever more severe counter-terror measures is any indication, the lid is perhaps on, in practical terms, for good (see especially Brodeur, 2005; Manning, 2006; Singh, 2000).

These issues raise broad concerns about the nature of the contemporary political economy of human security that we are presently revisiting in an ongoing series of investigations. On the more particular issue of understanding policing culture, the pertinent questions for now have less to do with settling the issue of whether private security is becoming more like the public police or vice-versa and more to do with *how* and *why* the worldviews, practices and impacts of these two industries are converging in some cases, diverging in others, and perhaps becoming increasingly complementary in many more. To set the stage for a continued discussion, we now turn to detailing the punitive and reactive institutional orientation that is manifested and deployed in the private security industry in South Africa.

On a practical level, private security in South Africa seeks to manage risky populations through a generalised logic of target hardening/situational crime prevention/deterrent patrols with the included threat of legal sanction (Singh, 2005a). Coercive interventions, for example armed guards (stationary and mobile) and perimeter security devices (electric fencing), aim to control behaviour by increasing the physical difficulty and risk associated with criminal activity. Where this fails to deter, private security has recourse to – and frequently makes use of – a broad repertoire of law enforcement tools, ranging from forced entry to search and seizure, arrest, physical force and even lethal force. It is interesting that in South Africa private security not only has routine access to extensive legal powers particular to their industry, but that much of this authority derives from their status as 'ordinary private citizens': the legal authority conferred on citizens in South Africa to use coercive force and to obtain and carry firearms is further reaching than in many jurisdictions in the Western liberal democracies.[3] The South African state does not exercise a monopoly over coercive force; indeed, the legitimate use of force has been extended to large swathes of the population. Thus, most guards operate firearms not because they are licensed as private security but rather because they possess a personal firearms license. In other cases, the police issue licenses to private security companies based on the records of the statutory regulatory body as to previous employee registration and company inspection records. These firms may then extend these permits to 'qualified' personnel; the question of who is qualified is left to the discretion of the security firm. Thus, while a minimum of five hours of training is required for guards to be armed on duty (Irish, 1999), in practice guards are not adequately trained, some reporting just five minutes of on-the-job 'instruction' (NIM, 1996). Lax regulatory controls means that private security operates within a much wider public gun culture in South Africa: estimates put the number of registered guns at four and a half million in a population of 43 million (Baker, 2002). The recently introduced Firearms Control Act (2004) has had little impact on this gun culture, at least in the short-term. In fact, the government was at pains to stress that its aim was to control gun possession 'without sacrificing legitimate needs of citizens to possess firearms', as the Minister of Safety and Security put it (http://archives.cnn.com/2000/WORLD/africa/10/12/safrica.guncontrol.ap/ index.html). The Act raises the minimum age from 16 to 21, restricts individuals to one hand-gun for self-defence, prohibits anyone with criminal records from owning a gun, and requires all licensed firearms holders to undergo a competency test involving basic training at an accredited facility and a police background check. Few licenses have been issued or renewed to date, not because applicants have failed to fulfill these conditions but because of huge licensing backlogs and a severe shortage of accredited trainers. In regards to the private security industry, until the end of December of 2006, firms can continue to issue firearms to employees, without competency certificates, as long as their existing licenses are valid.

As agents of property owners and managers, private security in South Africa operates with additional legal powers which likewise exceed corresponding parameters that would commonly pertain in Western liberal democracies. By virtue of their linkage to private property, private security agencies in South Africa have recourse to enhanced powers of arrest, with certain categories of guards (for example the aforementioned Key Point guards) operating with full powers of search and seizure, arrest and use of force. Despite the significant powers already at the disposal of private security agents to mete out physical penalties the industry's regulatory body has mounted a strong, though to date unsuccessful, lobby for the conferral of formal 'peace officer' status on certain categories of guards, in particular the armed response sector (Singh, 2005a). The additional powers would include full powers of search and seizure and arrest, along with 'emergency classification' for their vehicles which would enable guards to execute high-speed driving with flashing lights and wailing sirens. The emphasis on peace officer status is a further indication that industry leaders and representatives of the 'rank and file' alike regard reactive law enforcement and crime control as legitimate and saleable services, and consider traditional law enforcement approaches as effective means to achieve crime control and public order objectives. It is important to note that these debates over legal reform have been taking place against a backdrop of widespread public anxiety about crime with massive support for reactive and punitive policing interventions of both the state and non-state variety (Shaw, 2002; Singh, 2000, 2005b).

In its uniforms, weaponry and training private security in South Africa exhibits a punitive orientation. Guards are outfitted in blue uniforms similar to those of the South African police, with armed reaction units and Key Point guards in full combat attire. Automatic and semi-automatic weapons are standard items in the private security arsenal; most guards – not just the armed reaction segment – are heavily armed. Guards undergo a military style training programme intended to equip them with the necessary skills to perform their crime control function. The promotional material of one contract security firm outlined the standard training curriculum: this stresses legal powers, self-defence, weapons training, first aid and emergency procedures, report writing and record keeping, and, to a lesser extent, public relations and 'junior leadership' (Singh, 2005a). The training period is brief, however, with fully three quarters of all guards undergoing just one week of instruction. The result is that 'informal', on-the-job training by site managers and supervisors, along with informal communication between ground-level agents, constitutes an important aspect of job learning and socialisation – as commentators have also noted in other contexts (on Canada see especially Micucci, 1998; Rigakos, 2002; on Britain Wakefield, 2003).

Formal training is intended to transform recruits into skilled and useful guards but it also emphasises compliance and obedience. Indeed, a prominent industry member noted in an interview that training consisted chiefly of classroom instruction – with emphasis on 'input [by the instructor] rather than output [by the student]' – an instructional model where the guard is just a passive learner, with the focus on the teaching of the curriculum rather than on what, if anything, the recruit has learnt (Singh, 2000). Training and supervisory practices produce disciplined and docile guards groomed to function in a hierarchical and bureaucratic structure by complying automatically and without interruption with external directives for action. In addition to the training, coercive measures such as surveillance systems backed by sanctions for improper behaviour exert and maintain tight bureaucratic control over guards from a distance. Further, the rewards structure of the organisation reflects and helps solidify the self identity/image of the guard as both skilled and compliant: making arrests, recovering stolen goods, fighting fires and floods are all highly valued (by both security firm and client) and rewarded with pay increases and supervisory promotions. So too is long service, with 'loyalty' awards and cash gratuities (see the local South African trade magazine, *Security Focus*).

These observations on the nature and form of training and supervisory practices in South Africa resonate with Rigakos's (2002) findings in his study of Intelligarde in Toronto. It is therefore not surprising that parallel outcomes of these practices are evidenced in the worldviews and occupational mentalities of private security agents in both locales. In the accounts they give of the main purposes and practices of their jobs, few guards spontaneously emphasise 'prevention' in the sense of proactive and creative problem-solving; most confine themselves to an unreflecting reiteration of learned rules and strategies, with reactive law enforcement the dominant set. Thus the everyday cognitive business of most guards 'on the beat' is largely formulaic and mechanistic crime-fighting – seen and undertaken as low-paying 'grunt work' that, if done well, might lead to small pay increases within the lower echelons of the organisation. This despite representations (and probably desires) on the part of private security corporations that they tailor their services to clients' needs.

If that is the overarching nature of the organisational character of the private security industry in South Africa, the next question for us to consider is the profile of their actual employees. Historically and now, most rank-and-file security trainees in South Africa come from the black underclass. In more recent years, a number of former members of the (black) non-statutory liberation forces transferred to front-line jobs in the security industry – although, interestingly, the more specialised and prestigious front-line positions such as armed response continued to be dominated by white employees. Middle and upper management positions, on the other hand, are filled predominately by former members of the apartheid state security establishment. Indeed, some firms actively pursue a policy of reserving managerial appointments exclusively for personnel with police, intelligence and military backgrounds (Irish, 1999). Clearly, therefore, a racialised and class-based hierarchy exists. This divide is reflected in the fact that there are two cultures in the industry, both with a generally punitive orientation. The CEO of a prominent contract firm remarked on these two cultures in an interview, stating that, while creativity was a valued quality when exhibited by senior management, 'compliance' was the most common trait possessed and cultivated among entry-level employees. The finding that the South African private security industry is staffed largely by personnel whose skills lie in low-intensity warfare matches observations by Micucci (1998) and Rigakos (2002) in the Canadian context, where they found that significant numbers of personnel in both entry level and administrative positions have previous policing experience and are advocates of a traditional crime fighting approach to security.

In many ways, then, the culture of private security in South Africa bears some resemblance to the dominant professionalised public policing culture of the mid-twentieth century. In this period, the public police throughout the West developed a politically conservative, masculinist, punitive, and, in too many instances, racist culture that valued reactive crime fighting and action over service provision and working with the community (see, for example, Bittner, 1990; Bouza, 1990; Reiner, 2000). It is hardly surprising that this culture took hold in the then-dominant model of policing provision that isolated the police from their public, rendering them the 'expert' agency 'in charge' of the business of public order and crime control. How and why then have we seen some important parallels in the culture of private security agencies in the early twenty-first century? Correspondingly, what do these developments in private security signal about the emergent political economy of human security?

EXPLAINING PRIVATE POLICING CULTURE

In seeking to account for these parallel developments in private policing culture we might usefully begin by turning to traditional studies of public policing culture(s) for inspiration. The study of the dominant cultures of public policing is well developed (as attested by many of the other contributions to this volume) and has detailed both the sources and processes behind this culture, and the impacts it has had. Studies of the 'classic' dominant police culture in the professionalised era of public policing have traditionally had three main points of focus: individualistic/ psychological factors in recruits to the police profession (see, for example, Klockars, 1985), institutional and socialisation accounts that emphasise the structural and social processes that instill and exacerbate these tendencies in groups of officers (see, for example, Bittner, 1990; Marks, 2000, 2004, 2005; Reuss-Ianni & Ianni, 1983) and broader 'field' explanations examining cultural and legal influences (see, for example, Chan, 1997; Chan, Devery, & Doran, 2003). These approaches, adopted with caution, furnish possible starting points in accounting for the emergence of a punitive and reactive private policing culture.

Regarding individualistic factors, it has been suggested in classic studies of public policing cultures that persons with a particular psychological disposition – politically conservative, authoritarian and perhaps 'macho' – tend to be attracted to the well structured, disciplinary nature of the policing career (Klockars, 1985). This would help explain why such large numbers of public police officers exhibited the dominant authoritarian worldview. To date, few studies have explored whether this postulate has application to the private security industry. In our discussion of the South African case we have already indicated that the majority of entry-level positions in private security organisations are populated by black South Africans of the urban underclass, which raises the question of whether these employees themselves exhibit intolerant attitudes towards the same marginalised underclass that is also the target of private security practices.

A factor that argues for combining individualistic and institutional explanations of the dominant private policing culture in South Africa and elsewhere is the enormous staff turnover seen at the rank-and-file level. Wakefield (2003) highlights various reasons why people choose employment in the guarding sector including joblessness in itself, financial need, related work history and a special interest in security. In Canada, commentators (Micucci, 1998; Rigakos, 2002) have noted that the most recent recruits to the private security industry tend to see it as a stepping stone to a longer career in public policing, which in turn contributes to further staff turnover. Interestingly, these candidates tend to interpret a career in public policing as entailing reactive law-enforcement and 'responsiblised' use of force – functions associated with the aforementioned 'professionalised era' – while denigrating lower-level order maintenance, loss prevention and service provision as 'dirty work' (Huey et al., 2005). And it is also the case that many of these candidates end up in private security when they fail to get into the public police service (Micucci, 1998; Rigakos, 2002). This suggests that (at least amongst mid-level managers doing the private sector hiring, who frequently have prior service of their own in public policing) there is a prevalent view of *public* policing which owes more to private security priorities than it does to the nominal policies of contemporary public policing.

As we have mentioned, not all members of private security organisations exhibit these punitive, authoritarian attitudes that manifest themselves in reactive policing behaviour. In South Africa and elsewhere there is a variety of 'types' of private security officers ranging from guards, to bureaucrats, to enforcers (Micucci, 1998). This range suggests it is not so much a matter of a single particular kind of individual being attracted to this form of employment, nor of institutional factors *causing* such attitudes. Rather, it seems that, when, in at least some cases, individuals with authoritarian personalities are attracted to these positions, it is these recruits that are, in recent times especially, likely to flourish within private security organisations.

This is despite the fact that such orientations and practices often run counter to the best interests of the paying clients, where repressive outlooks and behaviours may not work in the interests of loss minimisation and harm reduction. The South African case would suggest that these recruits are able to flourish as they do because of inadequacies both in the training that they receive, and the regulatory regimes to which private security organisations are subject.

In South Africa, individualistic explanations combined with institutional histories seem particularly important in shaping private security culture, as former members of the apartheid security apparatus shift to private security management positions where they influence recruitment, training and promotion. As we have noted, this stands in contrast with the transfer of former members of the liberation forces into entry-level positions in private security. While these two groups hold different political views, what they have in common is that their primary skills-sets lie in low-intensity warfare[4] (for which they were indeed recruited in the first place) and this in large part contributes to the militaristic nature of private security. Beyond the case of South Africa, the broader issue arises of whether defectors from 'community policing' reform initiatives find their way into private policing organisations and so perpetuate the tradition of reactive law-enforcement policing.

Studies of public policing cultures have also emphasised the role played by institutional structures and institutionalised relationships in shaping the formation and propagation of the dominant authoritarian culture. In particular, training, promotion and reward structures, and informal relationships out 'on the beat' have been identified as critical for the formation of public policing culture. At the level of training, scholars point out that the emphasis on firearms use, close-range hand combat and legal procedures – at the expense of training in human rights, communication skills, and community relationships – has contributed to the militarised nature of classic policing culture (Brewer, 1991 ; Brewer & Magee, 1991; Marks, 2000, 2004, 2005). Further, the modicum of human rights training that is instilled soon dissipates in the lengthy 'apprenticeship' period where initiates are matched with more senior officers to learn the business of patrol. Little has been said in the literature about training procedures in private security organisations, apart from the general observation that without statutory insistence on a reasonable amount of training precious little of it occurs. Manzo (2004), for example, highlights the brevity of formal training for security guards operating at three Canadian shopping malls, ranging from limited classroom instruction to no training whatsoever. Our study of private security in South Africa indicates that the majority of guards have a mere week of training, with Key Point guards undergoing an additional two weeks. Within this limited training period, much time is spent on weapons and self-defense training, legal authority/powers and self-presentation skills in a public setting. Likewise, in his Canadian study Rigakos (2002) has observed a focus on legal powers, crowd control, weapons use, self-defense and legal note taking.

In terms of promotion and rewards structures, it is well known that public policing organisations have traditionally rewarded officers' accomplishments in the sphere of crime control, bravery and length of service (see, for example, Reiner, 2000) and promote officers upwards from within the organisation. In the South African case, as in other jurisdictions such as Canada (Micucci, 1998), the promotional structure of private security organisations favours external candidates for key managerial posts – and in particular ex-police and/or ex-army members. Further, the rewards structure also encourages a militarised culture, emphasising as it does reactive policing as well as obedience on the part of the guard.

Linking private security culture to broader social, political and economic relationships that influence the ascendancy of one policing regime over another, a number of studies in public policing culture offer us helpful starting points. Notably, Janet Chan demonstrates the connection, in the context of a neo-liberal political economy of crime control, between authoritarian and macho public policing culture in Australia and tolerant attitudes towards such behaviour in significant segments of the Australian public (Chan, 1997; Chan et al., 2003). For Chan, it is this broader socio-political and economic context that enables and sometimes encourages particular expressions of public policing culture – already present within policing organisations – to flourish. This same context frustrates more benign policing cultures, making it, for Chan, a critical aspect of reform to target the environment surrounding policing. In this regard, the legal environment is a critically important aspect of the broader socio-political and economic field of policing: where the police have been given extreme modes of authority (such as sweeping powers under counterterrorism legislation cf. Northern Ireland: Brewer, 1991; Brewer & Magee, 1991) their culture has observably become more isolated, militaristic and 'hostile' to 'enemy' populations.

These themes are very helpful for making sense of private policing culture. Most obviously, public attitudes of intolerance that support authoritarian public policing culture would have a similar (and, given the responsiveness of market controls, likely even more pronounced) effect on private policing culture. Our study of the South African case also indicates that conferring significant powers in law, especially coercive powers, upon private security agencies – will support the development of a similarly authoritarian culture in private policing organisations.

Building upon Chan's analysis, the South African case, along with studies of private policing in Canada (Rigakos, 2002) and Britain (Wakefield, 2003), reminds us that private policing culture is also shaped by the industry's relationships with other actors in the policing landscape. We have already noted how private security employees often view their positions as a stepping stone to a career in 'real' (i.e. public) policing. The question remains open of whether and in what ways variations in the treatment of private security agencies by public police authorities impact upon these views and attitudes. What can be said, at this point, is that the culture of private security organisations cannot be fully understood without also examining their relationships not only with the public police but also with community groups and other paid and voluntary agencies of various stripes (like public health organisations) that engage local security (on the breadth of the agencies involved, see especially Burris, 2006). The existing literature has tended to address the development of public police cultures in isolation from relationships with other security agencies. In an era where academic and practitioner commentators point to the 'networked', 'nodal' or 'partnership' orientation of contemporary policing, the study of the culture of any of these organisations must also take account of their relationships with other actors in the security landscape (see, further, Wood, 2006).

Thus the culture of private policing agencies develops in a broader 'field' of the socio-political economy of human security, namely the cultural, political, legal and economic regime in which particular forms of nodal associations of agencies engaged in policing arise to begin with, and then reciprocally support and perpetuate one another. The issue of understanding and reforming what may be problematic in private policing culture is therefore at least partially a matter of first delineating the relationships between policing agencies then regulating these interactions through legal, market, and other less formal social mechanisms. In the next section, we begin to develop these themes and identify some key empirical questions underlying them.

DIRECTIONS FOR RESEARCH AND POLICY REFORM

Relationships between state and non-state security organisations are often described as 'complementary' even if they are poorly coordinated – and it can in general be said that the combined impacts of state and non-state security policy and practice serve the interests of well-to-do segments of the population. Various commentators have observed that 'security regimes' reflect the priorities and concerns of a very limited 'public interest' (see especially Shearing, 2006; Singh, 2005b), to the point that 'security' increasingly stands as a 'club good' monopolised by the few (Crawford, 1998, 2006). The impacts of public and private security bodies cannot, in other words, be analysed in isolation from one another.

Nor, we have suggested, can the cultures of state and non-state security institutions be analysed in isolation from one another, as was the tendency in the classic sociology of public policing. Interventions to steer security policy and the culture of policing processes in the direction of serving a broadly *public* interest must accordingly address relationships between these organisations.

What knowledge, then, must we accumulate if we wish first to analyse and understand private policing culture and then take the further step of engaging with it to reshape and direct its development and, by extension, the character of policing processes as a whole? A necessary starting point for closer investigation of private security culture will be more detailed 'mapping' of its dominant characteristics across a range of sub-categories in the industry and in various national contexts. If we find that what we have observed in South Africa in the contract security industry (trends that resonate with other preliminary studies in Canada and Britain) is generalisable elsewhere in the private security industry, the next step in the research would be to extend the explanatory accounts that we have begun to explore here.

Ethnographies of private policing practices will need to determine whether persons with a particular disposition (distinguished possibly by socio-economic class, or, as individuals, from co-members of a class) are attracted to the profession. In particular, we would be interested to see a wider test of the impression we formed in our South African study that authoritarian members of the public security apparatus gravitate to management positions in private security organisations. But investigating line-management culture must not eclipse observations of rank-and-file behaviour. We need perspectives on both administrative and street level cultures and on the differences between them.

Then there is also the impact on private security culture of different training and regulatory regimes. How is private security culture affected when the industry is made accountable to public policing organisations? How is it affected by the introduction of minimum training standards or of statutory promotion protocols? Or, going beyond 'command-and-control' approaches to regulating the private security industry and other forms of policing, what other agencies contribute to shaping the market environment and the broader social fields in which private security operates? For example, do community organisations, civil business watchdog agencies (such as the Better Business Bureau in Ontario, Canada) or governmental bodies like Ombudsman's Offices have any kind of controlling or ameliorative influence on private policing culture, and could their roles be enhanced?

CONCLUSION

Private security plays an important role in policing contemporary urban existence. There is no function performed by the public police that is not, somewhere or sometimes also performed by private security. Mapping the contours of private security cultures is therefore of great importance, as is the development of explanatory accounts of the emergence of this culture. The classic literature on public policing provides a useful starting point for developing this understanding, although, as we have stressed, this should not be taken to imply that private security is becoming more like the public police. As we have argued, between the two there are elements of both convergence and complementarity; together, troublingly, they add up to an increasingly coherent security regime that both reflects and amplifies some of the most disturbing aspects of the marketised political economy of our day. Future work on both private and public policing cultures will therefore need to pay specific attention to the interpenetration of various policing agencies – state and non-state – in the security landscape, and to the current role and future potential of different regulatory regimes in controlling the most problematic aspects of this culture and limiting their negative consequences. For us, the South African example we have presented points the need to move beyond classically binary depictions of private and public police cultures.

NOTES

1. The material contained in this section derives from fieldwork conducted by one of us in South Africa in the middle-years of the 1990s (see Singh, 2000, 2005a, 2005b). This consisted of interviews with senior contract security management and analysis of private security advertisements and company promotional materials.

2. The incursion of private security forces into fully public spaces has not in all instances been met with open arms by the state or public security forces. In one notable example, in September of 2005, when private security companies blocked public thoroughfares that served as ingress into wealthy communities, the public police responded by laying (and threatening further) charges of treason against those agents involved (Kempa fieldnotes, 23 September 2005).

3. Thus, as 'private persons', security personnel are empowered, under the Criminal Procedure Act (51 of 1977), to arrest, without a warrant, anyone seen to be engaged in an affray and anyone 'reasonably' believed to have committed any offence who is fleeing a pursuing individual who 'reasonably' appears to be authorized to effect an arrest for that particular offence – the term 'reasonable' obviously being open to wide interpretation. Private security may also, without a warrant, arrest and pursue any person who commits, attempts to commit or is reasonably suspected of committing any Schedule 1 offence. Schedule 1 offences are wide ranging, falling (more or less) into three broad categories: property offences (arson, malicious injury to property, breaking or entering, theft, knowingly receiving stolen property, fraud and forgery); crimes against the person (murder, culpable homicide, rape, indecent assault, sodomy, robbery, kidnapping, childstealing, assault with grievous bodily harm); and offences against the state (treason, sedition, public violence, offences related to coinage). Further still, as agents of the owner, occupier or manager of property, private security may arrest without a warrant any person found committing any offence on or in respect of that property.

In order to effect an arrest in any of the above circumstances, security personnel are authorized to break open, enter and search any premises on which the person to be arrested is known or reasonably suspected to be. Furthermore, they are empowered to use reasonable force, and lethal force in relation to Schedule 1 offences, where an arrest can not be effectuated by other means and where resistance occurs, or where the suspect flees.

4. As one former guerrilla succinctly put it, 'We only know how to shoot' (Electronic Mail & Guardian August 5, 1995).

REFERENCES

Baker, B. (2002). Living with non-state policing in South Africa: The issues and dilemmas. *Journal of Modern African Studies, 40*(1), 28–53.

Bayley, D. H. (1994). What do the police do? In: D. H. Bayley (Ed.), *Police for the future* (pp. 29–41). New York: Oxford University Press.

Bayley, D. H., & Shearing, C. D. (2001). *The new structure of policing: Description, conceptualization and research agenda.* Washington, DC: U.S. Dept. of Justice, Office of Justice Programs, National Institute of Justice.

Berg, J. (2004). Challenges to a formal private security industry-SAPS partnership: Lessons from the Western Cape. *Society in Transition, 35*(1), 105–124.

Bittner, E. (1990). Florence Nightingale in pursuit of Willy Sutton: A theory of the police. In: E. Bittner (Ed.), *Aspects of police work* (p. x, 406). Boston: Northeastern University Press.

Bouza, A. V. (1990). *The police mystique: An insider's look at cops, crime, and the criminal justice system.* New York, NY: Plenum Press.

Brewer, J. D. (1991). Policing divided societies: Theorising a type of policing. *Policing and Society*, *1*, 179–191.

Brewer, J. D., & Magee, K. (1991). *Inside the RUC: Routine policing in a divided society*. Oxford: Clarendon.

Brodeur, J.-P. (1983). High policing and low policing: Remarks about the policing of political activities. *Social Problems*, *30*(5), 507–520.

Brodeur, J.-P. (2005). Trotsky in blue: Permanent policing reform. *The Australian and New Zealand Journal of Criminology*, *38*(2), 254–267.

Burris, S. (2006). From security to health. In: J. Wood & B. Dupont (Eds), *Democracy, society and the governance of security* (pp. 196–216). Cambridge: Cambridge University Press.

Carrol, R. (2006). Brutal divide: Fortified town plays on middle-class fear of crime. *Guardian Unlimited Newspaper*, 11 February. http://www.guardian.co.uk/southafrica/story/0,,1707548, 00.html. Accessed May 03, 2007.

Chan, J. (1997). *Changing police culture*. Melbourne: Cambridge University Press.

Chan, J., Devery, C., & Doran, S. (2003). *Fair cop: Learning the art of policing*. Toronto: University of Toronto Press.

Crawford, A. (1998). *Crime prevention and community safety: Politics, policies and practices*. Harlow: Longman.

Crawford, A. (2006). Policing and security as 'club goods': The new enclosures? In: J. Wood & B. Dupont (Eds), *Democracy, society and the governance of security* (pp. 111–138). Cambridge: Cambridge University Press.

Ericson, R., & Haggerty, K. (1998). *Policing the risk society*. Toronto: University of Toronto Press.

Grant, E. (1989). Private policing. *Acta Juridica*, (pp. 92–117). Cape Town: Juta & Co.

Huey, L. J., Ericson, R. V., & Haggerty, K. D. (2005). Policing Fantasy City. In: D. Cooley (Ed.), *Re-imagining policing in Canada* (pp. 140–208). Toronto: University of Toronto Press.

Irish, J. (1999). *Policing for profit: The future of South Africa's private security industry*. Johannesburg: Institute for Security Studies.

Johnston, L. (1992). *The rebirth of private policing*. London: Routledge.

Johnston, L. (2006). Transnational security governance. In: J. Wood & B. Dupont (Eds), *Democracy, society and the governance of security*. Cambridge: Cambridge University Press.

Johnston, L., & Shearing, C. D. (2003). *Governing security: Explorations in policing and justice*. London: Routledge.

Kempa, M., Carrier, R., Wood, J., & Shearing, C. D. (1999). Reflections on the evolving concept of 'private policing'. *European Journal on Criminal Policy and Research*, *7*(2), 197–223.

Kempa, M., & Shearing, C. D. (2002). Microscopic and macroscopic responses to inequalities in the governance of security: Respective experiments in South Africa and Northern Ireland. *Transformation: Critical Perspectives on Southern Africa (Special Issue on Crime and Policing in Transition)*, *29*(2), 25–54.

Kempa, M., Stenning, P., & Wood, J. (2004). Policing communal spaces: A reconfiguration of the 'mass private property' hypothesis. *British Journal of Criminology*, *44*(4), 562–581.

Klockars, C. (1985). *The idea of police*. London: Sage.

Manning, P. K. (2006). Two case studies of American anti-terrorism. In: J. Wood & B. Dupont (Eds), *Democracy, society and the governance of security*. Cambridge: Cambridge University Press.

Manzo, J. (2004). The folk devil happens to be our best customer: Security officers' orientations to 'youth' in three Canadian shopping malls. *International Journal of the Sociology of Law, 32*, 243–261.

Marks, M. (2000). Transforming police organisations from within: Police dissident groupings in South Africa. *British Journal of Criminology, 40*, 557–573.

Marks, M. (2004). Researching police transformation: The ethnographic imperative. *British Journal of Criminology, 44*, 1–24.

Marks, M. (2005). *Transforming the robocops: Changing police in South Africa*. Scottsville: University of KwaZulu-Natal Press.

Micucci, A. (1998). A typology of private policing operational styles. *Journal of Criminal Justice, 26*(1), 41–51.

NIM. (1996). *See* Network of Independent Monitors.

O'Malley, P. (1997). Policing, politics, post-modernity. *Social and Legal Studies, 6*(3), 363–381.

O'Reilly, C., & Ellison, G. (2006). Eye spy private high: Reconceptualising high policing theory. *British Journal of Criminology, 46*, 641–660.

Reiner, R. (2000). *The politics of the police* (3rd ed.). Oxford: Oxford University Press.

Reuss-Ianni, E., & Ianni, F. (1983). Street cops and management cops: The two cultures of policing. In: M. Punch (Ed.), *Control in the police organisation*. Cambridge, MA, London: MIT Press.

Rigakos, G. (2002). *The new parapolice: Risk markets and commodified social control*. Toronto: University of Toronto Press.

Rose, N. (1996). The death of the social? Refiguring the territory of government. *Economy and Society, 25*(3), 327–356.

Shaw, M. (2002). *Crime and policing in post-apartheid South Africa: Transforming under fire*. Bloomington: Indiana University Press.

Shearing, C. D. (1997). The unrecognized origins of the new policing: Linkages between public and private policing. In: M. Felson & R. V. G. Clarke (Eds), *Business and crime prevention* (pp. 217–229). Monsey, NY: Criminal Justice Press.

Shearing, C. D. (2006). Reflections on the refusal to acknowledge private governments. In: J. Wood & B. Dupont (Eds), *Democracy, society and the governance of security* (pp. 11–32). Cambridge: Cambridge University Press.

Shearing, C. D., & Ericson, R. (1991). Culture as figurative action. *British Journal of Criminology, 42*(4), 481–506.

Shearing, C. D., & Stenning, P. (1981). Modern private security: Its growth and implications. In: M. H. Tonry & N. Morris (Eds), *Crime and justice: An annual review of research* (pp. 193–245). Chicago: University of Chicago Press.

Shearing, C. D., & Stenning, P. (1983). Private security: Implications for social control. *Social Problems, 30*, 493–506.

Singh, A.-M. (2000). *Governing crime in post-apartheid South Africa, 1990–96*. Unpublished doctoral dissertation, Goldsmith College, University of London, London.

Singh, A.-M. (2005a). Private security and crime control. *Theoretical Criminology, 9*(2), 153–174.

Singh, A.-M. (2005b). Some critical reflections on the governance of crime in post-apartheid South Africa. In: J. W. E. Sheptycki & A. Wardak (Eds), *Transnational and comparative criminology* (pp. 135–156). London: GlassHouse.

South, N. (1997). Control, crime and the 'end of century criminology'. In: P. Francis, P. Davies & V. Jupp (Eds), *Policing futures: The police, law enforcement and the twenty-first century* (pp. 104–123). Basingstoke: MacMillan.

Spitzer, S., & Scull, A. (1977). Privatization and capitalist development. *Social Problems, 25*, 18–29.

Stenning, P. (2000). Powers and accountability of the private police. *European Journal on Criminal Policy and Research, 8*, 325–352.

Von Hirsch, D., & Shearing, C. D. (2000). Exclusion from public space. In: D. Garland & A. Wakefield (Eds), *Ethical and social perspectives on situational crime prevention* (pp. 77–96). Oxford and Portland, OR: Hart.

Wakefield, A. (2003). *Selling security: The private policing of public space.* Cullompton: Willan.

Walker, N. (2000). *Policing in a changing constitutional order.* London: Sweet & Maxwell.

Wood, J. (2006). Research and innovation in the field of security: A nodal governance view. In: J. Wood & B. Dupont (Eds), *Democracy, society and the governance of security* (pp. 217–240). Cambridge: Cambridge University Press.

CHAPTER 13

CONFLICT AND AFRICAN POLICE CULTURE: THE CASES OF UGANDA, RWANDA AND, SIERRA LEONE

Bruce Baker

ABSTRACT

The chapter argues that the values and practices of the Uganda, Rwanda and Sierra Leone police have been shaped by the experience of war. Following successful rebellion, Uganda and Rwanda chose to rely on a form of local popular justice, supplemented by the police. Sierra Leone, where the rebellion was defeated, has adopted a more western-style police model. All three have undertaken management reform. How its new values and approaches have been absorbed by senior, middle and lower ranks is explored. The chapter also investigates the role of policing agencies other than the police and the latter's relationship to them.

INTRODUCTION

In the violence and upheaval of war, structures of law and order, both state and non-state, are severely disrupted. Past values and practices are

Police Occupational Culture: New Debates and Directions
Sociology of Crime, Law and Deviance, Volume 8, 321–347
Copyright © 2007 by Elsevier Ltd.
ISSN: 1521-6136/doi:10.1016/S1521-6136(07)08013-X

prone to being abandoned as state police are targeted as defenders of the
regime under attack; customary chiefs with their court and policing systems
are driven out or flee; the social control of family, neighbours and clan
dissolves in the anarchy of displacement and bereavement; and young
men with guns assert their authority. Wars not only disturb the old order,
but may bring in a new order and a new way of regulating that order. If
the regime policing falls with its autocratic rulers, new doctrines may take
over – of popular justice or democratic policing or community participation,
or even, where insecurity persists, militarisation of policing. Post-war donor
reconstruction may bring a policing agenda that includes new styles of
policing, new approaches to management, new institutions of accountability
and new capital resources. Finally, in the course of regime change, there
may be a security vacuum between the discrediting and dismantling of old
forms of social control and policing and the introduction of new
alternatives. Depending on regime ideology, state policy, and capacity, this
law-enforcement vacuum may be filled by new or pre-existing non-state
policing agencies and commercial security, reordering security networks. It
would be very surprising if in all this turmoil police culture was not affected.

In this chapter I take the contested concept of police (sub)culture in its
broadest sense as, namely, the shared traditions and everyday practices
(physical and intellectual) that characterise the force. It is the shared
mentality concerning how the police see themselves, security rivals and the
public; it is the shared values that motivate and integrate the police and
sustain their self-esteem; it is the shared assumptions that determine the
meanings they attach to things and the attitudes they adopt or reject; it is the
shared organised knowledge about why and how things are done (and of
what was done before) that provides the model for their habitual actions.
Inevitably in large, complex, hierarchical organisations, there is a gulf
between the force mission statement and the police station conduct, between
the Inspector General and the rural constable. As others have before, I have
observed that there are divergences between the cultures of command,
middle management and lower ranks (Reuss-Ianni, 1983). I also concur with
Chan (1996) and others that police culture, far from being insular and merely
subversive of formal state directives, is shaped by its social context. In the
cases I refer to, experience of war, for the broad public and for government
leadership, engendered attitudes to the police that shape police officers'
outlook as much as do legal requirements. In other words, police culture is a
product of the interaction between their organisational knowledge and the
socio-political context.

Complexities like this make understanding police culture particularly difficult. I have interviewed large numbers of officers in Africa, but there is a limit to what will emerge from just *talking* to police officers as a gulf can exist between station talk and the street action (Waddington, 1999). The following account, therefore, is inevitably partial and tentative. It is this difficulty in understanding what police culture is, how it is established, and under what circumstances it might change that can lead governments, donors, police leaders and foreign police trainers to despair at how to tackle it in the introduction of reforms.

The chapter examines some aspects of everyday police practices along with some of the internal management and external state and donor influences that have sought to (re)shape them. It will seek to track where changes have occurred following conflict, why, and with what consequences. The impact of conflict on police culture is examined in the three African states of Uganda, Rwanda and Sierra Leone. The three have been chosen as providing contrasts in terms of outcomes (rebel or government victory), duration of major conflict (1–10 years) and post-conflict recovery time (6–20 years). The account is based on interviews and discussion groups held in each country with senior and junior ranks in the police, members of the executive, legislative and judicial branches of government, civil rights groups and large numbers of the general public. The interviews were conducted in 2005–2006.[1]

POLICING AND POLICE CULTURE BEFORE AND DURING THE CONFLICT

Prior to the Uganda civil war 1981–1986, the regimes of President Amin (1971–1979) and President Obote (1980 onwards) saw state initiated (or condoned) murder, torture, looting, rape, terrorism and imprisonment of opponents. Both Amin and Obote created several new security organisations which reported directly to them. These, along with the Military Police, are estimated to have killed between 100,000 and 500,000 (HRW, 1999 see Human Rights Watch). The head of state and the security forces were above the law; the judiciary were politicised and corrupted; the police were tribalised (dominated by the tribe of the president). Nor could the police bring suspects to justice, for fear of victimisation. Cases of army abuse against civilians 'could not be investigated by the police in case evidence was obtained to convict army personnel' (Kabwegyere, 1995, p. 228). And if the police were reluctant to investigate abuses by the state security forces and powerful political figures, the public were equally reluctant to report crimes by them. Serious crimes were thus committed with impunity. *The Times* of London observed that 'the ravages and apathy have left many Ugandans ... with little respect for law and life. Today many live only by deceit or by accommodation with violence'.[2] As a rebel officer at the time (now an Inspector of police) recalled, 'Before [the war] you couldn't arrest someone in Kawempe [district of Kampala] without a gun since there was no co-operation from the people'.[3]

In the case of Rwanda, until the civil war and the genocide ended in 1994, state policing was under three forces: the (paramilitary) *gendarmerie*, the (local) *police communale* and the (investigation/prosecution office) *police judicidaire*. Not only was there no harmonisation of training and standards, but, more seriously, the police were unaccountable, violent and sectarian. And in the case of the *police communale*, being locally recruited and managed allowed the entry of 'negative sentiments of sectarian recruitment and corruption ... . They were doing what they were not supposed to do. The people were afraid to approach [them]'.[4] In addition, President Habyarimana (1973–1994) maintained a presidential guard who were specially recruited and trained so as to defend him.

It was little better under President Stevens's authoritarian rule in Sierra Leone 1978–1991. The Sierra Leone Police (SLP) were tribalised and became an instrument of state oppression. The period was 'a litany of oppressive policing, nepotism and corruption' (Meek, 2003, p. 1). Further, 'with corruption and the appointment of friends and colleagues came the decline of the service – skills were not sought after and officers were illiterate' (Biddle, Clegg, & Whetton, 1998, p. 1). The Truth and Reconciliation Commission (set up after the war with a mandate to create 'an impartial, historical record of the conflict') describes the SLP before the war as 'incompetent', 'corrupt', 'a ready tool for the perpetuation of state terror against political opponents', and engaged in 'extortion of money' and 'the violation of basic human rights ... . All these factors served to widen the gulf between the public and the police' (TRC, 2006, 3a, p. 77; see Truth and Reconciliation Commission of Sierra Leone). As an SLP Commander observed,

Twenty-four years ago people were frightened of the police. They wouldn't come to the SLP even if they had a problem. They feared being taxed [having to pay a bribe]. There was no love lost between the people and the SLP.[5]

Like Obote and Habyarimana, Stevens established parallel policing systems to the civilian police to preserve his regime – in his case, a presidential guard and a party militia.

During the conflict in Uganda, the National Resistance Army (NRA), led by Yoweri Museveni against the Obote regime in Uganda, saw itself as a people's army leading a people's war. The bush war 1981–1986 was, according to an NRA political commissar, aimed at replacing the old regime, 'with structures moulded during the course of the struggle by the masses in accordance with their interests and the demands of the times' (Ondoga ori Amaza, 1998, p. 28). Those structures were to be institutions of self-government down to the village level that included justice and policing. Fresh from the Frelimo training camps of Mozambique, the NRA leadership was enthralled by the possibilities of 'popular' justice. It was seen as accessible, involving active community participation with judges drawn from the people (Museveni, 1997, p. 30). The NRA leadership was determined to start the new order by demonstrating strict discipline within its own ranks and then, when they had seized power, putting an end to the army and police being above the law, to judges being politicised and corrupted, and to self-serving exercise of judicial powers by customary chiefs. As the NRA took control of territory, they set up a tiered structure of Resistance Councils (RCs). The foundational administrative unit was the 'RC1', as it was known, for each village, formed of all the adults in the village. They elected a committee to run local affairs on a day-to-day basis. From the beginning, the RCs (subsequently renamed Local Councils – LCs, hence also 'LC1') were given responsibility not just for administrative functions but also for law and order. They undertook settlement of disputes and adjudication of cases within the local communities. They replaced not only Obote government structures but also roles formerly undertaken by the chiefs, who had been so discredited by political appointments and partisan activity as to have lost all legitimacy.

Whereas throughout the war in Uganda police numbers were maintained, in Rwanda the police forces abandoned the population as the genocide was prepared and executed. Indeed, the gendarmerie was removed from policing duties to the front line 'to facilitate the massacres'.[6] With the gendarmerie sidelined, the presidential guard in Kigali and the communal police in rural areas took an active role in leading the genocide. When the Rwanda Patriotic Front/Army (RPF/A) finally swept through Rwanda to halt the genocide, almost all the gendarmerie and communal police, along with a large number of the Hutu population, fled into the Congo. Yet the RPA was not unprepared. Already they had learnt the importance of community directed policing as a rebel organisation trying to survive on the northern border (and were to do so again in the insurgency that broke out in the northwest after the main civil war came to an end). As one former RPF fighter put it:

> We began as a very small group. We were poorly equipped and had no logistical support. We had to rely on the support of 'family members' ... . And they gave us food and cover and information about the movements of the enemy. We knew the population's support was crucial. In fact we were doing community policing! And it continued after we seized power.[7]

The lesson was so deeply impressed on the RDF leadership that they determined to incorporate community support into their new policing framework when they had seized control.

The Sierra Leone war experience was very different. The history of police abuse, together with their loyalty to the elected Kabbah government, resulted in their being targeted by the Revolutionary United Front (RUF) in their rebel attack on Freetown in 1999, when more than 300 police officers were killed. During the ten-year war 900 SLP officers were killed, and many had limbs hacked off (a common rebel punishment). As a result the SLP was reduced in numbers from 9,000 to 6,600. In addition, police stations, barracks and vehicles were destroyed. Yet the government under siege did not appear to learn any policing lessons from the conflict. Their only vision was for the war to stop so that they could rebuild the police that had existed before, albeit (in initially expressed intent, at least) with improved human rights. The changes in attitudes to policing that took place during the war happened not in government circles, but among citizens trying to cope in a situation where the state and its police (and the customary authorities) had largely abandoned them. As state and customary policing failed, in their place emerged armed militias (Civil Defence Force, CDF) and a resurgence of vigilante groups and anti-crime mobs. All were violent in their treatment of criminals (TRC, 2006, 3a, ch. 4; Amnesty International, 1999).

In all three countries, therefore, attitudes of suspicion and fear towards the police were forged among the public and the future governments alike, attitudes which the post-conflict police would be sensitive to and which would shape how the 'new' police saw themselves, the values they adopted to revive self-esteem, and the everyday practices they adopted to win support.

POST-CONFLICT POLICING MODELS

Following the wars, all three countries were left with disrupted social order, and state police forces that were discredited and either decimated or dissolved. As governments began reconstruction, the conclusions drawn (or not drawn) during the war had to be directed to specific policy choices: should it be a rebuilding of the old or the construction of something new; should it be the familiar actors of the past who resumed the authorisation and provision of policing or should new ones be encouraged; and should alternative policing systems be state planned and approved or left alone? Their answers were to have a profound effect on police culture.

Where a political class has survived rebel onslaught in a civil war, as in Sierra Leone, it very often, in the short term, relies for internal security on outside bodies such as the UN until it can rebuild its state police as the main provider of internal security. Where it is the rebel group that has been successful, as in Uganda and Rwanda, a different approach to policing reconstruction is often followed. The rebel experience can have a profound impact on the new regime's approach. Perceived success with popular justice methods in rebel-controlled areas can make it keen to incorporate the participation of local people into its state security and justice structures. From the beginning Rwanda chose, like Uganda, a policy of maximising popular participation in security.

A form of popular justice made practical and ideological sense to both rebel regimes. It was evident that it would take time to build a police force from scratch and that even when the process was complete, resources would not allow for such a force to be adequate in itself to provide all the policing needs of the nation. Ideologically, an incorporation of the public into the role of protecting and serving society alongside of and in co-operation with the police was seen as an instrument for both healing the aversion to the state police caused by the previous regime's oppressive and racist policing, and positively stimulating reconciliation and social cohesion through mutual co-operation (Mugambage, 2005).

The nature and the accompanying police culture of the state policing that has been provided in Uganda, Rwanda and Sierra Leone are a product of the process by which the three states have configured themselves after the wars. Sierra Leone's decision was to seek to improve pre-conflict policing institutions, to retrain their inherited cadre and replace the lost personnel. Uganda and Rwanda also sought to restore the old structures, but only alongside the introduction of a version of popular justice or informal community-based policing. As noted by the first Commissioner General of Police in the new Rwandan regime,

> The model chosen was the community-building approach which emphasized social as opposed to legal action thus recognizing informal social control mechanisms, in addition to modern policing, as a critical component of restoring and maintaining social order. (Mugambage, 2005, p. 40)

Reconstruction was easier in one sense in Rwanda, since there the former police force had been swept into the Congo forests and beyond. It offered the opportunity of a clean slate to reform the state police and to introduce a version of popular justice that fitted into already existing community structures.

Though having much in common ideologically, Uganda and Rwanda did differ for pragmatic reasons in the extent of the role assigned to their police. Whereas Rwanda was willing to transfer internal security to the ranks of a new civilian policing force it could trust, Uganda, with an inherited police force that it had limited respect for, held back. It preferred to look to its army or para-military structures for policing serious crime. President Museveni, doubtful of the loyalty and discipline of the police,[8] has kept them under constraint and instituted an array of military-style organisations more directly under his control. Where the Uganda and Rwanda governments do agree is that they are convinced of the necessity for community support and intelligence, and from the outset of their new regimes both were keen to incorporate the participation of local people into their security and justice structures. As the Deputy Commander of the Rwanda Police Training School said: 'If you fought for justice then your desire is to maintain it'.[9]

Yet the ruling elite of Sierra Leone has chosen not to avail itself of community participation to the extent that the two rebel armies of Uganda and Rwanda have systematically done. Their experience in the war was largely confined to the 'fortress' of Freetown and to relying on external advice and military support. They did not share the socialist principles that drove the Kagame and (initially) the Museveni regimes (see Museveni, 1986, 1997). They were a political class that under the tutelage of donors saw policing as the prerogative of the state police. Hence though there were changes in senior personnel and management structures, the state police (and even the customary policing) was to stay essentially the same. The war had taught them to defend the state institutions, not to overthrow them (Baker, 2005b, 2007).

These governmental decisions have set the context within which is developing the way the police see themselves. Yet though the countries differed on whether or not to follow the Western model of focusing on establishing a professional police force to undertake the majority of policing functions, they did agree that the return to insecurity must be avoided at all costs. Civil wars make new regimes nervous of political opposition and renewed conflict. Hence none of the three forces have fully cast off their regime-policing role. All forces discussed here are accused of political partisanship and of harassing and suppressing political opposition to the government. Regime insecurity is reflected, too, in state security structures other than the regular police force (paramilitary organisations with a focus on serious crime) that have variously emerged in these countries. If security is maintained in the long term then there is every reason to suppose that state policing will become increasingly demilitarised. These three different models have thus created the space for alternative policing agencies to emerge which we will now consider.

RELATIONSHIP TO OTHER POLICING AGENCIES

Whatever the range of policing agencies, the state police have to determine the relationship they are going to have with them, whether one of co-operation, indifference or conflict. This is a dynamic process, however, and initial suspicion and resentment can be followed by a degree of working relationship within the security networks.[10]

People in Uganda turn first to the patrols of the LC1 for prevention of crime and disorder, and to the LC1 courts for resolution of crime and disorder. As such the LC structure significantly relieves and supports the police, and the two work closely together. This is not to say that the police always respect the LC1 courts. Accusations of ignorance of the law, exceeding authority by hearing criminal cases, taking bribes and handing out sentences that are beyond their powers make some police dismissive of them.

Under a new initiative (called, confusingly, 'community policing programme') Crime Prevention Panels have been introduced where local residents are trained in crime prevention and accept responsibility themselves for law and order in their locality. Even though Panel members typically see themselves as existing to help the police to eliminate crime, initially there was resistance from the police – wary of empowering others in their own field of expertise and also of exposing police corruption. However, where they have been successful, the Panels are acknowledged as a valuable compliment to the police and one that has improved the public's perception of the police.

To address serious crime matters, the Uganda government frequently by-passes the police and turns to central military units, such as the Internal Security Organisation (ISO), which itself is part of Military Intelligence. They investigate, for instance, organised cattle theft, fictitious ('ghost') schools that still receive salaries and marijuana growing. With ISO operatives openly regarding the police as inefficient and corrupt there are inevitably tensions between the two agencies.

Work-based policing agencies are common in Uganda though they have a mixed relationship with the police. The mini-bus drivers used to have strained relations with the police as there had been a history of drivers facing police roadblocks and demands for money. Over time, however, the relationship has improved. The taxi drivers' association now polices taxi drivers and taxi parks, arrests thieves operating in the parks, and provides traffic wardens in Kampala. But the police ignore other groups such as local market traders associations that police markets through arbitration between traders and disciplinary interventions.

Commercial security companies have grown rapidly since the strategic withdrawal of the Uganda Police from guarding. Operating licences are renewed annually and subject to satisfactory inspection of the company by the police, though the regulations allow wide discretion (with corresponding opportunity for corruption). The larger companies sometimes undertake joint operations with the police (for example, when anticipating armed robbery). Yet their relationship with the police is variable. Some companies report that there is no co-operation because they are seen as rivals; some say the sharing of information is only one-way; others that the exchange is mutual.

In Sierra Leone policing other than by the state police is common. Civilian-led Partnership Boards have been introduced by the SLP. Yet there are doubts about how seriously they are treated at station level, with complaints that they fail to meet regularly, that local communities are not given a say in how they want to be policed, and that the police see the Boards only as intelligence providers.

Town markets in Sierra Leone, as in Uganda, have committees that act to control the conduct of vendors and customers. The police are largely absent from the markets and the vendors prefer it that way, regarding the police at best as 'a waste of time' and at worst, extortionist. The distrust seems mutual. On the other hand, the mini-bus drivers' association which controls many of the mini-bus parks and deals with disputes there has a better relationship. They take serious offenders to the police (though in some cases they 'give them lashes').

Since the civil war there has been a rapid expansion of commercial security in Sierra Leone, due to the prevailing sense of increasing crime, the weakness of the SLP and the many International NGOs requiring security for their staff. These services are rarely inspected and have little contact with the police. But at diamond mines, banks and some diplomatic missions, and for some rapid response teams, commercial operators work alongside the armed wing of the police to provide a mix of armed and unarmed guards.

Almost everywhere in Sierra Leone anti-social behaviour is regulated by customary chiefs. They use customary law to handle civil and customary matters such as family disputes, debt repayment, inheritance and land tenure. Since the war, there have been difficulties in re-establishing the chiefs' courts, for many chiefs had their authority undermined because of their failure to protect the people. The police ignore them for the most part, even though there are accusations of discrimination, illegal detention, excessive fines, and the illegal handling of criminal cases.

Not all non-state policing is state approved as the work-based and chiefdom courts are. In the absence of the SLP and sometimes in the failure of the customary structures, it is local (male) 'youths' (15–35 year olds) that frequently fill the security gap. According to one village leader, they 'ensure local policing where SLP do not go. They make arrest and take them to the SLP'. A local tribal headman in a poor Freetown area concurred that youths often intervened to stop fighting when the police failed to respond. Some police are reluctant to admit the contribution: one local police commander felt that youth representatives on the Neighbourhood Watch were 'criminals'. Yet I have witnessed another commander, following the 'arrest' of a cow on the main road, happily negotiate with the youths and the cow owner, until a financial settlement was reached.

There are far fewer non-state policing agencies in Rwanda. The informal local government structure is the most influential policing agency in the country; the one most people look to for their everyday policing. Its tens of thousands of local leaders keep watch over, manage and assist very small units of the population. Many different responsibilities fall within their remit: the mobilisation and sensitisation of the local community in law and order matters; night patrols; law enforcement; the local court system of justice to deal with minor anti-social behaviour, disputes and crimes (or directing them upwards); recording strangers to the neighbourhood; reporting deviant behaviour; punishment for misbehaviour; the establishment of by-laws that reflect local needs; a 'special constabulary' in the form of the Local Defence Force (LDF). This universal security system greatly relieves the police of a large number of cases and provides a rich source of intelligence. It is enthusiastically supported by the police at all levels.

The principle behind the LDF is of voluntary service by young people, trained by the police to provide local security for one or two days a week. Essentially they do patrols (usually in the rural areas with the local men; sometimes with the police in the towns). They gather information and take 'trouble makers' to the police. The police point of view is that 'We need them as a network spread around the countryside so that they can feed back information to us about what the problems are' (Superintendent); likewise, 'They are a valuable source of information. They are deep in areas where police can't go' (Chief Superintendent). Nevertheless, there are inevitable problems with an unpaid group of young people who have received minimal training and yet still bear arms. Many reported them to be 'rough', undisciplined and bribe takers. For some senior police officers, the answer was a smaller but better trained LDF.

Commercial security companies in Rwanda are licensed, renewably every year subject to satisfactory inspection by the police. The police speak of good co-operation, but when company mangers were asked whether companies co-operated with the police their replies were less affirmative: 'Not really'; 'We do not share. Actually exchange of information is zero. We don't share because they don't ask for information'.

Work-based associations are far less common in Rwanda than in Uganda and Sierra Leone. But where they do occur, the police are content to allow them to provide security within their own sectors without interference.

Whilst reform of the small state police forces proceeds slowly, the growth of these other policing agencies continues. It means that policing, as it is experienced in Africa, is a multi-choice affair. People are rarely users of just the state police. But that does not mean these alternatives can be simply characterised as non-state policing. As we have seen, some of the agencies are initiated by the state, some are private or customary initiatives supported by the state, and just a few are initiatives that are strictly illegal (which does not necessarily mean that they are suppressed by the police). For the most part these alternatives to the state police are a response to perceived deficiencies of the police: deficiencies either of conduct (such as corruption) or of resources and hence of ability to respond.

So what is the police shared mentality in regard to the way they see alternative security? For all that the police increasingly recognise the presence of these alternative policing agencies, they remain adamant that they are the police 'professionals' and should retain the core functions of policing and the status that this brings with it. Hence the other policing agencies are typically unsupervised and uncoordinated with the state police systems into any single security network. The state police have no common approach toward other policing agencies. Their relationships are *ad hoc*, taking into account the interests of the force or the individual officer as much as issues of legality.

POST-CONFLICT MANAGEMENT CHANGE AND INTERNATIONAL ASSISTANCE

Given the opportunity of introducing management change after the wars, all three countries looked to donor support for the training of senior personnel in strategic and operational planning. Sierra Leone relied largely on British influence through the Commonwealth Community Safety and Security Programme (CCSSP) and the UN CIVPOL (strengthening of civilian policing) programme. The SLP has received substantial donor support for rebuilding and re-equipment, but the focus of the support has been on training (or removing) senior personnel. The aim has not only been to impart skills, such as strategic and operational planning, but new values enforced by training and mentoring. One emphasis has been on lines of accountability: in the Change Management Plan, each of the 11 programmes has an Accountable Officer from the executive level and Project Managers from the senior level.[11] All the indications are that fresh attitudes towards corruption, accountability, responsibility, public service and human rights have been assimilated at the senior levels.

Uganda has made use of assistance from Britain, France, Germany, Egypt, and even North Korea. Here, too, there has been a concerted effort to improve accountability, co-ordination and effectiveness. Management units at directorate, departmental, regional, district and station level have been introduced. A number of new departments have also been established, including (in 1997) a separate Inspectorate to evaluate performance, a Community Affairs Department (in 1998), and a Human Rights Desk and Complaints Desk. The British contribution focused, after 1990, on institutional and management reforms, training, and the institution of 'community policing'. An independent review regarded the management reforms as valuable, though failing to make an impact on financial planning because of the 'painful realities of government budget planning'. It viewed training in particular as having been compromised by a prevailing culture in the personnel department that failed to recognise its importance. Policy, in this department, 'seems dominated by a compulsion to keep officers on the move, limiting perhaps their opportunities for corruption, but limiting also their chances to make use of specialist training' (Raleigh, Biddle, Mali, & Neema, 1998).

The big management change in Rwanda, prior to the advent of major donor help, was the merger in 2000 of the three police forces: the *gendarmerie* under the ministry of defence; *police communale* under the ministry of local administration and *police judicidaire* under ministry of justice. Reflecting on the merger, Frank Mugambagye, Commissioner General of police 1995–2005 made the comment that

> it aimed at making sure that we bring the service together, set the mission very clearly, harmonise the training, put in better and efficient use of the equipment; because in a scattered way it was very obvious that the efficiency was being undercut.[12]

With donor assistance (UNDP from 1995; UK from 2002; Sweden from 2003; South Africa from 2005) has come a focus on senior management, with training particularly in the four areas of crime scene investigation, accountability, management skills and 'community policing'. In the light of difficulties in getting new concepts to penetrate all levels of the force, senior management is now seriously questioning whether the focus should have been on lower ranks. Donor programmes of this kind are often accused of imposing western values and inappropriate practices on African forces, but this has been contested. The RNP Superintendent responsible for the Swedish–South African programme described a co-operative partnership: 'we discuss training with them. We sit down for two weeks. They bring their tools and together we work out a plan'.[13]

The direction of international assistance is moving away from support for individual projects to support of the justice and security sector as a whole, in particular encouraging reform and inter-agency co-ordination. In Uganda, a Justice Law and Order Sector was created in 1999 with a joint strategy and investment plan approved as part of the Poverty Eradication Action Plan. Donor assistance is provided in a manner that aims to respect national leadership, either through the national budget to which some donors directly contribute, or by confining funding to projects that fall within the national strategy. This is likely to be a sustained donor policy.

POST-CONFLICT RECRUITMENT, VETTING AND DISCIPLINE

War can dramatically reduce the numbers of state police. This was not such a serious matter in Uganda, where most of the 8,000 police force survived. In Sierra Leone, however, the SLP was reduced by nearly a third to just 6,600 survivors. Even more severe was the loss in Rwanda. The situation there in 1995 was that

> the material resources available to both forces [gendarmerie and communal police] have been almost totally destroyed during the civil strife. The majority of the two forces had fled to the Congo before the RPF rebel army. In terms of both quality and quantity, the human resources available to these agencies do not suffice to meet even basic requirements. (UNDP, 1995)

Even today the ratios of police officer to population in Uganda (1:2077), Sierra Leone (1:612) and Rwanda (1:1379) contrast unfavourably with England (1:402) or even South Africa (1:350).

On the positive side, the wartime disruption of police forces through death, displacement and flight opens the opportunity for personnel changes to legitimise the state police and the state itself. With very few of Rwanda's police force returning from the Congo, there was an opportunity for a totally new force, though the majority of the personnel at first came from the Rwanda Patriotic Army. On the other hand, Uganda (wholly so) and Sierra Leone (to a considerable degree) inherited police forces 'contaminated' by past human rights abuses and extortion. Yet to disband them would have proved costly and left a vacuum. Both governments, therefore, chose not to disband the old forces but instead to retrain the executive management team and to undertake a recruitment campaign. Sierra Leone did not undertake any vetting of existing officers, hoping that the complaints and disciplinary procedures would weed out the miscreants in time. It also, of course, relied heavily on the UNAMSIL force for internal security. Uganda was a little more careful. Of the 8,000 Ugandan police, screening revealed that only 3,000 were qualified to be retained. The reconstruction apparently saw an 'exceptionally high turnover of officers of Assistant Inspector and above' (Hills, 2000, p. 95). The government therefore augmented this force by contracting 2,000 retired police officers. Yet even at 5,000 personnel this force was too small to maintain law and order and the NRA had therefore to assume responsibility for internal security until 1989.[14]

Despite the reforms and vetting there are still hangovers from the past culture of abuse and corruption in the three countries. In Uganda, there are persistent accusations by the public of bribe-seeking (Baker, 2005b) and even the Inspector General of Government has called the police 'the most corrupt institution' in the country. In addition, the police are still troubled by charges of human rights abuses, especially excessive force. Even according to the police's own Human Rights Desk, complaints run into the hundreds each year; and the Uganda Human Rights Commission reports 541 complaints of police torture between 2000 and 2004. Likewise police were repeatedly charged with political partisanship in the debates over 'multi-partyism' and the presidential third term. Demonstrations in favour of Museveni were allowed whilst others held by the opposition were banned.

In Sierra Leone, complaints are common of officers engaged in acts of petty corruption, or in collusion with criminals (Baker, 2005b). It was the current Inspector General himself who closed down the rump of the Special Constabulary that had not been included in the SLP, because it was 'working with criminals'.[15] And in 2006 he admitted that the police were one of the most corrupt institutions in the country: 'We need a complete change in attitude and behaviour'.[16] The creation of the Complaints Discipline and Internal Investigation Department (CDIID) is one way that corruption has been addressed. As a result of public complaints about 100 officers have been removed from the force since 2001. Yet as Keith Biddle, the former (British) Inspector General, has stressed, changing attitudes in police culture in regard to corruption, brutality or public accountability is a personnel management problem, not just an operational matter. It requires line managers to accept responsibility for those under them rather than having the force leave it to an HQ Department like the CDIID. Said Biddle: 'It's a massive culture we've got to change. It's not only stopping corruption. It's changing culture'.[17] In other words, it is not just a matter of setting up new oversight institutions. As a CCSSP adviser noted, there is already in place an audit section that covers rules, governance and finance but 'It needs to be proactive, for example over the lack of fuel which might well be due to theft as much as lack of government payments. And CDIID covers professional standards, but that really should be a local problem not just a HQ concern'.[18] So despite the presence of these institutions the practice continues of charging complainants fees for papers and pens before obtaining statements from them, and 81 per cent of the public still claim that the traffic police arbitrarily demand money from drivers (SLP, 2004).

In contrast, the force in Rwanda is, generally, respected by the population for its discipline and lack of bribe taking to a degree that is very unusual in Africa (Baker, 2007). Few complaints were expressed by those interviewed and few are received by the Ombudsman. It seems that the culture of close monitoring and disciplinary procedures that prevailed in the RPA has been transferred to the police. Any complaint from the public about an officer leads to the officer's arrest. After investigation the case goes to a disciplinary committee which can impose a sentence of up to six months in prison or recommend dismissal. Police commanders' interviewed gave forthright accounts of the disciplinary policy:

> We are very strict about police officers. Also, because the Rwandan people are educated not to take things easily. No sooner does a traffic policeman ask for a bribe than the public just call you! Immediately I deploy to see if that man has that money. And sometimes we put someone in plain clothes on buses going up country [to see if police are asking for bribes].[19]

> When an officer committed a crime in the past it was tried in a military court and police officers felt secure in that environment. But now they are taken to the central prison just like any other criminal and it has created a lot of fear among the police.[20]

It may, then, be fear as much as democratic policing principles that shapes the shared values and everyday practices of the RNP.

PUBLIC–POLICE RELATIONS AND 'COMMUNITY POLICING'

The official policy of the three forces is very clear: the co-operation of the public is vital in providing intelligence to the police, keeping law and order and in implementing anti-crime strategies. The values incorporated in the policy have penetrated the mentality of middle management. A local commander in the Uganda Police expressed the view of many of his colleagues regarding the public:

> I believe the fear of the police has gone, as people have understood the law and discovered their rights. We act on their complaints. For instance there was an outcry over the torture of a suspect and that led to a PC being cautioned before the LC1 and the relatives of the victims.[21]

The same pro-public values are found in Sierra Leone. Asked how things had changed since the war, a local commander answered,

When I joined in 1984, the SLP were masters. Now people are masters. It is hard. 24 years ago people were frightened of the police ... . Now we try to be friendly to them.[22]

In Rwanda the biggest change, according to one superintendent, was

in how people respond to the police. We need their co-operation. How they feel about us is different. When I was in the military I couldn't go to the public. Now we [police] go to the schools. People feel the police is theirs. They trust them. Whether it is over the allocation of houses or land disputes we try to make justice. They appreciate it ... . Hence the public give many many information. We appreciate what they do.[23]

Even so, while the culture that the police exist only for the regime (or for themselves) may have been eroded, the pro-public outlook does not yet have the reach envisaged in the 'community policing' concept adopted as force policy. Community participation sometimes remains more of a mantra than a positively embedded value. One SLP Commander was apparently suspicious of co-operation with *anyone* outside of the SLP.

Q: Do you have a 'community policing' programme?

A: We have Neighbourhood Watch but it is not too effective since some of the youth on it are criminals! So people come directly to us.

Q: Are youth a problem in Makeni?

A: Yes too many are unemployed.

Q: How do you get on with commercial security companies?

A: I don't trust them. Some are into criminality.[24]

The SLP policy, as we have noted, has been to begin introducing Local Policing Partnership Boards but there is evidence that the station police in charge of the programme have not understood (or wanted to understand) the implications. The Boards were intended to give local communities a voice in how they want to be policed, yet when 26 people attended a Board in February 2005 to consider their local Community Action Plan, they were handed a printed copy of the Plan drawn up by the SLP beforehand. The Board was simply required to confirm it!

In Uganda, the so called 'community policing programme' is much broader and more effective. The emphasis has been on education in the law and on crime prevention. Community Liaison Officers (CLOs) are located at every police station and the keenest have been instrumental in initiating Crime Prevention Panels. These consist of local residents who are trained in crime prevention and the law and who accept responsibility for law and order for their geographical locality or employment group. In the latter case, they assume responsibility for policing their own members and handling public complaints (Baker, 2005a).

As one might expect, motivated officers share the participatory vision. A CLO in Katwe, Kampala, enthused that

> People don't fear the police anymore. Crime is reported better. We are sensitising them [about crime]. They preserve the evidence at the scene of the crime. And mob justice has gone down. There is very little now. None in the last 3 years. We intervene [in the Panels, only] when there is a problem.[25]

Yet not all are enthusiasts. There is evidence that some at the middle management and street level have doubts about the new institutional structures. One CLO Inspector commented that 'The success of Panels depends on the enthusiasm of the Liaison Officer in the District ... . Some are not active'.[26] Nor are Panels always popular when they intervene. The same Inspector admitted that as the trained 'crime preventers' started to use the direct phone line to senior police officers to report crimes or bribes demanded by police 'there was big resentment from the police at first about all this!'[27] And a chairman of a Crime Prevention Panel claimed that 'We work together with police and resolve problems. But bad police see us with a negative eye'.[28] The independent review already referred to considered that the police regarded community policing 'primarily as a means of instructing local populations, rather than of listening to them' (Raleigh et al., 1998).

In Rwanda the formal 'community policing programme' is open to the same criticism. From the police point of view,

> We go to schools and talk to them about drugs, about how to call the police, for instance to report domestic crime committed by their father. And we co-operate with the *résponsable* [local government official]. We encourage them to teach the people how to give information, how to solve problems; if they see a taxi man who is drunk, to call the police. They phone 112. It is free ... . We need intelligence so we have [hot] lines which are free, for example rape, traffic problems and the like.[29]

But again there are problems with translating the policy of close co-operation with the public into everyday police practice. Local commanders are reluctant to venture outside the station. A regional commander explained that his commanders' reports were vague because:

> they have never visited the areas they are reporting on. It means that when the community don't see us every day then if we do turn up then they think it is something unusual and strange! I ask the C/O how many meetings did you attend with local people; who did you visit? – tell me rather than just telling me crime statistics.[30]

Yet for all the problems of instilling in the police a frame of mind that views the community as partners, public testimony in all three countries nevertheless suggests that there has been a big cultural change in the police. In 2004, the SLP commissioned a small public perception survey (SLP, 2004; see Sierra Leone Police). Carried out in four urban areas (Freetown, Makeni, Bo, Kenema) it gives a snapshot of urban perceptions. Importantly, only 15 per cent felt that there had been 'no improvement' in SLP behaviour since the war, whilst 46 per cent thought there had been 'a great improvement in police attitude', particularly as regards human rights and 'rudeness'. Similar change is reported, too, from Uganda and Rwanda, showing that police culture can change quite rapidly in certain circumstances.

VALUES AND PRACTICES OF MIDDLE AND LOWER RANKS

Middle management is a key to understanding police culture (Neild, 2001, p. 29). This is the level where the new ideas coming from the highly trained senior management levels meet reality. Here is where the commander weighs the values of the new procedures and policies against tried and tested methods of 20 years in the force and against the very limited resources at his/her disposal. Here at middle management level the keen new constable, fresh from training school with new ideals, meets the brick wall of conservatism, well-established procedures and unchecked mal-practice that are not going to change at the suggestion of a junior (Reuss-Ianni, 1983).

One thing immediately apparent in all African police forces is that no amount of insistence on the importance of community/police relations has altered the reality that the police see themselves as largely reactive forces, based at police stations and posts, with patrols at a minimum. The other widespread police tendency is the slowness of middle management to (re)act – on account of their reluctance to make decisions and their preference either for seeking authorisation from above or for shifting the decision-making to a higher level. A Regional Commander in Rwanda admitted as much:

> We have realised that there is a gap at the middle management level. They are often confused on the scene. They ask: what can I do, and want those above them to tell them. They lack confidence. It has to do with training and our history.[30]

There may be elements of more general societal habit in this police reluctance to take initiative:

> Initiative can be developed. It is true in Rwandan society people want to look to the top. It is due to the way problems have been solved in the past – looking to the big man. This culture affects the police as well ... . At present O/Cs are being reactive. I tell them, map out your problems, prioritise, solve the cause of the problems! I have been given more officers this year but what do I see for it? ... of course we should not forget that many are ex-combatants and we should expect some confusion.[31]

In the effort to get values adopted at the senior level to penetrate middle and lower ranks Rwanda has in-service training but the missing element is post-training evaluation.

Problems afflict the SLP as well. The training at senior levels stresses the importance of station commanders getting officers out on the beat. But as a CCSSP Adviser observed,

> Getting them out of the station on patrols is 'challenging'. They want to hang around the station all the time. That is what they are used to – people coming to them, not them going to the people.[32]

Constable level is where the police meet the public. Perhaps unavoidably the values of the force command are diluted by the time they reach this level. Especially in isolated police posts, constables are often overwhelmed with the practical details of maintaining minimal policing activity and of personal survival. And considering that their basic training is only 12 weeks and that, in the case of Uganda and Sierra Leone, there is no in-service training, conformity to the new prescribed values is not uppermost in their minds. The following interview with a lone police constable in his two-room post in a village in eastern Sierra Leone underlines his pre-occupations:

Q: How many police are based here?

A: Four men.

Q: And what transport do you have?

A: One bike, which is damaged.

Q: What are the main problems you have to deal with?

A: Domestic violence, larceny and assault.

Q: What do you do in the case of domestic violence?

A: I call the elders to try to bring peace between the two. If they can reach no compromise then it goes to the magistrate's court but that causes delays – we have to gather evidence from the villages without transport. So I have to walk.

Q: How do you as a man deal with cases involving women?

A: We call the women's organisation leader.

Q: What improvements would you like to see at this post?

A: We have no toilet and no accommodation – I have to sleep here.

Q: How much do you get paid?

A: I will show you my pay slip. [it shows 130,000L p. month, i.e. £26, the equivalent of just over two bags of rice.]

Q: Is this enough to live on?

A: It is not enough. I depend on the help of others.[33]

Can such persons be agents of social change? Do they want to be? Certainly some profess noble aims and selfless service for the nation. Asked in a group discussion why they joined the police, 21 lower rank police of the RNP (17 men and 4 women from across Kigali) repeatedly said it was because 'we love our country and want it to be secure'. And what did they like about the job? It was the status and respect: 'The country has trusted us and given us a uniform'; 'Because we can protect people'. Probably closer to the truth was a woman police constable interviewed privately in a friend's home. As she expressed her motives: 'I was looking for a job and at that time they were looking for women in the police'. Her job-satisfaction: 'I like arresting criminals and not working in one place. And where you stay as a police officer there is peace – if drunkards and the like are there they move away'.[34]

Do these men and women looking for economic survival understand or want to understand issues like 'community policing'? Replies from RNP lower ranks to the question 'What is your understanding of "community policing"?' conveyed a range of perceptions: 'the community knows the police belong to them and they have been given a telephone number for close communication'; 'keeping the peace with the community by doing patrols with them'; 'when the community know their rights and give the police information'; 'when people see an increase in a particular crime and the police work with them to fight those crimes'; 'when police give seminars to schools about "community policing" and also use the radio'; 'when police use road signs to teach the community how the laws can be implemented'. What do answers like these tell us? As Seleti (2000) has pointed out, historical legacies of police cultural practices are not easily dispelled by reforms. It may be, as he observes in Mozambique, that such things yield more to public and media pressure than institutional changes or training programmes.

CONCLUSION

The shared traditions and everyday practices of all three forces have been significantly shaped by their experience of civil war, regime ideology and regime fear of conflict recurring. Change in police culture is far-reaching and inevitable following conflict, and for all the elements unique to each country there are common patterns.

Clearly conflict can decimate (Sierra Leone) or destroy (Rwanda) police forces such that more than just new recruits will be required to re-establish them. Yet war may create a window of opportunity to rethink policing policy, management, values and practice, and also to remove undesirable elements (as in Uganda). This kind of radical transformation is much harder in peacetime. Yet the post-conflict choices often reflect the war experience. Uganda and Rwanda chose to combine traditional western policing models with a form of popular justice because of rebel experience with it in the bush. And Sierra Leone chose to continue with western models alone because of the leadership's wartime experience of dependency on western assistance.

War reduces countries to poverty; it reduces poor countries to a state of dependency on international assistance for recovery. Post-conflict reconstruction of policing inevitably involves international financial assistance, and international values and procedures conveyed through experts. What we have seen in the three countries is the arrival not just of new equipment, but also of new ideas about force accountability, supervision and attitude to the public. Some of this may well fail to take root in the ranks of police personnel but it is unlikely that it will all fall by the wayside.

War offers some new opportunities but it also leaves scars. One such legacy is regime nervousness that conflict will repeat itself. All three regimes, having lived through regime change or attempted change, are well aware of how vulnerable they are. This explains the regime-defending role given to the police and to defensive internal security policies. Sierra Leone will not countenance (nor the UN arms embargo allow) arming the main body of its police or allowing commercial security companies to arm; Uganda has followed a militaristic policing policy to maintain its grip; Rwanda keeps a tight control on all forms of policing to prevent competition. The methods of disarmament, militarism and strict supervision are different, but the culture they foster in the police is the same: of being there to serve the regime as much as the public.

War unsettles the state police and alternative policing agencies alike. Some are undermined or destroyed because of their failure to provide services in the war (which happened with customary policing in Sierra Leone and Uganda). Some policing agencies are made by the war (the youth of Sierra Leone; the state appointed militias of Uganda and Rwanda; the commercial security companies) in that they fill the security vacuum left by the failure and withdrawal of others. War has transformed the security network of all three countries – a transformation not unnoticed by the police, but one which they have yet to adapt to or embrace.

And what of the future in this new security environment: new in terms of values and actors? Even when regimes strongly emphasise popular participation under state supervision (Uganda and Rwanda), and certainly where they do not (Sierra Leone), the gaps in security provision and differences over the definition of justice are such that policing other than that provided by the state will inevitably continue and probably grow. It may be that one of the biggest changes to police culture will come when the state police realise that they do not have a monopoly of policing and never will: when they learn to work in security networks with the other agencies.

Current police debates in the three countries largely concern management structures and accountability mechanisms, yet the debates have a different resonance at different levels of the forces. For example, all three governments have embraced the 'community policing' and 'sector policing' approach advocated by western advisers but in none of these countries has it taken hold seriously, because of state police suspicion, among the middle and lower ranks, of encroachment on their territory and, in the case of Uganda and Rwanda, because of strong community level participation in local government security structures. While such tensions remain within the forces themselves, police culture will be slow to change.

NOTES

1. In the research I undertook 82 interviews and 4 discussion groups in Uganda; 65 interviews and 6 focus groups in Sierra Leone; and 224 interviews and 8 discussion groups in Rwanda. The research in Uganda and Sierra Leone was funded by

the Economic and Social Research Council (Award Reference: R000271293) and Coventry University. The research in Rwanda was funded by the ESRC (Award Reference: RES000231102). Full transcripts of the interviews in Uganda and Sierra Leone can be found at the Economic and Social Data Service, http://www.esds.ac.uk/, under the title: Multilateral policing in Africa: its nature and socio-political impact in Uganda and Sierra Leone. The Rwandan interviews will be available at the same site from 2008.

2. Quoted in Kanyeihamba (2002, p. 211).

3. Interview, Inspector Ngako-Abbey Moiti, 11 March 2004.

4. Frank Mugambagye, Rwandan Commissioner General of Police 1995–2005, The Monitor, Kampala, 26 July 2004.

5. Interview with Local Unit Commander, Magburaka, 21 February 2005.

6. Hirondelle News Agency, Lausanne, 12 October 2004.

7. Interview with Assistant Commissioner of Rwanda National Police, Cyprien Gatete, Director of Training, 16 February 2006.

8. Museveni's first Minister of Internal Affairs claims that Museveni had such a low regard for the police that he wanted to replace them with military police when he took power in 1986 (The Monitor, Kampala, 5 April 2004).

9. Interview with the Deputy Commander of Police Training School, 22 February 2006.

10. The next section is based on interviews conducted in Uganda, Sierra Leone and Rwanda – see footnote 1.

11. Interviews with members of the CCSSP team, February 2005.

12. Frank Mugambagye, Rwandan Commissioner General of Police 1995–2005, The Monitor, Kampala, 26 July 2004.

13. Interview, Supt. Jimmy Hodari, Project Coordinator for the Swedish, South African, Rwandan tri-partite training project, 7 March 2006.

14. See, Uganda – National Security Index. www.photius.com/countries/uganda/national_security/

15. Interview, Inspector General of Police, Brina Acha Kamara, 12 February 2005.

16. Quoted in Concord, 10 March 2006.

17. Quoted in Sierra Leone Web, 17 June 2001.

18. Interview with Zimbabwean CCSSP Adviser, 18 February 2005.

19. Interview, Chief Spt. Jeanonot Ruhunga, Director of Intelligence, 15 February 2006.

20. Interview, Supt. George Rumanzi, Regional Police Commander, 13 February 2006.

21. Interview, O/C, Mityana Police Station, 31 March 2004.

22. Interview, Local Unit Commander, Magburaka, 21 February 2005.

23. Interview, Spt. Eric Kayiranga, Public Order and Security, Operations Unit, 10 February 2006.

24. Interview, Local Unit Commander, S Division, Makeni, 20 February 2005.

25. Interview, Inspector Ali Amote, CLO, Katwe Division, 5 March 2004.

26. Interview, Inspector Ngako-Abbey Moiti, CLO, Kawempe Division, 11 March 2004.

27. *Ibid.*

28. Interview, Jamil Sebalu, Crime Prevention Panel Chair for Katwe, 5 March 2004.
29. Interview, Spt. Jean Claude Kajeguhakwa, District Commander, Kigali, 9 February 2006.
30. Interview, Supt. George Rumanzi, Regional Police Commander, 13 February 2006.
31. *Ibid.*
32. Interview, British CCSSP Adviser, 16 February 2005.
33. Interview, PC, Police post, Tomodou, Kono District, 9 February 2005.
34. Interview, WPC, 7 March 2006.

REFERENCES

Amnesty International (1999). *Annual Report*, Sierra Leone.
Baker, B. (2005a). Multi-choice policing in Uganda. *Policing and Society*, *15*(1), 19–41.
Baker, B. (2005b). Who do people turn to for policing in Sierra Leone? *Journal of Contemporary African Studies*, *23*(3), 371–390.
Baker, B. (2007). Reconstructing a policing system out of the ashes: Rwanda's solution. *Policing and Society*, forthcoming.
Biddle, K., Clegg, L., & Whetton, J. (1998). *Evaluation of ODA/DFID support to the police in developing countries – synthesis study*. Swansea: Centre for Development Studies.
Chan, J. (1996). Changing police culture. *British Journal of Criminology*, *36*(1), 109–134.
Hills, A. (2000). *Policing in Africa: Internal security and the limits of liberalization*. Boulder: Lynne Rienner.
Human Rights Watch. (1999). *Hostile to democracy: The Movement system and political repression in Uganda*. New York: Human Rights Watch.
Kabwegyere, T. (1995). *The Politics of state formation and destruction in Uganda*. Kampala: Fountain Publishers.
Kanyeihamba, G. (2002). *Constitutional and political history of Uganda: From 1894 to the present*. Kampala: Centenary Publishing House.
Meek, S. (2003). Policing Sierra Leone. In: M. Malan, S. Meek, T. Thusi, J. Ginifer & P. Coker (Eds), *Sierra Leone: Building the road to recovery*. ISS, monograph 80.
Mugambage, F. (2005). *Community policing in a post-conflict society: A case study of post-genocide Rwanda*. Unpublished MA thesis, Institute of Diplomacy and International Studies, University of Nairobi, October 2005.
Museveni, Y. (1986). *Selected articles on the Uganda resistance war*. Kampala: NRM Publications.
Museveni, Y. (1997). *Sowing the mustard seed: The struggle for freedom and democracy in Uganda*. London: Macmillan.
Neild, R. (2001). Democratic police reforms in war-torn societies. *Conflict, Security and Development*, *1*(1), 21–43.
Ondoga ori Amaza. (1998). *Museveni's long march from guerrilla to statesman*. Kampala: Fountain Publishers.
Raleigh, C., Biddle, K., Mali, C., & Neema, S. (1998). *Uganda police project evaluation*. DFID. Available at: http://www.oecd.org/dataoecd/60/22/35097498.pdf

Reuss-Ianni, E. (1983). *Two cultures of policing: Street cops and management cops.* Somerset, NJ: Transaction Publishers.

Seleti, Y. (2000). The public in the exorcism of the police in Mozambique: Challenges of institutional democratization. *Journal of Southern African Studies, 26*(2), 349–364.

Sierra Leone Police. (2004). *An investigative perception survey on the performance of the SLP for the first half of the year 2004: A case study of the Western Area and the provincial towns of Makeni, Bo and Kenema.* Freetown: SLP.

Truth and Reconciliation Commission (TRC) of Sierra Leone (2006). *The final report of the Truth & Reconciliation Commission of Sierra Leone.* Available at http://trcsierraleone. org/drwebsite/publish/index.shtml

UNDP (1995). *Development assistance to the gendarmerie and communal police force of Rwanda: Background report to facilitate the elaboration of a final project document.* A Report By Lt-Col Cees De Rover for UNDP, December 1995.

Waddington, P. (1999). Police (canteen) sub-culture. *An appreciation. British Journal of Criminology, 39*(2), 287–309.

CONCLUSION: TAKING STOCK AND LOOKING AHEAD IN POLICE CULTURE STUDIES

Monique Marks and Anne-Marie Singh

In the first chapter of this book, David Sklansky cautions against schematic conceptualisations of police culture. Over-simplified assumptions about 'cop culture' have led to what Sklansky calls 'cognitive burn-in': mental schemas about the police which are difficult to change. Policing scholars and reformers, at least in the United States, now hold 'a broadly shared set of assumptions about the nature of the police subculture and its central importance in shaping the behaviour of the police', namely that police officers think alike, that they are paranoid, insular, and intolerant, and that they obstinately resist change.

In contrast to scholars such as Skolnick (1966) and Reiner (1992), Sklansky argues that while there certainly are defining qualities of police work, ways of coping are not uniform. Moreover, Sklansky continues, the police subculture schema obscures 'certain critical dimensions in policing and police reform, and changes in policing over the past few decades have made it more important than ever to rectify those blind spots'.

More than a decade ago, Dick Hobbs made a similar plea for a more nuanced and diversified way of understanding police culture. Following a detailed ethnographic study of detectives in the East End of London, he concludes that police subcultural manifestations differ in accordance with their specialist location and the 'daily grind' (1991, p. 597) that they are

Police Occupational Culture: New Debates and Directions
Sociology of Crime, Law and Deviance, Volume 8, 349–367
Copyright © 2007 by Elsevier Ltd.
ISSN: 1521-6136/doi:10.1016/S1521-6136(07)08014-1

confronted with. In order to avoid the blind spots that Sklansky points to, Hobbs argues that policing scholars need to

> tease out variations in policing styles rather than promote the perverse practice of identifying similarities across departments, cities, regions and countries. The assumption that there is something called 'police culture' is at best naïve, and results in crude generalisations in the quest for common characteristics so as to make the results virtually meaningless ... . Locating 'core characteristics' is hazardous, for as Fielding has noted, 'Police are not disembodied and culture free, but are more or less imbued with values and norms embedded in their milieu'. There is no homogenous milieu of policing. The public order specialist, the rural policeman, the traffic cop, the detective, all experience police work in different ways. Even individual police institutions then, are not concrete monochrome entities, but merely segmented spheres of activity that occasionally brush each other at information pick-up points and are bonded by a skeleton of concentric hierarchies. (Hobbs, 1991, p. 606)

Hobbs draws on the work of Nigel Fielding (1984, p. 569) who alludes to a 'patchwork of unofficial work practices, norms and relationships, existing in but still dependent on, the formal organisation'. The formal organisation, as distinct from the occupation itself, plays a crucial role in coordinating and disciplining police action, and levels some of the differences that might otherwise be more manifest. The generalised police response to a perceived demand for social control also creates commonality, based on a sense of shared purpose. But while organisational frameworks and public demands may constrain the breadth and depth of police subcultural diversity, they do not produce a monolithic police way of acting and thinking. The more individualised bubbling forth of new ideas about the policing occupation, police identity and good police practice that Jennifer Wood and Monique Marks describe in this collection will always be a feature of police organisations. And this is likely to be enhanced by new policing governance arrangements where police are encouraged (sometimes coerced) to work collaboratively with a range of public and private agencies and to rethink their own primacy in making communities safe and orderly.

Most authors in this book challenge the traditional characterisations of police culture, but the case still gets made that there are certain (usually negative) aspects of police culture that seem to persist over time (and even across space). Established cultural practices, both Jennifer Brown and Bethan Loftus argue, may even be reinforced when traditional identities and roles are challenged. Other contributors, like Bruce Baker and Maurice Punch, focus on the new circumstances that police find themselves in, both in their immediate organisational context and in their broader socio-political environment. They are interested in the way changed circumstances can lead to significant shifts in police practice and thinking. Mark Bevir and Ben Krupicka bring these two different approaches together. They focus on new governance arrangements and how change agendas may rub against existing practices and ways of thinking, making structural and cultural change difficult.

Avoiding the clichés about police occupational culture means, inevitably, that new and less easily assimilated complications have to be taken on board. More particularised understandings of police organisations and police culture are less amenable to generalisation, and also require research methodologies that give voice to individual agency and understandings – as recommended by Tom Cockcroft and by Jennifer Wood and Monique Marks. Janet Chan's chapter also points to the importance of ethnographic approaches in understanding more localised manifestations of police culture and in coming to grips with what police officers really think about their organisations and their occupations.

While the chapters in this book may be premised on a diversity of methodologies and philosophies, they all agree that police culture is not fixed. But there is always a tension between holding onto traditions (including schematic ways of thinking about police culture) that seem to work and responding innovatively to new circumstances, both as police practitioners and policing scholars. What we try to do in this concluding section is to suggest some of the themes that we believe are evident in this collection of essays and to suggest areas that still need to be explored in police cultural studies.

POLICE CULTURE AS 'SCRIPTED' AND DIFFICULT TO CHANGE: CONTINUITIES IN POLICE CULTURE?

Taking up the challenge that David Sklansky poses is not easy. As the introduction to this book points out, ingrained characterisations still inform contemporary writings on police culture. And there are can be good reasons for 'theories' to have sway and to continue to be influential in times of change; theories endure when they continue to have descriptive and explanatory value, as do many aspects of the classical conceptualisations of police culture and of the working police personality. Even when theories begin to be seen as too narrow they can still afford us a yardstick for measuring change and evaluating difference. Perhaps there is an unwillingness to set aside the lenses that have provided us with visual clarity in looking at 'police culture', but what some of the authors in this book demonstrate is that there does seem to be empirical validity in retaining some of the established schemas.

Jennifer Brown assumes in her chapter that machismo is a core characteristic of police occupational culture and she holds out little hope that this will change, reforms notwithstanding. Gender sensitive policy and managerial practices aimed at the promotion of women have not deterred police officers from embracing what Brown refers to as 'smart macho' – asserting established masculinist ideas and habits to cope with cultural change. Projecting police work as a masculine occupation lays down a certain measure of certainty in an organisational context of reform and change. For Brown, smart macho is more deeply entrenched than simply a cultural practice; it is about a hanging on to established identities as a way of asserting continuity and self-efficacy when broader occupational identity is under threat. For Brown smart macho runs deep because of the way machismo has become a part of the very basic assumptions (informed in part by organisational memory) that police officers have about the nature of their occupation and their working environment. Brown stresses the persistence of this macho element in police culture even while she insists that this occupational culture is a subtle, changeable, diverse thing and emphasises the individuality of the police men and women officers who are its makers.

Brown's chapter raises both empirical and theoretical questions for further investigation. What has been the impact of a changed field for policing itself on gendered relations and ideologies within the police? The advent of intelligence-led and community policing; emphasis on soft skills, on less physically oriented police work; gender and sexual orientation-based representative organisations within the police; managerialism; greater representativity in police organisations are changes that on the face of it would foster a less masculinist police culture. So is machismo a cultural security blanket? Is gendered cultural change more incremental and individualised than other aspects of cultural change?

Bethan Loftus also recalls more scripted understandings of police culture in her report on the persistence among police officers of discriminatory thinking and behaviour, often in defence of the police vocation. Loftus highlights a police cultural tradition that does not often feature in the police culture literature. There are numerous studies of racism and sexism in police organisations and of racist and sexist interaction with the public, but much less attention has been paid to the classist dimension of police culture. While the seminal studies by Reiner (1992), Emsley (1983) and Hall, Critcher, Jefferson, Clarke, & Roberts (1978) all point to the class-based nature of policing and the class location of police officers themselves, there has been very little scholarly investigation of issues of class-based police discrimination towards policed communities. Loftus chides the social sciences generally for not paying more attention to police treatment of the poor despite all the theorisation on growing class inequality.

Like Brown, Loftus concludes that discriminatory tendencies persist despite organisational commitments to equity. 'Class continues to permeate cultural knowledge and everyday practice', she argues, and this must be understood within a wider class-based social context. Harassment of working class people as 'roughs' and 'scrotes' springs from an entrenched cultural knowledge – classed-based tendencies that have, Loftus argues, become 'inscribed in police culture', rooted in very basic assumptions that shape the way police categorise people. Her work suggests that it would be very helpful to have more investigation of the degree to which police officers' own class location influences their attitudes and conduct towards working class persons. Her work begs the question whether there are times when police knowledge breaks with practice, for example when police are sympathetic with workers who protest? More broadly, what does the study of police culture tell us about the contradictory aspects of class consciousness?

Janet Chan reminds us in her chapter of the importance of 'solidarity' in understanding contemporary police culture in Australia. In this case the focus is on the preoccupation that police officers themselves have with what they consider a core tenet of their culture, namely 'solidarity' – which officers from the New South Wales police feel is under threat. The camaraderie that previously bonded relationships between rank-and-file police is, in the view of Chan's interviewees, being eroded by micro-management and the expectation that officers will 'tell on one another'. And because they hold solidarity to be synonymous with police culture itself, so they see police 'culture' too as diminished. Chan's chapter stands out for the way it uniquely foregrounds police officers' own understandings of the notion of 'police culture'. She actually asks officers themselves what they understand by the term police culture, and our impression is that not many other researchers try to do this. In this respect she sets a lead that we think would be extremely valuable to extend to other police constituencies.

The particular value of Chan's chapter is that it not only demonstrates how police officers bring their own schemas into police culture, but it brings their voices into the academic research discourse. And it also reminds us that outside researchers' assumptions about what the stressors are for police may not necessarily resonate with police experience: police may like to present their profession as 'unique' because of the threat of danger, and policing scholars may identify danger as a cornerstone of cultural adaptation, but what the officers in Chan's study are most concerned with is non-participatory management practice, lack of recognition, and the ongoing pressures on police organisations (and individual police officers) to reform themselves. These stressors are ongoing and impact significantly on the way that police officers feel about their work and the alliances they develop within the organisation. The much remarked-upon split between management and rank-and-file culture has perhaps intensified in this organisational environment. But a significant break with previous cultural traditions, at least according to police officers themselves, is that police now look beyond their immediate work peers for support.

All of this means that there is a special place for police unions and it is hardly surprising that where police unions do exist they have almost full organisational membership. In a context where police employees desire solidarity and where litigation suits against them are a common occurrence, unions as representative bodies are important and influential insider groups within police organisations (Marks & Fleming, 2006). Police representative organisations are the themes of the chapters by Megan O'Neill and Simon Holdaway and by Monique Marks. Both chapters question whether representative organisations such as police unions or the Black Police Associations (BPAs) pose any fundamental challenge to established police occupational culture. In raising this question, both chapters assume that there is a dominant or parent police culture in their search to evaluate the impact of these organisations, and in part this is because these organisations have positioned themselves both as challengers and as defenders of 'real' police work and 'true' police professionalism.

O'Neill and Holdaway argue that within the BPAs cultural practices have developed (like the eliding of rank distinctions) that go counter to those of the parent body, although these practices tend to be invisible to the more general police culture since BPAs usually take a non-confrontational approach to their work with the organisation. This is much the same case, Brown would argue, as with women police officers. The BPAs have, however, clearly had a notable impact in providing support to black officers, keeping a watch on discriminatory practices and policies, and challenging social relations both within the organisation and in the community. But BPA representatives seem not to regard the BPAs as cultural change agents, at least not in the near future. Their ability to foster cultural change is even more limited in non-urban areas where the numbers of minority officers are low.

What BPA representatives and even police leaders point out is that there has been a significant behaviour change in British policing where overt racist behaviour is now uncommon; white police officers seem to believe that this due to both the collective force of the BPAs and high profile investigations into police racism. As Chan (1997) and Marks (2006) argue, behavioural change can be merely mechanical with little bearing on deeper level assumptions and values, but the fact remains that BPAs are now part of the landscape of the British police and that their membership is growing. In themselves the BPAs are a strong reminder that the police are not homogeneous, and they signal the very considerable changes that distinguish present-day police organisations in the English-speaking democracies from those of 40 years ago (Sklansky, 2007).

While Sklansky and others have spoken about the changing demographics of police organisations, there is still a need for research into whether this has led to noticeable cultural change. A number of questions still need to be answered. Has demographic diversity impacted on cohesiveness and eroded notions of solidarity? Has greater diversity led to police organisations being more open, more prepared to engage with new ideas, more tolerant of dissent?

Maurice Punch's chapter addresses some of these questions. He argues that interesting cultural shifts been taking place in European police organisations since the 1960s. He is interested in the evolution of policing from a craft carried out by artisans to a profession which increasingly values higher education training. Even so, not just police managers but also policing scholars persistently disregard the thinking capacity of rank-and-file officers. Most police may not have university education (although increasingly they do) but they are still perfectly capable of being 'smart and savvy'. Academic researchers and police leaders alike need to understand how the 'brightness' of ordinary working officers can be tapped – a topic that is addressed in the chapter by Jennifer Wood and Monique Marks.

The important issue that Punch addresses is whether exposure to higher learning (particularly in the social sciences) impacts on thinking and practice in police organisations. His impression is that their university experience equipped officers to 'challenge conventional ways of thinking and acting', and he gives us a glimpse of the way that university-educated police bring fresh approaches, and in particular a more analytical bent, to police operations and procedures. More broadly, Punch's research underlines the capacity individuals can have to steer change in police organisations, particularly once they reach leadership roles.

It is debateable whether university-trained 'smart cops', as Punch refers to them, are anywhere the order of the day yet, and as Punch points out we need to distinguish what is happening in western democracies from the situation in more transitional societies. Bruce Baker's paper describes how police in transitional societies are concerned about police professionalism in ways that have little to do with tertiary education. In the transitional political environments that he refers to, being professional is about police acting ethically and playing by the rules, and it is about the development of basic police training and basic police infrastructure; the instances he cites from Uganda, Burundi and Sierra Leone highlight what are almost certainly widening distinctions between police occupational cultures in established democracies and in transitional societies. Questions also suggest themselves in relation to international police training projects and international donor assistance. What cultural differences distinguish police organisations around the globe and how might these differences impact on international interventions and cross-border policing programmes? What attempts are being made to make police officers 'smarter' in transitional societies? By what kind of international yardstick might we be able to say whether police forces in this or that country are less (or more) 'conservative' organisations now than they were two, or three, or four decades ago?

CONDUCTING RESEARCH ON POLICE CULTURE

Whether or not we conceive of police culture schematically is contingent on our broader philosophical starting points, and these framing tenets, particularly in regard to social agency, also govern our methodological approaches to understanding the culture. In turn, in an exegetical circle, the data and our analysis of it shapes the theories that we develop about the culture, the concepts we use to describe and explain this culture, and the questions we ask about police culture. But it is notable that scholarly work on police culture seldom interrogates the link between theory and methodology and initial tenets are not much discussed.

The chapters by Marks and Wood and by Tom Cockcroft both foreground the significance of the research approach and stress the inextricable link between the methods of research and the building of theory on police culture. Both of these chapters are concerned with how best to pursue our understanding of the police if we accept that police culture is diverse and changeable (even if incrementally) and that individuals have significant agency within police organisations. They also point to complex questions about the relationship of academic researchers to police organisations and the need for reflexivity in the research process.

Both these chapters make the case for direct engagement with individual police and for giving audience to non-elite voices within police organisations. But these voices need to be understood within a field of organisational and societal power relations. Wood and Marks talk about a situated understanding of 'webs of meaning', best developed when researchers enter into collaborative relationships with the police with mutual recognition and respect for the knowledge bases of both sides. They argue for a participatory action research (PAR) approach where individual police officers will be acknowledged as 'smart', 'savvy' innovators. Cockcroft also stresses the way that individual police officers are both actors and thinkers, coming together in time and space to respond to occupational demands and challenges. Not only does an oral history approach which he advocates allows for in-depth recording of individual experience and interpretation, its concern with recounting the past also limits the tendency to universalise police culture.

What links the oral history and PAR approaches is their conception of human agency. But more than that, they also share a pivotal concern with uncovering the more hidden voices of marginalised groups. While police in general are not themselves regarded as a marginal group in society, internally the voices of rank-and-file (non-elite) police are often silenced within the organisation (Walker, 2006). As we have already noted, this partly accounts for the high membership levels of police unions. But as Marks points out in her chapter, police unions are often oligarchal and their collective voice may likely as not transmit the viewpoint of long-standing union leaders who have held onto their positions sometimes as a way of avoiding being back on the beat. PAR and oral histories create the opportunity for rank-and-file police to narrate their understandings of their occupation, their organisations and the world around them.

Equally important, these approaches allow lower ranking police to talk about their perspectives of what Bevir and Krupicka refer to as 'elite' reform agendas, and also their sense of where reform should be headed. These perspectives are important for police reformers (both police leaders and outsiders) to know about because, as Bevir and Krupicka point out, initiatives that do not take account of rank-and-file knowledge are always likely to be incomplete. Taking stock of more individualised perspectives on reform may discourage broad-brush organisational strategies. It may also provide reformers with insight into why reform-weary police officers might forge identities and subcultures that look backward rather than forward.

None of this is to say that PAR and oral history approaches are without their difficulties. Wood and Marks and Cockcroft talk about the challenges of the approaches that they advocate. Cockcroft points out that the memories are subjective and selective. Getting a 'true' account of what happened, where things are at, is intrinsically elusive, as oral historians must always know. Nor can they disregard the way they as individuals and representatives of academic institutions influence how narratives are presented and what the narratives capture. Wood and Marks also point to the challenges of PAR. In the final section of their paper they talk about obstacles to collaboration created by the disparities in institutional objectives and practices between police and academia.

But the difficulties for police trying to make sense of academic enterprises and academics trying to make sense of the world of police should be more generally considered. In a recent book chapter, David Canter (2004) contends that police have become far more open to academic work and have embraced more 'scientific' approaches to police work. This has happened, in his view, because the police are now expected to enter into partnerships with a range of agencies and find more intelligent ways of dealing with 'volume crime' (2004, p. 111). This notwithstanding, Canter indicates very real differences between the academic/scientific culture and the culture of the police that limit this engagement. And these differences run very deep:

> The difficulty of interaction between what I am characterising as, on the one hand, the academic/scientific culture, and, on the other, the culture of the police is not merely a matter of vocabulary or engrained habits. It is a set of fundamental differences in thought processes, typical modes of action and the central objectives that shape the institutions in which these cultures thrive. (Canter, 2004, p. 111)

In many ways Canter buys into schematic depictions of police culture in describing the differences in modes of action between actors in these two institutions. But the key point he makes is that there is a fundamental difference in the 'ways of knowing' that makes an appreciation of one another's worlds difficult. Police, he says, search for evidence while scientists want data. Evidence is finite and conclusive while data often cannot be validified and its reliability varies.

The two institutions make use of information in very different ways because their objectives differ fundamentally. Police want information to make a conviction, academics want to contribute to knowledge building. Police focus on what is immediate, academics are concerned with lifetime achievement. For Canter (2004), then, there are 'rather different rhythms in the two different cultures and getting them synchronised can be difficult, although certainly not impossible' (p. 120). Canter offers no fixes for this cultural divide but he does make explicit some of the difficulties that researchers using PAR or oral history might face in their engagement with the police and his arguments reinforce our emphasis on the crux of theory and method for police culture research.

There is also room for more work on the cultural dissonance between police and academe. Whether this dissonance is increasing or on the wane in the present era of policing remains an open question, and has much to do with the way demands and expectations placed on the police and the self-identities that the police forge to cope with these.

THE NEW POLICING WORLD ORDER

The landscape of policing has altered significantly in the past few decades. Many of these changes are reflected in the chapters in this collection. Police organisations are now more representative and diverse, crime fighting technology has advanced dramatically, there is more academic involvement with both training and strategy, and management practices are being rapidly corporatised. All these changes derive from a complicated interplay of internal imperatives, external trends and pressures, and outsider 'expert' advice (Bayley, 2006), and not least of the changed circumstances is the way that the state police retain less and less of a monopoly in policing.

Responsibility for providing and authorising policing services and even for determining the architecture of security arrangements now falls to a range of state and non-state agencies, and there are various ways to understand and frame these 'new' governance arrangements: pluralisation (Bayley & Shearing, 1996), networked policing (Fleming & Wood, 2006), nodal policing (Shearing, 2006; Wood, 2006) and so on. We do not propose to debate these conceptualisations here, but there is convergence between broad public and political reassessment of the job of the police and internal reconsideration the police themselves are being asked to make of their roles and identities, with serious questions also being asked about whether, as researchers, we should grant the public police any primacy in our explanatory and normative work (Johnston & Shearing, 2003; Wood, 2006). In this context even police practitioners and their police representative groupings are trying to figure out what the core functions of the police are (Berry, 2006; Marks, this volume).

What exactly these new arrangements mean for expressions of police culture is not yet entirely clear. As different policing agencies come to interact more consistently their distinguishing cultural features become more shared. Jennifer Wood (2004) speaks of the 'melding of sensibilities within the governance of security as evidenced in the incorporation of risk-based thinking within state criminal justice agencies and, conversely, through the incorporation of punitive thinking within the commercial sector' (p. 37). A bifurcated or binary view of public and private police culture seems to have lost its descriptive and explanatory hold. As Kempa and Singh argue in their chapter, we need to rethink assumptions that the normative starting point of the public police is punitive and backward-looking and that private police culture is more future-oriented and preventive.

Whether or not this cultural osmosis provides the police with better cultural capital depends on our normative views on where policing should be headed. Private sector management techniques may increase the efficiency of the police and improve accountability mechanisms. But, as Sklansky argues, this could be at the expense of democratic gains that have been won by public police officers, including the right to unionise and to bargain collectively. The consequence might be a receding of what Sklansky refers to as the 'democratic inclinations' of the public police. This depends, of course, on whether or not extending labour and social rights to the police might spur more democratic police practice and thinking. While there have been normative arguments in this regard (see Marks & Fleming, 2006) there is an almost complete absence of empirical work to explore the relationship between police-officer rights and rights-based policing.

Nor have there been enough localised studies to clarify the direction in which the transfer of norms occurs between public and private police organisations. Michael Kempa and Anne-Marie Singh see a convergence of world-views and practices between public and private police. Focusing on South African developments they argue that both the private police and public police are becoming more punitive and militarised. This has occurred, they say, in a context where the socio-legal field enables private citizens to have guns and use force against others, in conjunction with very limited training for security employees. But is this kind of convergence apparent in other parts of the world? And how do we explain the differential accommodation and resistance of the public police to private police cultural encroachment?

But it is not just the melding of private and public police cultures that needs investigation. We also need to map the impact that community formations may have on policing cultures, with the democratic or retributive practices and world-views that they bring to the agenda (see Marks & Goldsmith, 2006). The extent and depth of community cultural influence depends on how the policing landscape is configured in law and in daily practice. Bruce Baker gives us a glimpse of the patchwork of public, private and community-directed policing in three post-conflict African countries.

What he shows is that there are significant differences in the policing arrangements and public police 'cultures' that have variously emerged in Sierra Leone, Rwanda and Uganda, shaped in large part by local differences in historical experiences, popular forms of justice, the capacity and resources of the state police, and the nature of the conflicts and their resolution, as well as by the interventions of international agencies.

In post-conflict Africa, experiences of war linked with pro-state or anti-state ideologies fundamentally shape the position of the public police in the security network and the way police officers view the world and their role in it. What Baker shows is how apparently similar country experiences can produce very different approaches to policing. His chapter sharply illuminates the way police cultures spring from a complex interplay of historical influences, global styles and fashions in governance, national legal and political particularities, and police community relations. The way police forces are constituted – creating something new or remaking something old – also has a massive effect on the police culture that is forged post-conflict. Baker also makes the important point that we need to take stock of the material circumstances of police officers before judging their capacity and willingness to be 'agents of change'. He shows how in Sierra Leone it is not uncommon for police officers to be without transportation, earn no more than the price of two bags of rice a month, and may even lack any toilet facilities at the police station. Agendas and initiatives for reform, top-down or bottom-up, are likely to be the last thing on their minds.

Baker talks about policing in Africa as a 'multi-choice' affair where there are a range of possible providers in the security arena. Citizens can choose between local community formations or the state police for resolution of 'security' problems, and the fluidity of policing arrangements can extend to the country as a whole. In Uganda, the public police have a reform programme to heighten accountability and service-levels, while on the other hand taxi drivers in that country regulate security within their industry with almost no 'interference' from the police.

The chapters by Baker and by Singh and Kempa raise questions about the core function of the police in this 'multi-choice' landscape. What core functions do the police want to hold on to, which are they prepared to let go of and how is this informed by existing police cultures? How are reconfigurations of the role and function of the public police likely to shape police culture for the future?

There can be little doubt, though, that police practice and knowledge has been greatly transformed by new police governance arrangements. Police members are increasingly exposed to new sensibilities, and police organisations and police unions are more or less compelled to adopt these sensibilities in defence of their role and function. What exactly these alternate sensibilities are and how readily the police espouse them are still areas that require empirical inquiry. The answers to these questions are likely to vary as local sensibilities and configurations of networks will differ.

The extent to which police are prepared to rethink their role, function and knowledge base is also heavily dependent on the demands the public makes of the state police, which may themselves be contradictory. Reflecting on his own expectations of the police David Canter remarks that

> As a member of the public I want action from the police. The constant public refrain for more Bobbies on the beat is a product of the belief that crime is prevented and solved by the hands-on acts of on-the-spot police officers. Yet there are many pressures that are making this less and less effective, however much the public and tabloid press still believe it is of operational value. The police are under pressure from many different directions to take more a strategic approach to their activities. There is consequently an inherent conflict between what populist politicians demand of the police and what is needed to manage the modern police service. (2004, p. 120)

With these contradictory demands it is not surprising that very substantial changes in the governance of policing should still leave key organisational characteristics intact. The chapters by Marks and by Bevir and Krupicka remind us that bureaucratic working modes persist despite managerial reforms that supposedly create flatter structures and top-down initiatives that stress partnerships and networks. Command and control is still well regarded as a management tradition in policing, and its continuance provides predictability and order in a new policing order.

When they are uncertain about just what is expected of them, and feel the core of their craft to be under threat, police hold onto the old narratives that transmit their ingrained self-identities and provide them with a connection to the past. This is certainly what Aogan Mulcahy (2000) observes of the police in Northern Ireland, faced with major reform initiatives, who glorify memories of a once-upon-a-time 'golden age' of policing.

Recently one of the editors of this collection attended an international police union network meeting in Texas. Police union officials outlined what they regarded as union responses to the pluralisation of policing. Acknowledging that the police no longer have a monopoly in the provision of policing services, they nonetheless refused to abandon their conviction that law and order are public goods best provided by the public police. This defence of the public police profession could be dismissed as conservative and backward-looking but it could also be seen as an invocation of public rights founded in the principles of social democracy. The point is to be wary of set interpretations of police cultural responses to their changing world. As Peter Manning insists in his chapter, police are 'no more bound to be conservative and self-interested in their discretionary acts than they are to be radical and other-regarding. We should no more demonise them than romanticise them'.

NEW DIRECTIONS FOR POLICE CULTURE STUDIES

This book is an attempt set in train new directions of thought on police culture. As editors we believed that it would be worthwhile to gather together a collection of authors from various different countries to reflect on continuities and breaks with tradition in theorising police culture. The theorisation varies from chapter to chapter with some more descriptive and others more analytical and/or normative. Some chapters emphasise the continuities in police culture and others consider breaks in traditions and the possibilities of producing cultural change from below.

As a collection the chapters demonstrate to us that police culture is a kind of patchwork quilt. No one schema makes sense for describing and explaining 'police culture', although both police and academic researchers continue to invoke what are perceived to be traditions of the policing trade or profession. The influences and pressures on police organisations vary hugely. Being a police officer in an established industrial democracy is a very different matter from being a police officer in a developing state dragging itself back from the trauma of war. Among the people who make up the police profession there are likewise huge disparities of educational attainment, and correspondingly in their views towards the 'intrusion' of academic researchers – and great inconsistencies, too, in their experiences of unionisation. Outside the force, their networking counterparts will invariably be local people with specifically local agendas, always different. And in what they think and do, individual officers themselves never cease to evolve, mostly in small, incremental ways.

Inadvertently, perhaps, this book as a totality meets some of the challenge that David Sklansky presents to us in the first chapter. What the book shows is that there are a range of different philosophical and methodological conventions to be used in understanding police culture. Each has its value. But going forward, what new directions can we discern or envisage in the approach to police culture, raised directly in chapters in the book, or hinted at in their implications?

A common, and not unhelpful, working assumption in policing studies (and for some of the discussion in this book) is that the zone of policing in which police cultures are forged is first of all the immediate organisational environment. So, in our present field, organisational studies tend to retain their primacy, to which case studies contribute important localised information, and with the national and political state context always present as a global parameter.

Peter Manning cautions us, however, not to conflate the police occupation with the police organisation. Police organisations 'house' the occupation and undoubtedly influence what officers think and do. But the trajectory of the occupation, and of its cultural expression, is influenced, too, by numerous factors beyond the organisation, only some of which have been touched on in this book: new fashions in corporate management; wider access to tertiary education; new standards of equity, and affirmative action to reinforce them; international police assistance programmes; greater pluralism in forms of governance.

Not least of extra-organisational parameters is the outright turn of history. One pre-eminent instance is the post-9/11 impact of terrorism on the policing of civil liberties. This is not a topic that contributors have particularly explored in this collection but it has been the subject of debate between P. A. J. Waddington (2007) and Dirk Haubrich (2007) in a recent edition of *Policing and Society*. New national and international threats to public order, coupled with a general surge in fear of crime (terror included) have impacted in two interlinked ways on the organisation of national police institutions. There are now denser and more intimate networks of collaboration between the law enforcement agencies of particular states (Sheptychi, 2000), and there is accelerated refiguring by national police forces of overall priorities, departmental structures and allocation of human and physical resources, all of which suggests further questions for police culture research. Do commonalities in police culture facilitate international collaboration? Does international police networking rub off at all on occupational culture? How do international pressures impact police cultural reform in local instances?

A common thread in this book is that continuities in police culture go hand-in-hand with continuities in the nature of police work and its meaning for police officers; as policing itself undergoes radical reconception, so too do conflicts begin to be manifest themselves in the culture. How do you juggle public (or political) expectations of a 24/7 servicing agency, on call to mop up just about any form of social malady, with professional participation in 'safety' networks as trained and authorised specialists in the use of force?

Jennifer Wood (2004) has suggested that cultural change debates have tended to focus somewhat narrowly on how to transform the institutional culture of the public police. This, she says, is 'despite the fact that the promotion of order and security is now considered highly pluralised, involving a range of state, corporate and volunteer auspices and providers that express different sensibilities' (2004, p. 44). She argues that we need to bring our analysis of culture and cultural transformation up to date with this reality. Most of the chapters in this book focus on public police officers and their organisations, whereas Wood calls for a more lateral perspective on police culture, thinking outside the box of the organisation, the force, the structure, and attending more closely to the myriad wider (cultural) influences constantly at play in the reactions of individuals as police officers and in the incremental consequences these have for the broader directions taken by their organisations.

The pluralisation of policing is now a background thing, a reality that is simply there (Cherney, O'Reilly, & Grabosky, 2006). It is a bit like the radiation emissions from computer screens, the frequency of mobile phone call signals and the international airlines flying above our heads. But taking this plurality on board there are important questions that still need to be answered: in this regulatory maze of networked actors and institutions where do we locate and identify changes in public police culture? What are the sticking points in police culture as pluralisation gathers momentum? To what extent do other network actors and agencies adopt cultural characteristics of the public police?

In the Introduction, we noted that one of the book's objectives has been to embrace the field from a range of different countries beyond just the regular Anglo-American location of police culture studies, and we hope that this volume may help to institute a trend in this respect. We could learn much from a more international range of police culture studies, but especially so from studies with a more explicitly comparative agenda: historically comparative police culture studies, or geographically comparative (within or between countries). Specifically comparative methodologies could tell us a great deal about whether there really are global shifts in police culture, how far they might reach, and their possible relation to globalising tendencies in the whole governance of security.

So what utility, in the end, does the term 'police culture' still retain? Everything in this book seems to confirm that it is highly relational, heavily contested, all too often very vague. No, it does not serve us well as a shorthand for describing or explaining everything the police do or think. Nor can it be an excuse for lumping together all police officers and all police agencies in time and space, or suggesting some sort of dubiously notional global police solidarity. Yet none of our contributors suggests that we should discard the term, and we suggest that their work vigorously confirms the importance of this continuing focus of inquiry.

REFERENCES

Bayley, D. (2006). Police reform: Who done it? Paper presented at the Conference on Police Reform from the Bottom-Up, University of California, Berkeley, 12–13 October.

Bayley, D., & Shearing, C. (1996). The future of policing. *Law and Society Review, 30*, 585–606.

Berry, J. (2006). Police reform from the bottom-up. Paper presented at the Police Reform from the Bottom-Up Conference, University of California, Berkeley, 12–13 October.

Canter, D. (2004). A tale of two cultures: Comparing the police and academia. In: P. Villiers & R. Adlam (Eds), *Policing a Safe, Just and Tolerant Society*. Winchester, UK: Waterside Press.

Chan, J. (1997). *Changing Police Culture*. Sydney: Cambridge University Press.

Cherney, A., O'Reilly, J., & Grabosky, P. (2006). Networks and meta-regulation: Strategies aimed at governing illicit synthetic drugs. *Policing and Society, 16*(4), 370–386.

Emsley, C. (1983). *Policing and its Context, 1750–1870*. London: Macmillan.

Fielding, N. (1984). Police socialisation and police competence. *The British Journal of Socioloogy, 35*(4), 568–590.

Fleming, J., & Wood, J. (2006). New ways of doing business: Networks of policing and security. In: J. Fleming & J. Wood (Eds), *Fighting Crime Together: The Challenges of Policing and Security Networks*. Sydney: University of New South Wales Press.

Hall, S., Critcher, C., Jefferson, J., Clarke, J., & Roberts, B. (1978). *Policing the Crisis: Mugging, the State and Law and Order*. London: Macmillan.

Haubrich, D. (2007). Anti-terrorism laws and slippery slopes: A reply to Waddington. *Policing and Society, 18*(4), 385–404.

Hobbs, D. (1991). A piece of business: The moral economy of detective work in the East-End of London. *The British Journal of Sociology, 42*(4), 597–608.

Johnston, L., & Shearing, C. (2003). *Governing Security: Explorations in Policing and Justice*. London: Routledge.

Marks, M. (2006). *Transforming the Robocops: Changing Police in South Africa*. Scottsville: University of KwaZulu-Natal Press.

Marks, M., & Fleming, J. (2006). The right to unionise, the right to bargain and the right to democratic policing. *The Annals of the American Academy of Political and Social Science, 605*(1), 178–199.

Marks, M., & Goldsmith, A. (2006). The state, the people and democratic policing: The case of South Africa. In: J. Wood & B. Dupont (Eds), *Democracy, Society and the Governance of Security* (pp. 139–165). Cambridge: Cambridge University Press.

Mulcahy, A. (2000). Policing history: The official and organizational memory of the Royal Ulster Constabulary. *British Journal of Criminology, 40*, 68–87.

Reiner, R. (1992). *The Politics of Police*. Toronto: University of Toronto Press.

Shearing, C. (2006). Reflections on the refusal to acknowledge private governments. In: J. Wood & B. Dupont (Eds), *Democracy, Society and the Governance of Security*. New York: Cambridge University Press.

Sheptychi, J. (Ed.) (2000). *Issues in Transnational Policing*. London: Routledge.

Sklansky, D. (2007). Not in my father's department. *Journal of Criminal Law and Criminology, 96*(3), 1209–1235.

Skolnick, J. (1966). *Justice Without Trial*. New York: Wiley.

Waddington, P. A. J. (2007). Terrorism and civil libertarianism pessimism: Continuing the debate. *Policing and Society*, *16*(4), 221–415.

Walker, S (2006). Why the neglect of police unions? Exploring one of the most important areas of American policing, Paper presented at the Police Reform from the Bottom-Up Conference, University of California, Berkeley, 12–13 October.

Wood, J. (2004). Cultural change in the governance of security. *Policing and Society*, *14*(1), 31–48.

Wood, J. (2006). Research and innovation in the field of security: A nodal governance view. In: J. Wood & B. Dupont (Eds), *Democracy, Society and the Governance of Security*. New York: Cambridge University Press.

NOTES ON CONTRIBUTORS

Bruce Baker is a senior research fellow at the Applied Research Centre for Human Security, Coventry University. He is currently engaged in a project examining informal and formal policing in post-conflict African states. He runs a web site on African policing at www.africanpolicing.org. His published articles and books cover African democratisation, governance, policing, security sector reform, popular justice and informal justice. He has conducted fieldwork in Zimbabwe, Mozambique, South Africa, Rwanda, Uganda, The Gambia, Sierra Leone, Cape Verde and the Seychelles.

Mark Bevir is a professor in the Department of Political Science at the University of California, Berkeley. He is author or co-author of *The Logic of the History of Ideas* (1999); *Interpreting British Governance* (2003); *New Labour: A Critique* (2005); and *Governance Stories* (2006). He is also the editor or co-editor of *Critiques of Capital in Modern Britain and America* (2002); *Markets in Historical Contexts: Ideas and Politics in the Modern World* (2004); *Modern Political Science: Anglo-American Exchanges since 1880* (2006); *Histories of Postmodernism* (2007); *The Encyclopedia of Governance* (2007) and *Public Governance*, 4 vols. (2007).

Jennifer Brown is currently working in the Department of Psychology at the University of Surrey where she holds a chair in Forensic Psychology and is Head of Department. She previously worked at Portsmouth University and contributed to distance learning programmes for police officers. She has an ongoing research interest in gender, ethnicity and sexual orientation within the police service and was the author of an early study of sexual harassment amongst women police officers in 1993. She held the post of research manager for Hampshire Police for eight years and was a syndicate director on the police senior command course at Bramshill.

Janet Chan is a professor in the School of Social Science and Policy, University of New South Wales, Australia. Janet's research interest has been in reforms and innovations in criminal justice, policing and, recently, creativity in the arts and sciences. Her publications include: *Changing Police*

Culture (1997); *e-Policing* (with Brereton, Legosz and Doran, 2001); *Managing Prejudicial Publicity: An Empirical Study of Criminal Jury Trials in New South Wales* (with Chesterman and Hampton, 2001); *Fair Cop: Learning the Art of Policing* (with Devery and Doran, 2003) and *Reshaping Juvenile Justice* (2005). She is a fellow of the Academy of Social Sciences in Australia.

Tom Cockcroft is currently senior lecturer in the Department of Crime and Policing Studies at Canterbury Christ Church University. He previously held the role of research officer at Kent Criminal Justice Centre at the University of Kent where he contributed to a number of evaluation studies of new criminal justice system initiatives. His other substantial area of interest remains the use of qualitative research methodologies within criminal justice contexts and he has published on the subject of police oral history.

Simon Holdaway is professor of Criminology and Sociology and director of the School of Law at the University of Sheffield. Before becoming an academic, he was a police officer for 11 years. His first book, *Inside the British Police: A Force at Work*, was the first ever published study of the occupational culture of the British Police. Since that publication, he has researched and published widely on many aspects of police race relations, including race relations within constabularies. His subsequent books have been about the recruitment of ethnic minorities into the police, their retention and the notion of racialisation. He has recently completed a study of Black Police Associations.

Michael Kempa is a lecturer in the School of Political Science, Criminology and Sociology at the University of Melbourne, Australia. He is particularly interested in the political contests that surround alternate policing forms. Building upon several journal articles, his first book on these matters (co-authored with Professor Clifford Shearing) will be published by Routledge in the coming year.

Ben Krupicka is a graduate student in the Department of Political Science at the University of California, Berkeley. His work focuses primarily on political ethics, democratic theory and the American presidency. He is also an editor of the academic journal *Critical Sense*. Ben received a BA from Willamette University in 2003, graduating Magna Cum Laude and being inducted into the prestigious Phi Beta Kappa honour society. He was a

Harry S. Truman Scholar Finalist in 2001 and an American representative on the 2004 British Debate Tour, sponsored by the National Communications Association (USA) and the English Speaking Union (UK).

Bethan Loftus is currently completing her Doctorate on contemporary police cultures at the Centre for Criminological Research at Keele University. She gained her BA (honours) 1st class degree in Criminology and Criminal Justice at the Centre for Comparative Criminology and Criminal Justice, University of Wales Bangor and a Masters (distinction) at the same centre. She won a young scholars academic award (£6k) from the James Pantyfedwen Foundation in 2003 and has written a number of reports for police audiences.

Peter K. Manning (PhD, Duke, 1966; MA, Oxon, 1982) holds the Elmer V. H. and Eileen M. Brooks trustees Chair in the College of Criminal Justice at Northeastern University, Boston, MA. He has been awarded many contracts and grants, the Bruce W. Smith and the O. W. Wilson Awards from the Academy of Criminal Justice Sciences, and the Charles Horton Cooley Award from the Michigan Sociological Association. His research interests include democratic policing and the rise of non-democratic policing, the rationalising and interplay of private and public policing, crime mapping and crime analysis, uses of information technology and qualitative methods. His book *Technology's Ways* is forthcoming in 2007.

Monique Marks holds a PhD in Sociology from the University of Natal, South Africa. She is currently a senior lecturer at the University of KwaZulu-Natal and is a visiting fellow at the Australian National University. She has also worked as a senior researcher at the Centre for the Study of Violence and Reconciliation in Johannesburg and at the Head Office of the African National Congress. She has published widely in the areas of youth social movements, ethnographic research methods, police labour relations, police organisational change and policing governance. Her recent book is *Transforming the Robocops: Changing Police in South Africa*.

Megan O'Neill is a lecturer in Criminology at the University of Salford, UK. She holds a PhD in Sociology from the University of Aberdeen and a BA in Sociology and Psychology from Albion College, Albion, Michigan. She worked as a research associate in the University of Sheffield Centre for Criminological Research for four years, two of which were spent on the Black Police Associations project with Simon Holdaway. Her interests include the police occupational culture, race and ethnicity in policing, the interplay between public and private policing groups, symbolic interactionism and the policing of football matches. The latter two topics are the focus of her book, *Policing Football* (Palgrave, 2005).

Maurice Punch has worked at universities in the UK, USA and the Netherlands where he has lived since 1975. He has researched corporate crime and police corruption – *Conduct Unbecoming* (Tavistock, 1985), *Dirty Business: Exploring Corporate Misconduct* (Sage, 1996) and *Rethinking Corporate Crime* (Cambridge University Press, 2003). After 18 years at Dutch universities he became an independent researcher and consultant and in 1999 he became a visiting professor at the London School of Economics. Forthcoming publications are on the motives of white-collar criminals, the 'transfer' of zero tolerance policing to the Netherlands, police accountability and on the experiences of British police officers attending university (*Policing by Degrees*. De Hondsrug Pers).

Anne-Marie Singh is an assistant professor in the School of Criminal Justice at Ryerson University, Toronto, Canada. She has considerable experience in South Africa, where she conducted fieldwork on the reconfiguration of policing in the post-Apartheid period. During this time, she contributed to numerous policy papers on policing transformations in post-Apartheid South Africa, as a research associate both at the University of Cape Town and at Technikon, South Africa. She has also been a researcher with the Centre for Urban and Community Research at the University of London, where she assisted in the evaluation of a local city challenge project. She is currently researching the place of coercive techniques in contemporary practices of rule.

David Alan Sklansky is professor of Law at the University of California, Berkeley and faculty director of the Berkeley Center for Criminal Justice. He teaches and writes about criminal procedure, criminal law and evidence, and is currently completing a book on the changing ideal of democratic policing. He joined the Berkeley faculty in 2005, following a decade at UCLA School of Law. Prior to that he spent seven years as a federal criminal prosecutor. In 2000, he served as Special Counsel to the Rampart Independent Review Panel, commissioned by Los Angeles Board of Police Commissioners to assess the operations, policies and procedures of the Los Angeles Police Department.

Jennifer Wood holds a PhD in Criminology from the University of Toronto, Canada. She is a fellow for the Regulatory Institutions Network at the Australian National University. Her research has focused on policing and governance, with an emphasis on new organisational and strategic approaches to the promotion of security and democracy. Her recent publications include *Democracy, Society and the Governance of Security* (co-edited with Benoît Dupont), *Fighting Crime Together: The Challenges of Policing and Security Networks* (co-edited with Jenny Fleming) and *Imagining Security* (co-authored with Clifford Shearing).

AUTHOR INDEX

SUBJECT INDEX